ISRAEL
& THE WEST BANK

GENEVIEVE BELMAKER

Contents

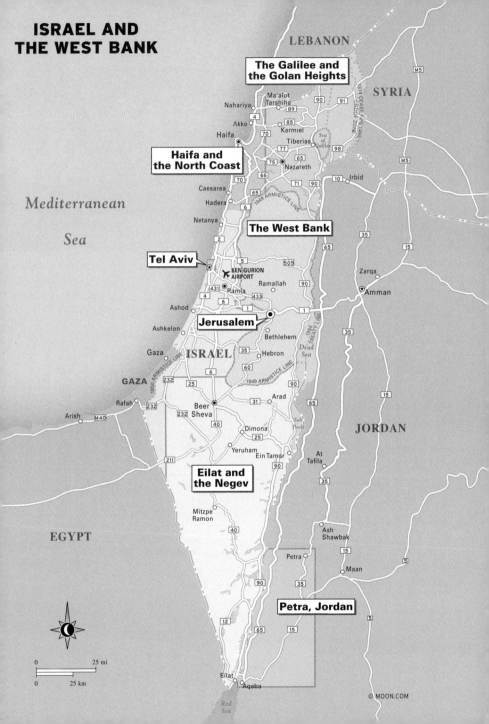

ISRAEL AND THE WEST BANK

The Galilee and the Golan Heights

Haifa and the North Coast

The West Bank

Tel Aviv

Jerusalem

Eilat and the Negev

Petra, Jordan

LEBANON

SYRIA

Mediterranean

Sea

Nahariya

Ma'alot Tarshiha

Akko

Haifa

Karmiel

Tiberias

Sea of Galilee

Nazareth

Irbid

Caesarea

Hadera

Netanya

BEN GURION AIRPORT

Ramallah

Zarqa

Amman

Ramla

Ashod

Bethlehem

Jerusalem

Dead Sea

Ashkelon

Gaza

ISRAEL

Hebron

GAZA

Rafah

Arish

Beer Sheva

Arad

JORDAN

Dimona

Yeruham

Ein Tamar

At Tafila

EGYPT

Mitzpe Ramon

Ash Shawbak

Petra

Maan

Eilat

Aqaba

Salt Pool

Red Sea

0   25 mi

0   25 km

© MOON.COM

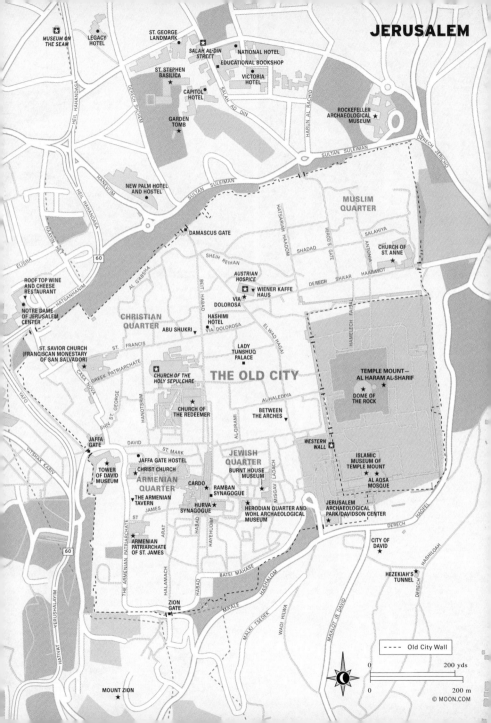

JERUSALEM

MUSEUM ON THE SEAM

LEGACY HOTEL

ST. GEORGE LANDMARK

SALAH AL-DIN STREET

ST. STEPHEN BASILICA

NATIONAL HOTEL

EDUCATIONAL BOOKSHOP

VICTORIA HOTEL

CAPITOL HOTEL

GARDEN TOMB

ROCKEFELLER ARCHAEOLOGICAL MUSEUM

DERECH SHCHEM

HEIL HAHANDASA

SALAH AD-DIN

HARUN AL-RACHID

SULTAN SULEIMAN

DERECH JERICHO

HANEVIIM

HEIL HAHANASA

NEW PALM HOTEL AND HOSTEL

SULTAN SULEIMAN

MUSLIM QUARTER

ELISHA

HAKVIN HEI

DAMASCUS GATE

60

HATSARIAH HAADOM

HERO'S GATE

SALAHIYA

CHURCH OF ST. ANNE

ROOF TOP WINE AND CHEESE RESTAURANT

SHEIH REIHAN

SHADAD

ANTONIA

NOTRE DAME OF JERUSALEM CENTER

AL G'ABSHA

AUSTRIAN HOSPICE

DERECH SHA'AR HAARAVOT

HATSANHANIN

BEIT HABAD

WIENER KAFFE HAUS

CHRISTIAN QUARTER

VIA DOLOROSA

HASHIMI HOTEL

ST. SAVIOR CHURCH (FRANCISCAN MONESTARY OF SAN SALVADOR)

ABU SHUKRI

VIA DOLOROSA

EL WAD HAGAI

ST. FRANCIS

GREEK PATRIARCHATE

LADY TUNSHUQ PALACE

CASA NOVA

CHURCH OF THE HOLY SEPULCHRE

THE OLD CITY

TEMPLE MOUNT— AL HARAM AL-SHARIF

HANOTSRIM

DOME OF THE ROCK

YAFO

ST. GEORGE

CHURCH OF THE REDEEMER

AL-HALEDIYA

ALQIRAMI

BETWEEN THE ARCHES

JAFFA GATE

DAVID

ST. MARK

WESTERN WALL

ISLAMIC MUSEUM OF TEMPLE MOUNT

YITSHAK KARIV

TOWER OF DAVID MUSEUM

JAFFA GATE HOSTEL

CHRIST CHURCH

JEWISH QUARTER

BURNT HOUSE MUSEUM

MISSAV LADACH

AL AQSA MOSQUE

CARDO

RAMBAN SYNAGOGUE

60

THE ARMENIAN TAVERN

JAMES

HURVA SYNAGOGUE

HERODIAN QUARTER AND WOHL ARCHAEOLOGICAL MUSEUM

JERUSALEM ARCHAEOLOGICAL PARK/DAVIDSON CENTER

ARMENIAN QUARTER

HABAD

HAYEHUDIM

DERECH

CITY OF DAVID

ARMENIAN PATRIARCHATE OF ST. JAMES

ST

ARAT

HAQEL

HEZEKIAH'S TUNNEL

THE ARMENIAN PATRIARCHATE

HALAMACH

HABAD

BATEI MAHASE

HASHALOM

DERECH HASHILOAH

YERUSHALAYIM

ZION GATE

MAALE

MALKI TSEDEK

WADI HILWA

MAALOT IR DAVID

HATIVAT

--- Old City Wall

0   200 yds

0   200 m

© MOON.COM

MOUNT ZION

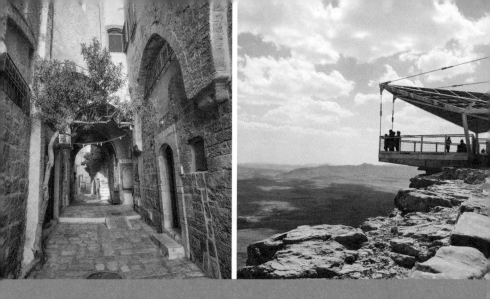

DISCOVER

Israel
& the West Bank

srael, the West Bank, and Petra all have one thing in common: They are lands frequented by pilgrims and painted by a tableau of stories stemming from ancient times through today. These are also places where modern, secular life thrives and some of the most advanced technology in the world is born.

This region is significant to the three largest monotheistic religions in the world—Judaism, Christianity, and Islam. As such, it is home to thousands of years of epic history. That history continues to unfold even today.

Many people dream their entire lives of journeying here. The archaeological and anthropological sites and museums also make it a prime destination for students and scholars.

The crown jewel for most visitors is Jerusalem, a city bursting at the seams with incredible historical and religious adventures alongside fine restaurants, excellent shopping choices, and an ever-increasing array of entertainment for every taste and age. As much as Jerusalem makes the past feel present, liberal, free-wheeling Tel Aviv is intently focused on the future. The fresh scent of sand and sea seems soaked into everything, and marketplaces smell of spices, falafel, and

Clockwise from top left: streets of Old Jaffa; the Ramon Crater in the Negev desert; ibex in the Ein Gedi Nature Reserve; Dome of the Rotunda at the Church of the Holy Sepulchre; spices for sale at the Carmel Market in Tel Aviv; Tel Aviv's beach and promenade.

Turkish coffee. It's an aromatic assault on the senses. North along the Mediterranean is sparkling Haifa, a city on a bay that is frequented by cruise ships filled with visitors from Europe. Often touted as a place in Israel where Jews and Arabs "coexist peacefully," Haifa is known for being a politically moderate city. The city's centerpiece is the world-famous Baha'i Golden Dome, of the people of the Baha'i faith.

The West Bank, with its ancient cities of Bethlehem, Jericho, and Hebron and the more modern city of Ramallah, offers a journey into another world—just as Petra's ancient stone facades do. On a hot summer day with the warm smell of olive trees and a backdrop of rolling brown hills, you can almost forget the centuries-long violence and political tensions that have troubled this area.

Is it any wonder this region has inspired such passions, such creativity, such devotion, such faith? Beyond the history books and news headlines, it must be experienced firsthand to be truly appreciated.

Clockwise from top left: the ancient Roman aqueduct at Caesarea; Old Town port of Jaffa; Turkish coffee in Tel Aviv; waterfall in Ein Gedi Nature Reserve.

16 TOP EXPERIENCES

1 Stepping into the dark, cavernous **Church of the Holy Sepulchre,** one of the most important sites in the Christian world. Also known as the Church of the Resurrection, it houses four stations of the Via Dolorosa. It's constantly filled with throngs of pilgrims, and its walls are filled with centuries of art (page 54).

2 Admiring the architecture of Tel Aviv's **White City,** a UNESCO World Heritage Site considered an outstanding example of new town planning in the early 20th century, adapted to the cultural and geographic context of Tel Aviv. A must-see for architecture aficionados (page 120).

3 Taking in the view and finding a contemplative corner in the gray-domed Roman Catholic church atop the **Mount of Beatitudes,** just outside of Tiberias, where Jesus is believed to have given the Sermon on the Mount (page 209).

4 Paying your respects at the **Western Wall,** the most famed religious site in all of Judaism. Named for its position as the outer western wall of the destroyed Second Temple's courtyard, the Western Wall is also called the Wailing Wall or the Kotel (page 58).

5 Roaming the terraced gardens in the looming shadow of Haifa's **Baha'i World Center,** which cover the northern slope on Mount Carmel. The Golden Dome is so massive that it acts as the unofficial center of Haifa (page 165).

6 Taking a photograph of the famous six-pointed star window at the gorgeous ruins of **Hisham's Palace,** a major archaeological site in Jericho (page 253).

<<<

7 Getting lost in the 125 acres of **Caesarea National Antiquities Park,** which contains archaeological remnants spanning a time period of about 2,300 years (page 191).

>>>

8 Taking in the history at the imposing, affecting **Church of the Nativity** in Bethlehem, one of the oldest working churches in the world. It is widely regarded as the location of Jesus's birth (page 242).

<<<

9 Exploring the winding streets and corners of **Old Jaffa,** Tel Aviv's port on a hill overlooking the Mediterranean. You'll find archaeological sites here, along with upscale shops, some of the best fine dining in Tel Aviv, an artists' quarter, renovated Ottoman-era houses, and several important landmarks (page 125).

10 Journeying back in time in Akko's magnificent **Acre Old City.** This UNESCO World Heritage Site is comprised of a complex network of buildings, archaeological and historical sites, and museums and takes about two days to tour completely (page 182).

11 Investigating the mysteries surrounding **Masada National Park.** A trip to the mountaintop fortress is enough to send the most jaded of travelers into another time and space with its epic views and equally epic history (page 269).

12 Navigating the art, religious relics, and historical lessons of the **Basilica of the Annunciation** in Nazareth, one of the largest churches in the Middle East (page 218).

>>>

13 Seeing bright, rare fish, including a dark room for viewing glow-in-the-dark sea life at Eilat's **Coral World Underwater Observatory** (page 287).

<<<

14 Educating yourself on the regional conflict that has long troubled this part of the world at the **Museum on the Seam,** along what was once a border between East and West Jerusalem (page 64).

>>>

15 Watching the sun rise or set at the **Mitzpe Ramon Observatory and Ramon Crater,** the largest of three massive geological craters in the Negev and home to the Ramon Crater Nature Reserve (page 279).

16 Marveling at the **Great Temple** of the Nabataeans, one of the most impressive and well-excavated sites in the "Rose City" of Petra (page 308).

Planning Your Trip

Where to Go

Jerusalem

A city of just over 800,000 people and an important locale to the three major religions of Judaism, Christianity, and Islam, Jerusalem seems older than time itself and is enthralling with its dozens of **archaeological, religious, and historical sites and museums.** When you tire of tours and history lessons, it is just as interesting to stroll through the unique districts of the city, such as the **German Colony,** with its many family entertainment options, lush greenery, unique homes, and numerous shops, and then stop for a **world-class meal** in one of the city's many restaurants. A classic destination for **religious pilgrimage,** Jerusalem also has a **lively arts scene** and some **nightlife** offerings, though it is tame compared to Tel Aviv. A claim

to fame is that it is home to more museums than anywhere else in Israel.

Tel Aviv

Tel Aviv isn't called the "center" for nothing. It boasts a dizzying offering of **restaurants, clubs, museums, performing arts venues** of all sizes, **nightlife, music, beaches, surfing,** and **outdoor sports.** The first modern Jewish city, Tel Aviv has earned its reputation as the core of contemporary Israeli life. It is a place known for its openly accepting atmosphere for people of all kinds, for its high-powered technical and business sector, and as the heart of the country's famed diamond industry. Tel Aviv's **world-class parks** and recreation offerings are at the heart of its many **summer festivals, events, and live**

Tel Aviv's Dizengoff Center

If You Have ...

- **One Week:** Jerusalem and Tel Aviv
- **10 Days:** Add Haifa, the Dead Sea, and Bethlehem
- **Two Weeks:** Add the Negev, the Sea of Galilee, and Akko
- **One Month:** Add Jericho, Ramallah, Eilat, and Petra

concerts. It is, far and away, the most popular place in Israel to party and just enjoy life.

Haifa and the North Coast

Once you're in Haifa, Israel's third largest city, situated on the coast about an hour north of Tel Aviv, you can easily jump off to other charming coastal towns and nearby historical and religious sites, such as **Akko, Caesarea,** and **Zichron Ya'akov,** with minimal hassle. The life of Haifa, the only city in Israel with any public transportation on the weekend, revolves around the dominating **Baha'i Gardens and Golden Dome.** You can spend days just going between exploring Haifa's **museums, restaurants, and beaches** and wandering through the serene and pristine grounds of the Baha'i Gardens.

The Galilee and the Golan Heights

The north of Israel encompasses the **Upper Galilee,** the **Lower Galilee,** and the **Golan Heights,** home **to gorgeous parks** and **nature reserves** that include countless **hiking and camping** opportunities. The area is known for its **world-class wineries** and numerous significant **archaeological, religious, and historical sites.** The Golan and the Galilee are also home to some **fascinating people,** like the Druze; important cities, like **Nazareth**; and spiritually moving locales, like the **Sea of Galilee.**

The West Bank

The West Bank is where many important **historic and religious sites,** including the towns of **Bethlehem, Jericho,** and **Hebron,** can be found. The Arab city of **Ramallah,** just a short drive from Jerusalem, is the hub of **Palestinian arts and culture** in the West Bank and known for the important cultural **festivals** it puts on every year. Because of the complex security situation, it is recommended that visitors travel to the West Bank with a licensed tour company and check the current recommendaitons from their consulate before planning a trip.

Eilat and the Negev

The bosom of the **Negev Desert,** which makes up more than half of Israel's landmass, the south is considered by many to be **wild and untamed** in many ways, though it is also an up-and-coming tech center. A popular destination for **desert ecotourism,** the Negev is the perfect place to experience **camping out under the stars** and to discover the unique beauty of the desert on **long hikes.** Home to the **Dead Sea,** the lowest point on Earth, the south is sparsely populated, but boasts the thriving tourist hub of **Eilat** at its far south end. Eilat has some of the best **coral diving** in the world and **tax-free shopping,** and it is the gateway to Petra, Jordan.

Petra, Jordan

Nothing can prepare you for the incomparable experience of seeing the **ancient Nabataean city** of Petra. Once the capital city of powerful and wealthy spice route merchants, modern Petra is a **massive archaeological site** that takes several days to explore thoroughly. Replete with **hikes** of varying lengths that end at gorgeous archaeological finds, Petra can be experienced in tandem with the immediately adjacent **Arab village of Wadi Musa,** with its many offerings of **Bedouin food and hospitality.**

Know Before You Go

High and Low Seasons

There are distinct high and low seasons in this region. The **high season** is **April-October** (approximately from Passover through Sukkot on the Jewish calendar), and the **low season** is **November-March.** Check the calendar carefully before planning your trip with an eye out for **major Jewish, Christian, and Muslim holidays.** The airfare and cost of hotels will be much higher during those times, and many businesses and tourist sites will be closed or have shorter hours.

The three **most challenging times** to visit are during the Jewish holiday of **Passover week** (approximately the end of March), which ends in the Christian holiday of **Easter Sunday,** and during the week of the Jewish holiday of **Sukkot** (approximately the end of October). The month-long Muslim holiday of **Ramadan,** around **July-August,** puts a bit of a damper on any sightseeing related to sites in the West Bank.

A generally **good period to visit,** when it is not too hot and not too cold, and there are not too many holidays to affect the opening and closing of sites, is in **April-June.**

Try to **avoid visiting Jerusalem during August,** when the heat coupled with the chaos of annual vacations and events among local residents make for an overwhelming (not in a good way) experience. Essentially, the city becomes **extremely crowded.**

Shabbat (Sabbath) and Weekly Closures

If you only have a few days in Israel, it's good to be aware of the Jewish Shabbat (or Sabbath), which starts on Friday at sundown and ends on Saturday night after three stars are out in the sky (when it is fully dark). All government offices

Easter observances draw many pilgrims to Jerusalem.

and services stop, including public transportation (except in Haifa, where some public buses run on a limited schedule throughout Shabbat). Also, any restaurant that is kosher is closed. Taxicabs still operate, but their fees are higher than normal. The exception is East Jerusalem, which is predominately Arab, where business continues as normal. Arab areas do shut down on Friday afternoon, which is their major prayer time during the week.

Passports and Visas

Many countries have a **visa waiver agreement** with Israel, including the United States, Canada, and the United Kingdom, which means you only need to purchase a round-trip ticket to show your future departure. You will be issued a **visa** upon entering Israel. Your **passport** must be good for at least six months past the date of your departure from the country.

Security

Check any travel advisories from foreign governments before departing. Sporadic violence might mean that you choose not to visit a certain area.

Transportation

The best and most common way to get to this region is by airplane, which will take you to Tel Aviv's **Ben Gurion International Airport.** Entry from Jordan or Egypt is also possible by **car,** and arrival by **cruise ship** over international waters commonly occurs via the **Port of Haifa. Eilat Airport** in the south handles domestic flights if that is your final destination.

Though the geographic area is fairly small (you can drive from the northern border to the southern border in one day), the complex security situation does require some advance planning, especially if you intend to visit multiple regions or cross international borders during your trip. Within most towns and cities—particularly Tel Aviv, Haifa, Jerusalem, and Eilat—**public transportation and taxis** make it fairly easy to get around. For travel beyond isolated locales, it is best to get a **rental car.** Long-distance **buses** will also get you around cheaply and efficiently, but they can require a sense of adventure and extra time for potential mishaps. The **Israel Railways train** is also an option, especially for going to and from the airport.

Best of Israel and the West Bank

If you are traveling to Israel and the West Bank with the intention of having a wide variety of experiences, mapping out at least a general strategy is a must. This itinerary describes how to get a taste of the best of the region in two weeks, and includes the major highlights and most popular sites in several cities and regions.

Jerusalem

DAY 1

Have breakfast at your hotel and get an early start to the **Old City** to beat the heat and crowds. Take the most accessible entrance at the Jaffa Gate, and stop by the information center for any current happenings and available tours. From here you can start to explore with a visit to either the **Rockefeller Archaeological Museum** or the **Tower of David Museum.**

Follow the main road downhill through the tightly packed shops selling all kinds of scarves, food, trinkets, jewelry, and souvenirs and try your hand at the regional custom of negotiating for a deal. Then head for the **Church of the Holy Sepulchre,** built on the spot where many believe Jesus was crucified, buried, and resurrected. From here, head to the **Austrian Hospice** for an incredible view of old and new Jerusalem from the rooftop and a piece of famous apple strudel in the quiet gardens.

After leaving the Austrian Hospice, wander around a bit as you work your way toward the **Western Wall, Al Aqsa Mosque,** and the **Dome of the Rock.** Pass the Western Wall and keep going toward the outer wall of the Old City, toward the **City of David** archaeological site. Here you can take a guided tour and walk through the ancient **Hezekiah's Tunnel,**

Dome of the Rock and the Western Wall in Jerusalem

Church of the Holy Sepulchre

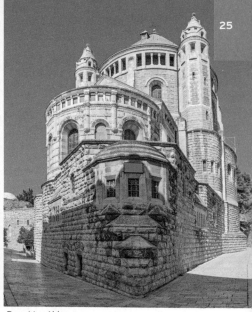

Dormition Abbey

knee-high in water. Skip the tunnel if you are claustrophobic, but if you're not, bring a flashlight.

Go back toward the Old City and take one of the many waiting taxis to dinner in City Center, preferably somewhere off King David Street or in the popular pedestrian plaza and historic neighborhood of **Nahalat Shiva.**

DAY 2

Take a taxi to the popular outdoor pedestrian shopping center **Mamilla,** where you can have breakfast alfresco at one of the restaurants with a vista of the new city and the landmark **Montefiore Windmill.** From Mamilla, it is a quick hop to the Old City, where you can check out anything you missed the previous day, such as the popular **Ramparts Walk tour** that circles the Old City along the top of the walls. Alternatively, there is the walk up the belfry tower at the **Church of the Redeemer** for one of the most highly rated and under-visited 360-degree views of the Old City.

Before it gets too late, exit the Old City through the Zion Gate and head up the hillside to **Mount Zion,** the site where some believe Jesus held the Last Supper and King David's Tomb can be found. Don't let anybody talk you into making a "donation" here; the site is free. At Mount Zion you will also find the lovely **Dormition Abbey** and great vistas of the city from multiple vantage points.

Take a taxi to the top of the **Mount of Olives,** where you will see the view of the Old City of Jerusalem that Jesus is said to have shed tears over when telling of its coming destruction. Go by foot into the nearby Arab village and have lunch at one of the many small restaurants serving Arab food before heading back down the hillside by taxi. Ask to be dropped off at the **Church of the Pater Noster,** and then walk downhill to the nearby **Dome and Chapel of the Ascension** and the **Garden of Gethsemane.**

From the Garden of Gethsemane, it is a long walk or a quick taxi ride to a City Center restaurant; try something near Tolerance Square this time.

DAY 3

Enjoy breakfast at your hotel before heading out to see some of Jerusalem's museums. Go by bus or taxi to **The Israel Museum,** about 20 minutes west of the Old City by car. Allow at least a half day to explore the museum and its rich, famed exhibits specializing in Judaica and Jewish history as well as regional history. Take advantage of the museum's restaurant for lunch and hop across the street to the **Bible Lands Museum.** Then take a taxi to the nearby and underrated **Monastery of the Cross,** located in the valley from which the wood for Jesus's cross is said to have been taken. From here take another taxi to **Yad Vashem** Holocaust memorial, or walk five minutes to the bus that will take you to the light rail. The light rail will deliver you to **Mount Herzl** and the associated Herzl museum, near the shuttle buses that take you down Yad Vashem's long drive. Allow at least four hours and some time for food or a cold drink at the cafeteria where you can meditate on the sweeping view of the Jerusalem forest.

From Yad Vashem, take the light-rail train to City Center and the famous **Machane Yehuda** Market (the *shuk*), where you can wander around and finish with dinner in one of the *shuk*'s many wonderful restaurants or cafés. In the evening, the *shuk*'s nightlife cranks up, and the quiet pubs turn into hopping parties, some with live music.

Tel Aviv
DAY 4
BUS FROM JERUSALEM (1 HOUR)

Go by bus from Jerusalem to **Tel Aviv** in the morning after breakfast (and after rush hour)—it's very easy to go back and forth between these cities by bus. After checking in at your hotel, take a stroll around **Dizengoff Center**'s great shopping district, and stop by the **Bauhaus Center** to pick up maps and information about Tel Aviv's famed **White City** and available tours. Stay near Dizengoff to enjoy one of the area's many outstanding restaurants for lunch.

After lunch, get ready for a late-afternoon beach session (in summer months, wait until after 2pm at the earliest). Take water and a change of clothes so you can go straight to dinner afterward. Try **Aviv Beach,** just north of Charles

dining at Machane Yehuda Market

Tel Aviv Museum of Art

Clore Park, or any of the beaches that are north of Charles Clore Park but south of the Marina. From Aviv Beach, take a nice 25-minute stroll to the **HaTachana Train Station Complex** for some shopping and dining; make sure to check out the **Made in TLV** store. Five minutes away, wander through Tel Aviv's historic **Neve Tzedek** neighborhood, the oldest neighborhood in the city, for a European-style dinner. If you can recharge at your hotel, head back out to party when things get started at the clubs around midnight.

DAY 5

Take a rest from the sun and nightlife of Tel Aviv to see the new and extremely popular addition of **Sarona** market for some shopping and cuisine. Self-described as the "heartbeat of Israeli culinary art," it is an assault of regional colors and smells. Stay for a wine-tasting, try some olive oil straight from the press, and enjoy a three-course gourmet meal.

From the market, take a taxi or bus to one of the city's museums, like the **Tel Aviv Museum of Art.** Take in the best view of the city at the **Azrieli Observatory** just before sunset, and then head back down to city level for dinner in one of the city's many restaurants. You can take the train back to your hotel from **Azrieli Center** after doing any shopping in the mall there if needed.

DAY 6
DRIVE TO HAIFA (1 HOUR)

Before checking out of your Tel Aviv hotel, head to the north of the city and have a breakfast of *shakshuka* eggs at one of the **Port of Tel Aviv**'s many seaside restaurants. If you time it right, you can catch the weekly **outdoor market.** Swing by **Old Jaffa** for an afternoon of sightseeing at one of the oldest ports in the world.

A good place to start in Old Jaffa is just off Yefet Street. From there you can wander around the center and the nearby promenade for some scenic wish-you-were-here photographs of the Mediterranean Sea. Look for the **clock tower,** surrounded by galleries and shops for browsing as an anchoring landmark. Stay in Old Jaffa for lunch at one of the many world-class restaurants that serve up Arab specialties, often with a European twist.

Pick up a rental car for the short drive to **Haifa,** about an hour north of Tel Aviv. Leave some daylight, because the road to Haifa hugs the scenic shoreline of the Mediterranean most of the way. Once you've settled into one of Haifa's gorgeous boutique hotels in the historic **German Colony,** have dinner under the twinkling lights of the **Baha'i Gardens and Golden Dome** at one of the area's many sumptuous restaurants.

Caesarea and Zichron Ya'akov

DAY 7

DRIVE FROM HAIFA (30 MINUTES TO CAESAREA, THEN 20 MINUTES TO ZICHRON YA'AKOV)

After breakfast, set out from Haifa for the **Caesarea National Antiquities Park,** where you can spend most of the day exploring the gorgeous **Roman ruins** by the sea that include the aqueduct, an amphitheater, mosaic floors, and bathhouses. There are many great options for lunch at the old **port,** which also has some nice shops showing off the work of local artisans.

Just 20 minutes up the coast is the charming Mediterranean village of **Zichron Ya'akov** with a redesigned town center created to foster sidewalk café culture, with street musicians and all kinds of **locally made arts.** There are also several places to enjoy **regionally produced wine.** After dinner, head back to Haifa.

Haifa

DAY 8

Plan to start your day early and spend it exploring Haifa by car or by one of the ample public transportation options, including the city's subway— the only subway in Israel.

Start at the top of the **Baha'i Gardens and Golden Dome** for an incomparable view of the Mediterranean Sea and the Haifa Port. Take the middle entrance if you want to explore more of

the gardens, but check visiting hours in advance as they fluctuate. For more views and strolling, the nearby **Louis Promenade** off Yefe Nof Street is fantastic and leads to the small but elegant **Mane Katz Museum** and the **Tikotin Museum of Japanese Art.**

At the top of **Mount Carmel** in Haifa is the **Stella Maris Carmelite Monastery,** with its small but extensively painted domed chapel and peaceful grounds filled with tropical plants and flowers. Just across the street from Stella Maris is the **San Francisco Observation Point** with a multilingual and comprehensive audio history of the area. Steps away is Haifa's **cable car,** which will take you down the mountainside to **Bat Galim Promenade.** Next to the promenade are **Elijah's Cave** and the **National Maritime Museum.**

For dinner, some of the best options in the most idyllic setting are located in the **German Colony,** at the base of the Baha'i Gardens. The area is small, so it's easy to wander through and find a range of options.

Akko (Acre)

DAY 9

DRIVE FROM HAIFA (30 MINUTES TO AKKO, THEN 1 HOUR TO TIBERIAS)

Leave your hotel by car for the 30-minute drive to Akko (also called Acre), where you can spend the day touring the **Acre Old City** and its network of **Crusader walls, fortresses, knights' halls, and tunnels.** Before lunch, take the long walk to the **Templars' Tunnel,** and stop near the *shuk* on the way back for some falafel and hummus. On your way out of Akko, you'll pass by the **Baha'i Gardens,** which are just as serene as their sister site in Haifa, but much smaller. Entrance is free and there is parking, so stop in for a look. Then make the one-hour drive from Akko to **Tiberias,** check into your hotel, and have dinner at one of the many restaurants in the town center on the shore of the **Sea of Galilee,** where you can enjoy the sunset and the moonrise over the waters if you time it right.

Tiberias
DAY 10

After breakfast in Tiberias, drive to the nearby grouping of historic and archaeological sites just 15 minutes away. Start at the archaeological site at **Magdala,** a 1st-century synagogue where Jesus is believed to have taught and where the earliest known depiction of the Second Temple in Jerusalem exists. Next head to the **Mount of Beatitudes,** where the Sermon on the Mount was given by Jesus, with its serene gardens and wonderful vista of the Sea of Galilee. Then head to the breathtaking archaeological and religious site of **Capernaum.** From Capernaum, leave your car and follow the footpath that hugs the shore of the Sea of Galilee for about 30 minutes until you reach **Tabgha** and the **Church of the Multiplication,** where bread and fish were multiplied by Jesus to feed thousands. Have dinner in Tiberias or take a short drive to one of the regional, family-run restaurants in the area.

The Dead Sea
DAY 11
DRIVE FROM TIBERIAS (2.5 HOURS)

Drive from Tiberias straight south to the Dead Sea for some rest and relaxation. It's a 2.5-hour run, so take a break along the way by stopping at the renowned archaeological site of **Beit She'an.** Once you've checked into your Dead Sea hotel, go to one of the many beaches to float in the **salty waters** and slather **therapeutic mud** on your body. Take your time and enjoy a leisurely dinner at an area restaurant before going back to your hotel.

DAY 12
DRIVE TO EILAT (2.5 HOURS)

Start out early before it gets too hot and take the tram to the famed archaeological site of **Masada** where it is said that a small band of Jews held off the Roman army. The views of the Dead Sea below and Jordan in the distance are incomparable. Take a picnic lunch and stop by the **Ein Gedi Nature Reserve** and its 2,000-year-old **natural**

Dead Sea

Ein Gedi Nature Reserve

Petra

spring that flows down the mountainside and forms multiple **waterfalls and pools** along the way. You can swim in many of the pools, the best of which is about a 15-minute walk from the park entrance. Drive from Ein Gedi to **Eilat** (2.5 hours) and stay overnight.

Petra, Jordan
DAY 13
DRIVE FROM EILAT (2 HOURS)

Start out early and get to the Eilat-Aqaba border by taxi (about 10 minutes). After crossing the border, go by taxi to one of Aqaba's many car rental offices and pick up a car for the two-hour drive to **Petra.** Once you are in Petra, take an afternoon hike, followed by a late-afternoon lunch in one of the restaurants in the village adjacent to Petra, **Wadi Musa.** Spend the rest of the afternoon exploring Wadi Musa, and do a bit of shopping. After a rest at your hotel, head back by foot to get dinner in town, and try some local Bedouin food.

DAY 14

Start off from your hotel early for a **morning hike** in Petra up one of the paths that leads to a high vantage point so you can see the area. Make sure to stop at the **Petra Nabataean Museum** and see the antiquities that have been found over the years. Go by foot back out to Wadi Musa for an early lunch and head out of town in your rental car for Aqaba and the Israel border.

A Middle East Feast

Certain towns in Israel and the West Bank are known for specializing in a regional cuisine. While there are long-standing debates over where the best of certain dishes originate, some undisputed reigning champions exist.

HUMMUS

For hummus, the Arab village Abu Ghosh just outside Jerusalem is high on the list. At **The Lebanese Restaurant** (65 Kvish Ha-Shalom, tel. 02/533-2019, 11am-11pm daily, NIS30), at the entrance to the village, the decor is spartan but the food is divine. Multiple additional options are within easy walking distance. Farther up the coast, Akko's hummus is known far and wide. A renowned favorite is **Hummus Said** (middle of the Old City market area off Salah ad Din St., tel. 04/991-3945, 6am-2:30pm Sun.-Fri., NIS30) for its traditional presentation, cheap prices, and central location.

FALAFEL AND PITA

Decent falafel can be found almost everywhere in the region, but if you really want to experience it hot and fresh, the *shuk* in almost any town will have offerings. In Jerusalem, a reigning falafel master is **Yemenite Falafel** (48 Hanevi'im St., tel. 02/624-2346, 9:30am-9:30pm Sun.-Thurs., 9:30am-3pm Fri., NIS40). Another extremely popular falafel joint is **Moshiko** (5 Ben Yehuda St., tel. 050/535-6861, 9am-midnight Sun.-Thurs., 9am-2pm Fri., NIS50), with its bright sign that is easy to spot.

No trip to the Middle East would be complete without pita. In south Tel Aviv's Jaffa, **Abulafia Bakery** (7 Yefet St., tel. 03/683-0958, 24 hours a day Sun.-Sat., NIS20) is renowned for its pita and Arab sweet treats.

SHAKSHUKA

Many try to claim the title of the best *shakshuka* ever created, but if you're new to the dish, Jerusalem's **Tmol Shilshom** (5 Solomon St.

the Arab sweet treat *knafe* for sale in the Old City of Nablus

through the back alley, tel. 02/623-2758, www.tmol-shilshom.co.il, 9am-1am Sun.-Thurs., 9am-3pm Fri., NIS55) has mastered this regional staple dish of eggs, tomatoes, and other vegetables. Tel Aviv's **Dr. Shakshuka** (3 Beit Eshel St., tel. 057/944-4193, http://shakshuka.rest.co.il, 8am-midnight Sun.-Thurs., NIS45) is widely known by reputation and considered a reigning champion of the cuisine. A very inventive and increasingly popular *shakshuka* option in Tel Aviv can be found at **Shakshukia** (94 Ben Yehuda St., tel. 03/522-3433, 10am-10pm Sun.-Thurs., 10am-4pm Fri., NIS60).

KNAFE

Ruin yourself on the popular Arab sweet treat *knafe* by trying it first in the West Bank Arab village of Nablus. Go anywhere in the Old City and you will easily find vendors preparing it fresh.

Journey into Jerusalem

Though six days is just enough to scratch the surface of what Jerusalem has to offer, this section maps out a travel strategy with an emphasis on archaeological sites alongside new attractions and places to eat and play. Think **ancient archaeological sites** in and around the Old City by day, and **rooftop drinks and food** overlooking the city or live music by night. It also includes a few notable places in the vicinity of Jerusalem. The time frame is divided by the days of the week, due to Jerusalem's more limited options during Shabbat (Fri. night-Sat. night).

Day 1: Sunday

After a good night's sleep at your hotel, put on your most comfortable shoes and get ready for some serious walking in the **Old City.** Start from the information center at the Jaffa Gate and pick a couple of key points in the Old City to explore, but allow for plenty of time to wander, take photos, and bargain for deals.

From the Jaffa Gate, you can easily explore the **Armenian Quarter** (mostly residential) and loop back up to the **Jewish Quarter** and the old Roman **Cardo,** which includes some high-end shopping. Keep going north to the **Christian Quarter** and you can see a number of churches, including the **Church of the Holy Sepulchre.**

Walk to **Nahalat Shiva,** where you can spend a couple of leisurely hours exploring the shops full of handmade crafts before you walk to the **Jerusalem Time Elevator** exhibit for an interactive trip through Jerusalem history. Stay in Nahalat Shiva for dinner to experience one of Jerusalem's most famous and authentically Middle Eastern restaurants, **Tmol Shilshom.**

Day 2: Monday

After a leisurely breakfast, get a picnic lunch and head to **The Israel Museum** by taxi or bus for a late-morning viewing session of antiquities and Jewish and regional history and

market in the Old City of Jerusalem

Station 9 on the Via Dolorosa

art, including the Shrine of the Book, which houses the Dead Sea Scrolls. Directly across the way is the **Bible Lands Museum** with its gorgeous ancient jewelry displays and emphasis on biblical history.

When you've had enough air-conditioning, take a quick taxi ride or a 25-minute walk to a free tour of the **Supreme Court of Israel**; the tour starts at noon. After that, hop over to the **Knesset (Israeli Parliament)** for another free tour, starting at 2pm, if you have time. Stop in the **Wohl Rose Garden** with its vast collection of roses on a gently sloping lawn overlooking Jerusalem for your picnic lunch. The roses will stay in full bloom late into the year, and after lunch you can explore the grounds and the approximately 400 varieties of roses.

Head back to your hotel by taxi and rest up before dinner at any one of the City Center restaurants near Tolerance Square. After dinner, take a stroll through **Tolerance Square** with its lively evening atmosphere including street musicians, and get dessert from one of the ice cream shops.

Day 3: Tuesday

Make sure you are conservatively dressed or have something to cover your shoulders and legs, but with pants that can be rolled up, then head back to the **Old City** in the morning (bring a flashlight). Take a taxi to the Damascus Gate in East Jerusalem, and enter the Old City through the gate to explore the **Muslim Quarter** and see some of the stations along the **Via Dolorosa,** where Jesus carried his cross on his way to be crucified. Continue along the Via Dolorosa to the northern side of the **Dome of the Rock, Al Aqsa Mosque,** and the **Western Wall,** holy sites to Christians, Muslims, and Jews. Just before the entrance to the Western Wall there are a number of restaurants where you can get lunch and rest before continuing.

Exit the Old City just past the Western Wall and you'll be in the East Jerusalem neighborhood of **Silwan,** where the **City of David** is located. Make sure you buy a ticket that includes a trip through **Hezekiah's Tunnel** (a good activity when the midday sun is out). After traipsing through the 2,700-year-old tunnel for 580 yards

looking up at Yad Vashem's Hall of Names

(530 meters) to the **Pool of Siloam** and touring the City of David, take a rest back at your hotel and freshen up for the evening.

Before dinner, take in the sunset at the swanky Mamilla Hotel's rooftop terrace bar and restaurant (make reservations in advance). You can stay for dinner after enjoying the view of the old and new cities, or head downstairs to try one of Mamilla's restaurants.

Day 4: Wednesday

Set out early to the **Mount of Olives** for an awe-inspiring sunrise. Get a taxi to take you to the top of the Mount of Olives' highest vista point, above the old Jewish Cemetery, right next to the Seven Arches Hotel. From here, enjoy the incredible view of old and new Jerusalem. Walk down the hill and go through the **Jewish Cemetery,** or just continue downhill to various vista points for photos. Continue downhill toward the Old City, stopping to peek inside the churches along the way. It's a long walk, but frequented by taxis if you get tired.

Take a taxi to **Mount Zion** just outside the Zion Gate at the Old City, and explore the

Dormition Abbey and the area near **King David's Tomb.**

For lunch, hop on the light-rail train bound for the **Machane Yehuda Market** (the *shuk*) where you can explore the massive array of stalls selling fresh produce, spices, and regional sweets and snacks. Stop off at one of the *shuk*'s many restaurants for lunch. From here, catch the light-rail train to **Yad Vashem** and **Mount Herzl.** Start with Yad Vashem, which can take several hours (children under the age of 10 are not allowed in the main hall).

If you have the energy, head back out just before dark to the Old City for the **Night Spectacular** light show at the Tower of David Museum citadel at the Jaffa Gate.

Day 5: Thursday

Use Thursday to visit the **Museum on the Seam** for a detailed and clear-eyed look at the juxtaposition of East and West Jerusalem. Go by taxi to the **L.A. Mayer Museum for Islamic Art** and then take a 15-minute walk downhill to the historic **German Colony** neighborhood either for a guided tour (arranged in advance) of the beautiful Templer-style buildings and homes or to do some shopping for essentials or souvenirs along popular Emek Refaim Street.

For lunch, walk 10 minutes to the popular **First Station** culinary-and-shopping complex, built from the foundation of Jerusalem's former main train station, which is more than 120 years old. There is more shopping to be had here in a lively atmosphere that often includes musical performances. Follow the adjacent trails in **Train Track Park** north to hilly **Bloomfield Garden** with its beautiful fountain and pathways. Walk through the park until you reach the **Montefiore Windmill** and its sweeping vista of East Jerusalem and the separation barrier in the distance. Continue on to the **King David Hotel** and the YMCA, both with historic architecture and idyllic outdoor seating for dinner.

Day 6: Friday

Friday in Jerusalem tends to be a bit frenzied as locals take care of last-minute shopping before the city shuts down for 24 hours. It is a good day to go back to the Old City's **Rockefeller Archaeological Museum** to see antiquities or take the **Ramparts Walk** along the top of the wall surrounding the Old City in the morning. A short taxi ride away, at the top of King David Street you will find the Bezalel Art Academy, where the **Bezalel Art Fair** with 150 local vendors selling locally made arts, crafts, and food is held. It is the perfect spot for souvenir shopping. There are numerous restaurants nearby for lunch, but plan to wrap things up by about 2pm.

For a quiet dinner and a glass of wine with a rooftop view of the city, go by taxi to the imposing Pontifical Institute Notre Dame's four-star **Roof Top Wine and Cheese Restaurant.**

Outward Bound: Excursions from Jerusalem

Using Jerusalem as your base, venture out to explore nearby areas including Tel Aviv, the West Bank, and the Dead Sea.

The West Bank (1-2 days)

GO TO THE WEST BANK BY BUS, SHARE TAXI, TAXI, OR WITH A TOUR GROUP (MAXIMUM OF 1 HOUR TO EACH LOCATION)

Go with a tour guide to **Bethlehem** for the day, where you can explore the various religious and cultural sites, focusing on the area near Manger Square in the town center. Bring your passport, as you'll have to cross through a checkpoint upon entering and exiting the town.

Stay overnight in either Bethlehem or **Ramallah,** and spend the next day exploring Ramallah's shopping and dining offerings in this modern Arab city. Get oriented at the Al Manara roundabout in town center and look for the **Stars & Bucks Café** if you feel lost or want

a destination to start from. It's a great place for **window-shopping and dining** at one of the city's many great restaurants, known for their east and west fusion.

Since Ramallah is only a short drive by taxi or bus to Jerusalem, dinner at **Rooftop** at the Mamilla Hotel is a good choice to round out the day one you've returned. It has an impressive view of Jerusalem and the Old City in a setting that feels more like Tel Aviv.

Tel Aviv (3 days)

DRIVE (1 HOUR) OR TAKE THE TRAIN (1.5 HOURS) FROM JERUSALEM

A good start in Tel Aviv is always one of the city's many **beaches** for some afternoon fun in the sun and water. The proximity of restaurants and cafés to the beachfront makes it easy to go straight from the Mediterranean to get a drink or something to eat. Tel Aviv's active and famously late **nightlife** (especially in the summer) means

an outdoor café on Dizengoff Street in Tel Aviv

you won't miss much if you take your time at your hotel before going out to dinner at one of the city's many fine restaurants. In fact, the later, the better.

If it's your first time in town, try one of Neve Tzedek's many European-style restaurants for dinner. From here you can easily walk to the lively nightlife and shopping scene at the **HaTachana Train Station Complex,** and you're also not far from **Dizengoff's numerous bars, pubs, and clubs.** For some of the most exciting nightlife in town, the north of the city at the Port of Tel Aviv has tons of seaside clubs, pubs, restaurants, and bars, as well as an enormous promenade right on the water with street performers, huge outdoor bars and restaurants, great stops for dessert, and plenty of strolling space.

Mornings in Tel Aviv are lovely for a stroll or bike ride and a leisurely breakfast on the waterfront, exploring **Old Jaffa** in the south, or getting out to **HaYarkon Park** in the north for a stroll before the heat becomes unbearable. The park has **bicycle and boat rentals,** and plenty of space for a **picnic lunch**. You can also dine in a restaurant by the lake, on the eastern side of the park, under massive trees.

If you're looking for some city tours, you can arrange to see Tel Aviv's famed **White City** with an English-speaking guide at the **Bauhaus Center,** or get a map for a self-guided experience through the area. There are always good shopping, dining, and entertainment options around **Dizengoff Street,** and on certain days of the week the Port of Tel Aviv has an **outdoor farmers market.**

Also worth exploring is the largest nonprofit art gallery in Israel in the **Shalom Mayer Tower** and its **Discover Tel Aviv Center,** with its general history of Tel Aviv. From the Shalom Mayer Tower, it's a short walk back to **Neve Tzedek,** where you'll find the **Nachum Gutman Museum of Art** and the **Rokach House Museum,** which offers a bit about the history of Neve Tzedek and how Tel Aviv's first neighborhood was founded.

For more suggestions on Tel Aviv, see page 109.

Hebron (1 day)

DRIVE FROM JERUSALEM WITH TOUR GUIDE OR GROUP (1 HOUR)

With a pre-hired tour guide only (due to long-standing security concerns), take the one-hour drive to Hebron to see some of the ancient city's sights, including the **Tomb of the Patriarchs** and **Ibrahimi Mosque.**

One of Hebron's highlights is the **Arab-style food,** but since it's a bit impractical to go there without a tour guide or group, you'll do whatever the tour group does, which will include a restaurant and shopping. You can also request to see one of Hebron's famed **ceramic or glass shops.**

The Dead Sea (2 days)

DRIVE OR TAKE THE BUS FROM JERUSALEM (1-2 HOURS)

Go from Jerusalem about an hour south to the Dead Sea, where you'll find a number of great **beaches** that offer different Dead Sea experiences. Check in advance for any road closures due to frequently occurring sinkholes in the area. About midway down the western shore of the Dead Sea just 15 minutes past Ein Gedi, you'll find the mountaintop fortress of **Masada.**

Masada is a good stop before hitting the beaches (there won't be much shade and it will be unbearable in the afternoon), where you can take in the vista of the Dead Sea from the vantage point of a high peak. The **Yigael Yadin Masada Museum,** which has a very interesting and easy-to-digest walk-through exhibit with an audio guide, is included with a full ticket to Masada and is a must-see.

Near most of the Dead Sea beaches you can have a light lunch or drink. In the area where hotels are concentrated, there are numerous restaurants to choose from, some of which are on the water.

Once you're in the sea, you can float in the salty waters and rub therapeutic mud onto your body. All of the beaches have outdoor showers where you can rinse off the salty water.

Just at the edge of where the Dead Sea meets the border of the West Bank is **Ein Gedi Nature Reserve,** with its 2,000-year-old spring and relatively steep hike up the mountainside. You can see ibex and hyrax on the way into the park, and take a 30-minute **hike** before reaching one of many **freshwater pools and waterfalls** where you can swim. It's always best to go as early in the day as possible, as the park attracts crowds of people and it gets punishingly hot in the summer after about noon. Do not take food into the reserve; park rangers patrol for and ticket violators.

Ancient Terrain: Desert Hikes and Magical Waters

Departing from Jerusalem, journey by car to the south on a route that will take you past the Dead Sea, Eilat and the Red Sea, and Petra, Jordan.

many beaches along its western shore. Spend the night in one of the Dead Sea hotels and luxuriate in the area's many offerings.

The Dead Sea

DAY 1

DRIVE TO EIN GEDI (1.5 HOURS)

Leave Jerusalem in the morning and go by rental car south to the Dead Sea, the lowest point on Earth. Stay in either **Ein Gedi,** exploring the ancient spring in Ein Gedi Nature Reserve, hiking, and swimming, or go to one of the **Dead Sea's**

Be'er Sheva

DAY 2

DRIVE TO BE'ER SHEVA (2.5 HOURS); BE'ER SHEVA TO MITZPE RAMON (1 HOUR); MITZPE RAMON TO EILAT (1.5 HOURS)

Continue southwest toward **Be'er Sheva,** the largest city in the south of Israel. Stop just north of Be'er Sheva, where you'll find the one-of-a-kind **Museum of Bedouin Culture at the Joe Alon Center.** After experiencing some Bedouin culture and history, drive south to the ancient archaeological site of **Tel Beer Sheba.** From here it is just a short drive to the city of **Be'er Sheva,** where you can have lunch at one of the many restaurants in the city center. Also near city center is the **Negev Museum of Art.** From Be'er Sheva, take the one-hour drive to the enormous **Ramon Crater** for a short desert hike and a look at the ancient crater before it starts to get dark. After your tour, drive the remaining approximately 90 minutes to **Eilat,** check into your hotel, and call it a night.

Eilat

DAY 3

Start off your morning in Eilat by taking breakfast at your hotel, then go by taxi to the **Dolphin Reef Diving Center** for a guided swim with the dolphins. Take a bus back to Eilat's city center for lunch and then head to one of the many **beaches** for a swim, or go diving. If you are new to diving, allow an entire day for it.

After freshening up at your hotel, go by foot or taxi to Eilat's version of Rodeo Drive, **La Boulevard,** for upscale shopping. One of the numerous nearby restaurants will be perfect for dinner.

DAY 4

Go by taxi to the **Coral World Underwater Observatory** to see the many varieties of bright, rare fish. You can easily spend half a day exploring this complex. Have an early dinner at one of the many beachfront restaurants in the city center and then take in an evening performance of **The WOW Show.**

Petra

DAY 5

DRIVE FROM EILAT (2 HOURS)

Start as early in the morning as possible with a prearranged tour guide who can escort you to the Eilat-Aqaba border where you will cross the border (about 10 minutes by taxi) and meet

swimming with dolphins in the Red Sea

Pilgrimage Sites

It isn't known as the Holy Land for nothing. Here is a list of some of the most important religious and spiritual sites.

- **Al Aqsa Mosque next to the Dome of the Rock** is the third holiest site in the Muslim world (Jerusalem, Old City; page 58).

- **Basilica of the Annunciation** is believed to be built over the site of the Virgin Mary's original home (Nazareth; page 218).

- **Capernaum** is home to an archaeological site believed to be the ruins of a village where Jesus and some of his disciples lived for a time on the shore of the Sea of Galilee (near Tiberias; page 209).

- **Church of the Holy Sepulchre** is widely recognized as the site of the crucifixion and resurrection of Jesus. The church has long been governed and used simultaneously by the Greek Orthodox, Armenian Orthodox, and Roman Catholic churches (Jerusalem, Old City; page 54).

- **Church of the Multiplication** is believed to be the location where Jesus turned a few fish and a couple of loaves of bread into enough food for thousands (Tiberias; page 208).

- **Church of the Nativity** is widely believed to be the location where Jesus was born (Bethlehem; page 242).

- **Mount of Olives** is the site of many miraculous occurrences and an extremely significant location in Judaism, Christianity, and Islam (Jerusalem, near the Old City; page 64).

- **Mount Zion** is one possible site of the Last Supper and the location of King David's Tomb (Jerusalem; page 62).

prayer in the women's section of the Western Wall

- **Tomb of Rabbi Meir** is significant to Jews all over the world as the tomb of the rabbi who was nicknamed "the miracle worker" and in whose name charity is often given (near Tiberias; page 207).

- **Tomb of the Patriarchs/Ibrahimi Mosque** is widely recognized as the burial place of Jewish and Muslim patriarchs and matriarchs, including Abraham. The site is sacred to both the Jews and Muslims (Hebron; page 258).

- **Western Wall** is a remnant of the western wall of the destroyed Second Temple. It is a popular destination for prayer by Jews and sometimes the site of large-scale religious events (Old City, Jerusalem; page 58).

up with another guide. During the two-hour ride to **Petra,** take note of all the unusual rock formations with ribbons of mineral deposits in the hills of the famous **Wadi Rum.** After arriving, spend a few hours taking a short hike into Petra, then have lunch in the modern neighboring village, **Wadi Musa.** Though it is small, Wadi Musa is geared heavily toward tourists, and you can find some interesting shopping in the town's center, especially if you gravitate toward the Shaheed roundabout. Take a break from the heat and rehydrate before going out for dinner in town at one of the home-style Bedouin restaurants.

the Petra by Night Show

DAY 6

Get an early start in Petra and take a hike up one of the paths that leads to a higher vantage point so that you can see the area from a different perspective. Make sure to stop at the **Petra Nabataean Museum** to see many of the antiquities that have been found over the years.

Go by foot back out to Wadi Musa by late afternoon and rest up at your hotel before dinner. Later in the evening, go back to Petra's **Treasury** for the idyllic **Petra by Night Show** with stories and music.

DAY 7

DRIVE TO EILAT (2 HOURS); EILAT TO JERUSALEM (4 HOURS)

Set out from Petra as early as possible in the morning with a rental car you picked up there for the two-hour trip back to Aqaba, where you will take a taxi to the border, cross by foot, and then take another taxi back to Eilat. Once in Eilat, pick up another rental car for the four-hour drive back to Jerusalem. Including stops to eat and logistics, the return trip will take an entire day.

Jerusalem

The region's religious, historical, and political

center, Jerusalem hosts a striking mixture of classical architecture, distinct regional cuisine, cultural treasures, and compelling tourist attractions.

Jerusalem has long been a place where history and faith collide, but in recent years, city leaders have led sustained efforts to also create space for arts, music, fashion shows, literary and brewing festivals, and more—alongside entrepreneurship and innovation. The city is an eternal work in progress, with a little something for everyone.

A city on a plateau in the Judean Mountains that sits at about 2,500 feet (750 meters), most visitors start by exploring the dusty, worn nooks and crannies within the Ottoman-era walls of the Old City. The

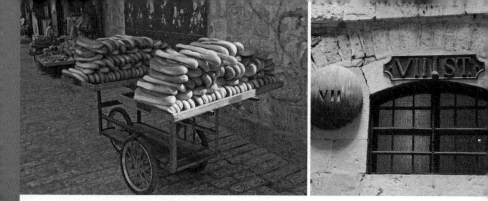

Highlights

Look for ★ to find recommended sights, activities, dining, and lodging.

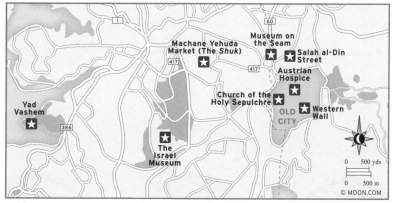

★ **Church of the Holy Sepulchre:** One of the most important sites for Christian pilgrims, this is the place where many believe Jesus was crucified (page 54).

★ **Austrian Hospice:** Ensconced behind a nondescript gray concrete wall, this calming neutral oasis in the midst of the Old City is a beloved place of respite and reflection for both locals and visitors (page 55).

★ **Western Wall:** One of the most important sites in Judaism, the Western Wall, also known as the Kotel or Wailing Wall, is at the southeastern corner of the Old City (page 58).

★ **Machane Yehuda Market (The *Shuk*):** An outdoor market by day and party central by night, the *shuk* is frequented by locals of all ages and backgrounds (page 63).

★ **Museum on the Seam:** One of the city's most politically relevant museums is situated along Jerusalem's traditional east-west border (page 64).

★ **Salah al-Din Street:** Experience some of East Jerusalem's best Arab food and browse bookshops with English-language literature by regional authors along this stretch just outside the Old City's bustling, central Damascus Gate entrance (page 66).

★ **The Israel Museum:** The museum's world-class exhibits on Jewish history, archaeology, and regional treasures are a must-see (page 68).

★ **Yad Vashem:** The largest Holocaust museum in the world is a solemn experience (page 70).

pungent aromas of spices, coffee, and regional dishes like falafel create a multidimensional experience for the scores of archaeological and pilgrimage sites. The Old City is a hub for shopping, entertainment, guided tours, concerts, and cultural activities like dining out. Some of the best and the worst can be found here, from Middle Eastern sweets made from centuries-old family recipes to cheap goods made in China. There are four distinct but partially overlapping quarters: Muslim, Jewish, Christian, and Armenian. The imposing Western Wall is overshadowed only by the Dome of the Rock on the elevated plaza of Haram al-Sharif in the background. There is also arguably nowhere else in the city where bargaining with vendors for a souvenir is quite as intense.

Jerusalem is an exciting place to shop for high-quality, regionally made usable items like ceramics, jewelry, and clothing. There are several world-class museums, spacious parks, and landscaped gardens. The rolling hills of the Wohl Rose Garden is a serene place for a picnic and a stroll, also within walking distance of tours of the Israeli parliament, the Israel Museum, and the Bible Lands Museum. City Center has many options for dining and sightseeing, as does the city's famed *shuk*, or market, which has emerged as another center of dancing, live music, drinking, and general Jerusalem-level partying. The sobering Yad Vashem Holocaust Memorial takes a toll on visitors with its descriptive exhibits and isolated location in the hills of the city's forest.

When too much history and culture start to overwhelm, the fun, family-focused, and more secular atmosphere of First Station in West Jerusalem has numerous dining, shopping, and entertainment options in a walkable area.

HISTORY

Jerusalem's history, like the city itself, is alive. The first evidence of human life in Jerusalem is around 4500 BC. The first reference to the name Jerusalem (Urushalimum) was in 1500 BC. In Arabic, it is called Al Quds. With a history full of winding twists and turns, for millennia it has been a religious stronghold for Muslims, Christians, and Jews. It has also long endured as a flashpoint of religious, ethnic, and geopolitical tension.

In ancient times, Jerusalem was mainly confined within the protective walls of the Old City. The city has long been an object of pursuit for ambitious rulers and empires and was conquered and destroyed multiple times.

In modern times, largely since the establishment of the Jewish state in 1948, political debates and armed battles of all sizes have raged over the question of who controls and can lay claim to the holy city. This is at the heart of the debate over foreign embassies there.

In 1948, soldiers from Transjordan's Arab Legion (which became the Hashemite Kingdom of Jordan in 1949) tried to capture the entire city during the War of Independence. Israeli fighters defended significant portions of the western part of the city. After the Arab Legion destroyed the Jewish Quarter of the Old City and expelled the residents, a cease-fire agreement was signed. The area outside the walls became known as the New City and was mostly Israeli-controlled.

In April 1949, an armistice agreement was signed along the 1948 cease-fire line between Israeli and Transjordan forces. The line between east and west was demarcated by concertina wire, concrete walls, minefields, and bunkers. East Jerusalem, including holy sites, was occupied by Transjordan and West Jerusalem became the capital of Israel.

In 1967, the Israeli Defense Force (or IDF) battled Jordan again to take control of East Jerusalem. The city came under full Israeli control, with a promise that religious sites for all faiths would be protected. For Jews this meant they gained access to Temple Mount

---

Previous: Dome of the Rock mosque on Temple Mount; bread cart in Old Jerusalem; Station 7 on the Via Dolorosa.

Jerusalem's Conquerors

The list of those who have conquered, occupied, or destroyed Jerusalem is lengthy.

- **King David** conquers Jerusalem in 1000 BC.

- **Nebuchadnezzar,** king of Babylon, conquers Jerusalem and destroys the First Temple in 586 BC.

- **Alexander the Great** conquers Jerusalem in 332 BC.

- **Antiochus III** conquers Jerusalem in 200 BC.

- **Pompeius** conquers Jerusalem in 63 BC and Roman rule begins.

- **Herod** occupies Jerusalem and fortifies significant public buildings in 19 BC.

- **Titus's army** destroys Jerusalem and the Second Temple in AD 70.

- **Transjordan** captures East Jerusalem in 1948.

- **Israel** annexes East Jerusalem to unify the city under Israeli rule in 1967.

and the Western Wall and could freely visit and pray at these sites. For Arabs, it meant that many who fled during fighting became homeless and stateless.

Today you can stand on Highway 50 and observe the line that still metaphorically divides the city.

Political and ethnic tensions between East and West Jerusalem are ongoing and marked by periods of violence on both sides. The Arab neighborhood of Silwan is a stark example. Immediately adjacent to the Old City at Dung Gate and home to an activist Arab community, outbreaks of violence and police actions here are fairly common. In the nearby West Jerusalem neighborhood of Baka, a pre-1948 home to some of the most prominent Arab families in the city, the sound of concussion grenades can sometimes be heard echoing across Kidron Valley under the dark cover of the wee early morning hours.

ORIENTATION

Jerusalem is thousands of years old and home to over 2,000 major and minor archaeological sites. Most visitors try to include the Old City, Yad Vashem, Salah al-Din Street, Machane Yehuda Market, the Western Wall, and City Center in their trip.

The Old City

The Old City is an unforgettable experience and quintessential Jerusalem, good and bad. Though you'll find that many major towns and cities in the region have an old city section, there's nothing on a comparable scale to Jerusalem. Though many claim to know its secrets, the real experts of Jerusalem's Old City are the lifelong native inhabitants from multigenerational families. Today, there are about 35,000 residents who are among the only Jerusalemites allowed to drive vehicles there. Even taxis aren't allowed on the narrow, stone streets worn slippery-smooth by time.

Above ground, the Old City is divided into four quarters that date back to Roman times: the **Muslim Quarter,** the **Christian Quarter,** the **Armenian Quarter,** and the **Jewish Quarter.** Though these quarters overlap somewhat, divisions are even more debatable below ground, as evidenced by the **Western Wall Excavations.** There are **free, paid, and self-guided tours** of the neighborhood, and snaking rows and corridors of **shops** that sell everything from scarves to antiquities.

Most find **Jaffa Gate** to be the easiest and most recognizable entrance. A broad, open plaza where the gate once stood makes a good

Jerusalem

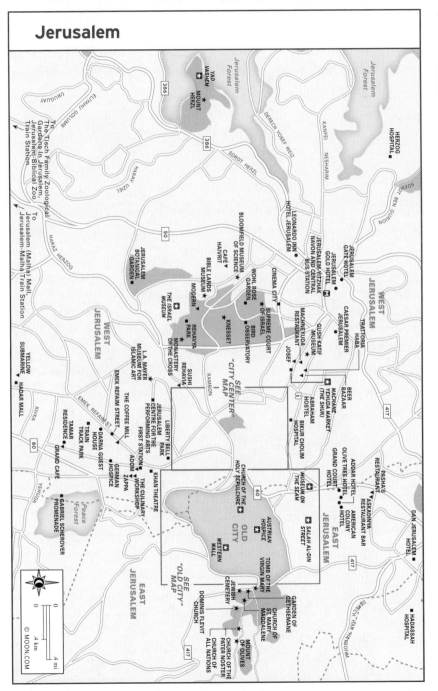

© MOON.COM

Old City

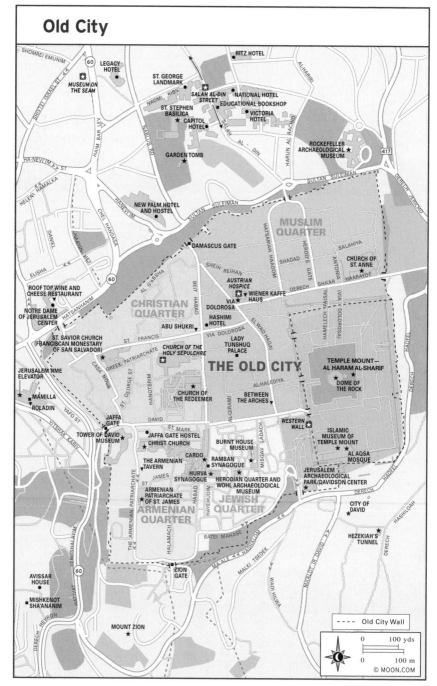

RITZ HOTEL

LEGACY HOTEL

ST. GEORGE LANDMARK

MUSEUM ON THE SEAM

SALAH AL-DIN STREET

NATIONAL HOTEL

EDUCATIONAL BOOKSHOP

ST. STEPHEN BASILICA

CAPITOL HOTEL

VICTORIA HOTEL

ROCKEFELLER ARCHAEOLOGICAL MUSEUM

GARDEN TOMB

SULTAN SULEIMAN

NEW PALM HOTEL AND HOSTEL

SULTAN SULEIMAN

MUSLIM QUARTER

DAMASCUS GATE

CHURCH OF ST. ANNE

SHEIH REIHAN

AUSTRIAN HOSPICE

WIENER KAFFE HAUS

ROOF TOP WINE AND CHEESE RESTAURANT

CHRISTIAN QUARTER

VIA DOLOROSA

NOTRE DAME OF JERUSALEM CENTER

ABU SHUKRI

HASHIMI HOTEL

VIA DOLOROSA

ST. SAVIOR CHURCH (FRANCISCAN MONESTARY OF SAN SALVADOR)

LADY TUNSHUQ PALACE

CHURCH OF THE HOLY SEPULCHRE

TEMPLE MOUNT— AL HARAM AL-SHARIF

JERUSALEM TIME ELEVATOR

THE OLD CITY

MAMILLA

DOME OF THE ROCK

ROLADIN

CHURCH OF THE REDEEMER

BETWEEN THE ARCHES

JAFFA GATE

WESTERN WALL

TOWER OF DAVID MUSEUM

JAFFA GATE HOSTEL

ISLAMIC MUSEUM OF TEMPLE MOUNT

CHRIST CHURCH

BURNT HOUSE MUSEUM

THE ARMENIAN TAVERN

CARDO

RAMBAN SYNAGOGUE

AL AQSA MOSQUE

HURVA SYNAGOGUE

HERODIAN QUARTER AND WOHL ARCHAEOLOGICAL MUSEUM

JERUSALEM ARCHAEOLOGICAL PARK/DAVIDSON CENTER

ARMENIAN PATRIARCHATE OF ST. JAMES

CITY OF DAVID

ARMENIAN QUARTER

JEWISH QUARTER

HEZEKIAH'S TUNNEL

AVISSAR HOUSE

MISHKENOT SHA'ANANIM

ZION GATE

MOUNT ZION

- - - Old City Wall

0   100 yds

0   100 m

© MOON.COM

City Center

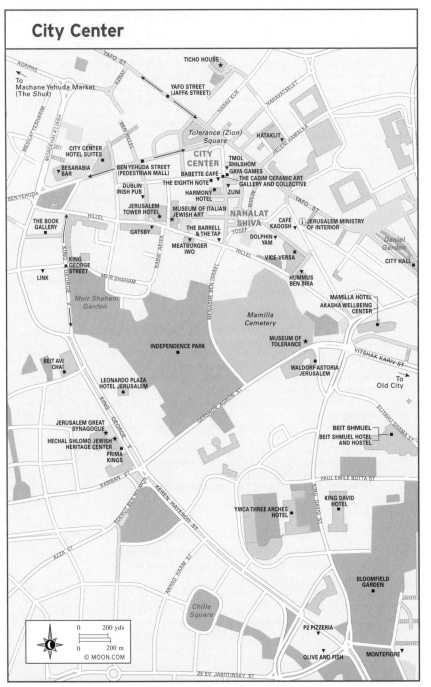

AGRIPAS

YAFO ST

TICHO HOUSE ★

To
Machane Yehuda Market
(The *Shuk*)

YAFO STREET
(JAFFA STREET)

MESILAT YESHARIM

MORDECHAI ALIASH

BEN HILLEL

EZRAT

HARAV KUK

HAHAVATSELET

Tolerance (Zion)
Square

HATAKLIT

HELEN HAMALKA

CITY CENTER
HOTEL SUITES

BESARABIA
BAR

BEN YEHUDA STREET
(PEDESTRIAN MALL)

CITY
CENTER

TMOL
SHILSHOM

BEN YEHUDA

DUBLIN
IRISH PUB

BABETTE CAFÉ

THE EIGHTH NOTE

HARMONY
HOTEL

GAYA GAMES

THE CADIM CERAMIC ART
GALLERY AND COLLECTIVE

ZUNI

JERUSALEM
TOWER HOTEL

HILLEL

THE BOOK
GALLERY

JERUSALEM
TOWER HOTEL

GATSBY

MUSEUM OF ITALIAN
JEWISH ART

NAHALAT
SHIVA

RIVLIN

YAFO ST

CAFÉ
KADOSH

ⓘ Jerusalem Ministry
OF INTERIOR

Daniel
Garden

RABBI AKIVA

YOSEF

THE BARRELL
& THE TAP

MEATBURGER
IWO

DOLPHIN
YAM

CITY HALL

KING
GEORGE
STREET

MEIR SHAHAM

HILLEL

VICE-VERSA

KING GEORGE

LINK

MENASHE BEN ISRAEL

HUMMUS
BEN SIRA

MAMILLA HOTEL

AKASHA WELLBEING
CENTER

*Meir Shaham
Garden*

*Mamilla
Cemetery*

INDEPENDENCE PARK

MUSEUM OF
TOLERANCE ★

YITSHAK KARIV ST

BEIT AVI
CHAI

LEONARDO PLAZA
HOTEL JERUSALEM

GERSHON AGRON ST

WALDORF ASTORIA
JERUSALEM

To
Old City

ELIYAHU SHAMA ST

JERUSALEM GREAT
SYNAGOGUE ★

HECHAL SHLOMO JEWISH
HERITAGE CENTER ★

PRIMA
KINGS

KING GEORGE V

BEIT SHMUEL

BEIT SHMUEL HOTEL
AND HOSTEL

RAMBAN ST

SDEROT BEN MAIMON

KEREN HAYESOD ST

PAUL EMILE BOTTA ST

KING DAVID ST

KING DAVID
HOTEL

AZZA ST

YMCA THREE ARCHES
HOTEL

AKHAD HAAM ST

BLOOMFIELD
GARDEN

*Chille
Square*

P2 PIZZERIA

OLIVE AND FISH

MONTEFIORE

ZE EV JABOTINSKY ST

0   200 yds

0   200 m

© MOON.COM

The First and Second Temples

No visitor to Jerusalem can escape references to the First Temple and the Second Temple, recalling historical time periods when two different massive Jewish temples stood approximately where Al Aqsa Mosque is now located. The main remnant of the Second Temple is the Western Wall, long known as the Wailing Wall or the Kotel. People flock from all over the world to pray and cram white paper notes to heaven into the wall's crevices.

According to Jewish tradition, both temples were destroyed hundreds of years apart in August or on the 9th of Av on the Jewish calendar. Every year, those destructions and other tragic disasters in Jewish history are marked by Tisha B'av, the day of mourning, when Western Wall Plaza fills with throngs of Jewish mourners.

FIRST TEMPLE PERIOD

The First Temple was built in 1000 BC by King Solomon after King David had conquered Jerusalem and made it his capital. It was destroyed in 586 BC by Nebuchadnezzar, the king of Babylon, when he conquered Jerusalem. The period between 1200-586 BC is now referred to as the **First Temple period.** There are scant remains of the temple on the south hill of the City of David. Evidence of the conquering and destruction of the city can be found in the Burnt House and the House of the Bullae.

Significant remains from the First Temple period include Hezekiah's Tunnel and the Broad Wall in the Jewish Quarter, made by King Hezekiah in preparation for an imminent siege on the city by the Assyrian king Sennacherib in 701 BC.

SECOND TEMPLE PERIOD

The beginning of the **Second Temple period** (586 BC-AD 70) is marked by the return of Jews to Jerusalem from their exile in Babylon. They were allowed to return under an edict issued by Cyrus, king of Persia. By 515 BC the reinstated Jewish residents had completed the Second Temple.

The time of the Second Temple and subsequent ages after its destruction are divided into different periods: the **Persian period** (586-332 BC), the **Hellenistic period** (332-63 BC), and the **Roman period** (63 BC-AD 324). In 37 BC, King Herod enlarged the Temple Mount and rebuilt the temple with the consent of the public. During the Roman period, in AD 70, the Second Temple was destroyed, along with the rest of Jerusalem, by Titus's army. It was also during this period that Jesus was in Jerusalem, where he was crucified about 40 years before the Second Temple's destruction.

Significant archaeological remains from the Second Temple period, including the Kidron Valley tombs, the Western Wall, Robinson's Arch, the Herodian residential quarter, numerous other tombs, and walls can be visited today.

BCE (Before Common Era) and CE (Common Era) are used throughout Israel and are numerically equivalent to BC and AD, respectively.

meeting spot and connects to nearby modern luxury shopping, dining, and entertainment. Free public **live performances** are often staged here, and there are nearby public restrooms, money exchange, taxi stands, visitors centers, and museums.

Once inside the Old City, the options are overwhelming. A possible good start is one of **Via Dolorosa's** 14 stations, believed to be the pathway that Jesus walked on his way to be crucified, or up above the city at **Temple Mount.** For a 360-degree view atop the Old City walls, the **Ramparts Walk** is a photographer's dream at sunset.

City Center

Jerusalem's City Center is part of many locals' lives, though portions are decidedly touristy and many area residents are either students or long-term visitors. Active visitors should find accommodations as close as possible to City Center. Home to a little of everything, its nightlife scene has recently exploded to include the renowned **Machane Yehuda Market** (the *shuk*). The area's shifting borders traditionally included King George Street on the west until it turns into Agripas Street in the north and meets with Agron Street in the south. Shivtet Israel Street loosely borders the east and Hanevi'im Street the north. The historic area **Nahalat Shiva** is also near City Center, within walking distance.

The most diverse mixture of Jerusalem **nightlife** is in or near City Center. There are dining, shopping, and entertainment options including live bands, open mics and street music, sports pubs, wine bars, fancy clubs, and every variety of restaurant. There are also several **museums,** numerous luxury **hotels,** and some of the best **shopping** in town. It's the most convenient place to go if you need small but important items. You can find everything from contact lenses to electric converters to money-changing and other banking services.

West Jerusalem

West Jerusalem consists of several distinctive neighborhoods attractive to visitors. Many start in the **German Colony,** encompassed by the triangle of Emek Refaim Street, Yehuda Street, and Hebron Road. The northern tip of the triangle, **Yemin Moshe-Mishkenot Sha'ananim,** is home to numerous important buildings that are surrounded and connected by **parks.** There is nearby family-friendly **entertainment.**

Originally settled by German Templers, the German Colony's **Emek Refaim Street** is popular for a diverse selection of kosher **restaurants and cafes** set amid breathtaking historic homes. A short cab ride uphill are **museums, theaters,** and the **Railroad Park,** which stretches from nearby **First Station** and its many daily **shopping** and **dining** offerings all the way to the enormous **Hadar Mall.**

Farther out into West Jerusalem are the **Israel Museum,** the **Bible Lands Museum,** the **National Campus for the Archaeology of Israel,** the **Museum for Islamic Art,** the **Museum of Tolerance Jerusalem,** and others.

East Jerusalem

Once you cross the line between East and West Jerusalem (unofficially delineated by Hebron Road or Highway 60), the city changes drastically. The condition of the roads, housing, public safety, and public services are undeniably inferior to those on the west side, largely due to conflict and the patterns of how Jewish and Palestinian neighborhoods developed over time. A major channel for buses and home of a promised future light-rail expansion, Hebron Road is a convenient starting point for West Bank or Jerusalem activities. Hebron Road runs north-south from the French Hill neighborhood to Bethlehem's main entry/exit checkpoint in the south.

East Jerusalem has a good selection of affordable **hotels, shopping** options, and a wide variety of regional Mediterranean-influenced **Arab and Persian food.**

Religious Muslims don't drink, so the atmosphere of East Jerusalem can feel conservative, but it's still an interesting place for a night out. Many places offer traditional *nargila* (water pipe) to smoke with a menu of flavored tobacco after a meal.

PLANNING YOUR TIME

Jerusalem is layered and complex. That makes for a fascinating challenge if you aim to visit major city highlights in fewer than three days. Six days allows you to comfortably visit all of the best sights and get in a nearby day trip while enjoying some culture, cuisine, and entertainment.

When to Go

There are two major considerations when planning a visit to Jerusalem: the weather and the holiday calendar. The climate is generally pleasant unless there is rain, usually between late November to late March. In the summer months, the average temperature typically goes above 80-90°F (26-32°C) daily, but when the sun goes down, pleasant, cool, breezy evenings in the mid-70s are the norm.

The best time of year to visit is late April to early July, though this is high season for hotel and tour prices. August-September is hot, unpredictable, and filled with major Jewish and Muslim holidays.

Getting Around

Be especially cautious when driving around Jerusalem, as it has some tricky aspects. There are numerous one-way streets, rough roads, and dense foot traffic. Getting around by foot works well in areas like City Center, particularly along Yafo Street where only pedestrian foot traffic and the light-rail are allowed. When getting around other more remote sections of the city, like Museum Row, be prepared to walk longer distances on steeper hills or travel by car.

Jerusalem is easier to navigate if you set a transportation plan, budget, and curfew ahead of time. Taxicabs are readily available, but cost 25 percent more and are harder to hail on Friday and Saturday between 9pm and 5am. Not all taxis have meters or will use them. Many people prefer to use one taxi company and establish a relationship with a driver. It's wise to keep a few taxi company numbers on hand. Tourists can get a discounted public transportation ticket for both the light-rail (which is being expanded) and public buses. Most city bus drivers don't speak English, but they are usually happy to help visitors.

Itinerary Ideas

Jerusalem is a city that demands a little bit extra—energy, time, money, patience, curiosity, understanding, and critical thinking. If some of the popular sights leave you feeling more exhausted than exhilarated, pause for a leisurely cappuccino and dessert at a sidewalk café and people watch. Slow down and ask a couple of locals for their highly recommended restaurants or park or bar. If you give it a chance, you'll discover your own way through this complex, charming, utterly magical city.

JERUSALEM ON DAY 1

Ease into your surroundings a bit by starting out with breakfast in City Center, followed by a few Old City highlights. Finish with drinks and an elegant dinner at a rooftop restaurant or bar with the sunset in the background.

1 Start with breakfast at city treasure **Tmol Shilshom** for true Jerusalem flavors and the café's book collection, which showcases this institution's important role in local literary culture.

2 Just around the corner is Jaffa Street, perfect for a post-breakfast stroll to take in the **Old City.** In the center of the Old City, the **Church of the Holy Sepulchre** is a solid, relatively low-pressure introduction to the neighborhood's densely packed, cobblestoned storm of activity.

3 Head back out to the foot of the Jaffa Gate where you can take in the air-conditioned shops and bookstores at modern and upscale **Mamilla,** and have lunch and a coffee.

4 On the way out of the Old City, take an hour to venture up to the elevated plaza of **Al Aqsa Mosque** and **Haram al-Sharif,** which offers a great view of the surrounding area.

5 Return to your hotel to wash off the dust of the day and rest for the hotter part of the afternoon. When the sun starts to go down, get a window table at the **Notre Dame**

Itinerary Ideas

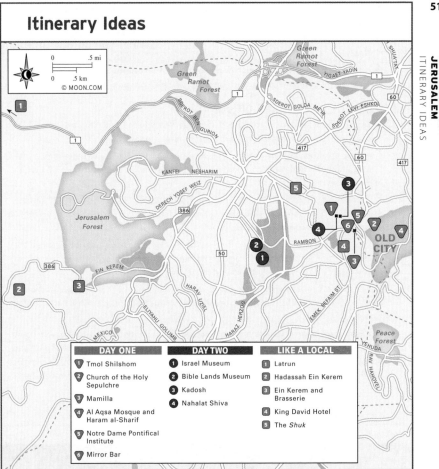

DAY ONE	DAY TWO	LIKE A LOCAL
1 Tmol Shilshom	1 Israel Museum	1 Latrun
2 Church of the Holy Sepulchre	2 Bible Lands Museum	2 Hadassah Ein Kerem
3 Mamilla	3 Kadosh	3 Ein Kerem and Brasserie
4 Al Aqsa Mosque and Haram al-Sharif	4 Nahalat Shiva	4 King David Hotel
5 Notre Dame Pontifical Institute		5 The *Shuk*
6 Mirror Bar		

Pontifical Institute's rooftop wine-and-cheese restaurant for the finest selection of cheese in the city, impeccable service, and gorgeous views of the Old City.

6 Later, take in after-dinner drinks and a cigar in the humidor room at the nearby **Mirror Bar,** just around the corner in the Mamilla Hotel.

JERUSALEM ON DAY 2

Venture to the outskirts of the city to spend the day exploring the region's history, politics, and religion at Museum Row. Plan on a late-afternoon cappuccino before a quiet evening of rest at your hotel.

1 Plan to get to the **Israel Museum** by mid-morning, where you can explore thousands of years of archaeological and anthropological history. The museum's elegant restaurant is the perfect place for a leisurely lunch.

2 Cross the street to the **Bible Lands Museum** and explore the range of Bible-centric and regionally specific exhibits.

3 Grab a taxi to the City Center for a coffee and French pastry at another local treasure, **Kadosh.**

4 Afterward take a stroll through nearby historic area **Nahalat Shiva** for shopping and easy exploring by foot. Head back to your hotel and plan on room service and rest.

JERUSALEM LIKE A LOCAL

Take a rental car and head to the outskirts of the city where you can find vineyards, forest hiking, and communities that battle for title of "best hummus in town."

1 After breakfast at your hotel, head straight to **Latrun,** just 20 minutes outside the city, in a taxi or rental car. Here you can get a close-up look at a vineyard run by a group of monks.

2 From there, head back toward the city to **Hadassah Ein Kerem,** about a 30-minute drive that will take you to the Jerusalem Forest. At Hadassah you can see the famous **Marc Chagall Stained Glass Windows.**

3 Next, head back to the nearby village of **Ein Kerem** for a late afternoon lunch on the outdoor terrace at **Brasserie.** Take your time and plan for some exploration around the quaint forest village that includes several interesting sights.

4 Drive back to Jerusalem, and after returning your rental car, have a late-afternoon coffee and dessert within the classic architecture of the politically historic **King David Hotel.**

5 Head back to your hotel to rest and change before doing that most Jerusalem of all things: a late dinner at one of the many ever-changing restaurant choices in **the *shuk*.** Your options will range from posh to trendy to rough around the edges. After dinner you can stroll through the area and hear numerous live music performances for free, most nights of the week, year-round.

The *shuk* at night becomes a street party of sorts.

Sights

You could spend days sightseeing in Jerusalem and never run out of experiences and lessons of all kinds. This is especially true for those who have a love of history, archaeology, geopolitics, human rights, and spirituality. It is one of the most overwhelming cities in the world and demands your full attention.

The trick to sightseeing in Jerusalem is to pace yourself, especially in the scorching-hot summer months. There are no advertised special combination tourism tickets unless you hire a tour company, and the sights with entrance fees range on average NIS20-50 per person. Many sights are run or managed by organizations with political or religious agendas.

Many museums stay open late one day each week or have windows of limited free admission, as well as discounts for seniors, children, and Israeli military.

THE OLD CITY
Via Dolorosa

One of the most revered sites among Christian pilgrims visiting Jerusalem is the Via Dolorosa (Way of Sorrows), the path Jesus is said to have walked on his way to his crucifixion over 2,000 years ago. Along the path, fourteen numbered "stations" mark locations of significant moments during Jesus's journey as he bore his own cross. The Via Dolorosa begins just inside the Lion's Gate in the Muslim Quarter and ends in the Christian Quarter inside the Church of the Holy Sepulchre, where the last five stations are located. Pilgrims kneel to pray at some stations, most of which are points along the streets of the Old City marked with Roman numerals. Much of the Via Dolorosa is accessible 24 hours, and the entire route is free to access. Part of the living history of the Old City, the stories connected to the Via Dolorosa are part of Christian tradition passed down through generations.

You can take a guided tour or join the **Via Dolorosa procession** led by Franciscan friars on Fridays starting from Station 1 (3pm Oct.-Mar., 4pm Apr.-Nov., Church of the Flagellation just inside Lion's Gate, free). Check with the **Christian Information Centre** in the Old City (Omar Ibn el-Khattab Square at Jaffa Gate, www.cicts.org, 9am-5:30pm Mon.-Fri. and 9am-12:30pm Sat.).

STATION 1

Located at the northwest corner of Temple Mount, just inside the Lion's Gate in front of El Omariye School, is a round, black seal imprinted with the Roman numeral I on an outer wall. The station is where Pontius Pilate condemned Jesus to death.

STATION 2

Across the street is the Roman numeral II. Here Jesus was given his cross, whipped, and mockingly dressed in a robe and given a crown of thorns by Roman soldiers. It's situated near a compound of buildings including the Roman Catholic Church of the Condemnation and the Convent of the Flagellation.

STATION 3

The corner of Via Dolorosa and El Wad (Hagai) Street marks where Jesus fell under the weight of the cross for the first time. The route then traces the western side of the Temple Mount. The Polish Catholic church, the Austrian Hospice, and a 15th-century chapel are nearby.

STATION 4

On El Wad Street, at Our Church of the Lady of the Sun, is the Roman numeral IV, where Jesus is believed to have encountered his mother, Mary. The Armenian church is home to a floor from the 5th century and two sandal footprints said to have belonged to Mary.

STATION 5

At the western end of El Wad Street is the Roman numeral V and a small Franciscan church built in 1229 to mark the location where Simon bore the cross for Jesus. An old square stone to the right of the door of the church is believed to bear the handprint of Jesus.

STATION 6

Midway down Via Dolorosa just before Souq Khan al-Zeit Street (the market street) is the Roman numeral VI and Our Church of the Holy Face with its restored Crusader arches. This is the station where a woman named Veronica wiped the face of Jesus.

STATION 7

At the intersection of Souq Khan al-Zeit Street and Via Dolorosa is the Roman numeral VII, marking where Jesus fell for the second time. Just beyond a massive Roman column is the Chapel of the Seventh Station.

STATION 8

The Roman numeral VIII is at Aqabat al-Khanqah, across from the Station VIII souvenir bazaar. The station is marked by a stone embedded in the wall of the Monastery of St. Charalambos bearing the engraving IC-XC NI-KA, which means "Jesus Christ conquers." This is where Jesus spoke to the women of Jerusalem and told them not to weep for him, but for themselves and their children.

STATION 9

A zigzag route down Souq Khan al-Zeit Street and up 28 stone steps leads to Station IX with its cross painted on a stone pillar next to an archway where Jesus fell for the third time. Adjacent to the Church of the Holy Sepulchre, the route here winds around the building of the Coptic Patriarchate. Nearby is the Ethiopian Church of St. Michael and a Coptic church with paintings that depict scenes from the Bible.

STATION 10

At the southern end of Souq Khan al-Zeit Street to the right is Souq al-Dabbagha. Cross the courtyard to the entrance of the Church of the Holy Sepulchre, where the last five stations are located. Start at Station X, the Chapel of the Franks, where Jesus was stripped of his clothes.

STATION 11

Station XI is the interior of the Church of the Holy Sepulchre where Jesus was nailed to the cross.

STATION 12

A Greek Orthodox crucifixion altar inside the church marks Station XII in the Church of the Holy Sepulchre where Jesus was crucified and died on the cross. A silver disk with a central hole under the altar marks where the cross stood. Pilgrims kneel and kiss the spot.

STATION 13

A large stone marks Station XIII in the Church of the Holy Sepulchre where the body of Jesus is said to have been laid and prepared for burial after he died. The station is encased and has an open top for pilgrims to touch.

STATION 14

The tomb of Jesus and the final station of the Via Dolorosa is located in the rotunda inside a small inner chamber past the Chapel of the Angel in the Church of the Holy Sepulchre. A marble lid covers the tomb, which was restored in 2017.

The Christian Quarter

TOP EXPERIENCE

★ CHURCH OF THE HOLY SEPULCHRE

Suq Khan e-Zeit and Christian Quarter Rd.; tel. 02/627-3314; 5am-9pm daily Apr.-Sept., 4am-7pm daily Oct.-Mar.; free

One of the most popular destinations in the Old City, the Church of the Holy Sepulchre is also one of the most important sites in the

Christian world. Also known as the Church of the Resurrection, the dark, cavernous structure houses four stations of the Via Dolorosa and is constantly filled with throngs of pilgrims. Its walls are also filled with centuries of art, much of which badly needs restoration.

Just past the church's outdoor courtyard is the end of the Via Dolorosa. At the entrance is the Chapel of the Franks, and the looming interior includes a Greek Orthodox altar where Jesus is said to have been crucified. A large stone (stone of unction) to the left is the place where, according to tradition, the body of Jesus was prepared for burial. In the rotunda inside a small inner chamber, past the Chapel of the Angel, is a marble-encased tomb said to be the place where Jesus was buried. A massive vaulted dome rises above the tomb with a center of light that streams downward.

The church was one of many commissioned by Constantine the Great after he converted to Christianity. Work on the church began in AD 326, and some historians believe that Constantine's builders dug around the tomb of Jesus. Since then, it has suffered tremendous neglect, desecration, and damage as the city has changed hands and rulers. The current church is the result of the joint efforts of the Latin, Greek, and Armenian communities, who banded together in 1959 for a major restoration project. The current church is a mixture of Byzantine, Crusader, medieval, and modern styles. Control of the church is shared by three Christian denominations: Roman Catholic, Greek Orthodox, and Armenian Orthodox.

ST. SAVIOR CHURCH (FRANCISCAN MONASTERY OF SAN SALVADOR)

1 St. Francis St.; tel. 02/626-6595; http:// catholicchurch-holyland.com; 8am-5pm daily; free
The Franciscan Monastery of San Salvador, also known as St. Savior Church, is easy to find next to the New Gate. The visit of St. Francis of Assisi to the Holy Land in 1219 marked the beginning of the Franciscan monks following in his footsteps, and to this day the San Salvador Monastery in the Old City is the center of the Franciscan Order in the Holy Land and the Middle East.

The monastery, which visitors cannot enter, does have a church that is free to go into with a magnificent vaulted ceiling and pipe organ. Construction on the church was completed in the 19th century.

You might see members of the Franciscan Order while walking about the Old City. They are distinguishable by their simple brown robes with a rope belt knotted three times in honor of the vows of their order: obedience, poverty, and chastity.

CHURCH OF THE REDEEMER

24 Muristan Rd.; tel. 02/627-1111; www.elcjhl.org; 9am-1pm and 1:30pm-5pm Mon.-Sat.; NIS15
The Lutheran Church of the Redeemer is easy to spot with its distinctive bell tower that can be reached by trekking up almost 200 steps. The bell rings most mornings at 9am. The church's interior walls are made of simple and relatively unadorned white stone with massive arches. The church was built by Kaiser Wilhelm in the late 1800s, and he later brought his wife with him to personally dedicate it in 1898. He was the first Western ruler to visit Jerusalem and infamously ordered the door of Jaffa Gate be removed so he could enter the Old City unimpeded while riding his horse wearing a tall, spiked helmet. The gate was never repaired, making it the only entrance point in the Old City without a full gate.

The church is home to Lutheran congregations that speak Arabic, German, English, and Danish, and it is the site of frequent musical performances.

★ AUSTRIAN HOSPICE

37 Via Dolorosa, near Damascus Gate; tel. 02/626-5800; www.austrianhospice.com; 24 hours daily, free
The well-known Austrian Hospice is hidden in plain sight; any merchant will know its location if you ask for directions.

Situated behind a set of tall double wooden doors is one of the most serene spots in the Old City. Ring the bell to the right of the door and you will be buzzed into an inner gate. The location was chosen by Austria's first consul general as a place to build (and establish a local presence) in Jerusalem and was opened as a pilgrims' house in 1856. The hospice functions as a high-end hotel. Outside visitors can wander the hallways filled with photographs of the Holy Land.

Two spots in the hospice not to miss: the garden café with its apple strudel and the easily accessible rooftop with its view of the Old City and the Dome of the Rock. Other rooftop access points aren't as accommodating: If you're not a guest you might be asked to pay at least NIS10 for entry and viewing. The hospice rooftop is accessible by elevator and then a short flight of stairs. Once on the roof, you can enjoy the moderately high bird's-eye view of the Old City. You can also take as long as you like at one of the many outdoor tables in the garden near the entrance (which is elevated two stories above street level) for a quiet coffee, beer, or snack. The rooftop here also makes a fine lookout spot when there is commotion or a procession of some kind in the streets below.

The Muslim Quarter
CHURCH OF ST. ANNE
near the Lion's Gate in the Old City off Sha'ar HaArayot St.; 8am-noon and 2pm-5pm Mon.-Sat.; NIS12
Near the beginning of the Via Dolorosa and adjacent to the Pool of Bethesda is the remarkably preserved Crusader-era Church of St. Anne. According to Catholic tradition, this is the birthplace of the Virgin Mary, preserved as a cave dwelling located beneath the crypt of the church.

The **Pool of Bethesda** (included with paid entry to the Church of St. Anne) is mentioned in the New Testament as the place where Jesus cured a crippled man. The area is an archaeological site that includes five pools and ruins of Byzantine, Crusader, and medieval churches.

ROCKEFELLER ARCHAEOLOGICAL MUSEUM
27 Sultan Suleiman St.; tel. 02/628-2251; www.imj. org.il/en under Archaeology; 10am-3pm Sun.-Mon. and Wed.-Thurs., 10am-2pm Sat., closed holiday eves; free
The Rockefeller Archaeological Museum is recommended by most locals (it's free) and is home to thousands of artifacts displayed in chronological order from prehistoric times to the Ottoman period. Many items were unearthed between 1919-1948 during the British Mandate period. Treasures include a 9,000-year-old statue from Jericho, jewelry from the Bronze Age, and Stone Age eating utensils. There is limited signage on exhibits, which frustrates some visitors.

LADY TUNSHUQ PALACE
off Al Wad St. on Aqabat al-Taqiya; 24 hours; free
The 14th-century Lady Tunshuq Palace was built by Muslim Sufi mystics under the direction of Lady Tunshuq. The complex includes large archways with intricate inlaid marble work and also houses a working school.

TEMPLE MOUNT—AL HARAM AL-SHARIF
main access for non-Muslims is between the Western Wall and Dung Gate; tel. 02/628-1248; www.noblesanctuary.com; 7:30am-11am and 1:30pm-2:30pm Sun.-Thurs. Apr.-Sept., 7:30am-10am and 12:30pm-1:30pm Sun.-Thurs. Oct.-Mar.; dress modestly, bring passport; entrance subject to change; free
On the eastern side of the Old City is Temple Mount—Al Haram al-Sharif. The complex consists of about 100 buildings known as the Noble Sanctuary and an open plaza with ancient paving stones. The current construction dates back 1,400 years and includes the Dome of the Rock, Mount Moriah, Al Aqsa Mosque, and many other significant religious and cultural sites. The area's history dates back much

1: interior of the Church of the Holy Sepulchre
2: Austrian Hospice 3: Church of the Redeemer
4: etchings from pilgrims in the Church of the Holy Sepulchre

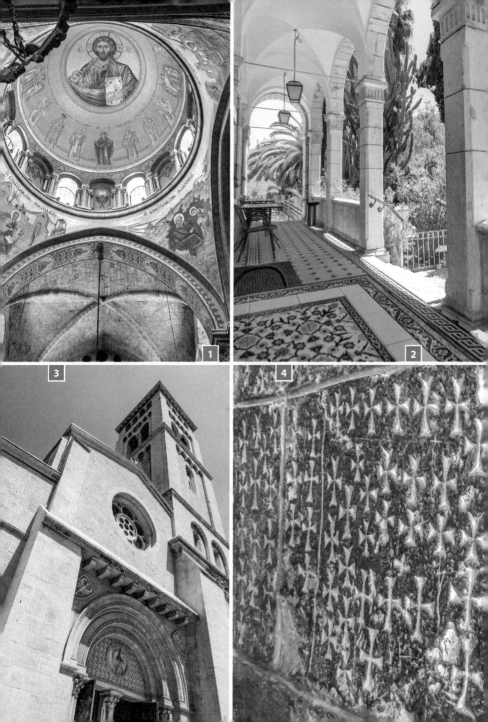

earlier, though, as it was the site of the first and second Jewish temples, and is one of the most hotly disputed pieces of territory in the world. Exercise caution doing anything resembling praying or showing skin (that includes men, too) in the area because of these tensions. Guided tours are sometimes available through information boxes on the plaza. The best bet for a visit here is to hire a guide in advance. Most hotel front desks in the area will help you.

The **Dome of the Rock** is easily recognizable from many points in Jerusalem by its enormous golden dome. Situated atop Temple Mount on the edge of the Old City, the Dome of the Rock is built over the rock where, according to tradition, Prophet Muhammad ascended to heaven and Abraham attempted to sacrifice his son.

Al Aqsa Mosque is the third holiest site in Islam and a popular place for Muslims in Israel and the West Bank to pray, particularly during Friday prayers and major holidays. Israeli-controlled border police sometimes limit access to the mosque to men under the age of approximately 40 as a control tactic.

The Islamic Museum of Temple Mount (southwest corner of the compound grounds, near the Western Wall, tel. 02/628-3313, 8am-11:30am and 2pm-4pm Mon.-Sat., NIS38 at stone kiosk between Al Aqsa Mosque and the Dome of the Rock) is one of the oldest museums in the country and houses a large collection of Korans, coins, glassware, guns, swords, daggers, and Islamic ceramics. The admission fee will also allow you to enter the mosque depending on the security situation at the time.

Jerusalem Archaeological Park

Ma'ale HaShalom St. at Old City's Dung Gate; tel. 02/627-7550; www.rova-yehudi.org.il; 8am-5pm Sun.-Thurs., 8am-2pm Fri.; adult NIS30, senior, student, and child NIS16

The Jerusalem Archaeological Park covers a vast area near the Old City. The park extends from the north at Temple Mount to the slope of the Mount of Olives and the Kidron Valley

on the east, and on the west and south to the Valley of Hinnom.

Considered one of Israel's most significant antiquities site, it includes 5,000 years of history from the Canaanite (Bronze) Age and through the days of the Israelite monarchy in the First Temple period. At the entrance to the park is the **Davidson Center,** a virtual reconstruction and exhibition center that uses state-of-the-art computer technology to give visitors a historical and archaeological orientation.

The Jewish Quarter

TOP EXPERIENCE

★ WESTERN WALL

Jewish Quarter of the Old City; tel. 02/627-1333; http://english.thekotel.org; 24 hours daily; crowded on holidays, modest dress required; free

Just below Temple Mount is the most famed religious site in all of Judaism. Named for its position as the outer western wall of the destroyed Second Temple's courtyard, the Western Wall is also called the Wailing Wall or the Kotel.

The Wall is considered particularly significant to Jews because it is the last remaining piece of the outer courtyard wall of the Second Temple, the most significant site in all of Judaism. The imposing 62-foot (18.9 meter) wall is a destination for the faithful to pray. Modest dress is required at all times. The plaza can hold 60,000 people, but closest to the wall it is divided between men and women. Visitors are permitted to leave small pieces of paper with prayers or messages in the crevices of the wall. You can walk (mostly) freely about the plaza and take photographs, but don't be surprised if you are approached by an official for some minor infraction. An upper plaza in the southeastern corner offers an excellent view of the wall and the golden Dome of the Rock behind it. It also makes a good perch during large-scale events.

On the northern end of the Kotel is the **Chain of Generations Center** (near the

Western Wall, tel. 02/627-1333, http://english.thekotel.org, visits by reservation in advance Sun.-Thurs. and Fri. morning, NIS30, children and seniors NIS15.5). It uses a light and art show to tell the story of the Jewish people over 3,500 years, from exile to statehood. The center uses a combination of music, sculpture, archaeology, and light effects and is divided into several rooms. Each room covers a different period and has art made from layers of glass lit by rays of light that shine from dark rooms. There is also a view of the Western Wall from one portion of the center.

South of the Western Wall near Dung Gate are the **Western Wall Excavations** (Western Wall, Jewish Quarter, tel. 02/627-1333, http://english.thekotel.org under Tunnels, 7am-11pm Sun.-Thurs., 7am-noon Fri. and holiday eves depending on reservations, adult NIS42, child and seniors NIS20). This 75-minute underground tour of excavations tells the story of ancient Jerusalem and explores hidden layers of the Western Wall. Tours are led by a guide and given only by advance reservation.

HERODIAN QUARTER AND WOHL ARCHAEOLOGICAL MUSEUM

1 Ha-Karaim St.; tel. 02/626-5906; www.rova-yehudi.org.il/en; 9am-5pm Sun.-Thurs., 9am-1pm Fri. and on eve of Jewish holidays; NIS18, combined ticket with the Burnt House NIS37

A six-house compound on the slope of the hill facing the Temple Mount makes up the Herodian Quarter and Wohl Archaeological Museum. Here you'll find three main attractions: the Western House, the Middle Complex, and the Palatial Mansion. All thought to be homes of aristocrats and priests during the Herodian period, they are designed in the Hellenistic/Roman style. The 600-square-meter Palatial Mansion is the largest and gives clues to the lifestyles of the wealthy of that time. It includes rich floor mosaics and remarkably preserved wall frescoes. Also unearthed here were utensils, artifacts, decorated plates, and imported wine jugs.

HURVA SYNAGOGUE

89 Ha-Yehudim St.; tel. 02/626-5906; www.rova-yehudi.org.il; 9am-5pm Sun.-Thurs. and 9am-1pm Fri.; NIS32

The distinctive domed, white roof of Hurva Synagogue is home to the world's tallest Holy Ark and boasts a 360-degree view of Jerusalem from the synagogue's roof rampart. The synagogue, which literally means "ruin" in Hebrew, has a long and winding history. Construction began on it in 1700, but 20 years later it was still not complete, and the unfinished building was torched and destroyed for the first time. It was rebuilt in the mid-1800s, only to be blown up by the Transjordan Legion Army just after the War of Independence in 1948. When the Old City was recaptured by Israel in 1967, the site of the ruins was commemorated but nothing was rebuilt there until 40 years later. In 2005, construction on the current Hurva Synagogue began, and it was finished in early 2010. The basement of the synagogue is home to antiquities, and the masterfully renovated building integrates stones from the ruins of the old building with the new. Entry for women is restricted at certain times, less so at prayer time.

BURNT HOUSE MUSEUM

Tiferet Israel St.; tel. 02/626-5906; www.rova-yehudi.org.il; 9am-5pm Sun.-Thurs., 9am-1pm Fri. and on eve of Jewish holidays; NIS30, combined ticket with Herodian Quarter NIS35

The Burnt House Museum is the excavated remains of the home of an upper-class priestly Jewish family that burned during the destruction of the Second Temple in 70 BC. The home was later excavated and features unique period archaeological artifacts and a multimedia presentation about the daily life of the people who lived in the house. The movie is screened every 40 minutes starting at 9am.

RAMBAN SYNAGOGUE

enter via Jewish Quarter St.; tel. 02/627-1422; call in advance to visit, modest dress required; NIS10

The Ramban Synagogue is the second oldest working synagogue in the Old City. It is

believed to have been built on Mount Zion and then moved to the Old City in the 14th century. Closed by the Ottomans in 1589, it was reopened in 1967. The synagogue is a small, modest building that many see as a symbol of the enduring power of faith, hope, and tradition.

CARDO

HaKardo St.; tel. 02/626-5900, ext. 102; www. rova-yehudi.org.il; 8am-6pm Sun.-Thurs., 8am-4pm Fri., closed for Shabbat; free

The Cardo is the impressive remnants of an ancient Roman double-columned main street (always called a *cardo maximus*) and its shops that were a fixture in many Roman cities. The Old City's Cardo stretched from the Damascus Gate to the Zion Gate.

The southern section of the Cardo was excavated and buildings from later periods were removed to reveal the Byzantine Cardo. Some of the columns from that period were reconstructed and restored, allowing visitors to experience a taste of the 6th-century Cardo.

The covered section of the Cardo, which dates back to the Crusader period, includes shops located in the same place they were during ancient times. Most of the Old City is like this, actually. Many Cardo shops sell higher-end items like fine jewelry and Judaica.

At the end of the Cardo at David Street are ruins of five Roman columns and paving stones that date to the Byzantine period. Farther on is a reproduction of a section of the Madaba Map, the oldest known map that depicts Jerusalem in the 6th century.

The Armenian Quarter

This section of the Old City is largely residential and makes for a lovely and distinctive place to take a quiet stroll.

1: the Western Wall 2: the Hurva Synagogue 3: Cardo Street 4: the Night Spectacular light show at the Tower of David

ARMENIAN PATRIARCHATE OF ST. JAMES

Zion Gate, inside the Old City; tel. 02/628-2331; www. armenian-patriarchate.org, nourhan@netvision. net.il; 6:30am-7:30am and 3pm-3:30pm Mon.-Fri., 8:30am-10:30am and 3pm-3:30pm Sat.; free

Just inside Zion Gate and west until the city wall is the Armenian Patriarchate of St. James, or St. James Cathedral, a magnificent cathedral built on the tombs of St. James the Apostle and St. James the brother of Jesus. The interior of the cathedral is decorated with ancient hanging oil lamps and includes three chapels and two thrones at the front of the church. The church served as a bomb shelter for residents of the Armenian Quarter during the War of Independence in 1948.

CHRIST CHURCH

Omar Ibn Al Hatab St. just inside Jaffa Gate; tel. 02/628-7487; www.itraveljerusalem.com/the-old-city; hours vary, call in advance before visiting; NIS10

Near the intersection of Armenian Patriarchate Road and David Street is Christ Church, a compound on the right of the street. This is the oldest Protestant church in the Middle East, and it houses a hostel, a heritage center, and a coffee shop. There is a tunnel beneath it dating to the Second Temple period.

Christ Church was completed in 1849 in preparation for the return of Jews to Israel. The believers of the church wanted to establish themselves in Jerusalem in order to be in a position to help the Jews when they returned. Due to its history, there are Hebrew inscriptions inside the church, and modern services have incorporated some Hebrew.

RAMPARTS WALK

Jaffa Gate; tel. 02/627-7550; 9am-4pm Sun.-Thurs., but call in advance as tours vary widely by season; self-guided ticket good for two days NIS20, tickets for guided tours at tourist service office

For a unique view of Jerusalem, climb up onto the narrow catwalk on the 16th-century wall surrounding the Old City and try the Ramparts Walk. The southern route starts at the Tower of David and ends at the Dung

Gate; the northern route starts at Jaffa Gate and ends at the Lion's Gate. You can walk around the entire rampart in 3-4 hours or descend at any one of the gates along the way at approximately 20-minute intervals. On the ramparts you will get a bird's-eye view of the city, the ancient niches in the wall that used to be used by shooters to defend the city, and many steep steps. There are modern, secure railings along the way, but it would be a tiring route for the very young or infirm.

TOWER OF DAVID MUSEUM

Jaffa Gate, inside the Old City; tel. 02/626-5333; www.tod.org.il; 9am-4pm Sun.-Thurs., 9am-2pm Fri. and holiday eves and Aug., 9am-4pm Sat. and holidays and Aug.; adult NIS40, child NIS20

At the southern side of Jaffa Gate is the Tower of David Museum, located in a medieval citadel. The museum tells the story of Jerusalem and includes the archaeological site of the citadel. It is also home to a unique sound and light show, the **Night Spectacular** (9pm and 10:30pm, adult NIS55, senior and child NIS45, museum admission plus show adult NIS70, senior and child NIS55).

Mount Zion

Ma'aleh Hashalom Rd.; 052 -538-8342; 8am-noon Mon.-Sat.; free

Outside the walls of the Old City at **Zion Gate** is a hillside path to Mount Zion, a series of sites run by different entities that can be visited in succession as part of guided tours or alone bit by bit. At the bottom of the hill is **Mount Zion Catholic Cemetery,** the final resting place of Oskar Schindler, famed for saving 1,098 Jews during the Holocaust. **Dormition Abbey** (Mount Zion, tel. 02/565-5330, www.dormitio.net, 8am-noon and 2pm-6pm daily, free) is an active abbey with a distinctive bell tower and lead-covered cupola that can be seen from many points in the city. According to Christian tradition, Mount Zion was an important meeting point in Jerusalem for Jesus and his disciples.

At the Abbey you can tour the German Benedictine basilica completed in 1910.

Several mosaics can be seen inside the abbey, including some from a former Byzantine church that was once at the same location.

A small room known as the site of **King David's Tomb** (Mount Zion compound, 8am-6pm Sun.-Thurs. and until 2pm on Fri., free) is a religious site in Judaism and requires men and women to use different entrances. **St. Mark's Church** (Ararat St., tel. 02/628-3304, 8am-6pm daily, free) or the Monastery of St. Mark is thought to be the site of the Last Supper. Claims about both the tomb and the supposed Room of the Last Supper are unreliable due to centuries of war and subsequent destruction and rebuilding. Some guides openly say the actual sites are likely farther downhill.

CITY CENTER
Museum of Italian Jewish Art

25 Hillel St.; tel. 02/624-1610; http://ijamuseum.org; 10:30am-4:30pm Sun., Mon., Tues., Wed., noon-7pm Thurs.; NIS15

Conveniently situated in the midst of City Center, the Museum of Italian Jewish Art is renowned as a repository of the history of Italian Jewry. Most famous among its treasures of ritual Jewish objects from the baroque and Renaissance periods is a lavish gold 18th-century synagogue that was transported from Italy to Israel. The museum features permanent and changing exhibitions and is part of the Jerusalemite Star, five boutique museums that are physically connected and form the shape of the Star of David.

Museum of Tolerance

Gershon Agron St.; www.wiesenthal.com

Slated to open sometime around late 2019, the Museum of Tolerance Jerusalem will be part museum and part commercial and residential housing units. The venture is connected to a group of museums of tolerance, all run by the Simon Wiesenthal Center. The controversial project faced criticism during construction due to its location on the site of an old Muslim cemetery.

Jerusalem Time Elevator

37 Hillel St., Agron House; tel. 02/624-8381; www. time-elevator.co.il/en; 10am-5pm Sun.-Thurs., 10am-2pm Fri.; adult NIS54, senior NIS46, Internet booking NIS46, ages 5 and up only, reservation recommended

The unique trip through Jerusalem's history offered by the Jerusalem Time Elevator is a sensory overload of 3,000 years of history in a 2-D surround sound, interactive environment. Using crashing ceilings, splashing water, and other special effects, the Time Elevator is a good break from visiting archaeological sites in the hot sun. It is located just outside of the Old City, a 5-minute walk from Jaffa Gate.

Ticho House (Israel Museum)

9 Harav Kook St.; tel. 02/624-5068; www.imj.org.il/ en/wings/arts/ticho-house; 12pm-8pm Sun.-Thurs., 10am-2pm Fri.; free

One of the first buildings constructed outside of the Old City walls in the latter half of the 19th century, the Ticho House is now at the modern city center. Home to regionally well-known painter Anna Ticho in the early 20th century, Ticho House is part of the Israel Museum. The outer courtyard is perfect for a private reverie, and inside there are cozy art galleries, a collection of Hanukkah lamps, and a **reference library** of books about art, literature, and Jerusalem.

Jerusalem Great Synagogue

56 King George St.; tel. 02/623-0628; www. jerusalemgreatsynagogue.com; tours by appointment by emailing jgs@zahav.net.il; free

The unmistakable facade of the Jerusalem Great Synagogue is an imposing structure on a main thoroughfare in central Jerusalem. Adorned with massive stained-glass windows, it was opened in 1982 and is dedicated to the memory of the six million Jewish victims of the Holocaust. The synagogue's annual operating budget of more than US$1 million comes entirely from donations, and their internationally acclaimed choir is one of the world's chief repositories for Jewish Ashkenazic liturgical music.

Hechal Shlomo Jewish Heritage Center

58 King George St.; tel. 02/588-9007; http://eng. hechalshlomo.org.il; 9am-3pm Sun.-Thurs.; adult NIS20, senior and child NIS15, family NIS50

A landmark building in the city is the Hechal Shlomo Jewish Heritage Center, which serves as a Jewish spiritual and cultural center. Aside from Hechal Shlomo's cultural events, which include live music and several permanent exhibits, the active synagogue is decorated lavishly in 18th-century Italian style. It is home to the **Wolfson Museum of Jewish Art** with its permanent exhibit of Jewish ceremonial art and temporary exhibits of Israeli artists.

AROUND MACHANE YEHUDA MARKET

★ Machane Yehuda Market (The *Shuk*)

between Yafo St. and Agripas St. at Beit Ya'acov and Eitz HaChaim; www.machne.co.il/en; 8am-7pm Sun.-Thurs., 8am-3pm Fri.

This open-air market, world-famous for its colorful produce stands, restaurants, and characters, is known to locals as the *shuk*. Machane Yehuda Market is overwhelming in its sights, sounds, and tastes. At every entrance (and there are about a dozen of them), you will find yourself in a seemingly endless maze of bins overflowing with fruits and vegetables, sweets and olives, and all kinds of spices and teas. It's wonderful to just browse the ordered chaos of the market's many restaurants, cafés, coffee shops, pubs, and shops for produce, spices, or sweets.

The secret to enjoying the *shuk* is picking the time of day that suits your preferences. The most intense time of the week is 11am-3pm on Friday. The level of activity reaches a fever pitch as closing time gets closer; vendors want to sell more goods and shoppers want to buy their last items before the weekend.

The most low-key time to visit is generally any weekday before about 10:30am. You will have plenty of space to move about and enjoy the market without worrying about battling the crowds. You won't get many deals, though. The best deals begin during the market's final open hour.

Later in the day, especially on Thursdays and Fridays, the level of chaos in the *shuk* crescendos as college kids sit down in the middle of the pathway to drink beer and hang out, tourists and last-minute shoppers rush in for the weekend, and live music cranks up.

Gush Katif Museum

5 Sha'arei Tsedek; tel. 02/625-5456; www. gushkatif.022.co.il; 10am-5pm Sun.-Thurs., 10am-1pm Fri.; NIS20

The small but extremely unusual Gush Katif Museum is the only museum in the world that tells the story of the Jewish settlement Gush Katif in the Gaza Strip before it was broken apart in the 2005 unilateral disengagement, when Israel pulled out of the region.

EAST JERUSALEM

TOP EXPERIENCE

★ Museum on the Seam

4 Chel Handassa St.; tel. 02/628-1278; www.mots. org.il; 10am-5pm Mon., Wed., Thurs., 2pm-8pm Tues., 10am-2pm Fri.; adult NIS30, senior and student NIS25

Along the line where there was once a border between East and West Jerusalem is the Museum on the Seam, a sociopolitical contemporary art museum that focuses on the social situation created by regional conflict. Established in 1999, the museum is internationally known and is highly recommended for those who want to learn more about conflicts in the region and artistic interpretations of their effect on the residents of Jerusalem. The museum is a 10-minute walk north of Damascus Gate.

Mount of Olives

Stretching from the **Kidron Valley** (24 hours daily, free) where the tombs of Zechariah,

Bnei Hezir, and Absalom can be found, to the uppermost ridge at the end of E-Sheikh Street due east from the Lion's Gate of the Old City is the Mount of Olives (24 hours daily, free) a lookout point with one of the most impressive panoramic views of the Old City. Due to the sacredness of the Mount of Olives to Christianity, Judaism, and Islam, there are several holy sites in the area. This is the site where Jesus is said to have looked out over Jerusalem and wept at its future destruction. It is recommended to avoid the temptation to buy a turn on the camel ride often at the lookout.

Jewish Cemetery

The largest, oldest, and holiest cemetery in the Jewish world with approximately 70,000 graves, the Jewish Cemetery (tel. 02/627-5050 for help locating a grave) is considered by some to be the sacred future location of the resurrection. It is divided into sectors and covers the entire western and much of the southern slope of the Mount of Olives and is not technically open for public access. The cemetery is the final resting place of several well-known historical figures including Eliezer Ben-Yehuda and Rabbi Abraham Isaac Kook. Groups and those visiting a grave to pay respects are allowed.

Tomb of the Virgin Mary

intersection of Jericho Rd. and Al-Mansuriya Rd.; 6am-noon and 2:30pm-5pm Mon.-Sat.; free

Starting from the base of the Mount of Olives, go north along Al-Mansuriya Road and then west along El Monsuriyya toward the **Church of the Assumption** or the Tomb of the Virgin Mary, an underground tomb thought to be the resting place of the Virgin Mary. The site also includes a place for Muslims to pray, as St. Mary is highly regarded in Muslim tradition. Above the tomb is the 12th-century church. You can enter the tomb area via a set of wide steps that go underground.

1: old olive trees in the Garden of Gethsemane
2: the Tomb of the Virgin Mary

Church of All Nations

Jericho Rd.; tel. 02/628-4371; 8am-noon and 2pm-4:30pm Mon.-Sat.; free

Just south of Mary's Tomb on Jericho Road is the **Basilica of the Agony** or the Church of All Nations, with a magnificent mosaic on the front and a row of pillars directly facing the road. The church was completed in 1924 with donations from a dozen different countries. The impressive interior of the church includes massive frescoes painted on vaulted walls and a large rock believed to be the place where Jesus prayed the night he was betrayed. The symbols of the 12 countries that contributed to the building of the church are woven into the 12 inlaid gold cupola ceilings.

Garden of Gethsemane

Jericho Rd.; 8am-noon and 2pm-6pm Mon.-Sat.; free

Accessible from an alley toward the north side of the Church of All Nations is the Garden of Gethsemane, where Jesus is said to have betrayed by Judas. The garden is a grove of ancient olive trees, some of which are over 2,000 years old. It is completely surrounded by a wrought-iron fence, making it impossible to touch the trees or sit or walk among them.

Dominis Flevit Church

accessible by a footpath from the base of the Basilica of Agony or from the top of the Mount of Olives; tel. 02/626-6540; 8am-noon and 2pm-5pm Mon.-Sat.; free

The Franciscan Dominus Flevit Church is located on a site considered holy as far back as the Bronze Age. The current structure was built in 1954 over the ruins of other buildings that have stood at the location, including a Byzantine-period monastery and church whose mosaic floor can still be seen to the left of the entrance. The building was designed by Italian architect Antonio Barluzzi and has a roof with a distinctive tear-shaped dome to symbolize Jesus's tears over the coming destruction of Jerusalem.

Church of the Pater Noster

E-Sheikh St.; tel. 02/628-3143; 8am-noon and 2pm-4pm Mon.-Sat.; NIS10

The Church of the Pater Noster is built on the location where Christian tradition says Jesus taught his disciples the Lord's Prayer. Famed for its display of the Lord's Prayer in 140 different languages, it is a partial reconstruction of the Byzantine-era Constantine's Eleona church. The main building and its cloister are situated above an unearthed cave that's believed to have existed in the time of Jesus.

Church of St. Mary Magdalene

Al-Mansuriya Rd.; tel. 02/628-4371; www.jerusalem-mission.org; 10am-11:30am Tues. and Thurs., free

The golden-domed Russian Orthodox Church of St. Mary Magdalene is easily recognizable as an example of Russian architecture, built in the Muscovite style with golden onion domes or cupolas.

★ Salah al-Din Street

between the Old City's Damascus Gate and the American Colony Hotel at Louis Vincent St. 1; shops generally open 9am-9pm daily

More an adventure than a destination, Salah al-Din Street is an ideal gateway to East Jerusalem for independent travelers. It is easy to spend several hours browsing the shops for souvenirs and regional specialties like falafel and Arab sweets.

City of David

off Ophel St. in Silwan; tel. 02/626-8700; www.cityofdavid.org.il; 8am-5pm Sun.-Thurs., 8am-2pm Fri. Nov.-Mar., 8am-7pm Sun.-Thurs., 8am-4pm Fri. Apr.-Oct., closed for Shabbat and holidays; adult NIS45, senior and child NIS15, 3-D film add NIS13, guided tour adult NIS45 and senior and child NIS35, combination tickets available

Just south of the Old City, the City of David is home to numerous historical and archaeological treasures, but there has been controversy about the approach taken to establish a Jewish presence in the predominately Arab neighborhood, including accusations of land grabbing.

The Separation Barrier

At several points near the Old City and along the often-invisible border between East and West Jerusalem that runs through the new part of the city, the Separation Barrier is clearly visible. Also known as the Security Barrier or Separation Wall, it cuts Israel and the West Bank off from one another. The barrier directly abuts neighborhoods and villages along its route, and has been under construction and extended for many years. It serves multiple purposes for the ruling Israeli authority in the region: security from would-be attackers, a method to control the movement of people in the region, and a possible future border if a two-state solution is ever reached with Palestinian leaders and the international community. If completed, it would span a distance of about 708 miles (1140 km) from north to south. It is currently about 440 miles (700 km) long, and the structure varies, from fence with barbed wire to massive, towering walls of concrete. The best view of the Separation Barrier from Jerusalem is just outside the city on the drive to Rachel's Tomb in Bethlehem. The wall encloses the Jewish holy site and cuts through the corner of Bethlehem, a majority-Christian, Palestinian Authority-controlled city.

HEZEKIAH'S TUNNEL

Among the highlights in the City of David is the epic and claustrophobia-inducing Hezekiah's Tunnel, considered a wonder of clever and persistent ancient engineering. The tunnel starts at Gihon Spring, a major source of water for ancient Jerusalem for 1,000 years. Armed with an essential flashlight, you can wade through the 2,700-year-old tunnel for 580 yards to the Pool of Siloam, the place to draw water in biblical times. King Hezekiah ordered the tunnel to be built in preparation for the Syrian siege. Two groups of workers painstakingly dug out the tunnel, starting from opposite ends and meeting in the middle, almost 3,000 years ago.

Garden Tomb

Conrad Schick St.; tel. 02/539-8100; www. gardentomb.com; 8am-noon and 2pm-6pm Mon.-Sat.; free

Though a slight detour from flashier attractions, the Garden Tomb is the only place in Jerusalem other than the Church of the Holy Sepulchre that claims to be the site of the resurrection of Jesus. You can enter the cave in the hillside where it is said that Jesus was buried and inspect clues said to correlate with historical references to the true burial place of Jesus. The garden and sitting areas built up around the tomb make for a very pleasant place for a private contemplation of the absurdities of historical debate. The Garden Tomb is just north of the Old City.

St. Stephen Basilica

6 Nablus Rd.; tel. 02/626-4468; www.ebaf.edu/en; call in advance to visit, free

Home to the world-famous École Biblique (French Biblical and Archaeological School) is St. Stephen Basilica. The original church at this location was built at the end of the 5th century as a resting place for the relics of St. Stephen, the first Christian martyr. The massive adjacent monastery was home to 10,000 monks by the end of the 6th century. Destroyed in the 12th century by Crusaders, it was not until 1900 that a new church was rededicated at the site on the base of the ruins. Founded in 1890, the École is the oldest research institute in the Holy Land, hosts visiting biblical scholars, and has an extensive research library and a collection of 20,000 glass photo plates dating from 1890 that are partially on exhibit. The church is just north of the Old City, about a 10-minute walk from Damascus Gate.

WEST JERUSALEM
German Colony

available tours vary; tel. 02/531-4600

The Templer neighborhood known as the German Colony is home to numerous historically significant buildings constructed in the mid-1800s by a group of German Protestants who came to the Holy Land in anticipation of the return of Jesus. (There is also a German Colony in Haifa to the north). The buildings in one of Jerusalem's most affluent and religious neighborhoods are a mix of residential and business. It is fairly easy to reach from either the outskirts of the city, such as Bethlehem, or the center. Even without a guide, it's possible to take a very safe and leisurely stroll night or day, and end up shopping and dining on Emek Refaim Street, the main road that cuts through the heart of the German Colony.

L.A. Mayer Museum for Islamic Art

2 HaPalmach St.; tel. 02/566-1291; www.islamicart. co.il; 10am-3pm Mon.-Wed., Thurs. 10am-7pm Thurs., 10am-2pm Fri.-Sat., closed Sunday, adult NIS40, student NIS20, child NIS20

Home to a smaller but exquisite collection of Islamic art and antique watches and clocks, the L.A. Mayer Museum for Islamic Art also features rotating exhibitions. In addition, the museum helps visitors arrange certain types of tours in the city.

★ The Israel Museum

11 Ruppin St., near the intersection with Kaplan St.; tel. 02/670-8811; www.imj.org.il/en; 10am-5pm Sun.-Mon. and Wed.-Thurs., 4pm-9pm Tues., 10am-2pm Fri. and holiday eves, 10am-5pm Sat.; adult NIS55, student NIS40, senior, child, and disabled NIS27, NIS27 on repeat visit within 3 months only at box office

The crown jewel of Jerusalem's so-called museum district is The Israel Museum. Even among locals, the Israel Museum is lauded as one of the must-see spots in the city. Home to the Shrine of the Book and the Dead Sea Scrolls, the museum finished a major renovation in 2010 throughout its 20-acre (81,000-square-meter) campus to increase exhibition space, expand structures, and add exhibits.

The museum was founded in 1965 and is Israel's largest cultural institution. It's also considered by some to be among the best art and archaeology museums in the world. It is home to artifacts from prehistory to the present time, and has the most extensive biblical and Holy Land archaeology collection in the world.

Among the museum's most spectacular collections are the Dead Sea Scrolls, housed in a distinctive-looking building called the Shrine of the Book. It was designed to emulate the shape of the lids from the jars where they were discovered. An outdoor model of the Second Temple nearby covers almost one acre. There is enough here for several hours with a meal at the restaurant along the way, where you can rub shoulders with famous locals who are known to be frequent diners.

Bible Lands Museum

25 Avraham Granot St.; tel. 02/561-1066; www.blmj. org/en; 9:30am-5:30pm Sun.-Tues. and Thurs., closes at 9:30pm Wed., 10am-2pm Fri. and holiday eves, 10am-2pm Sat.; NIS44, under 18 NIS22

The first museum in the world dedicated to the history of the Bible and the ancient Near East is the Bible Lands Museum. The permanent exhibition, which is made up almost entirely of the former private collection of Dr. Elie Borowski, art collector and academic, spans from earliest civilization to the early Christian era in the lands of the Bible. The classical art collection features Etruscan, Greek, and Roman art from the 7th century BC through the 2nd century AD. A collection of well-preserved frescoes is believed to be from a village near Pompeii. Guided tours are available and there is a kosher dairy café on premises.

Bloomfield Museum of Science

Hebrew University on Museum Blvd.; tel. 02/654-4888; www.mada.org.il/en; 10am-6pm Mon.-Thurs., 10am-2pm Fri., 10am-5pm Sat.; NIS45, children under 5 free

The rather compact but ambitious Bloomfield

1: an exhibit at the Bloomfield Museum of Science 2: entrance gate of Holocaust Shoa memorial Yad Vashem 3: the Israel Museum

Museum of Science is a ruggedly hands-on, interactive museum designed for children about age 4-12. The museum's three above-ground levels and two below-ground levels include outdoor seating and interactive play space, and science lessons are communicated with mechanical demonstrations through experimentation such as a mirrored room, a ball drop machine, an air gun target practice machine, and a walkable circular rotating disk. Some exhibits are a bit worn from excessive play or get temporarily shut down for repairs, but there's plenty to entertain. The museum also hosts rotating exhibits and special events, and has an underground auditorium for shows. A small cafeteria is located inside where you're allowed to bring your own food.

National Government Compound

A grouping of significant government buildings, some of which are open for tourists to visit, is known as the National Government Compound.

THE KNESSET (PARLIAMENT)

intersection of Kaplan St. and Rothschild St. in Givat Ram; tel. 02/675-3337; www.knesset.gov.il, tours@knesset.gov.il; tours 8:30am-2pm Sun.-Thurs., English tours 8:30am, noon, and 2pm Sun.-Thurs., reservations not needed for individuals, just show up 30 minutes before tour starts; free

A visit to The Knesset (Parliament) should include a guided tour, as you will be unable to enter the building unaccompanied. The very general tour touches on the workings of the Knesset, artwork in the Knesset, architecture, and a combined tour with the Supreme Court. The only independent tour is the Knesset Archaeology Park tour, which includes findings from the Second Temple period through the Ottoman period.

SUPREME COURT OF ISRAEL

intersection of Yitzhak Rabin St. and Rothschild St. in Givat Ram; tel. 02/675-9612; www.court.gov.il; English tours noon Sun.-Thurs.; free

Known for its grand architectural design created by the sister-brother team of Ada Karmi Melamede and Ram Karmi from Tel Aviv is the Supreme Court of Israel. Opened in 1992, the building includes a massive restored mosaic, a panoramic window, and the unique library that is an architectural representation of the Second Temple. The overall structure was created to integrate postmodern architectural elements and reflect Jerusalem's rich architectural history. It was also designed to express the values of justice, law, and righteousness.

Monastery of the Cross

enter on Shota Rustaveli St. in Rehavya Valley; tel. 02/679-0961; 10am-4:30pm Mon.-Sat.; NIS10

Resembling a fort, the Greek Orthodox Monastery of the Cross was most recently rebuilt in the 11th century. The monastery is on the site where Christian tradition says the tree grew that was used to make the cross to crucify Jesus.

It was originally built in the 6th century, destroyed in the Persian invasion in 614, and rebuilt again in 1038. An important Christian theological seminary through the 20th century, it has 16th- and 17th-century frescoes and mosaics and includes a courtyard café.

★ Yad Vashem

enter via the Holland Junction, on the Herzl Route opposite the entrance to Mount Herzl and the descent to Ein Kerem; tel. 02/644-3802; www.yadvashem. org; 8:30am-6pm Sun.-Wed., 8:30am-8pm Thurs., 8:30am-2pm Fri. and holiday eves, closed Sat. and all Jewish holidays, last visitor one hour before closing; free, no children under 10 years old in Holocaust History Museum and main exhibits; paid parking, free shuttle from Mount Herzl stop on the light rail

Nothing can prepare you for the enormous psychological and emotional impact of visiting Yad Vashem. More of an institution than a museum, the Yad Vashem complex is an astounding window into Jewish history and culture. Given the size of Yad Vashem and the amount of information, it is advisable to plan to spend at least half a day there.

Start with the **Holocaust History**

Free Saturday Tours

Saturday is one of the best days of the week to go on a free tour in Jerusalem. Most of the city shuts down and doesn't start opening again until late Saturday evening, so there is very little foot and vehicular traffic. It's also a good time to explore some of Jerusalem's neighborhoods (for detailed tour listings by type, go to the **city's official tourism website** at www.itraveljerusalem.com).

Several types of three-hour-long Saturday tours depart at 10am from **Safra Square** (24-26 Yafo St., tel. 02/531-4600, call in advance, free).

- **The Explore Ethiopia Tour** showcases Eliezer Ben-Yehuda's old neighborhood (he was instrumental in reviving the Hebrew language) and also goes through the Russian Compound, The Ticho House, Ethiopia Street, Bnei Brit Library, and Beit Tavor Street.

- **The German Colony Tour** takes you through the neighborhood built by German Templers at the end of the 19th century and includes a route from King David Street down through Emek Refaim Valley.

- **The Hanevi'im Tour** takes visitors through the history of Hanevi'im Street and its ties to the British, Germans, Italians, and Ethiopians. Some of the buildings on the tour help tell the stories of famous leaders, ambassadors, doctors, poets, artists, and hermits.

- **The Kidron Valley Tour** explores the burial grounds of the Second Temple period, the Kidron River and its streams, and the story behind four rock-hewn graves here. The route goes through Jaffa Gate, the Jewish Quarter, Dung Gate, Kidron Valley viewpoint, and Kidron Valley proper.

- **The Muslim Quarter Tour** takes you from Damascus Gate in the Old City to the Western Wall.

- **The Rehavya Walking Tour** comprises national institutions in the Rehavya neighborhood, including a monastery and the president of Israel's home.

- **Sandeman's New Jerusalem Tour** meets just inside the Old City's Jaffa Gate by the tourism information stand (11am and 2pm daily) and covers a broad range of sights during this two-hour tour. Look for the guides in the red Sandeman's T-shirts; guides might encourage you to tip them.

Museum, the building behind the main entrance. You can rent an audio guide (NIS20) and buy a guide map (NIS10) and work your way through the 45,200-square-foot (4,200-square-meter) spike-shaped linear structure that stretches mostly underground. The museum includes an overwhelming collection, some of it interactive, of artifacts, firsthand testimonies, and personal possessions from the Holocaust.

After you work your way through the main museum, it ends in the **Hall of Names,** a circular repository lit by skylight for the names and testimonies of the millions of Holocaust victims. Two million testimonies are included, with room for four million more. The somber and impressive **Hall of Remembrance** features basalt boulders from the Sea of Galilee and the always-burning Eternal Flame, surrounded by a mosaic of 22 names of the most notorious sites where Nazis committed murder. In front of the flame is a stone crypt with the ashes of Holocaust victims.

Home to the largest and most wide-ranging collection of Holocaust art in the world, the **Holocaust Art Museum** displays some of its more than 10,000 pieces of work by artist and subject matter. There are plenty of comfortable benches for lingering reflection, and the first computerized archive of Holocaust art and artists is adjacent to the museum's galleries.

Mount Herzl

*Herzl Blvd., Mt. Herzl; tel. 02/632-1515; www.wzo.org.
il/mount-herzl; first-come, first-served basis; adult
NIS25, child NIS20*

At the entrance to the Yad Vashem campus is Mount Herzl. The museum is dedicated to the story of famed Zionist Theodor Herzl and gives visitors an audiovisual history through a live-action one-hour program. The four rooms of the small museum explore Herzl's path from a European to the modern father of the State of Israel and include artifacts and memorabilia. Mount Herzl is an easy stop on the way to Yad Vashem.

SOUTHERN JERUSALEM
The Tisch Family Zoological Gardens in Jerusalem

*1 Aharon Sholov Rd.; tel. 02/675-0111; www.
jerusalemzoo.org.il; 9am-6pm Sun.-Thurs.,
9am-4:30pm Fri. and holiday eves 10am-6pm
Sat. and holidays; adult NIS58, child, senior, and
student NIS44*

The Tisch Family Zoological Gardens in Jerusalem is a remarkably diverse zoo and aquarium spread out over several square miles of rolling hills. A small train offers rides around the grounds for a few shekels. The fairly new aquarium can only be reached by vehicle and there are typically no shuttle buses for zoo patrons. Opened in 1993, it is home to an impressive collection of vertebrates and invertebrates. Among the zoo's most popular exhibits are the kangaroos, giraffes, elephants, lions, and lemurs.

SPECIAL TOURS
Tour Guides

As with any major tourist destination, there are a number of fly-by-night tour guides and companies in Jerusalem selling their services. A good rule of thumb is to work with someone who is a licensed tour guide or get recommendations from the front desk at your hotel.

The **official travel website of Israel** (https://info.goisrael.com) has a complete listing of tour guides authorized by the Ministry of Tourism who offer services in a wide range of languages. You can also choose a guide who has a car as part of their services. Check under the "Before You Go" tab on the website, and choose "Tour Guide Search" from the left tab.

Sandeman's New Europe (www.newjerusalemtours.com) is a large, international company with a good reputation that offers a variety of tours in Jerusalem, including free daily tours of the Old City. They can be contacted online in advance of any special tour you'd like to arrange.

Nature Tours

*tel. 02/625-2357 or 03/638-8688; natureisrael.org;
NIS120-220*

The **Society for the Protection of Nature in Israel** gives urban walking tours in English, but not on a fixed schedule. Call to see if an English tour is available, as they typically only take groups of 10 or more. Their website has a green map that contains useful information about green spaces within the city. They also give ecotours throughout Israel, and operate relatively cheap places to stay called field schools in more remote regions of the country. They can also be contacted in their U.S., Canadian, French, and British offices.

Archaeological Tours

*tel. 02/586-2011; www.archesem.com; US$200 and
up, plus VAT and entrance fees*

For tours with an archaeological twist, try **Archaeological Seminars Institute Ltd.** for one of their varied half- and full-day private walking tours for up to 10 people. Some of the tour types include archaeology as it relates to religion, and retracing the footsteps of ancient Jewish residents of the city.

Underground Archaeological Tours

Above the ground, Jerusalem is rich and fascinating. Underground lies another layer of the city that will convince even the most frugal traveler of the value of paying for a tour. These are some of the best underground tours in Jerusalem:

- **Burnt House:** Part of a larger complex under the Old City's Jewish Quarter, the charred remains date back to AD 70 (www.rova-yehudi.org.il/en).

- **Herodian Quarter and Wohl Archaeological Museum:** The basement of a Jewish seminary covers the remains of a mansion from the Second Temple period (www.rova-yehudi.org.il/en).

- **Hezekiah's Tunnel:** You can wade through the water in this 2,700-year-old tunnel, part of the City of David, for 580 yards (520 meters) (www.cityofdavid.org.il/en).

- **Warren's Shaft:** An underground waterworks system that dates back to the age of the kings of Judea was discovered in 1867 by British engineer Sir Charles Warren (www.cityofdavid.org.il/en).

Herodian street in the Western Wall tunnels

- **The Western Wall Tunnels:** This 75-minute tour explores hidden layers of the Western Wall (english.thekotel.org).

Entertainment and Events

Jerusalem, with its emphasis on ancient tradition and spiritual and family life, hasn't typically been known for its nightlife scene, but that's slowly changed in recent years with new business, community, and municipal government initiatives. For evening entertainment, there are a variety of bars, pubs, live music venues, and clubs, as well as performing arts venues.

PERFORMING ARTS
Cultural Centers
BEIT AVI CHAI
*44 King George St.; tel. 02/621-5300; www.bac.
org.il/eng; box office open 1pm-9:30pm Sun.-Thurs.,
9:30am-noon Fri.*
If you're in the mood for something focused

on the Jewish experience in Israel and the diaspora, Beit Avi Chai features a 270-seat auditorium and stage. Their programming includes a range of speakers, film screenings, and artists. Israeli musicians perform weekly, and a popular summer music concert series showcases free concerts and evening concerts by Jerusalem and Israeli musical favorites in the courtyard.

BEIT SHMUEL
*6 Eliyahu Shama St.; tel. 02/620-3455; www.
beitshmuel.com; NIS65-120*
Encore performances in English are hosted by the World Union for Progressive Judaism at Beit Shmuel. They host plays, musicals, ethnic music, and educational and cultural activities.

MISHKENOT SHA'ANANIM

9 Yemin Moshe St.; tel. 02/629-2220;
www.mishkenot.org.il/en; prices vary,
sometimes free

One of Jerusalem's largest and most prominent centers for international cultural activities is the Mishkenot Sha'ananim complex, which is backed by the Jerusalem Foundation. The stair- and hill-filled grounds are home to a public park with paved pathways for strolling and the landmark "lion fountain," the INFO Press Club for foreign journalists, and a guest house for artists and writers. The area is the location of the first Jewish settlement outside of the Old City walls, founded in the mid-19th century. Numerous historic structures from that time survived, including the iconic and recently restored Montefiore Windmill. An international convention center just next to the windmill hosts the International Writer's Festival and other prominent events, festivals, screenings, and lectures.

FIRST STATION

4 David Remez St.; tel. 02/653-5239;
http://firststation.co.il; open daily; free

A magnet for the many young and secular Jewish families in Jerusalem and those looking for indoor-outdoor dining, shopping, and live music is the First Station, in Hebrew **HaTachana.** It's all centered around an outdoor stage under a tent where bands perform year-round for free.

Theaters and Cinemas
JERUSALEM CENTRE FOR THE PERFORMING ARTS

20 David Marcus; tel. 02/560-5757;
www.jerusalem-theatre.co.il; NIS220-250

The Jerusalem Centre for the Performing Arts is the largest center for performing arts and cultural performances in Israel. Its five halls host everything from concerts and dance, to festivals, lectures, plays, and films. It's also home to the Jerusalem Symphony Orchestra.

THE KHAN THEATRE

2 David Remez Sq.; tel. 02/630-3600;
www.khan.co.il; NIS220

Ensconced in a classic Jerusalem stone building with arched entryways and an inner courtyard, The Khan Theatre is the city's only repertoire-producing theater company. A regular ensemble of actors manages, produces, and performs three to six performances every year.

CINEMA CITY

10 Yitzhak Rabin Blvd.; tel. 074/752-6700;
www.cinemacity.co.il; NIS65

Always fun-filled, Cinema City includes movie theaters, a small shopping mall, multiple restaurants, and specialized theaters designed for children for special events. It also features live stage performances, live high-definition broadcasting, and 3-D movies.

FESTIVALS AND EVENTS

Year after year, Jerusalem continues to host a number of festivals, musical and performance events, concert series, and more. Many of the more accessible festivals and events are geared toward the Jewish or secular communities in the city in particular. Depending on level of access, event fees vary but generally run on the more expensive end, between NIS50-200 per person.

Spring

The annual **International Writer's Festival** (Mishkenot Sha'ananim, http://mishkenot.org.il/writersfestival2019/en, late spring, NIS140-300) is known for its breadth and length. The multiday festival is held in late spring at Mishkenot Sha'ananim and features talks with a slew of well-known international authors, film screenings, and an extensive collection of books. Many of the events are in English.

The exact dates vary slightly, but the **Palestine Festival of Literature** (various locations in the West Bank and Israel, usually Apr., http://palfest.org, free) has been held annually for over a decade, often around the month of April. Dubbed PalFest, the multiday cultural and literary festival aims to "break the cultural siege imposed on Palestinians" by featuring artists, authors, activists, and musicians for discussions, readings, talks, and performances. Events happen by day and night at various locations that change each year.

Summer

The **Jerusalem International Film Festival** (Jerusalem Cinematheque, www.jff.org.il, prices vary) has been running for over 30 years and is thus a bit more traditional. The festival's flavor is primarily Israeli film, with a European flair.

Now a highly anticipated annual event, the **Jerusalem Beer Festival** (Independence Park, tel. 050/594-8844, www.jerusalembeer.com/en; NIS85 pp) has been running for about 15 years. Centrally staged near Jerusalem's First Station, the festival features over 120 different beers, both international and local. It lasts two days and includes live music.

A bit more refined crowd can be found at the **Jerusalem Wine Festival** (Billy Rose Garden of the Israel Museum, tel. 02/625-9703, 8:30pm-11pm, 3 days in July, NIS80/evening pp, includes a wineglass, unlimited tasting, and admission to the museum's galleries until 9pm on Tues.), which takes place over three days at the end of July. The festival brings together some of the best wines from Israel's varied collection of local wineries.

The **End of Summer Festival** (20 David Marcus, tel. 02/560-5755, www.jerusalem-theatre.co.il; NIS55-110) is three days at the end of August featuring Israeli and foreign artists and performers. The festival consists of some of the latest work in performance art and film. It's hugely popular amongst locals.

One energetic and fascinating night a year, **Contact Point** (Israel Museum, Aug.) connects artists and audiences through interactive art installations around the sprawling campus of the Israel Museum. Activities start at dusk and end around 3am. The interactive art experiences are just part of the fun. Guests lucky enough to get tickets—they are in extremely high demand—also get to hear live music and gain access to the museum's permanent exhibitions.

Fall

The **Jerusalem International Chamber Music Festival** (YMCA Mary Nathaniel Hall, tel. 02/625-0444, www.jcmf.org.il, Sept., NIS80-150) is a several-days-long concert series that highlights a different area of classical music every year.

For an interesting peek at Israeli culture, head to the **President's Open House** (Presidential residence, Hanasi St. in Talbiyeh, Sukkot week; free) for photo taking, food, and live music. You can peek into the president's formal sitting room and wander a couple of tightly controlled hallways and rooms. The main events take place in the backyard of the house, just past the lavish Sukkah decorated for the Jewish holiday of Sukkot.

A series of other events take place during Sukkot week; check with the official tourism site of the **Jerusalem Municipality** (www.itraveljerusalem.com) for details and listings of events.

The **Abu Ghosh Vocal Music Festival** (Abu Ghosh, www.agfestival.co.il/en, Oct., free) takes place every year in the Arab village of Abu Ghosh just outside Jerusalem. Concerts are performed in the 12th-century Crusader-Benedictine Kiryat Ye'arim Church in the heart of the village.

Winter

Now going for more than three decades, **The Jerusalem International Book Fair** (central locations throughout Jerusalem, www.jbookfair.com; free) brings together agents, authors, and exhibitors of all kinds for a multiday event. Tickets are difficult to get; purchase them in advance. The festival's Jerusalem Prize is awarded to a writer who exhibits the principles of individual freedom in society.

Shopping

Jerusalem has a variety of shops, but the most accessible and common are merchants who sell religious ornaments and objects, clothing, regional spices and nuts, and locally handmade ceramics. Types of shopping can be divided mainly into outdoor markets, the Old City and City Center shops, and extremely upscale and high-end souvenirs and jewelry. Home decor and houseware shops, electronics shops, money changers, shopping malls, grocery stores, and furniture stores are largely concentrated around King George Street in City Center, and the neighborhood district of Talpiyot. When buying anything of value, get the proper receipt and paperwork for customs, including the **tax rebate** calculation that you can collect at the airport.

THE OLD CITY
Jaffa Gate
MINISTRY OF TOURISM INFORMATION CENTER
1 Jaffa St.; tel. 02/627-1422; 8:30am-5pm Sun.-Thurs., 8:30am-noon Fri.

The Ministry of Tourism Information Center is just at the start to HaNotsrim Street, a narrow pedestrian and merchant walkway in the Christian Quarter that abounds with **religious items, souvenirs, clothing, and jewelry** for minor shopping and beginner bargaining. Follow the main road from Jaffa Gate at David Street until you reach the second-to-last right turn, and you'll get to the **Cardo** (tel. 02/626-5900, ext. 102, business area and shops 8am-6pm Sun.-Thurs., 8am-4pm Fri.) with its numerous high-end gift shops and galleries for Judaica. This is the border between the Jewish and Armenian Quarters, the latter of which has some interesting shops that sell jewelry, antiques, and textiles.

Damascus Gate
For a vibrant shopping experience (as in, loud and extremely physical), just inside of Damascus Gate at the intersection of Beit Habad Street and El Wad Hagai Street is the gateway to the **Arab Souk,** where you can find trinkets, clothing, spices, sweets, jewelry, raw meat, and other food. Watch out for merchants barreling through with carts!

Mamilla
street entrance is at the intersection of Shlomtsiyon HaMalka and Shlomo HaMelech, just across the street from the David Citadel Hotel; shop hours are generally 9am-10pm Sun.-Thurs., 9am-3pm Fri.

Just off the hectic Jaffa Gate plaza is the mellow atmosphere of Mamilla, an indoor-outdoor mall. The Old City and Mamilla feed off each other, siphoning hungry, tired tourists from the dusty heat to cool air-conditioning. Many shops here are Israeli brands and international chain stores for clothing, jewelry, and makeup, which makes it a convenient place.

Brands represented include Rolex, MAC, H. Stern, Nike, Polo Ralph Lauren, Gap, Nautica, bebe, and Tommy Hilfiger, as well as local brands like Fox, Castro, and Ronen Chen. Midway along the plaza is a public restroom. There are often street performances or free public performances, which makes it a fun place to wander and window-shop. It stays active late into the evening and is home to great places to grab a burger and a beer.

Take a look inside **Eden Fine Art** (Alrov Mamilla Ave., tel. 02/624-2506, www.eden-gallery.com; 10am-6pm Sun.-Thurs and until 3pm Fri.) for a glimpse at this international art representative. The shop sponsors artwork, sculptures, and photographs from select leading Israeli and international artists. The bright, small venue caters to upper-crust clients and art collectors, and has some interesting pieces from Israeli artists.

The **Stern House** (33 Jaffa St. in Mamilla shopping center; 10am-6pm, Sun.-Thurs and until 3pm Fri.) is a charming and interesting preserved and reconstructed building that played host to Theodor Herzl during his visit

Mamilla's Numbered Stones

Throughout Jerusalem you will see stone buildings with numbers scrolled by hand on each stone. These are historically significant buildings that have been disassembled, preserved, and reassembled. In that typical Jerusalem fashion of blending sentimentality with history, the numbers have been left to advertise the act of preservation and to distinguish the building among its neighbors for special historic value.

Stroll through **Mamilla Alrov Quarter** and you will see five examples of buildings preserved this way, either in their entirety or by being incorporated into new buildings. The preservation was done under the guidance of the Israel Antiquities Authority.

Two buildings in Mamilla that have been left in place are particularly notable:

- **The Stern House,** situated at about the center of Mamilla's pedestrian promenade, was built in 1877 and hosted Zionist Theodor Herzl on his only trip to Israel.

- **The Clark House** was constructed by American evangelicals in the late 19th century.

to Jerusalem in 1898, and now houses an outlet of **Steimatzky Books** (tel. 02/625-7268), a bookstore chain that has a good selection of English books and magazines, and **Café Café** (tel. 02/624-4773), a chain coffee shop for a bite to eat or coffee.

CITY CENTER
Tolerance (Zion) Square

Shopping in City Center rotates on the axis of Tolerance Square, which runs between **King George Street** and **Yafo Street** and is at the foot of both **Ben Yehuda Street** and **Yoel Moshe Salomon** pedestrian malls. The square's name was changed in 2016 to honor the victim of a stabbing attack at Tel Aviv's annual gay pride parade, but it is still referred to as Zion Square. Most shopping areas shut down from Friday late afternoon to late Saturday night and Jewish holidays. There are a few exceptions. Shopping in the area is decidedly geared toward tourists, and it is largely limited to stores that sell souvenirs and Judaica, embroidered *kippot* and T-shirts, camera equipment, electronics and housewares, and local brands of clothing and shoes.

THE BOOK GALLERY

6 Schatz St., at corner of 26 King George St.; tel. 02/623-1087; www.bookgallery.co.il; 9am-7pm Sun.-Thurs., 9am-2pm Fri.

At the top of Zion Square, check out The Book Gallery, the largest secondhand bookstore in Israel. It includes two floors with a separate section for old and rare books and a large basement.

King George Street

A main street leading into Jerusalem's heart is King George Street, filled with shops of all kinds selling items from electronics to clothing to food, and nearly every side street has additional storefronts for everything from salons to restaurants.

Yafo Street (Jaffa Street)

Busy Yafo Street (also known as Jaffa Street) is the main artery of the city's center and home to the light-rail train. Only pedestrian and train traffic are allowed to go through the length of the street that runs through the heart of town, passing always-happening **Tolerance Square** (formerly known as **Zion Square**) near where Yafo intersects with Shamai Street, which is full of tourists, souvenir shops, ice cream shops, juice bars, and sidewalk cafés.

Ben Yehuda Street (Pedestrian Mall)

A main pedestrian artery that leads to Tolerance (aka Zion) Square, Ben Yehuda Street is full of shops that tend to cater to tourists and sell items such as souvenirs and

Judaica. In the past, the highly trafficked area made it a target for terrorist bombings—look for silver plaques on the ground and sides of buildings marking spots where bombings took place. The triangle formed by Ben Yehuda, King George, and Yafo Streets is partially inhabited by shops founded after attacks on the Mamilla commercial center, just days after the UN vote on the partition of Palestine in 1947.

Nahalat Shiva
VICE-VERSA
1 Shim'on Ben Shetach St.; tel. 02/624-4412; www.viceversalib.com; 9am-6pm Sun.-Thurs., 9am-1:30pm Fri.

Small and mostly stocked with books and materials in French, Vice-Versa is a sweet shop with a warm atmosphere that highlights Jerusalem's subculture of French residents. Mostly fun for browsing, the shop does sell some gift-related merchandise, like cards and items for children.

GAYA GAMES
7 Yoel Moshe Solomon St. at the end of Shamai St.; tel. 02/625-1515; www.gaya-game.com; 10am-10pm Sun.-Thurs., 10am-3pm Fri., 10am-10pm Sat.

For a truly unique souvenir and just plain fun with some super cool locals, Gaya Games has dozens of unique wooden games and brain teaser toys. Staff demonstrate the games by playing them with you. The cavernous feel of the Israeli chain's Jerusalem store caters to adult customers who are interested in challenging play. Their **Creative Thinking Seminars** (contact Galit, tel. 03/903-3122, galit@gaya-game.com) allow you to play with some of their games and challenge your brain.

THE CADIM CERAMIC ART GALLERY AND COLLECTIVE
4 Yoel Moshe Solomon St; tel. 02/623-4869; 10am-10pm Sun.-Thurs., 9am-3pm Fri.

The Cadim Ceramic Art Gallery and Collective is a smaller gallery and shop that serves as the storefront for a cooperative of 15 Israeli ceramic artists, who also serve as staff and management. Objects are displayed in groups by artist and every purchase includes the story of the artist. Prices start on the affordable end and go up for objects including functional pottery, decorative objects, sculptural pieces, Judaica, and jewelry.

THE EIGHTH NOTE
12 Ze'ev Raban St.; tel. 08/919-9555; www.tav8.co.il; 10am-6pm Sun.-Thurs.

Often missed by visitors to Jerusalem, The Eighth Note was established in 1993 before becoming a national brand with locations around Israel. The original store has a small black-and-white sign on its storefront and a basement store packed to the brim with a broad collection of Arabic, Greek, Turkish, and other Middle Eastern CDs and DVDs. The friendly and knowledgeable sales staff will help you with listening samples and recommendations.

MACHANE YEHUDA MARKET (THE *SHUK*)
between Yafo St. and Agripas St. at Beit Ya'acov and Eitz HaChaim; www.machne.co.il/en; 8am-7pm Sun.-Thurs., 8am-3pm Fri.

Known to locals as the *shuk,* this open-air market is world-famous for its colorful produce stands, restaurants, and characters. At every entrance (and there are about a dozen of them), you will find yourself in a maze of bins overflowing with fruits and vegetables, sweets and olives, and all kinds of spices and teas. Browse the ordered chaos of the market's many restaurants, cafés, coffee shops, pubs, and shops for produce, spices, or sweets.

SALAH EDDIN STREET
EDUCATIONAL BOOKSHOP
19 and 22 Salah Eddin St.; tel. 02/627-5858; www.educationalbookshop.com; 8am-8pm daily

Renowned as an oasis of books in English on a wide range of subjects about Israel, the West Bank, and the conflict in the region,

---

1: Shopping options abound in the City Center.
2: sausage for sale in Machane Yehuda Market

Shopping in the Old City

Shopping in the Old City can be exciting or intimidating. There are seemingly endless streets of shops and cavernous stalls that are open seven days a week, and they have very similar items. Most visitors enter the Old City area from Jaffa Gate and turn down HaNotsrim Street, a narrow pedestrian street in the Christian Quarter.

The stores fall mainly into the categories of jewelry, religious items, souvenirs, clothing, antiques, and food. For gifts to take back home, you can find nice scarves, sweets, and cute trinkets. Be aware, though, that in many cases, aggressive shop owners won't allow you more than two seconds to glance at their products before pushing you to buy. It is also a notoriously expensive place for English-speaking customers, particularly Americans. Despite that, it's good fun and a bit like gambling: The trick is to know when to stop.

a shop in the Old City

BARGAINING

Be prepared in advance to do the dance of bargaining if you plan to buy something, which might include literally walking away to get the best price. You can bargain if you are confident, but the best bet for avoiding some serious unplanned spending is to decide in advance on your limit.

A good approach to shopping in this area is to walk past vendors and stores, and only slow down if you are seriously interested in buying something. Otherwise you will spend a lot of time extricating yourself from negotiations with shop owners.

ANTIQUES

Shops selling antiques and artifacts, including Roman-glass inlaid jewelry and other locally handmade items, can be found mainly in the Christian and Jewish Quarters, although such stores are scattered throughout all four quarters. Be very cautious when purchasing antiques. You need a legal certificate to take the item out of the country, in part due to problems with grave robbers and theft of antiques from archaeological sites. Check with the information center about the proper documentation necessary or visit the Israeli Antiquities Authority website.

CURRENCY AND OPENING HOURS

Most vendors are more than willing to take American dollars. One of the great advantages to shopping in this area is that almost everything is open on the weekend.

Educational Bookshop is a combination of two bookshops, a small coffee shop, and a space for events in English. A third location down the road at Louis Vincent Street is on the American Colony Hotel grounds in a small, historic building. The friendly, knowledgeable staff at all three locations can help you find a book on nearly any subject. The main bookshop-coffee shop location is very tight on space but is the perfect place to relax with a book and a cappuccino and hosts regular talks with authors.

OUTDOOR MARKETS
BEZALEL ART FAIR

Schatz St. and Bor Shiber Garden by the Mashbir; 10am-4pm Fri.

Every Friday, local and regional vendors

converge at the outdoor Bezalel Art Fair to sell paintings, wood crafts, textiles, jewelry, glasswork, unique handicrafts, and food. The lively fair consists of carefully chosen vendors to maintain an overall atmosphere and a varied selection of art and artistic displays. Staged next door to the historic campus of the Bezalel Art Academy, the outdoor fair also includes a tour at noon from Bezalel to City Center.

FARMERS AND ARTISTS STREET MARKET

12 Emek Refaim St.; 10am-2pm Fri.

A popular stop before the weekend is the Farmers and Artists Street Market that includes vendors selling jewelry, ceramics, toys, food, and a wide variety of other items for very affordable prices.

SOUTHERN JERUSALEM

JERUSALEM (MALHA) MALL

Agudat Sport Beitar 1, across from Teddy Stadium; tel. 02/679-1333; 9am-10pm Sun.-Thurs. and 9am-3pm Fri.

The massive Jerusalem (Malha) Mall has the feel of a Southern California shopping mall in its size, parking, range of stores, and dining options. With 215 stores that include local and international brands for everything from clothing to groceries, it is Jerusalem's largest mall. It is on the outskirts of the city, making public transportation there tedious.

HADAR MALL

26 Pierre Koenig St.; http://hadar-mall.co.il; 9am-11pm Sun.-Thurs. and 9am-3pm Fri.

Very easy to reach by bus, taxi, walking, or some combination, Hadar Mall sells everything from basic necessities to medical services.

Sports and Recreation

Jerusalem's higher elevation means that even in the hot summer months there's a cool, soothing breeze most mornings and evenings. This makes outdoor activities a common pastime, including visiting natural springs, hiking, biking, swimming, camping, and cooking out (which is practically a national sport). Many Jerusalemites enjoy taking long walks through the city's scenic (and often hilly) terrain. Playing soccer, having a picnic, or simply sitting and relaxing are common pastimes.

PARKS AND GARDENS

SHEROVER-HAAS PROMENADE

enter off Daniel Yanovski St. at Olei HaGardom St.; tel. 02/626-5900, ext. 102; www.tclf.org; 24 hours daily; free, free parking

A paved walking trail with fantastic vistas, the Sherover-Haas Promenade overlooks East Jerusalem, the Old City walls, and the Judean Desert. The winding walkway of the promenade zigzags down the hillside for about one mile (1.6 km). There are stairs at different points. The area is landscaped with native plant and flower gardens, quiet places to sit, and viewing pergolas. The bottom of the promenade is the edge of the Judean Desert and a local neighborhood.

BIRD OBSERVATORY

just south of Eliezer Kaplan St. and Rothschild St.; tel. 02/653-7374; http://natureinisrael.org; 9am-3pm Sun.-Thurs., and by appointment; free

The one-acre (4050-square-meter) Bird Observatory is run by the Society for the Protection of Nature in Israel. The observatory is home to the Israel national bird-ringing center and features a wildlife blind to watch the myriad wild animals that spend time in this richly preserved and fortified natural habitat. Night hikes, sketching workshops, guided birdwatching, and photography workshops are all held here.

LIBERTY BELL PARK

crossroads of Keren HaYesod and King David St.,
down to the beginning of Emek Refaim St.; 24 hours
daily; free

The popular and always lively Liberty Bell Park is often the site of Ethiopian wedding parties and huge family cookouts. The western end of the park is home to a reproduction of the Liberty Bell (hence the park's name), and there are several different playgrounds, walking paths, basketball courts, and picnic areas. It also hosts festivals, performances, and fairs, and is home to the Train Theater.

TRAIN TRACK PARK

between First Station and Teddy Stadium; 24 hours
daily; free entry, paid parking

The nearly 4-mile-long (6.5-km-long) linear Railroad Park follows the old Turkish railway train tracks from the cultural and entertainment center at the First Station to near Malha Mall. Since the park was established, various forms of entertainment have popped up along the way. It is also a singular glimpse into local life, architecture, and customs. The paved jogging and bike path is always busy, and a boarded walkway atop the old railroad tracks is good for more leisurely strolling. The park is filled with plants, flowers, and benches to stop off for a rest and has easy access to numerous dining and shopping venues along the route.

BLOOMFIELD GARDEN

runs along King David St. from the base of Keren
HaYesod St. to Elimelech Admoni St. and west to
Mishkenot Sha'ananim St.; 24 hours daily; free

Full of character and history, Bloomfield Garden features massive agave plants, the family tomb of King Herod, and the remains of an ancient aqueduct. A unique landmark on the southern end of the 17-acre (69,000-square-meter) park is a fountain with distinct bronze lions (the symbol of Jerusalem) encircling it. At the north end of the park is the venerable artist colony and cultural center Mishkenot Sha'ananim and the little-known **Gozlan Garden,** a small,

precisely designed park with fountains behind the world-famous King David Hotel.

WOHL ROSE GARDEN

Government Center opposite the Knesset; tel.
02/563-7233; www.jerusalem.muni.il; 24 hours daily;
free, paid parking

Magical Wohl Rose Garden covers an area of almost 20 acres (81,000 square meters) and is home to about 400 varieties of roses on 15,000 bushes. The park also has a variety of charming nooks and crannies, including an observation point and an ornamental pool. It is adjacent to other major tourist spots, including the Supreme Court and the Israeli Parliament.

INDEPENDENCE PARK

bordered by Gershon Agron St. and King George St.;
24 hours daily; free

Just on the edge of City Center, you will find the sprawling Independence Park, with some good places to sit and enjoy a picnic after exploring nearby. Its terraced landscaping is dotted with a waterway system of an artificial creek and pools and frequented by families, but is rarely crowded except during an outdoor concert or event.

JERUSALEM BOTANICAL GARDEN

1 Yehuda Burla St.; tel. 073/243-8914; http://
en.botanic.co.il; 9am-5pm Sun.-Thurs., 9am-3pm Fri.
and holiday eves, 9am-5pm Sat. and holidays, hours
and price subject to change for special events; adult
NIS30, senior and child NIS20

A trip to the Jerusalem Botanical Garden includes exploring 30 acres (122,000 square meters) of landscaped grounds that include a renowned bonsai collection and about 10,000 varieties of plants from Europe and North America. Inside the grounds of the garden you can ride the Flower Train or walk along leafy paths. It also includes an indoor tropical conservatory, plants of the Bible trail, an herb and medicinal plant garden, and an African savanna grass maze.

1: Lions Fountain by sculptor Gernot Rumpf in Bloomfield Garden **2:** segway tour of Jerusalem

BICYCLING AND SEGWAY RIDING

Getting around the city on self-propelled and guided wheels is a great way to see and experience Jerusalem, especially at night for the more experienced and adventurous bicyclists. Bicycle and Segway tours cover a fair amount of ground in a compact period of time, and for a reasonable price. Take the climate into account when planning to factor in exposure to the elements, particularly sun exposure in the summer months.

A **bike share rental** program sponsored by the city has been in the works since 2016. Once launched, it will initially include about 500 bicycles at 15 stations, largely in and around City Center.

JERUSALEM MIDNIGHT BIKING

departs from the Karta parking lot; tel. 02/566-1441; http://jerusalembiking.com; call for upcoming rides; NIS115, NIS230 with bike and helmet

For those already comfortable on a bike, the Jerusalem Midnight Biking tour offers exercise and a chance to socialize. The three-hour tour covers about 5 miles (8 kilometers) on a circular route that passes through the neighborhood districts of Abu-Tor, Yemin Moshe, and parts of the Old City.

GORDON ACTIVE BIKE TOURS

tel. 03/765-9000 ext. 118; www.gordonactive.com; NIS300-500 pp

Although its offices are based in Tel Aviv, Gordon Active offers tours that range from Jerusalem road biking to night biking and trips between Jerusalem and Eilat.

SMARTTOURS

tel. 02/561-8056; www.smart-tour.co.il; tours daily; NIS180-330 pp

One way to experience Jerusalem for those who have good hand-eye coordination and a sense of balance is by Segway. A popular Segway option among several in town is SmartTours, with options for night and day in both the old and new city.

HIKING AND WALKING

For very serious hikers, the **Jerusalem Trail** (www.israeltrail.net) forms a circular route about 26 miles (42 km) long through the city as part of the larger **Israel National Trail** that runs from the north to the south of the country. The trail should be marked with blue-and-white or blue-and-gold signs along the route. There are maps and recommended resources on the trail's website.

REHAVYA PARK

off Ben Tsvi St.; 24 hours daily; free

Rehavya Park has extensive trails that are easy to navigate with sturdy shoes. The views of the Valley of the Cross and its monastery below are magnificent. Walking in this area is better suited to cloudy days or early evening during the summer months.

SWIMMING

There are several public and private pools in the city, but most options are on the expensive end. Check beforehand about restrictions due to different hours for men and women.

AMERICAN COLONY HOTEL

1 Louis Vincent St.; tel. 02/627-9777; www.americancolony.com; 7:00am-7:00pm daily; NIS125

The American Colony Hotel swimming area is closer to an oasis than a pool. Built from classic Jerusalem stone and lined with Italian glass tiles, cascading water features complete the serene scene.

MAMILLA HOTEL

11 King Solomon St.; tel. 02/548-2222; www.mamillahotel.com; 7am-7pm daily except Jewish holidays; NIS11

The luxurious indoor swimming pool for adults and children at the easily accessible Mamilla Hotel is fully equipped with Egyptian-cotton towels, a relaxed atmosphere, comfortable deck chairs, and a side baby and toddler pool.

JERUSALEM YMCA

26 King David St.; tel. 02/568-6960;
http://ymca.org.il; 6am-11pm Sun.-Thurs.,
6am-7pm Fri., 10am-11pm Fri.; NIS85

Housed in a historic building in the center of the city, the Jerusalem YMCA is a half Olympic pool open to both hotel guests and visitors.

GYMS AND SPAS

DAN JERUSALEM HOTEL

32 Lehi St., Mt. Scopus; tel. 02/533-1234;
6:15am-9pm Sun.-Fri. and 8:45am-9pm Sat.; NIS80

The Dan Jerusalem Hotel has a range of facilities including a gym, Turkish bath, whirlpool bath, saunas, and indoor and outdoor pools (in season).

AKASHA WELLBEING CENTER

11 King Solomon St.; tel. 02/548-2222;
www.mamillahotel.com; call for hours and
entry fees

The Akasha Wellbeing Center is inside the Mamilla Hotel and includes a state-of-the-art gym, Turkish spa, health bar, massages, and treatments.

Food

Restaurants, coffee shops, and other dining options in Jerusalem tend to group together according to various factors, such as whether they are kosher. Along a main artery like Emek Refaim Street, which is home to at least a dozen dining options, all the restaurants are kosher. As a result, it is extremely busy on Friday and closed for the entire weekend. In City Center, a grouping of solid nonkosher mainstays ensures that there are options seven days a week.

CITY CENTER

Contemporary Middle Eastern

CAFÉ KADOSH

6 Shlomtsiyon HaMalka; tel. 053/809-1548;
7am-midnight Sun.-Thurs., 7am-4pm Fri., 1 hour after
Shabbat-Midnight Sat.; NIS50

Long a Jerusalem icon, Café Kadosh traces its establishment to 1967. One of the longest-running restaurants in the city, Kadosh is a popular date restaurant. In the style of a European patisserie, it has a tight floor plan with a large display of baked goods and a variety of espresso drinks. Hearty Mediterranean-style breakfasts with salad, eggs, fresh bread, juice, and coffee are augmented by one of the best selections of croissant and *burekasim* (flaky pastry-crust-filled savory treats) in the city.

★ ZUNI

15 Yoel Moshe Solomon St., 2nd Fl.; tel.
053/934-5582; 24 hours daily; NIS60

Beloved by visitors and locals, Zuni is easy to find and friendly. Beyond being open 24 hours a day and serving bacon, Zuni staff always aims to please and improve. Housed on the second floor of a historic building, Zuni is decorated in rich, dark wood with a smoker-friendly bar, worth visiting even if you aren't having dinner, enclosed from the main dining room. English-speaking wait-staff and a rotating set of menus for different times of day mean Zuni's offerings include everything from bacon, coffee, and eggs for breakfast to handcrafted cocktails and chicken and beef dinner entrees. The late-night menu accommodates snacking, desserts, and coffee.

MEATBURGER IWO

28 Hillel St.; tel. 02/622-2513; http://iwos.co.il;
10am-3am Sun.-Thurs., 10am-7pm Fri., 10am-4pm
Sat.; NIS50

A fast-food chain called Meatburger Iwo serves up hefty Israeli-style hamburgers, wraps, and grilled chicken sandwiches. It offers English-speaking service, delivery, and a convenient online ordering system.

Restaurants and Cafés Open Weekends

From late Friday afternoon to late Saturday evening, it can be a challenge to find a great meal because most places in the city are closed for the Jewish Sabbath, or Shabbat. Scattered about are some outstanding establishments that do stay open.

CITY CENTER AND VICINITY OF THE OLD CITY

Many establishments open on the weekend are part of international hotel chains. Those and independent restaurants are largely concentrated in the space around and between City Center and the Old City:

- **First Station Restaurants** (4 David Remez St., tel. 02/653-5239, http://firststation.co.il/en)
- **Austrian Hospice Café** (Old City near Damascus Gate, 37 Via Dolorosa, tel. 02/626-5800, www.austrianhospice.com)
- **Barood** (31 Jaffa St. in Feingold Courtyard, tel. 02/625-9081)
- **Blue Dolphin** (7 Shim'on Ha'tsadik St., tel. 02/532-2001)
- **Chakra** (41 King George St., tel. 02/625-2733, www.chakra-rest.com/en)
- **Dublin Irish Pub** (4 Shamai St., tel. 057/944-3740)
- **Focaccia Bar** (4 Rabi Akiva St., tel. 057/944-3123, bar.focaccia.co)
- **Lavan Restaurant at the Cinematheque** (11 Hebron Rd., tel. 02/673-7393)
- **Link** (3 Hama'alot St., tel. 053/809-4510)
- **Meatburger Iwo** (28 Hillel St., tel. 02/622-2513, http://iwos.co.il)
- **Notre Dame Roof Top Wine and Cheese Restaurant** (3 Paratroopers Rd., tel. 02/627-9111, www.notredamecenter.org)
- **YMCA Three Arches Restaurant** (26 King David St., tel. 02/569-2692, http://ymca.org.il)
- **Zuni** (15 Yoel Moshe Solomon, 2nd Fl., tel. 053/934-5582)

EAST JERUSALEM

Most places in East Jerusalem are open on the weekend, and here are a few choice places to start:

- **American Colony** (1 Louis Vincent St., tel. 02/627-9777, www.americancolony.com)
- **Askadinya Restaurant Bar** (11 Shim'on Ha'tsadik St., tel. 02/532-4590)
- **Pasha's Restaurant** (13 Shimon Siddiq in Sheikh Jarrah, tel. 02/582-5162, www.shahwan.org)
- **Educational Bookshop Café** (19 Salah Eddin St., tel. 02/627-5858)

GERMAN COLONY AND WEST JERUSALEM

The farther away from City Center, the fewer the pickings:

- **The Culinary Workshop** (28 Hebron Rd. in the JVP Media Quarter, tel. 053/934-4990, http://hasadna.rest-e.co.il)
- **Landwer Café** (4 David Remez St., tel. 02/587-7988, www.landwercafe.co.il)
- **P2 Pizzeria** (36 Keren HaYesod St., tel. 02/563-5555)
- **Scottish Guesthouse Restaurant** (1 David Remez St., tel. 02/673-2401, www.scots-guesthouse.com)

★ TMOL SHILSHOM

5 Yo'el Moshe Salomon St.; tel. 02/623-2758; www.
tmol-shilshom.co.il; 8:30am-11pm Sun.-Thurs.,
8:30am-3pm Fri., NIS55

One of Jerusalem's most treasured mainstays, this restaurant-café includes books for sale, tables where well-known authors have written, and frequent public events in both Hebrew and English hosting famous Isreali writers. One of the café's several rooms allows indoor smoking, and there is also a small outdoor patio. The menu features a variety of vegan and vegetarian dishes, American-style desserts, and regional favorites like *shakshouka*. Drinks include everything from regional wines to a chai latte milkshake. The 19th-century Jerusalem stone building is perfect on both hot summer days and chilly nights.

HUMMUS BEN SIRA

3 Ben Sira St., tel. 02/625-3893, 10:30am-2am
Sun.-Thurs., 10:30am-4:30pm Fri., NIS25

A kosher favorite for hummus and falafel in the heart of city center is Hummus Ben Sira. The interior is simple and spare like most falafel restaurants, and there are a range of affordable options.

DOLPHIN YAM

9 Shim'on Ben Shetach St., tel. 053/809-4765,
11am-midnight daily, NIS80

For non-kosher seafood in a convenient location, Dolphin Yam is one of the best-known seafood restaurants in the city. The menu also includes an array of meat and pasta dishes including bouillabaisse, appetizers, and entrées offering seafood dishes for every taste. There are also some vegetarian options.

★ ROOF TOP WINE AND CHEESE RESTAURANT

3 Paratroopers Rd., tel. 02/627-9111, www.
notredamecenter.org, noon-midnight daily,
reservations recommended, NIS80

The Pontifical Institute Notre Dame of Jerusalem Center's massive building, just outside the Old City, looks more like a castle than a hotel. It's home to the Roof Top Wine and Cheese Restaurant, where diners can choose from 40 types of imported cheese and a large selection of wines from all over the world, including Notre Dame's private label, on a rooftop terrace with a breathtaking view of the Old City. Start with a drink in the bar's luxurious lounge. The menu offers a range of French and Italian options, including beef carpaccio, salmon tartare, a delectable Roquefort salad, pasta, lamb, and filet mignon.

TRATTORIA HABA

119 Yafo Street, tel. 02/623-3379, www.haba.co.il,
7am-midnight Sun.-Thurs., 7am-3pm Fri., NIS60

Headed by world-class chef Michael Katz, Trattoria Haba occupies prime territory on the edge of the *shuk* facing busy Yafo Street. The kosher milk establishment serves a huge array of wonderful breads, pasta, meat, and vegetable dishes. Cheese plays a supporting role in many of Haba's entrées, including for cuts of meat. The atmosphere is bright and sunny with counter space facing Yafo Street in the front and outdoor garden seating facing the *shuk* in the back.

YMCA THREE ARCHES

26 King David St., tel. 02/569-2692, http://ymca.org.
il, 7am-11pm daily, NIS50

The draw for dining at the YMCA Three Arches restaurant is largely about the setting. The menu is very limited, so it is the perfect place to enjoy a peaceful afternoon coffee or a light lunch on the massive veranda set back on the grounds from the street.

MONTEFIORE

Yemin Moshe St., below the windmill, tel.
053/943-8439, http://montefiore.rest-e.
co.il, 8am-midnight Sun.-Thurs., 8am-3pm Fri.,
7pm-midnight Sat., NIS100

A fine dining Italian restaurant with a seafood menu that includes salmon, Montefiore also offers a variety of pasta and pizza dishes. The linen-tablecloth restaurant is just steps away from the Old City, the Jerusalem Cinematheque, the conference center, and the Montefiore Windmill and has outdoor balcony seating with views of the Valley of Hinnom and the Old City.

Restaurant Culture

Deciphering the rules of Jerusalem restaurants can be a challenge:

- **Closed for Shabbat:** This means several things, chief among them that the establishment is kosher and closes sometime on Friday afternoon anywhere between 3pm-5pm depending on the time of year. This type of restaurant often (but not always) reopens for business on Saturday night around 8pm-9pm, again depending on the time of year. Shabbat is from sundown on Friday evening until it gets dark on Saturday evening; precise time calculators are available online and Jerusalem has a Shabbat alarm that sounds on Friday afternoon.

- **Shabbat Reservations:** From Thursday night until Saturday night, whether the restaurant is kosher or not, it's a good idea to make reservations. You can still get a table in some cases if you walk in without a reservation, but you will be asked to leave when it's time for the next reservation to arrive. It's typically allowed to take a reserved table if there is at least one hour before arrival.

- **Check:** You will probably never get your bill until you ask for it.

- **Coffee Shops:** Israel has a few national chain café-coffee shops, but you can get a good cappuccino at almost any non-kosher or kosher milk restaurant.

- **Business Hours:** Advertised business hours tend to be loosely interpreted unless it's a longstanding establishment. It's a good idea to call ahead and check if you're planning on being someplace near opening or closing time.

- **Kosher:** The kosher system dictates keeping dairy and meat separate, and kosher restaurants serve either milk or meat. Kosher certification is officially issued by a governing Rabbinate and has degrees of strictness. If you dine at a kosher steak restaurant, you can't get a cappuccino with milk or cream for your coffee.

- **Restrooms:** A cup with handles next to a restaurant's bathroom sink is for religious hand washing and indicates the establishment is kosher.

- **Security:** Some places tack a security fee onto your bill, usually a few shekels. It is optional and you can ask to have it removed.

- **Service:** It is common to have more than one waitperson attend you, so feel free to call on any staff member for help.

- **Tipping:** There is often a large note in English on the bottom of bills stating that "service is not included." A standard tip is about 15 percent.

- **Water:** Typically, you need to ask for tap water and refills. Most places will give you a bottle of tap water for free that they filled.

- **Wi-Fi:** Almost every restaurant and coffee shop in Jerusalem has free wireless Internet.

Seafood
OLIVE AND FISH

2 Jabotinsky St.; tel. 02/566-5020; noon-11pm Sun.-Thurs.; NIS80

Olive and Fish is conveniently located and features special seafood dishes as well as salads, chicken, and kebabs. Try the hot salmon salad or the St. Peter's fish filet. The interior of the restaurant is decorated with antique photographs of Jerusalemites through the generations, and is spacious and classy, with an indoor veranda.

Pub Fare and Burgers
DUBLIN IRISH PUB

4 Shamai St.; tel. 057/944-3740; 5pm-3am Sat.-Thurs., 5pm-5am Fri.; NIS50

The spacious interior floor plan of Dublin

Irish Pub features the typical wooden pub chairs and booths, a large bar, and big screen TVs for sports games. The pub serves hamburgers, pizza, sandwiches, desserts, and a wide variety of bottled and draft beer. Cocktails and every kind of hard liquor you could want are also available.

★ LINK

3 Hama'alot St.; tel. 053/809-4510;
11:30am-midnight Sun.-Thurs., 10am-midnight
Fri.-Sat.; NIS60

A dining hotspot that somehow maintains a serene atmosphere, Link can feel a bit like hanging out at your cool cousin's house. A favorite of local celebrities, the Israeli version of pub dining is fronted by a spacious wooden deck. The restaurant's main dining room has a greenhouse-like feel, complete with trees growing up to the roof. A wood-paneled back section has nice nooks and crannies for a quiet drink with friends. The hamburger is a consistently delicious menu option, but there's also a nice selection of fish and chicken, appetizers like calamari, and Middle Eastern-style dishes.

Italian
P2 PIZZERIA

36 Keren HaYesod St.; tel. 02/563-5555;
noon-midnight daily; NIS40

P2 Pizzeria is a small restaurant with a menu featuring mostly pizza and some pasta dishes. The pasta is made on the premises in a large pasta machine at the front of the restaurant. The thin-crust pizza is served up with high-quality ingredients and expert care. There's limited seating, including bar stools and outdoor chairs.

Dessert
BABETTE CAFÉ

16 Shamai St. at Yoel Moshe Solomon St.; tel.
02/625-7004; 4pm-2:30am Sun.-Thurs., 11am-3pm
Fri.; NIS30

The perfect place to stop off for dessert, Babette Café is one of the coolest little hangouts in City Center—*little* being the

operative word. Its small size is easy to overlook once you taste one of their famous waffle dessert combinations with chocolate and whipped cream.

WIENER KAFFE HAUS

37 Via Dolorosa; tel. 02/626-5800;
www.austrianhospice.com; 10am-10pm daily;
NIS40

A Viennese-style café with indoor seating and an expansive outdoor terrace under a canopy of trees in the heart of the Old City is the Wiener Kaffe Haus. Run from inside the Austrian Hospice, it has a limited menu that includes soups, salads, and toast. Tea in a pot, wine, and beer are also available, but their locally famous Viennese apple strudel is the real star.

ROLADIN

Alrov Mamilla Ave.; tel. 02/623-1553;
www.roladin.co.il; 7:30am-11pm Sun.-Thurs.,
7:30am-3pm Fri.; NIS40

Always hopping with customers hungry for sweet treats is Roladin bakery and café. They also have a typical Middle Eastern selection of egg dishes, sandwiches, and pasta. During Hanukkah, customers flock to buy holiday doughnut treats. The view of the city with both indoor and outdoor seating is fantastic, and it's just a short walk from the Old City's Jaffa Gate.

AROUND MACHANE YEHUDA MARKET
Contemporary Middle Eastern
MACHNEYUDA

Beit Yaakov 10, tel. 02/533-3442,
12:30pm-4:30pm and 6:30pm-midnight Sun.-Thurs.,
noon-4pm Fri., 8:30pm-midnight Sat., NIS100

Unlike many new, trendy restaurants that pop up, Machneyuda has managed to endure. It is run by three Jerusalem chefs with ingredients brought in fresh daily from the *shuk*. The delicious menu changes daily, and the kitchen is open for viewing. Reservations are recommended on the weekend, as it gets packed and loud in the evenings.

Pub Fare and Burgers
JOSEF
123 Agripas St.; tel. 073/758-4219; 11am-2am
Sun.-Thurs., 11am-3pm Fri., 7pm-2am Sat.; NIS45

Known primarily for its hamburgers, Josef serves up a selection of generous burgers in a warm, inviting, well-lit pub atmosphere. The menu also features gluten-free buns and vegan and veggie burgers. They serve a modest selection of beer, liquor, and wine.

EAST JERUSALEM
Middle Eastern
HEART OF THE OLD CITY
end of Cardo; tel. 02/627-3408; 8am-8pm daily; NIS35

Easy to find by its large sign outside the southern entrance, Heart of the Old City is a family-owned restaurant that has friendly staff and serves falafel, hummus, *shawarma*, and the like. It is also known as Afandi Restaurant.

ABU SHUKRI
Al Wad St. in the Old City, next to Station No. 6 on Via
Dolorosa; tel. 02/627-1538; 10am-8pm daily; NIS25

A longtime hummus-and-falafel restaurant in the Old City, Abu Shukri is decidedly on the touristy side, but a solid option if you need something quick and delicious.

GEO'S ESPRESSO BAR
Muristan St., within the row of sidewalk cafés
near the Church of the Holy Sepulchre; generally
10am-8pm daily, hours vary; NIS20-75

Serving up chicken dishes, hummus plates, sandwiches, salads, falafel, and kebabs just inside the Old City's Jaffa Gate, Geo's Espresso Bar is part of a row of several cafés and small eateries, many of which specialize in freshly squeezed juice drinks. Their hours vary depending on customers, but they are generally open from 10am-8pm daily.

THE ARMENIAN TAVERN
79 Armenian Orthodox Patriarchate Rd., turn right at
the Tower of David and the restaurant is downstairs,
Armenian Quarter; tel. 02/627-3854; 11am-10:30pm
Tues.-Sun.; NIS50

For meat dishes with special touches like mint and grape leaves, The Armenian Tavern works well. The charming interior is festooned with arched ceilings that date to the Crusader period and an indoor fountain.

BETWEEN THE ARCHES
174 HaGay St. at HaKotel HaMaaravi St.; tel.
053/809-4584; 9am-6pm Sun.-Thurs.; NIS65

At Between the Arches, kebab, hummus and pita, falafel, pizza, and pasta are served up in an underground dining room that's inside part of a system of 13th-century tunnels. The interior features an array of fish tanks, warm lighting, and nice decorative touches for a relaxed and leisurely atmosphere.

PASHA'S RESTAURANT
13 Shimon Siddiq in Sheikh Jarrah; tel. 02/582-5162;
www.shahwan.org; noon-11pm daily; NIS70

For a taste of home-cooked regional food, Pasha's Restaurant serves traditional Arab fare including lentil and other soups, hot and cold appetizers, lamb dishes with mint, and a variety of international dishes such as beef Stroganoff. Their sister establishment, **Borderline,** stays open until about 1:30am and offers a menu of *nargila* water pipes to smoke for after-dinner relaxation.

Contemporary
★ THE AMERICAN COLONY
1 Louis Vincent St.; tel. 02/627-9777; www.
americancolony.com; 9am-10pm daily; NIS110

An idyllic five-star setting at The American Colony provides several levels of dining and drinking options in numerous spots throughout the hotel's impeccably manicured gardens and grounds. The outdoor enclosed garden courtyard with its cascading flowers and fountains is the perfect place for a quiet lunch or drink with unparalleled multilingual service (English, Hebrew, Arabic, French), all set in classic Jerusalem opulence and charm. The generous Saturday brunch includes bacon.

1: the counter at Machneyuda restaurant **2:** plates of eastern traditional sweets in a street café **3:** Jerusalem mix with hummus **4:** a café in Nahalat Shiva

Other dining options at the hotel include the Arabesque Restaurant, The Courtyard, Val's Brasserie, The Cellar Bar, The Summer Bar, and The Terrace Café.

ASKADINYA RESTAURANT BAR

11 Shim'on Ha'tsadik St.; tel. 02/532-4590;
noon-midnight daily; NIS80

For a nice gastropub with courtyard dining and vegetarian options, Askadinya Restaurant Bar has a special blend of East-meets-West with meat dishes served with an Asian flair in addition to more common pasta and salad dishes. A specialty is the steak with a raisin-and-caramel sauce.

WEST JERUSALEM

Contemporary

CAFÉ HAIVRIT

Cossell Center at Givat Ram, across from the
Bloomfield Museum of Science; tel. 02-566-9124;
8am-10pm Sun.-Thurs., 8am-2:30pm Fri.; NIS45

Café Haivrit is one of the few restaurants in the vicinity of Museum Row. Directly across the street from the Bloomfield Museum of Science, Haivrit offers health-conscious food to complement the large number of customers coming and going from its sports center, including light menu options like salads and juice drinks. There is nice, shady outdoor seating with a grassy area for children.

ADOM

4 David Remez St., tel. 02/624-6242, 12:30pm-2am
daily, NIS80

Part of the First Station complex, local favorite Adom has a food and drink menu and decor that add up to an experience just on the verge of fine dining. Adom specializes in wine and international cuisine with French and Italian influences and features their take on a variety of lamb and filet mignon dishes.

MODERN

Ruppin 11 inside the Israel Museum; tel. 02/648-0862;
http://en.modern.co.il; 11am-5pm Sun.-Thurs.,
6pm-midnight Tues.-Wed.; NIS85

A simple and elegant choice in combination with a visit to the Israel Museum is Modern. The restaurant includes a huge patio area and a small, chic interior of clean, modern decor. A favorite of local VIPs, including high-level politicians, Modern's menu makes regional fish, pasta, and meat dishes with a decidedly European flair. The menu offers business lunch, a children's menu, wine tastings, and live music.

★ THE CULINARY WORKSHOP

28 Hebron Rd. in the JVP Media Quarter;
tel. 02/567-2265; http://www.sdnrest.com,
6:30pm-Midnight daily, NIS90

It would be a shame to miss out on The Culinary Workshop. Tucked away just slightly off the beaten track, the restaurant's atmosphere is both elegant and cozy with its enormous open kitchen, multilayered floor plan, soft lighting, and outdoor deck seating. The small, extremely inventive and well-executed menu features European-style dishes including fish tartare, seafood bacon, and pork belly with butternut squash, all prepared to give just the right balance of flavors. There is also a nice selection of steak cuts at reasonable prices, a rare find in Jerusalem.

Asian

SUSHI REHAVIA

31 Azza St.; tel. 02/567-1971; http://sushirehavia.co.il;
noon-11pm Sun.-Thurs., 11am-3pm Fri.; NIS80

The flagship location of the popular Sushi Rehavia is one of several branches throughout Jerusalem. In addition to sushi, the restaurant features delectable noodle dishes, Japanese-style grilled chicken, *gyoza*, and stir-fried dishes. The modern Asian-style interior and atmosphere caters to trendsetters looking for new gastronomic experiences.

Cafés and Coffee Shops

THE COFFEE MILL

23 Emek Refaim St.; tel. 02/566-1665;
7:30am-11pm Sun.-Thurs., 7:30am-3pm Fri.,
7pm-midnight Sat.; NIS30

A visit to Jerusalem wouldn't be complete without a trip to The Coffee Mill, a local institution. The very small shop's walls are plastered with old *New Yorker* magazine covers, and the menu is a bright and creative mix of pictures for the myriad espresso and coffee drinks as well as the food, which is largely pastries. The late weekday hours make it a great place to stop in for a coffee after dinner nearby.

★ **GRAND CAFÉ**
70 Beit Lechem Rd.; tel. 02/570-2702; 7:30am-11pm Sun.-Thurs., 7:30am-3pm Fri., 7pm-11pm Sat.; NIS50
A favorite amongst locals and visitors, Grand Café is one of West Jerusalem's busiest neighborhood spots, preparing a robust selection of Middle Eastern food in a French café style. Mouthwatering Israeli salads go perfectly with the café's signature eggs Benedict. Nowhere else holds a candle to the espresso drinks made by some of the friendliest baristas in the city, alongside French-style desserts and pastries. The modern, warm European decor includes plenty of outdoor seating year-round, a long marble bar, and several nice nooks and crannies for long conversation. Make a reservation if you plan to eat there on Friday.

Bars and Nightlife

CITY CENTER

City Center at night is a much different place than it is during the day. If you're not sure what you're in the mood for and don't want to waste any time, Machane Yehuda (the *shuk*) never fails to entertain. After daytime shops close, the *shuk's* main pedestrian thoroughfare—and several side passageways—turn into party central for dining, drinks, and music. Not much of it is very organized or on a schedule of any kind. But there is arguably no wilder, louder, or more entertaining place in the city to party on a Thursday night than the *shuk*. An added advantage is that if you want to move on to something else, four-star elegant drinks or more local experiences are all nearby. A visit to the same place on a Saturday morning will afford a view of the dozens of graffiti paintings on the front of metal shop doors.

BEER BAZAAR
3 Etz Hayyim St.; tel. 02/671-2559; 11am-2am Sun.-Wed., 11am-4am Thurs.-Fri., 8pm-4am Sat.; no cover
Right at the heart of the action in the *shuk* is the easy-to-find Beer Bazaar, a tiny brewery-style beer counter with sidewalk tables and a spot for open-mic performers. Part of an Israeli brewery chain, the menu includes some of the brewery's more than 100 beers, regional microbrews, takeaway options like growler refills, and small food items.

GATSBY
18 Hillel St.; tel. 054/814-7143; peacock-cb.com; 6pm-1am daily; no cover
Gatsby is an atmosphere-rich, upscale craft cocktail bar tucked away in the heart of City Center. Gatsby has an extensive craft drink menu, a buffet, live DJs, and other events. A reservation is recommended.

HATAKLIT
7 Heleni HaMalka St.; tel. 02/624-407; 8pm-last customer; no cover
The trendy HaTaklit was founded by three music-industry Jerusalemites who adorned the walls with vinyl record sleeves. The full bar serves cocktails, and there is beer on tap, English football screenings, live music, DJs, and independent performers. They also have happy hour (4:30pm-9pm daily).

THE BARRELL & THE TAP
33 Hillel St.; tel. 052/316-0404; http://thebarrelph. com; 5pm-4am daily; no cover
The Barrell & The Tap is an age-23-plus venue with lots of room to smoke outside and a variety of draft beers inside. They also boast a

selection of cognacs, whiskeys, scotches, and bourbons. The food menu features pub standards including schnitzel, hamburgers, and french fries.

OLIVER TWIST

59 Haneviim St.; tel. 054/521-2044; 10pm-4:30am Thurs.-Sat.; no cover

Oliver Twist is a popular DJ club housed in a 150-year-old building that also serves food and has outdoor seating.

BESARABIA BAR

34 Ben Yehuda St.; tel. 052/431-9695; 8pm-2am Sat.-Thurs., 10pm-3am Fri.; NIS25

Popular among locals for its rustic Jerusalem flair, Besarabia Bar uses its dance floor for Balkan, neofolk, ska, indie, and electroswing music. It also hosts DJs, live music, and events like Purim parties with costumes, poetry readings, and stand-up comedy, and had a full bar of top shelf liquor.

MAMILLA HOTEL

11 King Solomon St.; tel. 02/548-2222; www. mamillahotel.com; hours vary by venue; NIS60-120

The Mamilla Hotel has a few nice spots for drinks and mingling. **Winery** (2nd Fl., 3pm-8pm Sun.-Thurs., 2pm-6pm Fri., NIS40) has a selection of 300 Israeli wines that gives a nice introduction to the region's vines, and it sells kosher wines. The **Rooftop** (8th Fl., noon-11pm Fri.-Sat. with a cold Shabbat menu, NIS85) offers a commanding view of Jerusalem and the Old City and caters to the wealthy and elite set. A long bar is complemented by a wooden deck and a row of small bar tables and stools near the front, while the back area (with the better view) has a larger area with seating for dinner.

The posh **Mirror Bar** (2nd Fl., 8pm-last customer Sun.-Thurs., 9pm-last customer Sat., no cover) features a stylish, modern interior and a selection of cigars that can be enjoyed in a glassed-in smoking room.

WEST JERUSALEM
ZAPPA

28 Derech Hevron; tel. 03/762-6666; www. zappa-club.co.il; open after 5pm for shows; price varies by show but generally NIS50 and up

The stylish and upscale Zappa is the Jerusalem branch of a chain of live music venues with locations in Tel Aviv, Herzliya, and Binyamina. Zappa features high-quality local and international musicians as well as some major names in jazz, rock, and reggae. It serves light food and drinks near a sizable stage where performers can get close to the audience.

SOUTHERN JERUSALEM
HAOMAN 17

17 Haoman St.; tel. 02/678-1658; 9pm-3am Tues., 9:30pm-5am Thurs., 9:30pm-3am Sat.; NIS80

The bustling, warehouse-size Haoman 17 is part of a chain of clubs with a location in Tel Aviv. The club features Israeli, house, and funk music. They regularly host international DJs.

YELLOW SUBMARINE

13 Herkevim St.; tel. 02/679-4040; http:// yellowsubmarine.org.il; shows daily from around 8pm or later; NIS35 and up depending on show

The Yellow Submarine hosts concerts and events that range from heavy metal to Israeli pop and folk musicians. It's also a multidisciplinary music center and is home to rehearsal rooms, recording studios, and an annual international music showcase.

Accommodations

Accommodations in Jerusalem tend to be located either in and around City Center or close to major tourist sites. Types of accommodations vary, from four-star hotels to hostels, hospices, guesthouses, *zimmers* (bed-and-breakfasts), and kibbutz hotels. Most places in Jerusalem will accept payment in U.S. dollars, and often list rates in dollars, rather than shekels, for tourists. Non-Israeli passport holders are exempt from the VAT tax on their hotel bill, or are entitled to a refund with a receipt at the airport upon leaving the country. Jerusalem accommodations, even the grittier options, are on the expensive side. Many offer a small discount for booking through their website.

OLD CITY
Under US$100
HASHIMI HOTEL

73 Khan El Zeit St.; tel. 054/547-4189; www.
thehashimihotel.com; US$99 d

The 275-year-old building that's home to the Hashimi Hotel is a renovated structure at the epicenter of the Old City. The hotel's intimate rooftop bar and restaurant offers a fantastic panorama view of the Old City. The modern interior features marble throughout, even though the rooms in this medium-size hotel are quite bare. Wireless Internet, cable TV, and air-conditioning are included and the hotel can help with arranging guided tours.

JAFFA GATE HOSTEL

Jaffa Gate in front of David's Tower; tel.
02/627-6402; www.jaffa-gate.hostel.com; US$78 d

Jaffa Gate Hostel includes linens in the price, towels and hair dryers for rent, a place to park bicycles, a tour desk, luggage storage, currency exchange, and a postal and fax service. Dormitories and private rooms are

available and are as simple and tiny as you can get, but they have a certain Middle Eastern atmosphere and charm. The hostel has evening movie screenings, free wireless Internet, *nargilot* (hookahs), a terrace area, and space for barbecues.

AUSTRIAN HOSPICE

37 Via Dolorosa, near Damascus Gate; tel.
02/626-5800; www.austrianhospice.com; US$98 d

A little on the plain side but still elegant, the Austrian Hospice is in one of the best locations in the Old City. The hotel itself is clean and very secure. The rooms and dormitories with bunk beds have only the bare minimum of amenities, and the small lobby is abutted by private, outdoor garden seating for guests and customers of the Austrian Hospice Café. Many staff are Austrian, and the hotel caters to European travelers in general. The rooftop is a popular place to check out the Old City from about five stories up.

Over US$200
★ MAMILLA HOTEL

11 King Solomon St.; tel. 02/548-2222; www.
mamillahotel.com; US$440 d

Mamilla Hotel is a top choice for discerning travelers, with its rooftop restaurant and its wine bar, Saturday disco, and live weekly jazz. Subtle artistic touches throughout the hotel invite you to interact with your surroundings. Rooms have modern, sleek furnishings, free wireless Internet, and large-screen televisions, and guests have access to the Akasha Wellbeing Center and gym, a luxurious indoor hotel pool, and a Turkish hammam. There is also a business center and 24-hour concierge service. Try the outdoor patio for a swing in a hammock seat and a view of the stars.

CITY CENTER
Under US$100
★ ABRAHAM HOSTEL

67 Hanevi'im St.; tel. 02/650-2200;
www.abraham-hostel-jerusalem.com; US$35 d

Recommended by locals and travelers alike, the Abraham Hostel is a medium-size hostel in the heart of Jerusalem offering a range of rooms from private singles to 10-bed dorms. The rooms are austere and sparsely furnished, but include Wi-Fi and a common area, dining hall, kitchen, laundry facilities, rooftop terrace, and a TV room with a bar and space for hanging out, all open 24 hours a day. The hostel also offers tours and activities, live music, and an open mic night. Private rooms are often booked well in advance.

US$100-150
CITY CENTER HOTEL SUITES

2 Hahistadrut St. on the corner of 13 King George St.; tel. 02/650-9494; www.citycentervacation.com; US$145 d

If you're looking for luxury at an amazing price, check the City Center Hotel Suites. It has elegant and modern apartments for short stays and long-term visits. Just at the base of Ben Yehuda Street, City Center Hotel Suites' rooms include studio, deluxe studio, and suite, and feature kitchenettes or kitchens, balconies, closet space, toiletries, and housekeeping service. The apartments have clean, modern lines and enough space for a comfortable stay.

US$150-200
JERUSALEM TOWER HOTEL

23 Hillel St.; tel. 02/620-9209;
www.jerusalemtowerhotel.com; US$175 d

The Jerusalem Tower Hotel is right in the middle of City Center, making it an ideal place to stay if you want easy access to nightlife, an array of restaurants, and an easy jumping-off point. The rooms are decorated in a very stark, modern style with large, bright paintings on very white walls. Of the 120 rooms in the hotel, those on the higher floors have views of the Old City. Amenities are very basic, such as wireless Internet in the lobby only.

Over US$200
PRIMA KINGS

60 King George St.; tel. 02/620-1201;
www.prima-hotels-israel.com; US$217 d

Conveniently located Prima Kings is in an ideal location for visitors who plan on extensive sightseeing. The lobby is small, but the 217 units in the hotel range in size from rooms to suites, some with balconies. The hotel provides various tourist booklets and restaurant coupons for free. The hotel caters to observant Jewish guests with a synagogue on the premises and a Shabbat elevator. There is also a kosher dining room, coffee shop, and business center.

YMCA THREE ARCHES HOTEL

26 King David St.; tel. 02/569-2692;
http://ymca.org.il; US$249 d

The broad veranda that wraps around the historic lobby of the YMCA Three Arches Hotel gives way to a massive lobby of classic Middle Eastern arched and tiled ceilings. The hotel is part of a larger complex including a pool, gym, restaurant, and fenced-in playground for children. The rooms are a bit austere but include free wireless Internet and cable television, and some have garden views. The location is convenient to some of the best dining and entertainment in City Center and the Old City.

HARMONY HOTEL

6 Yoel Moshe Solomon St.; tel. 03/542-5555;
www.atlas.co.il; US$350 d

Popular, trendy, and smack in the middle of Nahalat Shiva is the kosher Harmony Hotel, part of an Israeli-wide chain. Preferred for its downtown location and modern urban style in a traditional setting, it has a business lounge with a billiards table, free computer for Internet use, free wireless access, a rooftop lounge, and rooms with a mini-fridge, safe, and multichannel LCD TV. Harmony's 50 rooms are decked out with bright, modern bedding, rugs, and furniture.

NOTRE DAME OF JERUSALEM CENTER

3 Paratroopers Rd.; tel. 02/627-9111; www.
notredamecenter.org; US$350 d

The Notre Dame of Jerusalem Center hotel is part of the massive, towering Pontifical Institute Notre Dame of Jerusalem, located just outside the Old City. The hotel's 150 rooms cater to Christian guests making a pilgrimage to the Holy Land, so though anyone can book a room, it is recommended to book at least three months in advance. Amenities include a cafeteria, an excellent rooftop restaurant, a chapel, wireless Internet, and complimentary breakfast. The rooms are somewhat plain, but most are spacious and full of light.

★ KING DAVID HOTEL

23 King David St.; tel. 02/620-8888; www.danhotels.
com; US$620 d, includes large breakfast

The King David Hotel is one of the most elegant in the city. Look for the massive table in the rich, lavish lobby where Israeli prime minister Yitzhak Rabin and Jordan's King Hussein signed their historic peace agreement in 1994. The pool area behind the hotel is a charming, surprisingly affordable place for an outdoor lunch. Some of the rooms include balconies with views of the Old and New City. All are richly appointed with sitting areas, modern furniture, and large-screen televisions. The garden behind the hotel is a hidden gem. The staff is classy, multilingual, and gracious.

LEONARDO PLAZA HOTEL JERUSALEM

47 King George St.; tel. 02/629-8666; www.
leonardo-hotels.com; US$450 d

The iconic and easy-to-spot tower of the Leonardo Plaza Hotel Jerusalem in the middle of City Center overlooks the rolling green lawns of Independence Park. The hotel's 270 rooms are decorated in rich, bright colors, and there are three restaurants on the premises. Guests have access to a spa, seasonal pool, fitness room, and whirlpool tub.

BEIT SHMUEL HOTEL AND HOSTEL

6 Shamai St., at the corner of 13 King David St.; tel.
02/620-3455; www.beitshmuel.co.il/he-il; US$215 d

Designed by renowned architect Moshe Safdie, the Beit Shmuel Hotel and Hostel features a landmark glass dome that covers the building's main dining area. The modern, clean, bright interior of Beit Shmuel makes for a welcoming atmosphere, and the location is central to sights, food, and entertainment in both the Old City and New City. Small overall, but with a variety of accommodations, the guesthouse has 28 rooms for up to six people each. There are 12 hotel rooms for up to four guests each, and one apartment for a family or group visiting for a long-term stay.

WALDORF ASTORIA JERUSALEM

26-28 Agron St.; tel. 02/542-3333; www.
waldorfastoriajerusalem.com; US$455 d

The Waldorf Astoria Jerusalem is the height of luxury in the center of the city and a Condé Nast Best Hotel in the Middle East pick. The hotel's 223 rooms for guests exist alongside 30 luxury private residences. Rooms feature Italian marble bathrooms, 46-inch flat-screen televisions, a private wet bar, an espresso coffee machine, free wireless Internet, and crystal chandeliers. In addition to every amenity imaginable, the elements of each room can be controlled by the guest.

AROUND MACHANE YEHUDA MARKET
US$100-150

CAESAR PREMIER JERUSALEM

208 Yafo St.; tel. 02/500-5656; www.caesarhotels.
co.il; US$149 d

The Caesar Premier Jerusalem is a three-star hotel with 150 rooms and an intimate atmosphere. A standard room includes a mini-refrigerator, cable TV, breakfast, and wireless Internet.

JERUSALEM GATE HOTEL

43 Yirmiyahu St.; tel. 02/500-8500; www.
jerusalemgatehotel.com; US$150 d

The 298-room Jerusalem Gate Hotel is in

close proximity to the city's central bus station, making it a great jumping-off point to travel around the region. The hotel caters to business travelers with its understated interior and proximity to the city's convention center. The rooms are a decent size and simply decorated. Every room has wireless Internet, a safe, and hair dryers.

Over US$200
JERUSALEM GOLD HOTEL
234 Yafo St.; tel. 02/501-3333; www.jerusalemgold. com; US$240 d

The Jerusalem Gold Hotel is a classy, medium-size hotel with a bit of European sass. The rooms are decorated with heavy drapes and rich tapestries, and have extra-long beds, blackout curtains, and double-glazed windows for extra quiet. Guests can select their pillow from a menu, and video games and a laptop-size safe are available. The hotel is also close to several restaurants, shops, and entertainment venues.

EAST JERUSALEM
Under US$100
NEW PALM HOTEL AND HOSTEL
4 Hanevi'im St.; tel. 02/627-3189; www. newpalmhostel.com; US$79 d

The simple accommodations at the New Palm Hotel and Hostel can be upgraded to package deals that include airport transportation and other amenities like guided tours and a hotel breakfast. Private and shared rooms are available as well as free wireless Internet. This smaller hostel offers free luggage storage, a common-area TV, and a fully equipped kitchen. It's well-located—less than a five-minute walk from the Old City.

VICTORIA HOTEL
8 Al Masoudi St.; tel. 02/627-4466; http://4victoria-hotel.com; US$95 d

Close to numerous convenient amenities and just north of the Old City, Victoria Hotel is a stone's throw from the central bus station, shops, and banks. The hotel has 49 renovated rooms, most with a balcony. Breakfast, free

wireless Internet, 24-hour room service, cable TV, and hair dryers in the rooms are included.

CAPITOL HOTEL
17 Salah Eddin St.; tel. 02/628-2561; http://capitol. thejerusalemhotels.com/en; US$99 d

Small, elegantly proportioned, and centrally located Capitol Hotel is a 54-room property on East Jerusalem's famed Salah Eddin Street. Along with 24-hour room service, there's satellite TV and air-conditioning, as well as minibar and laundry service. The interior of the hotel is simple and the ground floor features an idyllic garden dining area with a fountain and a large interior dining room.

US$150-200
ADDAR HOTEL
53 Nablus Rd.; tel. 02/626-3111; www.addar-hotel. com; US$175 d

The boutique family-run Addar Hotel was rebuilt from a 19th-century structure that features a plush, richly appointed interior and a marble lobby. VIPs have been known to stay in this medium-size hotel just five minutes from the Old City. Some of the rooms are equipped with marble whirlpool bathtubs, balconies, French windows, a sitting area, free wireless Internet, and a safe. Some rooms also include a kitchenette. The hotel restaurant has outdoor garden seating.

LEGACY HOTEL
29 Nablus Rd.; tel. 02/627-0800; www. jerusalemlegacy.com; US$175 d

Set up with an array of familiar comforts in a central location north of the Old City, Legacy Hotel has 49 rooms with sitting areas and hair dryers, a fitness center, and a restaurant with Middle Eastern food and an outdoor panoramic view of the city. There is also a bar, buffet, sushi bar, coffee shop, and garden restaurant.

NATIONAL HOTEL
4 Al Zahra St.; tel. 02/627-8880; www.nationalhotel-jerusalem.com; US$199 d

A simple, modern boutique hotel with luxury and design features, National Hotel is close to some of the best shopping in East Jerusalem, as well as the Old City. The spacious rooms feature large beds, and guests have access to free newspapers and parking, hotel shops, and a gym.

RITZ HOTEL
8 Ibn Khaldoun St.; tel. 02/626-9900; www. jerusalemritz.com; US$175 d

The Ritz Hotel is a renovated 104-room hotel that boasts a lovely rooftop terrace dining area, a bar, 24-hour reception service, satellite TV, and free wireless Internet in the rooms. Each room has a personal safe, and the hotel is within easy walking distance to the Old City.

Over US$200
ST. GEORGE LANDMARK
6 Omar Ibn Al Aas St.; tel. 02/627-7232; www. stgeorgehoteljerusalem.com; US$285 d

Known for its rooftop pool and outdoor restaurant with a panoramic view of the city, the St. George Landmark features 130 rooms and a Lebanese restaurant. Every room has free wireless Internet, an espresso machine, and tea and coffee machines. Many rooms also include balconies and views of the city. The hotel is just north of the Old City.

GRAND COURT HOTEL
15 St. George St.; tel. 02/591-7777; www.grandhotels-israel.com; US$216 d

The enormous Grand Court Hotel has 446 rooms, including rooms equipped for families and others for disabled travelers. There is free wireless Internet and a pool and sundeck that overlook the Old City. The hotel has a restaurant, garden terrace, and lounge bar.

OLIVE TREE HOTEL
23 St. George St.; tel. 02/541-0410; http:// olivetreehotel.com.my; US$325 d

The Olive Tree Hotel is built around an ancient olive tree, which, according to legend, shaded pilgrims on their way to Jerusalem in ancient times. This large hotel has 304 renovated rooms throughout eight floors. Rooms have over 50 international channels on the televisions, capability to dock laptops using the TV

screen, and bathtubs. There is also a business center, babysitting service, and a large, inviting lobby with accents of Jerusalem stone.

★ THE AMERICAN COLONY
1 Louis Vincent St.; tel. 02/627-9777; www. americancolony.com, US$420 d

A gathering place for foreign dignitaries and business executives, The American Colony is a world unto itself. Full of quiet corners and lushly landscaped, it's the perfect place to escape the heat and chaos of Jerusalem. This five-star hotel includes an outdoor pool and sauna, fitness and business centers, a wine cellar, and an antique shop. The 93 luxurious rooms offer rich wood furnishing, arched ceilings, and satellite TV, and some have sitting areas and balconies. The hotel has a decidedly Middle Eastern feel, with beautiful tile flooring and stone walls, and the overall atmosphere is seriously upper-crust.

WEST JERUSALEM
Under US$100
GERMAN HOSPICE
12 Lloyd George St.; tel. 02/563-7737; http://www. deutsches-hospiz.de/en; US$90 d

Hidden behind a stone wall in the heart of the German Colony is the German Hospice, a Christian guesthouse that caters to German-speaking pilgrims and features limited amenities. The small guesthouse offers rooms at a very low rate, and it is just around the corner from several popular restaurants on nearby Emek Refaim Street. It is also just steps away from the miles-long Railway Park and numerous popular shopping and entertainment options at First Station.

US$100-150
DARNA GUEST HOUSE
12 Hanania St.; tel. 054/565-7001 or 054/227-2370; http://bnb.co.il/darna; US$115 d

In keeping with the overall trend of guesthouses in the historic German Colony, Darna Guest House offers three different locations with furnished apartments in central locations around the neighborhood. A member of the Home

Accommodation Association of Jerusalem, Darna offers flexible rates for long stays with advance inquiries. The nicely furnished apartments include all the amenities of home and some include bonus features like outdoor patios.

★ TAMAR RESIDENCE

70 Beit Lechem Rd.; tel. 077/270-5555; http://tamar-residence.thejerusalemhotels.com/en; US$144 d

Far enough off the beaten path to be more affordable, but not inconvenient, the Tamar Residence is situated above the popular Grand Café and some package stays include breakfast there. Long-term stays are also available, but book in advance, especially for stays during the Jewish holidays as they are kosher residences. Each of the modern, bright rooms comes equipped with a kitchenette and plush furniture, and several also have an outdoor terrace. Most rooms have a separate living room area.

US$150-200
AVISSAR HOUSE

12 Hamevasser St., Yemin Moshe; tel. 02/625-5447; www.jeru-avisar-house.co.il; US$190 d

With four small do-it-yourself vacation suites, Avissar House's location is unique. Situated in the Yemin Moshe Artists' Quarter, Avissar is a natural choice for writers and artists, or those with artistic souls. Each suite can accommodate several people and features a balcony, free wireless Internet, lush green plants, and comfortable furnishings. There are views of the walls of the Old City, the Valley of Hinnom, and surrounding villages, and it's a short, easy walk to the City Center.

LEONARDO INN HOTEL JERUSALEM

4 Vilnay St.; tel. 02/655-8811; www.leonardo-hotels. com; US$170 d

The Leonardo Inn Hotel Jerusalem is a 200-room hotel situated at the entrance to Jerusalem near the Knesset. Some amenities include a spa and health club with sauna, whirlpool tub, and outdoor and indoor swimming pools. The light rail has a stop in front of the hotel, which seriously ups its level of convenience even though it is not situated in the heart of town. The decor of the rooms is plain and simple, and the hotel caters to practical guests who are also looking for a certain level of comfort, but nothing ostentatious.

Over US$200
JERUSALEM HARMONY

various locations; tel. 02/621-9999; www.atlas.co.il; Skype revamann, reva@jerusalemharmonyapartments.com; US$220 d

For a more customized experience, Jerusalem Harmony presents some interesting options. Accommodations have chic furnishings and include an array of deluxe guesthouses and vacation apartments fully equipped for longer stays in prime spots throughout the German Colony; sizes vary from small to very large and can accommodate up to eight people. The emphasis is on spaces conducive to fostering creativity.

SOUTHERN JERUSALEM
Over US$200
HOTEL YEHUDAH

Haim Kulitz Rd. 1; Givat Massuah; tel. 02/632-2777; www.byh.co.il; US$210 d

Hotel Yehudah is in the hills of Jerusalem, close to the zoo, Yad Vashem, and Malha shopping mall. The 129 rooms offered by the hotel include satellite TV and minibars, and many have a view of the gardens and the Jerusalem hills. A swimming pool and café are also on-site. It is the perfect setting if you want to visit Jerusalem in style but prefer to be a bit removed from the hustle and bustle of the city.

RAMAT RACHEL KIBBUTZ HOTEL

Kibbutz Ramat Rachel, Tzfon Yehuda; tel. 02/670-2555; www.ramatrachel.co.il; US$240 d

The Ramat Rachel Kibbutz Hotel feels like a getaway in the city. The 165-room, four-star hotel is situated on the grounds of one of the oldest settlements outside the Old City walls. Hotel amenities include an outdoor swimming pool, a variety of room types, a country club, a kosher restaurant, money-changing services, and a synagogue.

Information and Services

INFORMATION

Tourist and Travel Information

The hotline of the Jerusalem municipality is **106** (or tel. 02/531-4600). It covers advisories and basic information for tourists. There are several places throughout Jerusalem that act as information centers to some degree. In the Old City, the **Jaffa Gate Tourist Information Center** (1 Jaffa Gate, tel. 02/627-1422, 8:30am-5pm Sun.-Thurs., 8:30am-noon Fri.) is in a convenient location but has limited information and resources. The **Christian Information Center** (Jaffa Gate, tel. 02/627-2692, www.cicts.org, 9am-5:30pm Mon.-Fri. and 9am-12:30pm Sat.) is nearby and can also offer some help.

The **Abraham Hostel Information Center** (67 Hanevi'im St., tel. 02/650-2200, www.abraham-hostel-jerusalem.com) has a 24-hour front desk and an information center that caters to independent travelers very close to the Machane Yehuda market.

Tourist Visas

Most visitors to Israel automatically get a three-month tourist visa at Passport Control depending on the country of the passport holder, which can be renewed at the **Jerusalem Ministry of Interior** (1 Shlomtsiyon HaMalka St., tel. 02/629-0231). A tourist visa can usually be extended for up to 24-27 months, but only in increments of 3-6 months, and there is a fee of about NIS400 every time you extend your visa.

Media and Internet Resources

The **Jerusalem Development Authority** (www.jda.gov.il) and the **City of Jerusalem** (www.jerusalem.muni.il) are the driving forces behind the **Official Tourism Website of Jerusalem** (www.itraveljerusalem.com). All three websites have useful information for tourism in the city, but the City of Jerusalem site has very relevant information on basics in its "Visitors" section. Another helpful site is **Go Jerusalem** (www.gojerusalem.com), with its listings of everything from restaurants to tourist sites.

There are several local radio stations, including 101.3FM and 88.2FM. A relay of the international broadcast Reshet Hey to shortwave overseas listeners can be had on an additional 10pm broadcast on 88.2FM. **IBA World Service Israel International Radio and TV** (www.iba.org.il/world/#) has an English news radio broadcast online and a TV broadcast at 5pm Sunday-Thursday on Israel Channel 3 (33 on cable) and 6pm Friday-Saturday. On Israel Channel 1, a nine-minute version broadcasts at 4:50pm Sunday-Thursday.

The official tourism website of Israel is **https://info.goisrael.com.**

Maps

The best place to find tourist maps in Jerusalem is through information centers or from the information racks that many hotels have in their lobbies. No matter which map you use, you will find many differences in the names of streets and sights, which are not errors but the result of the city's long history, as well as differing spellings for street names and the inconsistencies in translating words and names from Arabic and Hebrew to English. Sometimes there are political factors at play.

Holidays

There are several major holidays during the calendar year that draw visitors to Jerusalem from all over the world or greatly impact services and access if you are already in the city. The most impactful are Jewish holidays, and their dates vary slightly from year to year because they are based on the Jewish calendar. It's necessary to check a calendar to see when the holidays will occur.

The most major holidays are **Sukkot** (Oct.), **Yom Kippur** (Sept.), **Passover** (late

Mar. or early Apr.), **Easter** (late Mar. or early Apr.), and **Ramadan** (one month around June-July).

Hospitals

There are a number of hospitals in Jerusalem: **Bikur Holim Hospital** (tel. 02/646-4111, www.szmc.org.il); **Hadassah Hospital** (tel. 02/584-4111, www.hadassah.org.il/Hadassa) at Mount Scopus; and **Herzog Hospital** (tel. 02/531-6875, www.herzoghospital.org).

Emergency Services

You can dial emergency services from any phone by calling **Police**, 100; **Ambulance**, 101; **Fire Department**, 102; **Electric Company Hotline**, 103; and **Municipal Emergency Situation Room**, tel. 02/625-6202 (for information during emergencies).

SERVICES

Currency Services and Money Exchange

There are several "Change" stands located throughout the city that will change foreign currency into New Israel Shekels (shekels for short) and vice versa. Change offices are concentrated in and around Zion Square and in the German Colony and Bak'a. If you are in the Old City, a trustworthy and very easy-to-find money exchange office is **Abu Ghazeleh Money Exchange** (Old City at Damascus Gate, tel. 02/628-2479, 9am-6pm daily) just inside Damascus Gate to the right. The owner speaks perfect English and has been in business at the same location for 40 years.

Post offices (www.israelpost.co.il) cash foreign currency checks and traveler's checks. The official symbol of the post office is a red sign with white writing and an ibex leaping with its horns above the title of the post office. A complete listing of the post office branches in Jerusalem can be found on the post office website.

Banks are open 8:30am-12:30pm Sunday-Friday (closed for Shabbat and holidays), and some also open from late afternoon until evening. There are several bank branches in Jerusalem that change money, including the **Jerusalem Center Branch** (33 Jaffa St.), the **City Center Shamai Branch** (6 Shamai St.), and the **Old City Jewish Quarter Branch** (69 Hayehudy St.). Near Nahalat Shiva and directly next door to the Ministry of Interior is **Hillel Change** (1 Shlomtsiyon HaMalka St., tel. 02/623-0656; 10am-5pm Sun.-Thurs. and until 2pm Fri.), which operates under the supervision of the Bank of Israel.

ATMs

There are ATMs outside of most banks that take foreign bank cards. There is a fee of US$3-9 charged by most banks for using their card at a foreign ATM.

Zion Square has two conveniently located banks with outdoor ATMs that take foreign cards. **Bank Hapoalim** (www.bankhapoalim.co.il) has red, blue, and white colors on its sign, and other branches can be found throughout Jerusalem, including at the base of the square where it meets with Yafo Street. The **Israel Discount Bank** (www.discountbank.co.il) has a green-and-white logo with branches throughout Jerusalem.

Internet

Free wireless Internet (often without a password) is available almost everywhere in the city, particularly in restaurants and cafés. City Center has free Wi-Fi provided by the municipality.

There are also about 100 Wi-Fi hotspots in convenience stores adjacent to gas stations, and other hot spots are available at universities, colleges, museums, visitors centers, convention halls, marinas, tourism sites, and shopping malls.

Postal Service

There are more than 20 branch **post offices** (main branch at 23 Yafo Street opposite Safra Square, tel. 02/629-0676, www.israelpost.co.il, 9am-3pm Sun.-Thurs., 9am-2pm Fri.) throughout Jerusalem. Check the branch for hours; most operate 9am-3pm Sun.-Thurs., 9am-2pm Fri.

Transportation

GETTING THERE

Air

The airport closest to Jerusalem is the **Ben Gurion International Airport** (tel. 03/975-2386, www.iaa.gov.il) outside Tel Aviv.

Known as the de facto national airline, **El Al Airlines** (www.elal.co.il) has frequent flights to Tel Aviv from all over the world and provides kosher meals. Most major international airlines offer at least one flight a day to Tel Aviv.

There are several ways to reach Jerusalem from the airport if you are not staying at a hotel with a shuttle service. Jerusalem is about one hour by car from the airport, about two hours by train, and a little over one hour on the many frequent, convenient, and comfortable buses. Follow the official signs to transportation and the information desk at the airport. Public transportation does not run during Shabbat (from Fri. afternoon through 8pm or 9pm Sat.), but it is possible to get a service taxi from certain locations during that time.

SHABBAT AND HOLIDAYS

Be careful when planning a flight around Shabbat or on a major Jewish holiday. You will have a more difficult time reaching your final destination if you plan to arrive or depart during these times.

SECURITY CHECKPOINTS AND VEHICLE SEARCHES

Jerusalem is under ongoing threat of terrorist attack, and it is not unusual to be stopped and questioned coming and going from a public place or to have your bag searched before entering a building. Metal detectors at building entrances are common. If you are in a car, the trunk might be searched, you might be asked for your ID, and you might be questioned. Refrain from joking with security personnel or saying you have a package given to you by someone else.

Train

Israel Railways (www.rail.co.il, NIS25) has three train stations in Jerusalem. **Jerusalem-Malha** and **Jerusalem-Biblical Zoo** are located in the southwestern outskirts of the city and are about a 15-minute car, cab, or bus ride to City Center. **Jerusalem-Yitzhak Navon** (6 Shazar Ave.), where the new direct train from Ben Gurion Airport arrives, is located west of City Center, about a 15-minute walk from Machane Yehuda Market.

Before late 2018, the train from Ben Gurion airport to Jerusalem took at least two hours, with a stop of at least 30 minutes at a train change location. A direct train line now operating between the airport and Jerusalem-Yitzhak Navon station takes less than 30 minutes.

Share Taxi

Just north of Tolerance Square on Harav Kook Street is an unofficial **way station** for share taxis going to and from Tel Aviv and other locations. The cost is about NIS30, and the vans will not leave until they are full, so you might have to wait for a while. Check with the driver before getting in that they are going to your destination.

GETTING AROUND

Jerusalem can be tricky to maneuver if you take a wrong turn, particularly if you're traveling by car. It's highly recommended to go by foot or the city's fairly efficient bus system, taxis, or the light-rail train.

Car Rental and Driving

Visitors to Israel are allowed to drive with their foreign license for up to one year from arrival in the country. As most street signs are in English, it is relatively easy for someone who can't read in Hebrew or Arabic to drive in Jerusalem. A car in Jerusalem is useful on days you plan to hop to nearby cities, such as Bethlehem, for an afternoon or visit other areas that are slightly farther away or spread out.

With three locations in Jerusalem, **Hertz** offices can be found in King David and Romema. The King David branch (19 King David St., tel. 02/623-1351, www.hertz.co.il) is centrally located in the city, and you can get compact Suzukis and Hyundais starting at US$40 a day.

Budget (23 King David St., tel. 03/935-0015, www.budget.co.il) has a variety of car models, from compact cars to SUVs, and is on centrally located King David Street.

The **parking** system in Jerusalem has some strict rules, and some you can break fairly safely. For instance, you might see cars parked on the sidewalk or facing the wrong direction on the weekend or when spots are at a premium due to a crowd. One rule you break at your peril, though, is to not feed the meter anytime except between Friday afternoon and Saturday evening. Red and white stripes mean no parking, blue and white stripes mean paid parking by a street meter, and gray is free parking. Other paid parking in certain neighborhoods or small lots will have a yellow-and-black sign with hours of paid parking; for these, you must buy a ticket and leave it on your car dash with the date stamp showing. These machines often take nothing but coins.

If you are going to be in Jerusalem and driving on a daily basis, yellow gas stations sell an automatic pay-in-advance parking meter that you leave on the side of your vehicle for NIS100. You can add more credit as needed. There is also a city parking app if you have a cell phone and a local number.

Taxis

Taxis in Jerusalem are white midsize cars with a yellow light on the roof and are often BMWs. You can get almost anywhere in the city (without heavy traffic) for NIS50 or less. Drivers might offer you a fixed rate or simply not turn their meter on, but you can rarely beat the meter with a set rate. There is a NIS15 (about US$1.50) drop charge at the start of every ride, and an additional NIS5 charge for summoning a taxi to a hotel. There can be an additional charge for luggage, and some drivers might try to charge more for two or more passengers.

The legal fare system is 25 percent higher during Shabbat and holidays (sundown on Fri. until it is dark on Sat. night, usually about 8pm). Fares are also 25 percent higher at night, 9:01pm-5:29am.

Tips are not expected, but always appreciated. If you need a taxi for a long distance, it is better to call and order a cab and do be prepared to tip for the longer distance.

Two reputable taxi companies in Jerusalem are **Rehavia Taxi** (3 Agron St., tel. 02/622-2444) and **HaPisga Taxi** (2 HaPisga St., tel. 02/642-1111).

Public Transportation

Jerusalem's city bus system, **Egged** (tel. 03/694-8888 or *2800 from any local phone, www.egged.co.il), provides fairly extensive and reliable service throughout the city and country. Within the city, it costs about NIS7 for a one-way trip. The Rav Kav ticket can be purchased and filled for multiple trips and works in both Tel Aviv and Jerusalem. Bus stops throughout the city have a timed arrival chart for every impending arrival, but the bus line explanations are only posted in Hebrew.

The **Central Bus Station** (218 Yafo St., tel. 054/797-1147) is a typical transportation hub with several levels that also support shops and places to eat or get a snack. Bus tickets can be purchased at the information window on the second level or directly from your driver if you are paying cash. Bus seats are on a first-come, first-served basis, and people stand and sit in the aisles if the seats run out.

Overseas visitors can buy Israbus tickets, valid on all Egged bus lines and on the Light-Rail Train. They are available at all branches of Egged Tours.

The **Light-Rail Train** (tel. 073/210-0601 or

*3686 from any local phone, www.citypass.co.il, NIS6.90) is a fast and convenient way to get around in certain parts of the city. It is the most convenient way, for example, to get from City Center to Yad Vashem. But the route is rather limited and does not include many major tourist sites. As it runs roughly along the old border between East and West Jerusalem, it is very convenient if you want to get somewhere in East Jerusalem. The ticket purchasing system is tricky, so leave extra time to get it right the first time.

Around Jerusalem

Not far from Jerusalem are several small towns, some with notable history, archaeology, spiritual traditions, and natural adventures. Many communities just outside of Jerusalem have open restaurants and tourist sights on the weekend.

You can take a **taxi** to any of the locations outside of Jerusalem, but the fare will be very costly. A 20-minute ride will cost about NIS120 or more. A **rental car** is a good option, as all of the signs are posted in English.

EIN KEREM

About 20 minutes west of Jerusalem is the scenic valley village of Ein Kerem, believed to be the birthplace of John the Baptist, whose mother was the Virgin Mary's cousin. Ein Kerem is a fun diversion during the weekend when much of Jerusalem is running in first gear. You can do a little sightseeing, take a stroll amongst the village's steep streets, get a drink, or have dinner and dessert.

Sights
HADASSAH EIN KEREM
off Route 396 near Ein Kerem; tel. 02/677-7111; www.hadassah.org.il; visitors hours 10am-5pm daily; free
If you're a serious art lover, a detour to Hadassah Ein Kerem, one of the leading research hospitals in the world, might be in order. The hospital is home to the famous **Marc Chagall Stained Glass Windows**, a series of 12 arched, stained-glass windows surrounding the hospital's synagogue. They can be viewed for free inside the hospital's main lobby. Chagall called the windows his "modest gift to the Jewish people," and numerous other works of art throughout the hospital were donated by other artists or supporters.

MARY'S WELL
southern end of HaMa'ayan St.; 24 hours; free
A popular draw in Ein Kerem is Mary's Well, which Christian tradition says was visited by the Virgin Mary when she stopped here to drink from the spring. There is a 19th-century mosque above the spring.

SHRINE OF THE VISITATION
southern hill facing the village at the top of the pedestrian extension of HaMa'ayan St; tel. 02/641-7291; www.custodia.org; 8am-noon and 2:30pm-6pm Mon.-Sat.; NIS5
The Shrine of the Visitation is a church with a facade on the front with a series of arches, a bell tower, and a painting of the Virgin Mary riding a donkey and accompanied by angels on the front outer wall. The two-story church has large color paintings throughout depicting biblical scenes. It is also home to a guesthouse run by nuns.

GORNY MONASTERY
Ein Kerem, 10am-5pm daily; NIS10
The iconic Gorny Monastery, also known as Moscavia for its distinctive gold onion domes that are clearly visible from the village, can be reached by taking a short hike up a steep, winding footpath. The 19th-century Russian Orthodox church is also home to a convent. The compound's buildings are closed to the public, but you can get an excellent view from the parking lot on HaOren Street next to Shibboleth Lane.

CHURCH OF ST. JOHN

Mevo Hasha'ar; tel. 02/632-3000; 6am-noon and 2pm-5pm daily; free

The Church of St. John is built at the location where John the Baptist was believed to have been born. The church has a grotto beneath it with the remains of a Byzantine mosaic.

Food

The main concentration of restaurants and bars here is on two roads: to the end of HaMa'ayan Street and along the part of Ein Kerem Road 74 where it passes through the village. Most of them are not listed on travel websites.

CHARLOTTE

25 Ein Kerem Rd.; tel. 02/643-4545; noon-11pm Sun.-Thurs.; NIS70

Offering a nice array of chicken and beef dishes, Charlotte is perfect if you're in the mood for something grilled. Though they are one of the few places not open on the weekend, Charlotte has the unusual offering of goose breast skewers. All of their entrées are served with salad, and their interior is large and spacious with wood paneling and huge windows that give it the feeling of a cabin.

★ BRASSERIE

15 HaMa'ayan St.; tel. 02/566-5000; http:// brasseriejer.wp.2eat.co.il/en; noon-last customer Sun.-Wed., 10am-lasts customer Thurs., 9:30am-last customer Sat.; NIS60

Specializing in seafood and meat dishes in a French-style atmosphere, Brasserie boasts a large outdoor patio on its second level with a view of the scenic valley and church. It's the perfect setting for a get-together with friends. The restaurant also has a broad selection of steak, chicken, and French-inspired dishes (try the camembert croissant). Brasserie's liquor and wine selection is extensive, and customers can arrange a menu for wine-tasting. Several beers are served on tap, as well as an array of signature cocktails.

1: Herodium **2:** floor mosaic in the Shrine of the Visitation in Ein Kerem

KARMA

74 Ein Kerem Rd.; tel. 02/643-6643; www.karma-rest. co.il; 10am-midnight Sun.-Wed., Thurs.-Sat. 10am-1am; NIS70

Karma has a nice layout and very accommodating waitstaff. The menu is a fairly typical blend of pasta, salad, and meat selections with some delightful surprises. Try the *taboon*-baked flatbread covered with vegetables and eggs or the Druze-inspired appetizer platter, which consists of a thin pita overstuffed with lamb cuts, pine nuts, red sauce, tahini, and roasted eggplant. Karma also has enclosed veranda seating on the first floor and tons of balcony seating on the second floor.

Getting There and Around

To get to Ein Kerem, take an **Egged** bus (www.egged.co.il, bus number 17, NIS15) from City Center; the trip takes about 25 minutes. Once there, the village is easy to navigate by foot and there is no need for a vehicle.

If you're driving, note that parking is extremely limited on the weekend. Navigate west on Betsal'el Bazak Street to Shmu'el Bait Street and turn left on Route 386, which will take you to Ein Kerem.

HERODIUM

south of Jerusalem and east of Bethlehem on the edge of Judean Desert; tel. 050/623-5821, www. parks.org.il; 8am-5pm daily Apr.-Sept., 8am-4pm daily Oct.-Mar.; NIS27

About eight miles (13 km) south of Jerusalem is King Herod's palace-fortress Herodium. According to one historical account, he built it after winning a victory over the Hasmoneans and Parthians. The palace is 2,490 feet (758 meters) above sea level. The site contains extensive palatial ruins, including a living quarter complex, an ancient synagogue, and underground tunnels, and it can be accessed by foot.

Getting There

If you are venturing to Herodium, you can go and return by bus, though you will also have to do a fair amount of walking. A 40-minute

Egged bus ride (www.egged.co.il, bus number 266, NIS17.5) toward Karmei Zur will get you close, followed by a 20-minute walk.

ON HIGHWAY 1 TO TEL AVIV

If you have a car and are traveling between Jerusalem and Tel Aviv, there are a few good places to stop, such as Latrun Monastery and the Arab village of Abu Ghosh.

Latrun Monastery

tel. 08/922-0065; 9am-1pm and
2pm-5pm Mon.-Sat., free

Just off of Highway 1 between Jerusalem and Tel Aviv is the Latrun Monastery, founded in 1890 and home to an order of silent monks up until the 1960s. The site consists of a large church and living quarters on the monastery grounds, a garden, a vineyard, and orchards. In late 2012, the monastery was vandalized by Jewish settlers angry over being removed by the government from their settlement. As you enter the site, you will find a shop selling Domain de Latroun wines, liqueurs, spirits, and olive oil and honey made at the monastery. It's a 25-minute ride on Egged bus (www.egged.co.il, bus number 403, 433, or 434, NIS16) from Jerusalem's Central Bus Station.

Ein Hemed (Aqua Bella)

off the main Highway 1 from the Hemed off-ramp,
opposite Kibbutz Kiryat Anavim and the town of Abu
Ghosh; tel. 02/534-2741; 9am-6pm daily; NIS20

Just outside Jerusalem near the villages of Bet Nekofa and Abu Ghosh is Ein Hemed (Aqua Bella) national park, which was once used as a way station for Crusaders. You can still find the remains of a ruined Crusader farmhouse and a park with an olive press.

Abu Ghosh

Abu Ghosh is a quiet Arab village just off Highway 1 between Jerusalem and Tel Aviv, famed for its hummus and other Arab delicacies. It's about 25 minutes northwest of Jerusalem.

THE ORIGINAL ABU SHUKRI

15 Hashalom Way; tel. 02/652-6088;
8am-8pm daily; NIS45

The Original Abu Shukri gets its name from a dispute with another restaurant. The dispute is that one restaurant (nobody is sure which one anymore) has the reputation for the best hummus in the land. The interior of the restaurant is very simple and homey, and the dining experience is, like most hummus dining, without much fanfare. But the food is delicious and comes to your table quickly, the service is good, and there is free parking.

THE LEBANESE RESTAURANT

65 Kvish Ha-Shalom; tel. 02/533-2019; 11am-11pm
daily; NIS30

The Lebanese Restaurant is another favorite for hummus. The decor is spartan but the food hits the spot. You are guaranteed to leave with a full stomach and money still in your wallet, no matter how much you eat.

ELVIS AMERICAN DINER

near the Neve Ilan gas station; tel. 02/534-1275,
7am-7pm Sat.-Thurs., 7am-5pm Fri.; NIS80

If you're tired of Middle Eastern food, you can find the Elvis American Diner in Abu Ghosh serving up what are widely reputed to be some of the best hamburgers in the area. A large statue of Elvis is outside the building, and Elvis pictures cover the walls inside.

Getting There and Around

To get to Abu Ghosh, take **Superbus** (www.superbus.co.il, bus number 185 or 186, NIS27). It's about a 40-minute ride. Once you are there everything is within fairly easy walking distance.

For the gorgeous parklands of Ein Hemed (Aqua Bella), the Superbus (bus number 185, NIS22) leaves Jerusalem every hour. It's about a 30-minute ride. Just get off at Beit Nekufa and walk 10 minutes over the bridge that goes over Road 1.

The major hub for Superbus in Jerusalem is in East Jerusalem near **Damascus Gate.**

Tel Aviv

The first modern Jewish city, Tel Aviv (or Tel

Aviv-Jaffa) is seen by some as a beacon of progress and modernity, by others as a den of iniquity, and by others as a beach town with a more laid-back atmosphere the closer you get to the water. It can certainly feel like a breath of fresh air in the midst of some very heavy culture and history.

The Tel Aviv-Jaffa metro area has managed to bridge the gap between old customs and traditions and Israel's more modern and forward-looking perspective. Often called "the center" by locals, there's a little bit of everything here.

Home to roughly half a million people, Tel Aviv-Jaffa is a buzzing mix of finance, tech and defense professionals, fashionistas,

Highlights

Look for ★ to find recommended sights, activities, dining, and lodging.

★ **White City:** A preeminent example of Bauhaus architecture and a UNESCO World Heritage Site, Tel Aviv's White City is a draw for urban architecture and design enthusiasts (page 120).

★ **Neve Tzedek:** Old-world European charm meets modern city life in this charming slice of traveler heaven, with cobblestone streets, distinctive architecture, exquisite dining, and first-class shopping. The lovely neighborhood is also home to excellent museums (page 121).

★ **Sarona:** Intended as a new cultural and culinary center for Tel Aviv-Jaffa, Sarona is a favorite of visitors and locals (page 123).

★ **Old Jaffa:** One of the world's oldest port cities, Old Jaffa is home to authentic Arab culture, including a renowned bakery (page 125).

★ **Carmel Market:** Tel Aviv's massive indoor-outdoor Carmel Market is a delight for the senses—the air is filled with the smells of exotic coffee, spices, and other intoxicating aromas amid the colorful mountains of fruit, baklava, and all manner of goods and wares (page 132).

★ **HaYarkon Park:** North Tel Aviv's massive HaYarkon Park is a playground for all kinds of outdoor sports and recreation. When the sun goes down, it's a great place for an evening stroll or a drink at one of the outdoor cantinas along HaYarkon River (page 136).

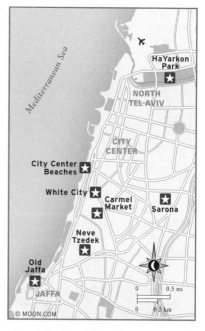

© MOON.COM

★ **City Center Beaches:** This part of the coastline has several clean, easy-to-find beaches that are well-equipped with changing facilities, lockers, and restrooms (page 138).

well-developed beach culture, world-class fine dining and entertainment, art and music, and a diverse range of people.

A magnet for talent and ambition from all over the region, Tel Aviv boasts an impressive mixture of nightlife hotspots, business and commercial sectors, massive parks, endless beaches, and a large secular population. On any given day of the week Tel Aviv has offerings for every taste and budget. Its nightlife scene is legendary and doesn't really get started until after midnight.

Adjoining Tel Aviv and under the same municipality is Jaffa, one of the oldest cities in the world. Jaffa is predominately Arab and Christian and home to some of the most memorable dining experiences in the area. Just after Israel became a state in 1948, the southern neighborhood of Jaffa was annexed to Tel Aviv to form the municipality of Tel Aviv-Jaffa. Jaffa is home to some important Christian pilgrimage sites, ancient architecture, authentic Arab-style food, and eclectic shopping opportunities. Its beachfront offers sightseeing, shopping, and dining options.

Literally translated from Hebrew as "new city," Tel Aviv was founded by a group of families who divvied up the land area before Israel was established. The very deliberate blend of old and new is what makes Tel Aviv so unique. It's a place where you can find ancient traditions and customs alongside new and modern ways.

ORIENTATION

Tel Aviv is a beach city on central Israel's coast directly adjacent to Jaffa. It's just a couple hours' drive south from Haifa, 30 minutes away from Ben Gurion International Airport by car, and about an hour by train or bus. It is about one hour from Jerusalem by car, taxi, or bus, and about two hours by train. The rectangle-shaped city stretches down the western border of the Mediterranean Sea. Throughout Tel Aviv, there are miles of boardwalks, in addition to pathways and trails in parks and beaches.

North Tel Aviv

North Tel Aviv generally consists of residential neighborhoods with pockets of shopping, entertainment, and food. It all culminates at the Marina with its shopping, sightseeing, dining, and nightlife options before giving way to the city's center. The city's north is also home to the massive HaYarkon Park and its myriad outdoor diversions. A number of nice museums can also be found here.

City Center

Tel Aviv's City Center begins just south of the Marina and north of Charles Clore Park. Much of the city's entertainment, shopping, and nightlife, and most of the lifeguard-monitored beaches and nicer hotels are located here. It is a good base if you are only visiting the city for a few days.

South Tel Aviv

South Tel Aviv extends approximately from Charles Clore Park down to Jaffa, and is home to the lovely and entertaining Neve Tzedek neighborhood with its high-end shops, European-style cafés and restaurants, and varied nightlife options that include a converted train station compound with shops, dining, and live entertainment.

Jaffa

South of Tel Aviv is Jaffa, one of the oldest cities in the world. Today it is part of the Tel Aviv-Jaffa municipality and intertwined with Tel Aviv's daily life. Jaffa's predominately Arab population distinguishes this part of the city. Jaffa is home to some of Israel's best chefs, many of whom are internationally renowned.

PLANNING YOUR TIME

Tel Aviv really comes alive when the sun starts to go down, particularly in the sweltering

Tel Aviv

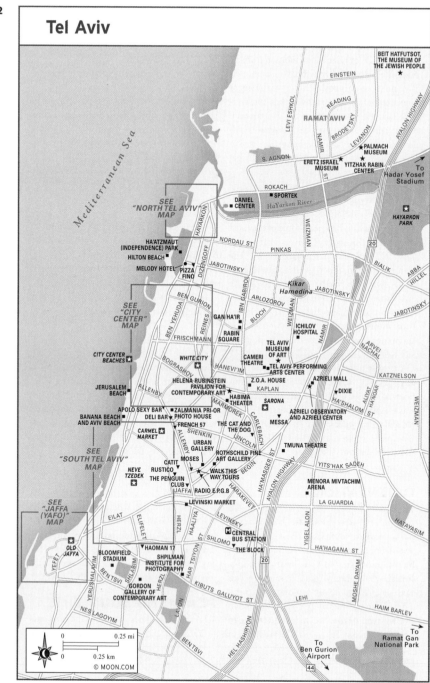

BEIT HATFUTSOT,
THE MUSEUM OF
THE JEWISH PEOPLE ★

EINSTEIN

RAMAT AVIV

READING

BRODETSKY

LEVI ESHKOL

NAMIR

LEVANON

AYALON HIGHWAY

S. AGNON

★ PALMACH
MUSEUM

ERETZ ISRAEL ■
MUSEUM

★ YITZHAK RABIN
CENTER

To
Hadar Yosef
Stadium

ROKACH

■ SPORTEK

DANIEL ■
CENTER

HaYarkon River

WEIZMAN

20

BIALIK

HAYARKON
PARK

ABBA
HILLEL

Mediterranean Sea

HAYARKON

HA'ATZMAUT
(INDEPENDENCE) PARK ■

NORDAU ST

PINKAS

WEIZMAN

JABOTINSKY

HILTON BEACH ■

MELODY HOTEL ■   ● PIZZA
FINO

DIZENGOFF

Kikar
Hamedina

JABOTINSKY

SEE
"NORTH TEL AVIV"
MAP

BEN GURION

ARLOZOROV

IBN GABIROL

BLOCH

WEIZMAN

JABOTINSKY

SEE
"CITY
CENTER"
MAP

BEN YEHUDA

REINES

FRISCHMANN

GAN HA'IR ■

RABIN
SQUARE

ICHILOV
HOSPITAL

NAMIR

ARVEI
NACHAL

CITY CENTER
BEACHES ✪

BOGRASHOV

WHITE CITY ✪

HANEVI'IM

TEL AVIV
MUSEUM
OF ART

CAMERI
THEATRE

TEL AVIV PERFORMING
ARTS CENTER

KATZNELSON

WEIZMAN

JERUSALEM
BEACH ■

ALLENBY

HELENA RUBINSTEIN
PAVILION FOR
CONTEMPORARY ART ■

Z.O.A. HOUSE ■

KAPLAN

AZRIELI MALL ▼

▼ DIXIE

HA'SHALOM

ALIYAT
HANOAR

BANANA BEACH
AND AVIV BEACH ■

APOLO SEXY BAR ■

CARMEL ✪
MARKET

■ ZALMANIA PRI-OR
▼ PHOTO HOUSE

DELI BAR ■

▼ FRENCH 57

SHENKIN

URBAN
GALLERY

HABIMA
THEATER

MARMOREK

CARLEBACH

▼ SARONA

MESSA ▼

AZRIELI OBSERVATORY
AND AZRIELI CENTER

THE CAT AND
THE DOG ▼

LINCOLN

HA'MASGER ST

AYALON HIGHWAY

TMUNA THEATRE ■

YITS'HAK SADEH

SEE
"SOUTH TEL AVIV"
MAP

NEVE
TZEDEK ✪

CATIT
RUSTICO ▼

MOSES ▼

THE PENGUIN
CLUB ▼

JAFFA

RADIO E.P.G.B ▼

ROTHSCHILD FINE
ART GALLERY ■

★ WALK THIS
WAY TOURS

BEGIN

HARAKEVET

MENORA MIVTACHIM
ARENA ■

LA GUARDIA

HATAYASIM

SEE
"JAFFA
(YAFO)"
MAP

EILAT

ELIFELET

HERZL

■ LEVINSKI MARKET

HAALIYA

HAR TSIYON

LEVINSKY

SHLOMO

LEVINSKY

Ⓜ CENTRAL
BUS STATION

THE BLOCK ■

20

YIGEL ALON

HA'HAGANA ST

MOSHE DAYAM

OLD
JAFFA ✪

YEFET

BEN TSVI

SHLABIM

■ HAOMAN 17

BLOOMFIELD
STADIUM ■

SHPILMAN
INSTITUTE FOR
PHOTOGRAPHY ■

HERZL

LAVON

KIBUTS GALUYOT ST

LEHI

HAIM BARLEV

YERUSHALAYIM

GORDON
GALLERY OF
CONTEMPORARY ART ■

NES LAGOYIM

BENTSVI

HEL HASHIRYON

To
Ramat Gan
National Park

To
Ben Gurion
Airport

44

0   0.25 mi

0   0.25 km

© MOON.COM

summer months. Plan to spend at least two days and nights in the city to get the right amount of sand, sun, food, and nightlife. In the summer, plan on air-conditioned downtime in the afternoon to keep your energy up for any late nights. The summer heat and humidity in Tel Aviv can be brutal, so pace yourself and keep drinking water. The city is active year-round, but as temperatures go down a bit during the winter months from November through March, people naturally move indoors.

Most of the sights and activities are concentrated in and near City Center, but it is a small city, so you don't have to go far to find a museum, a tour group, outdoor sports, or good food. If you stick somewhat close to the beach and promenade between Old Jaffa in the south and the port in the north, you won't run out of things to do. The best bet for getting around efficiently is to use the trains and buses. Taxis are also easy here.

Itinerary Ideas

TEL AVIV ON DAY 1

1 Start out at the famous clock tower to explore Arab culture, food, and shopping at the **Old Jaffa Port.**

2 Have a treat from **Abulafia Bakery** for breakfast. You can also take home some of the famed baked goods, along with regional souvenirs like ceramics, metalwork, and handwoven rugs from the famous flea market.

3 For a rare taste of Israeli-style Mexican food, **Mezcal** serves up tacos, nachos, and great beer.

4 After lunch, take a taxi to the **Tel Aviv Museum of Art,** where you can peruse the wide array of exhibits. Don't miss the sculpture garden and works by old masters.

shops along the Old Jaffa Port

Itinerary Ideas

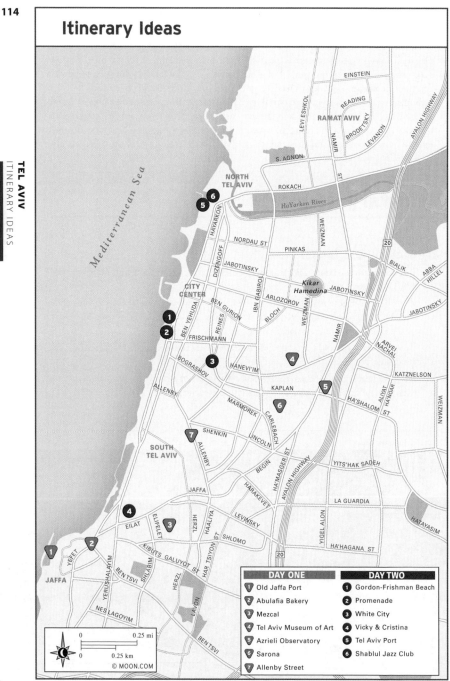

DAY ONE	DAY TWO
1 Old Jaffa Port	**1** Gordon-Frishman Beach
2 Abulafia Bakery	**2** Promenade
3 Mezcal	**3** White City
4 Tel Aviv Museum of Art	**4** Vicky & Cristina
5 Azrieli Observatory	**5** Tel Aviv Port
6 Sarona	**6** Shablul Jazz Club
7 Allenby Street	

0.25 mi
0.25 km

© MOON.COM

5 For a different view of Tel Aviv, head to **Azrieli Observatory** where you can capture a view of Tel Aviv from the 49th floor of the tallest building in Israel.

6 Nearby, open-air **Sarona** will work up your appetite again with its food shops and many restaurants to choose from for dinner.

7 End your day by hitting up some of the bars and clubs, like the quirky **Deli Bar** along **Allenby Street.**

TEL AVIV ON DAY 2

1 There is no better way to spend a morning in Tel Aviv than at one of Tel Aviv's many beaches, like **Gordon-Frishman Beach.** Bring all the essential beach items, plus about NIS100 for food, drinks, and chair rental.

2 After some time in the sand and surf, pack your things into a rental locker and take a **stroll down the promenade,** or use one of the city's bike share programs to rent a bike. Get lunch at one of the various options along the promenade.

3 In the afternoon, take a walk through the **White City,** a UNESCO World Heritage Site for its planning and architecture. Leave time to recover from the sun and nap at your hotel in the hot hours of the late afternoon.

4 For dinner, spend the evening enjoying Middle Eastern tapas done Tel Aviv style in the gardens of popular **Vicky & Cristina.** The Spanish wine bar has over 100 bottles to choose from.

5 After dinner, the **Tel Aviv Port** is a lovely place to stroll on the boardwalk with an ice cream.

6 From there, head over to one of the port's clubs for some live music, like jazz at the **Shablul Jazz Club** at Hangar 13.

the Tel Aviv promenade

Sights

Tel Aviv proper is shaped like a rectangle with a curving eastern border and a pin-straight western border where the land meets the Mediterranean Sea, buffered by 13 beaches and boardwalks that stretch for almost nine miles (14 km). Each pocket of the city is generally known for its distinct offerings, such as world-class museums in the north, a huge variety of shopping and dining options in the center, and historical points of interest in the south.

NORTH TEL AVIV
Port of Tel Aviv

where HaYarkon St.'s most northern point turns east and becomes HaTa'arucha St.; tel. 03/544-1505; www.namal.co.il

The object of a recent major transformation, the Port of Tel Aviv was once desolate but is now a hub of activity with its Marina and boardwalk. It is one of the most happening and family-friendly places in the city, where you can get right up to the water's edge on the boardwalk. There is no swimming (legally) in the area, but Tel Avivians come out in droves in the evening to enjoy the seaside; the massive, sloping boardwalk; street performers; and the many restaurants and sweet shops.

During the hot summer months, the boardwalk is crowded late into the night with everyone—even children. Most of the restaurants in the boardwalk area serve typical Israeli food.

Ramat Aviv

The area of Ramat Aviv, at the northern tip of Tel Aviv, is home to some fantastic museums.

THE YITZHAK RABIN CENTER

8 Chaim Levanon St.; tel. 03/745-3322; www. rabincenter.org.il; 9am-5pm Sun.-Mon. and Wed., 9am-7pm Tues. and Thurs., 9am-2pm Fri.; adult NIS50, senior and child NIS25

Start with The Yitzhak Rabin Center, which includes the **Israeli Museum** (tel. 03/745-3345), which deals with the development of

North Tel Aviv

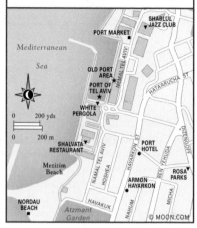

the State of Israel as a young democracy. Smart audio guides (NIS10) recognize where you are as you move in a downward spiral through the 1,500 striking photographs, extensive memorabilia, and documentary films on assassinated prime minister Yitzhak Rabin and the history of the State of Israel. The building is adjacent to the **Eretz Israel Museum,** and you should allow 2-3 hours for a visit to both.

ERETZ ISRAEL MUSEUM

2 Chaim Levanon St.; tel. 03/641-5244; www. eretzmuseum.org.il; 10am-4pm Sun.-Wed., 10am-8pm Thurs., 10am-2pm Fri.-Sat.; adult NIS52, student NIS35, under 18 free

The Eretz Israel Museum is an eclectic structure built partly on top of an archaeological site. It bills itself as a spiritual and cultural center in Tel Aviv and Israel. The museum features several exhibition pavilions, each dedicated to a different cultural field and subject in Israel, including archaeology, Judaica, and ethnography, as well as more modern art and cultural pieces. Some key permanent exhibitions are the ceramics exhibit and the ethnography and folklore pavilion. The museum's running theme is to highlight life in Israel from ancient up through modern times. It is easy to walk through the various exhibits. The outdoor archaeological

Tel Aviv's Coastal Culture

Israelis love to say that Tel Aviv is "their version of New York City" because of its bustling pace. In fact, it more closely resembles a beach town that just loves to party. Tel Aviv's surf-loving, partying atmosphere is apparent everywhere, from the scantily clad pedestrians to those crossing the street with a surfboard.

It is a city that has good reason to be so obsessed with the sea. Tel Aviv's entire western border is the Mediterranean, and it has a tremendous influence on the city's lifestyle, leisure activities, and atmosphere.

There are two types of Tel Aviv beaches: official and unofficial. Official beaches are designated as safe areas for swimming and have lifeguards. Unofficial beaches have no lifeguards and are often blocked off (such as at the Old Port of Tel Aviv). Some beaches, such as Hilton, are gay-friendly, others are brimming with surfers, and others are jam-packed with tourists.

Four major points of reference on the Tel Aviv coast are the Jaffa Port, the Dolphinarium, the Tel Aviv Marina, and the Port of Tel Aviv.

JAFFA PORT

The Jaffa Port is on the southern end of the city and near the Old City of Jaffa and the tip of Tel Aviv. Here you can find restaurants, ancient architecture, and general sightseeing in the scenic setting of what is believed to be one of the oldest ports in the entire world.

DOLPHINARIUM PARK

The Dolphinarium Park is just north of the oldest part of the *tayalet* (promenade) and the spacious Charles Clore Park, with gorgeous views of both Jaffa and Tel Aviv. The Dolphinarium was the site of a horrific terrorist bombing in 2001 during the Second Intifada. There is a park and playground there now that was established by the Tel Aviv Yafo Foundation. Nearby is the Israel Surf Club, where you can rent equipment and take lessons. Just southeast are the hip and happening adjacent districts of Shabazi Street, Neve Tzedek, and HaTachana.

TEL AVIV MARINA

Due north up the coast is the Tel Aviv Marina, another hub of activity and central launching point for activities. Here you will find the heated saltwater Gordon Swimming Pool, Atarim Square, and more excellent surfing spots and beaches.

PORT OF TEL AVIV

Continue north to the Port of Tel Aviv to a tremendous center of activity, including a scenic board-walk, restaurants, shops, a farmers market, and a couple of beaches. The area has been revitalized in recent years and is a hive of activity, especially in the late summer evenings when locals looking to escape the stifling heat get out and about.

exhibit is accessible even after closing. The gift shop's unique items and the building's open-air pavilions are popular draws, making this an excellent spot for a leisurely visit.

PALMACH MUSEUM

10 Chaim Levanon St.; tel. 03/643-6393;
http://info.palmach.org.il; 9am-5pm Sun.-Mon.
and Wed., 9am-8pm Tues., 9am-2pm Thurs., 9am-1pm
Fri.; adult NIS30, child NIS20

The extremely popular Palmach Museum is an experiential museum documenting the history of the elite underground Jewish fighting forces in pre-state Israel. Instead of displays or documents, a 90-minute group tour includes fascinating personal accounts of historical characters alongside three-dimensional decor, films, and special effects that incorporate documentary materials. Visits must be arranged in advance, especially for English-speaking visitors.

A Brief History of Israel's "New City"

Tel Aviv draws at least some of its inspiration for being vibrant and exciting from its status as Israel's "new city." The name Tel Aviv literally translates as "spring mound," but the more intuitive meaning is "old new city," as its name was inspired by founding father Theodor Herzl's book bearing that title. The founding and creation of Tel Aviv was, and is, seen as the center of the revival of the new Jewish state in the ancient homeland.

Tel Aviv's official name, Tel Aviv-Yafo, stems from its connection to the ancient port city of Jaffa (or Yafo) that is at the southern end of the city. Jaffa, which is predominately Arab, is estimated to be about 4,000 years old.

The first modern Hebrew city, Tel Aviv was established in 1909 by a group of 60 families who simply took plots of land through a group self-assignment process. But as the population of Tel Aviv grew, so did tensions with Arab neighbors in Jaffa who had already been living there for years.

Suffering from a long history of instability and insecurity, Jewish and Arab forces battled for control of Tel Aviv on the eve of the establishment of an independent Jewish state in 1948. Ultimately, Arab forces and residents were violently pushed into Jaffa. In 1949, Tel Aviv's second mayor, Israel Rokach, united Tel Aviv and Jaffa under the auspices of the Tel Aviv-Yafo municipality.

Today, Jaffa accounts for about 12 percent of Tel Aviv's total area and is home to about 45,000 Arab, Christian, and Jewish residents. It is famed for having some of the best fine dining in the country.

BEIT HATFUTSOT, THE MUSEUM OF THE JEWISH PEOPLE

Tel Aviv University campus, Klausner St.,
in Ramat Aviv, entrance through Matatia Gate 2;
tel. 03/745-7808; www.bh.org.il; 10am-4pm
Sun.-Tues., 10am-7pm Wed.-Thurs., 9am-1pm Fri.;
adult NIS70, senior NIS30, child NIS55

A good way to combine a museum visit with a visit to the campus of Tel Aviv University is a stop at Beit Hatfutsot, The Museum of the Jewish People. The permanent and rotating exhibits that trace the story of the Jewish people over the last 2,500 years include models, short films, and texts on the history and ongoing stories of the Jewish Diaspora. A lack of upgrades in years past have now led the museum to initiate renovations, but it is still possible to spend hours exploring. Don't miss the miniature synagogue exhibit with models of famous synagogues from all over the world including Europe, Asia, and the Middle East. Also of interest is the genealogy section where you can research on computers and add information to the database.

CITY CENTER

Ben-Gurion House

17 Ben-Gurion Blvd.; tel. 03/522-1010; www.bg-house.
org; 8am-3pm Sun. and Tues.-Thurs., 8am-5pm Mon.,
8am-noon Fri., 11am-2pm Sat.; free

The former home of one of the fathers of the nation of Israel, David Ben-Gurion, is still intact for visitors. The very modest Ben-Gurion House includes Ben-Gurion's library of approximately 20,000 books and is an example of the Bauhaus/International design so well-preserved in Tel Aviv. The museum's signage is mostly in Hebrew, but it is still worth a visit to explore the residence and some of the photos, letters, and gifts from world leaders. Call in advance to ask about the possibility of an English-speaking guide.

Old Town Hall

27 Bialik St.; tel. 03/517-3052; http://beithair.org;
9am-5pm Mon.-Thurs., 10am-2pm Fri.-Sat. and
holidays; free

The beautiful, grand Bauhaus building that served as Tel Aviv's Old Town Hall (*Beit Ha'ir*) with grand colonnades and facing entrance staircases is home to the **Beit Ha'ir** and part

City Center

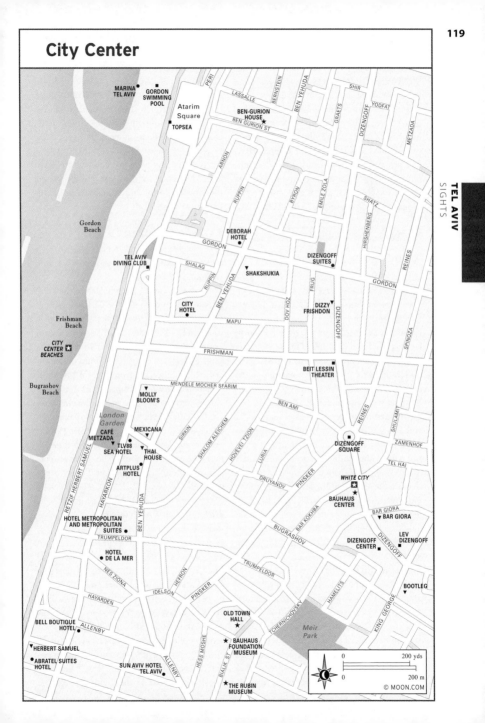

MARINA TEL AVIV
GORDON SWIMMING POOL
Atarim Square
TOPSEA
BEN-GURION HOUSE
BEN GURION ST

PERI
LASSALLE
BERNSTEIN
BEN YEHUDA
SHIR
GRAETS
DIZENGOFF
YODFAT
METZADA

Gordon Beach

ARNON
RUPPIN
BYRON
EMILE ZOLA
SHATZ
HIRSHENBERG
REINES

DEBORAH HOTEL
DIZENGOFF SUITES
TEL AVIV DIVING CLUB
SHALAG
RUPPIN
BEN YEHUDA
SHAKSHUKIA
GORDON
GORDON

CITY HOTEL
MAPU
DOV HOZ
FRUG
DIZZY FRISHDON
DIZENGOFF
SPINOZA

Frishman Beach

CITY CENTER BEACHES

FRISHMAN

Bugrashov Beach

BEIT LESSIN THEATER

MENDELE MOCHER SFARIM

London Garden

MOLLY BLOOM'S

BEN AMI
REINES
SHULAMIT

CAFÉ METZADA
MEXICANA
SIRKIN
SHALOM ALEICHEM
HOVEVEI TZION
LURIA
DIZENGOFF SQUARE
ZAMENHOF
TEL HAI

RETZIF HERBERT SAMUEL
TLV88
SEA HOTEL
THAI HOUSE
ARTPLUS HOTEL
HAYARKON
BEN YEHUDA
DRUYANOV
PINSKER
WHITE CITY
BAUHAUS CENTER
BAR GIORA
BAR GIORA

HOTEL METROPOLITAN AND METROPOLITAN SUITES
TRUMPELDOR
BAR KOKHBA
BUGRASHOV
DIZENGOFF CENTER
DIZENGOFF
LEV DIZENGOFF

HOTEL DE LA MER
NES ZIONA
TRUMPELDOR
HAMELITS
BOOTLEG

HAYARDEN
IDELSON
HEFRON
PINSKER
KING GEORGE

BELL BOUTIQUE HOTEL
ALLENBY
OLD TOWN HALL
TCHERNICHOVSKY
Meir Park

HERBERT SAMUEL
ABRATEL SUITES HOTEL
HESS MOSHE
BAUHAUS FOUNDATION MUSEUM
BIALIK ST
SUN AVIV HOTEL TEL AVIV
ALLENBY
THE RUBIN MUSEUM

0   200 yds
0   200 m

© MOON.COM

of the **Bialik Complex** UNESCO World Heritage Site. The collection of photos and old video clips from Tel Aviv residents chronicles the history of the city in the last 100 years and includes an "old" and a "new" wing. The office of Tel Aviv's first mayor, Meir Dizengoff, has been restored with a view of Bialik Square and Bialik Street's Bauhaus architecture. Rotating exhibitions of local and international artists and designers are also on display. The museum is designed as an open house for area artists and thinkers, and is a pleasant, easy-to-reach stop on the way to see the White City.

TOP EXPERIENCE

★ White City

between Allenby St. in the south, Begin Rd. and Ibn Gabirol St. in the east, the Yarkon River in the north, and the Mediterranean Sea in the west; www.bauhaus-center.com

Tel Aviv's White City is a UNESCO World Heritage Site and considered an outstanding example of new town planning and architecture in the early 20th century, adapted to the cultural and geographic context of Tel Aviv. It is a must-see for architecture aficionados. The **Information Center** (46 Herbert Samuel St. at the corner of 2 Geula St., tel. 03/516-6188) will assist in getting you oriented with tours and knowledge about the area. Based on a design by Scottish urban planner Sir Patrick Geddes, the 4,000 buildings of the White City were built between the early 1930s through the 1950s. They are a definitive part of Tel Aviv's character and what UNESCO calls an "outstanding architectural ensemble of the Modern Movement in a new cultural context."

The buildings in the White City were designed by European-trained architects who practiced their profession abroad before immigrating to Israel. Most of the buildings are 3-4 stories high and have flat roofs, plaster rendering, some decorative features, and a monochromatic color scheme of cream to white. The buildings are located mainly along Rothschild Boulevard, around Dizengoff Circle, and on Bialik Street.

BAUHAUS FOUNDATION MUSEUM

21 Bialik St.; tel. 03/620-4664; 11am-5pm Wed., 10am-2pm Fri.; free

On Fridays, the one-room Bauhaus Foundation Museum offers free two-hour tours, but call ahead for specific times. Otherwise, the one-room establishment dedicated to the Bauhaus movement through the display of Bauhaus objects and furniture is a worthwhile stop for architecture buffs. It is housed on the ground floor of a renovated Bauhaus building and is also home to the Bauhaus Foundation.

BAUHAUS CENTER

99 Dizengoff St.; tel. 03/522-0249; www.bauhaus-center.com; 10am-7:30pm Sat.-Thurs., 10am-2:30pm Fri.; free

The Bauhaus Center is dedicated to the public recognition of the White City as a unique architectural and cultural site. The center is small and tightly packed with an interesting array of Bauhaus memorabilia and a second-floor gallery with permanent and changing art exhibitions. The ground floor gift shop sells books in English on the subject of the White City and Bauhaus. Guided tours in English (10am Fri., NIS60) are available here either with a tour guide or by renting audio headphones (any time, NIS60). Both types of tour take about two hours. The center also offers other tours in Tel Aviv and other areas of Israel.

WALK THIS WAY TOURS

White City tour: meet at 46 Rothschild Blvd. on the corner of Shadal St.; tel. 03/516-6188; www.visit-tlv.com; 11am Sat.; free

The City of Tel Aviv also hosts a variety of free Walk This Way Tours that include a route in the White City. Other tours include Tel Aviv University, Tel Aviv by Night, Tel Aviv Art and Graffiti, and Old Jaffa. There is no need to book in advance; you just meet up at the starting point about 10 minutes before the scheduled departure time. Check the website for updated times before you go.

The White City

In 1925, as Tel Aviv grew and developed, Scottish urban planner Sir Patrick Geddes was brought in to help design a modern urban city to work against sprawling expansion and lack of cohesion. Geddes's vision of a master plan for Tel Aviv was a garden city with clear separations between main streets, residential streets, and vegetation-filled pedestrian boulevards. One of the plan's key elements was creating shared public spaces in parks, squares, and residential blocks. It was a significant part of the Bauhaus movement, a highly influential, modernist approach to art and design that also manifested itself in architecture and the design of purposeful buildings centered on integration with the modern city's needs and surroundings.

Using Geddes's urban plan from the early 1930s until the 1950s, the White City came into being. Designed by architects who had trained and practiced in Europe, the White City reflects modern organic planning principles and ultimately became what UNESCO calls "an outstanding architectural ensemble of the Modern Movement in a new cultural context."

Declared a UNESCO World Heritage Site, the White City can be seen by guided tour, and its buildings are protected structures.

The Rubin Museum

14 Bialik St.; tel. 03/525-5961; www.rubinmuseum. org.il; 10am-3pm Mon. and Wed.-Fri., 10am-8pm Tues., 11am-2pm Sat. and holidays; adult NIS20, senior NIS10, under 18 free

In the heart of old Tel Aviv, The Rubin Museum operates out of the house of famous and popular Israeli modern artist Reuven Rubin, and the four floors house works by Rubin, a reading room, a children's gallery, and changing exhibits of other Israeli artists.

SOUTH TEL AVIV
★ Neve Tzedek

Decades before Tel Aviv was formally established as a city, Neve Tzedek (which means "oasis of justice") had already sprung up in 1887. It is Tel Aviv's oldest neighborhood, and the first one inhabited by Jewish residents. Prominent artists and writers like S. Y. Agnon and Nachum Gutman called Neve Tzedek home during the early 20th century, and it still has a distinctly bohemian, European vibe. It is by far one of the coolest places in the city to stroll around and take in the atmosphere; browse designer boutique stores, crafts shops, and bookstores; and enjoy one of the area's fine cafés or restaurants. The main (very narrow) throughway in Neve Tzedek is Shabazi

Street, an excellent place to see historic Tel Aviv architecture.

NACHUM GUTMAN MUSEUM OF ART

21 Shim'on Rokach St.; tel. 03/516-1970; www. gutmanmuseum.co.il; 10am-4pm Sun.-Thurs., 10am-2pm Fri., 10am-3pm Sat.; entrance fee, NIS24

Start at the Nachum Gutman Museum of Art with its distinctive bright-yellow colonnade fence around a historic house dating to the founding of the neighborhood. The charming, small museum showcases works by Nachum Gutman, a beloved Israeli artist and children's author. You can see hundreds of his illustrations and drawings as well as oil, watercolor, and gouache paintings.

ROKACH HOUSE MUSEUM

36 Shim'on Rokach St.; tel. 03/516-8042; www. rokach-house.co.il; 10am-2pm daily, schedule English tours in advance; NIS10

The Rokach House Museum was built in 1887 and is famous for its domed roof. Now a museum named for Shim'on Rokach, a prominent Jewish public servant and cofounder of Neve Tzedek, the museum focuses on Rokach's notable artist and sculptor granddaughter, Lea Majaro-Mintz. There's also an English video and photographs depicting Neve Tzedek's history.

South Tel Aviv

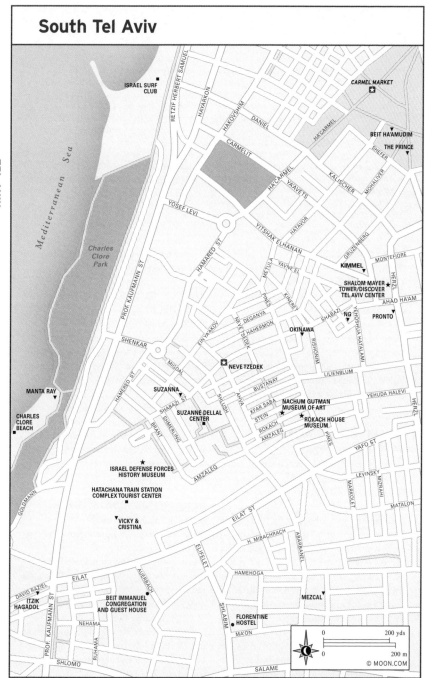

ISRAEL SURF CLUB

RETZIF HERBERT SAMUEL

HAYARKON

HAKOVSHIM

DANIEL

CARMEL MARKET ✪

HACARMEL

BEIT HA'AMUDIM ▼

THE PRINCE

SHEFER

CARMELIT

YOSEF LEVI

HACARMEL

YAAVETS

KALISCHER

MOHALIVER

Mediterranean Sea

Charles Clore Park

PROF. KAUFMANN ST

HAMARED ST

YITSHAK ELHANAN

HATAVOR

GRUZENBERG

MONTEFIORE

KIMMEL ▼

SHALOM MAYER ★ TOWER/DISCOVER TEL AVIV CENTER

HERZL

AHAD HA'AM

PRONTO ▼

METULA

YAVNE'EL

PINES

KINERET

SHABAZI

NG ▼

YEHOSHUA HATALAMI

SHENKAR

NEVE DEGANYA

HAHERMON

OKINAWA ▼

RISHONIM

NEVE TSEDEK

EIN YAAKOV

MIGDAL

HAMERED ST

NEVE TZEDEK ✪

SHLUSH

AHVA

BUSTANAY

LILIENBLUM

MANTA RAY ▼

SUZANNA ▼

SHABAZI ST

SHIMERING

SUZANNE DELLAL CENTER ▪

KFAR SABA

STEIN

ROKACH

AMZALEG

NACHUM GUTMAN ★ MUSEUM OF ART

ROKACH HOUSE MUSEUM ★

YEHUDA HALEVI

HERZL

CHARLES CLORE BEACH ▪

BRANT

AMZALEG

ISRAEL DEFENSE FORCES ★ HISTORY MUSEUM

PINES

YAFO ST

HATACHANA TRAIN STATION COMPLEX TOURIST CENTER

LEVINSKY

MARKOLET

MIZRAHI

MATALON

VICKY & CRISTINA ▼

EILAT ST

H. MIBACHRACH

ABARBANEL

HAMEHOGA

GOLDMANN

EILAT

EILFELET

DAVID RAZIEL

ITZIK HAGADOL ▪

PROF. KAUFMANN ST

AUERBACH

BEIT IMMANUEL CONGREGATION AND GUEST HOUSE ●

SHLAIM

MEZCAL ▼

FLORENTINE HOSTEL ●

NEHAMA

RUHAMA

MA'ON

SHLOMO

SALAME

0   200 yds
0   200 m

© MOON.COM

Shalom Mayer Tower

9 Ahad Ha'am St.; tel. 03/510-0337; www.
migdalshalom.co.il/eng; 8am-7pm Sun.-Thurs.,
8am-2pm Fri. and holidays; free

An interesting stop for art enthusiasts, the Shalom Mayer Tower has a spacious, modern layout that includes exhibits in the lobby and a first-floor **art gallery.** It is one of the largest nonprofit art galleries in Israel. Works include pieces from contemporary Israeli painters, sculptors, and photographers and a dozen permanent and alternating exhibits from Israel's best museums.

DISCOVER TEL AVIV CENTER

9 Ahad Ha'am St.; for tours email tiki@
discover-telaviv.co.il; 10am-5pm Sun.-Thurs.; free

The tower also houses the Discover Tel Aviv Center on the ground floor with an interactive multimedia display about Tel Aviv's development, history, and famous residents. It depicts the history of the city through paintings and photographs and offers professionally guided tours in Tel Aviv and throughout Israel.

Israel Defense Forces History Museum

Shimtat Shlush St. at the corner of Ashkelon St.; tel.
03/517-2913; toldot_zahal_museum@mailto.mod.gov.
il; 8:30am-3:30pm Sun.-Thurs.; free

A good option for military history buffs and those who want to know a bit more about the Israeli military in particular, the Israel Defense Forces History Museum depicts the history of the Israeli army from 1948 through today. With a bunker-like exterior, the museum is spread out through five buildings and includes extensive outdoor pavilions with exhibits that comprise films, photographs, maps, historic documents, and authentic tanks, cars, and weapons.

EASTERN TEL AVIV

Azrieli Observatory and Azrieli Center

132 Menachem Begin Rd., 3rd Fl. designated elevator;
tel. 03/608-1990; http://mitzpe49.co.il/home; adult
NIS22, senior and child NIS17

The highest observation point in the Middle East is the Azrieli Observatory on the 49th floor of Azrieli Center, a multilevel mall with a train stop and multiplex cinema. The observatory, located in the center's round tower, has a commanding view of the coastline from Gedera in the south to Hadera in the north of Tel Aviv. Some vantage points are only accessible from the bar and restaurant, often closed for private events. It makes for a good sunset visit in combination with a trip to the mall in the same building, or drinks and dinner at the 2C Restaurant on the same floor.

★ Sarona

3 Kalman Magen St.; tel. 03/624-2424; http://
saronamarket.co.il/en; 9am-11pm Sun.-Thurs.,
8am-6pm Fri.

Conceived as a renewed cultural center of the city, Sarona is part popular village-like gathering place, part high-end food market. Designed to emulate ventures such as Eataly in New York City, Sarona is an open-air commercial center in the midst of a residential area. A former German Templer colony, Sarona was created from 37 renovated Templar-era buildings that were converted into upscale modern shopping and dining venues and art galleries. The ample public space features live street music, and tours are offered at the visitor's center. Nestled among lower-rise buildings, it is the perfect spot to get the old and new of Tel Aviv, with a clear view of the distinctive Azrieli Center high-rise building and tree-lined paths for a stroll on the way to have a drink or dinner outdoors.

A good place to start is the **Visitor's Center** (14 Alber Mendler St.), which will help guide you through the restoration work done on the area and some of the history of Tel Aviv and the general area through its exhibitions. Maps of the area will also get you oriented, and you can check about available tours.

Helena Rubinstein Pavilion for Contemporary Art

6 Tarsat Blvd.; tel. 03/528-7196; www.tamuseum.org.
il; 10am-6pm Mon.-Thurs., 10am-2pm Fri.; NIS10

Part of the Tel Aviv Museum of Art, the Helena Rubinstein Pavilion for Contemporary

Art is home to contemporary art by Israeli and international artists. In addition to changing exhibits, the upper level houses permanent exhibits of porcelain and glassware artwork. The building is part of Tel Aviv's so-called "culture square" that includes the Habima Theater and the Bronfman Auditorium.

Tel Aviv Museum of Art

27 Shaul HaMelech Blvd.; tel. 03/607-7020; www. tamuseum.org.il; 10am-6pm Mon., Wed., and Sat., 10am-9pm Tues. and Thurs., 10am-2pm Fri.; adult NIS50, senior NIS25, under 18 free

Opened in 1932 in the home of Tel Aviv's first mayor, Meir Dizengoff, and since moved to a distinctive, futuristic-looking building, the Tel Aviv Museum of Art hosts a vast collection of art from the 16th century through modern times, including contemporary Israeli art. Made up of a main building, a new wing opened in 2011, an art education center, and a sculpture garden, this vast art museum hosts at least half a million visitors a year. The old masters collection is on par with European museums, and in general there is a surprising array of pieces in both the permanent and changing exhibits.

JAFFA (YAFO)

The port city of Jaffa (Yafo) is believed to be one of the most ancient cities in the world. An area with a strong Arab flavor, Jaffa is an important part of a visit to Tel Aviv. It is directly adjacent to the rest of the city and easy to reach by bus or car. It is full of charming, interesting sights, restaurants, and shopping. For a scenic route to reach Jaffa, walk on the paved beachfront boardwalk at Charles Clore Park and cross the pedestrian bridge that is the unofficial boundary between Tel Aviv (the new city) and Jaffa (the old city).

1: Neve Tzedek neighborhood **2:** Tel Aviv Museum of Art **3:** Old Town Hall **4:** old town and port of Jaffa

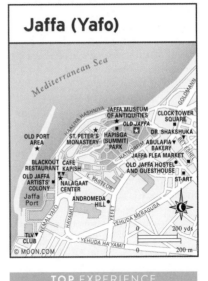

TOP EXPERIENCE

★ Old Jaffa

Old Jaffa (access through the promenade or off Yefet St.) is contained largely near the port on a hill overlooking the Mediterranean and has numerous corners to explore. You'll find archaeological sites here, but also upscale shops, some of the best fine dining in Tel Aviv, an artists' quarter, renovated Ottoman-era houses, and several important landmarks.

Start on the east side of Old Jaffa at **Clock Tower Square,** which is a popular meeting place and home to the **clock tower,** built in 1901 by Turkish Sultan Abed-el-Hamid II and one of Jaffa's most easily recognizable sites. Here you will also find the **former governor's house** and a jailhouse used by the Turks and British known as the **Kishle.** The plaza area is encircled by several galleries, restaurants, and souvenir shops, and you can hear free concerts here during the summer.

ABULAFIA BAKERY

7 Yefet St.; tel. 03/681-2340; NIS20

On Yefet Street in the immediate vicinity is the famous Abulafia Bakery, which also runs a 24-hour street bakery nearby.

VISITORS CENTER

Clock Tower Square; tel. 03/603-7686; www.
oldjaffa.co.il; 10am-5pm Sun.-Thurs., 10am-3pm Fri.,
10am-5pm Sat. Nov.-Mar.; 9am-7pm Sun.-Thurs.,
9am-4pm Fri., 9am-7pm Sat. Apr.-Oct.

In the Clock Tower Square is the Visitors
Center, a good place to get started. It is also
an archaeological site and a museum about
the area's history. The Visitors Center is
in an underground building that includes
exhibits of archaeological ruins from the
Hellenistic and Roman eras and three-
dimensional illustrations of Jaffa's legends
and historical events of the past 2,000 years.
There are also eight paintings done over the
past 300 years of Jaffa from the perspective
of the sea. The Visitors Centers' light and
sound show tells the story of the past and
present of the Old City.

JAFFA MUSEUM OF ANTIQUITIES

10 Mifrats Shlomo St.; tel. 03/682-5375; www.
oldjaffa.co.il; 4pm-8pm Mon.-Wed., 4pm-9pm Thurs.,
10am-4pm Fri.-Sat.; NIS30

Along **Mifrats Shlomo Promenade** you
will find a large structure that is historically and architecturally unique and made
up of several historical buildings, built
over Crusader-era remnants. Dating to the
18th century, it has served as the seat of
the Ottoman governor, a post office, and a
guard house. A well-known Christian family by the name of Demiani bought part of
the building in 1733 and converted it into a
successful soap factory. Abandoned during
Israel's War of Independence, it now houses
the Jaffa Museum of Antiquities with permanent exhibits on archaeology and changing exhibits on modern art. It is small and
comprehensive enough to be informative but
not exhausting.

ST. PETER'S MONASTERY

1 Mifrats Shlomo St. next to Clock Tower Square; tel.
03/682-2871; 8am-noon and 3pm-6pm daily Apr.-Oct.,
8am-noon and 3pm-5pm daily Nov.-Mar.; free

Built over medieval fortress remains and
the ruins of a Byzantine church, St. Peter's
Monastery is a Franciscan church from the beginning of the 20th century. It features a unique
brick facade and towering belfry that overlooks
the sea from where it sits at the top of Jaffa
mound. The iconic building's silhouette is visible from the southern end of Tel Aviv, and the
picturesque view is frequently photographed.
The location has been a center for Christianity
for thousands of years, and it is believed that
Napoleon once stayed here. The church has
a spectacular interior with a vaulted ceiling,
stained glass windows, and marble walls.

Old Port

From Jaffa's Clock Tower Square, you can
find small, winding streets leading down to
the Old Port area, one of the most ancient
ports in the world. The Bible's Book of Jonah
mentions Jaffa's port; Napoleon's army destroyed it in 1799, and it was later rebuilt by
the Ottomans. The port has served as the
main point of entry for thousands of Jewish
immigrants, and it has boating excursions
and good seafood restaurants. The main
hangars were restored to house art galleries,
cafés, restaurants, and shops.

THE NALAGAAT CENTER

Retsif Haaliya Hashniya at Jaffa Port; tel.
03/633-0808; www.nalagaat.org.il; call for
reservations

A highly popular draw is the startling and unusual Nalagaat Center. It is an artistic complex
operated by the deaf and blind community,
complete with a unique restaurant and café.

Entertainment and Events

PERFORMING ARTS, VISUAL ARTS, AND CULTURAL CENTERS

City Center

LEV DIZENGOFF

50 Dizengoff St., Dizengoff Center Mall; tel. 03/621-2222; www.lev.co.il/en; NIS40

An easy cinema to reach is Lev Dizengoff. Most movie theaters in Israel will have some mainstream movies in English with Hebrew subtitles.

BEIT LESSIN THEATER

101 Dizengoff St.; tel. 03/725-5333; www.lessin.co.il

The country's second largest theater, Beit Lessin Theater was founded in the early 1980s as a club for Israel's Workers Union. It is home to Israel's annual **New Israeli Drama Festival** called Open Stage. Numerous award-winning playwrights have shown their work at Beit Lessin or have been discovered on the venue's stage.

South Tel Aviv

SUZANNE DELLAL CENTER

5 Yehieli St.; tel. 03/510-5656; www.suzannedellal.org.il

A centerpiece of the famed Neve Tzedek bohemian neighborhood is the Suzanne Dellal Center, recipient of the prestigious Israel Prize and home to modern and experimental productions and top Israeli dance troupes. The carefully restored older buildings that make up the center play host to events, festivals, performances, a restaurant and coffee shop, and a large outer piazza.

Eastern Tel Aviv

TEL AVIV PERFORMING ARTS CENTER

19 Shaul HaMelech Blvd.; tel. 03/692-7777; www.israel-opera.co.il

The Tel Aviv Performing Arts Center is home to the Israeli Opera and the Israel Ballet. It offers a wide variety of operatic performances for all ages, and hosts other varied performances almost nightly, year-round. It is particularly known for its dance performances by the Israel Ballet and the international performers and festivals it brings in throughout the year.

Z.O.A. HOUSE

1 Daniel Frisch St.; tel. 03/695-9341; http://zoatlv. co.il; 9am-11:30pm daily

The Z.O.A. House is a charming mixture of cinema, theater, café, and history. With construction that was started in the presence of Israel's first prime minister, David Ben-Gurion, the Zionist Organization of America House now holds a movie theater, a theater for stage, and a ground-floor café that is reputed to serve some of the best cappuccinos in all of Tel Aviv. There is a surprising array of performances that range from old Shakespeare classics to folk performances that are done in Yiddish.

There are several movie cinemas in the city; you can find current listings by searching online or buying an English newspaper.

TMUNA THEATRE

8 Shonzino St.; tel. 03/561-1211; www.tmu-na.org.il; tickets vary

The Tmuna Theatre is a community theater that hosts a variety of stage performances including plays, performing arts showcases, live music, literature, and fine art that are considered less mainstream and often fringe. Tmuna hosts over 550 theater shows, 80 dance performances, 270 music events, and 50 literature and poetry nights every year.

CAMERI THEATRE

19 Shaul HaMelech Blvd.; tel. 03/606-0960; www.cameri.co.il

Part of one of Tel Aviv's largest cultural complexes is the renowned Cameri Theatre. The theater puts on Israeli and classic plays, musicals, concerts, and modern theater.

HABIMA THEATER

19 Leonardo da Vinci; tel. 03/526-6666; www. habima.co.il

The Habima Theater is Israel's national theater and was rebuilt and reopened in 2009. All productions are in Hebrew, but you can call ahead for productions that are translated simultaneously into English.

ART AND PHOTOGRAPHY GALLERIES
Eastern Tel Aviv
URBAN GALLERY

72 and 74 Ben Yehuda St.; tel. 03/524-4110; www. urbangallery972.com; 9am-8pm Mon.-Thurs., 9am-3pm Fri., 9am-8pm Sun.; free

The Urban Gallery has two locations in Tel Aviv and one in Jaffa and specializes in classic and contemporary Israeli and international art. It is also home to a large selection of works by famed Israeli artist Menashe Kadishman, known for his offbeat paintings of sheep.

ROTHSCHILD FINE ART GALLERY

48 Yehuda Halevi St.; tel. 052/372-9431; www. rgfineart.com; 11am-6:30pm Mon.-Thurs., 11am-2pm Fri.-Sat.; free

Very near the center of town and easily accessible, the Rothschild Fine Art Gallery features a range of fine art by various Israeli and international artists and displays mostly paintings.

GORDON GALLERY OF CONTEMPORARY ART

5 Hazerem St. and 6 Hapelech St.; tel. 03/529-0011; www.gordongallery.co.il; 11am-6pm Mon.-Thurs., 10am-2pm Fri., 10am-1pm Sat., by appointment Sun.; free

The internationally known Gordon Gallery of Contemporary Art was established in 1966 and became home to Israel's first auction house in 1977. Their new location in South Tel Aviv opened in 2018 on Hapelech

Street, and is open by appointment only. The nearby Hazerem St. location focuses on newer Israeli artists. The gallery has published two of the most respected and authoritative art books in Israel. Today it emphasizes exhibitions of photography, works by top contemporary Israeli artists, and several permanent exhibitions.

ZALMANIA PRI-OR PHOTO HOUSE

5 Tchernichovski St.; tel. 03/517-7916; zalmania@ gmail.com; 10am-6pm Sun.-Thurs., 10am-1pm Fri.; free

The Zalmania Pri-Or Photo House is home to one of the largest and most important private photography archives in Israel with a collection of historical photographs and over one million negatives. It was established in 1940 by photographer Rudi Weissenstein, who documented the creation of the State of Israel.

SHPILMAN INSTITUTE FOR PHOTOGRAPHY

27 Shoken St., 3rd Fl.; tel. 03/728-3737; 10am-2pm Sun.-Thurs.; free

At the heart of the Tel Aviv art scene is the Shpilman Institute for Photography, a major modern photography institute with a vast exhibition space. The institute hosts lectures and exhibits by a range of international photographers.

Jaffa (Yafo)
ST-ART

3 Rabbi Pinkhas St.; tel. 03/516-9599; www.st-art. co.il; 9:30am-6pm Sun.-Thurs., 10am-2pm Fri.; free

An incubator project for Israeli artists, ST-ART supports mostly young graduates of Israel's leading art schools. It features largely contemporary Israeli art from 1986 onward.

OLD JAFFA ARTISTS' COLONY

Yefet St. in Jaffa Old Port area, free tour every Wed. at 10am, starts at Visitors Center office in Old Jaffa's Clock Tower Square; tel. 03/603-7700

The Old Jaffa Artists' Colony is a collection of several independent spaces centered around the port area of the Old City.

1: Tel Aviv Performing Arts Center **2:** the garden of Suzanne Dellal Center

FESTIVALS AND EVENTS

Spring

WHITE CITY MUSIC FESTIVAL

Hangar 11 at the Port of Tel Aviv; tel. 03/602-0888;
May; ticket packages from NIS2,500

Tel Aviv comes alive with festivals and events in the spring. The new White City Music Festival features major international and Israeli acts covering a range of musical genres including jazz, funk, rock and roll, and ethnic world music.

TASTE OF TEL AVIV FOOD FESTIVAL

HaYarkon Park; tel. 03/642-2828; www.park.co.il;
8pm-midnight for three days in May; free entry

The Taste of Tel Aviv Food Festival is the largest food festival in the country.

FELICJA BLUMENTHAL INTERNATIONAL MUSIC FESTIVAL

Tel Aviv Museum of Art, 27 Shaul HaMelech Blvd.; tel.
03/620-1185; NIS45 and upward per show

Also in May is the Felicja Blumenthal International Music Festival, a week-long classical array including chamber music, orchestras, solo ensembles, and folk music. Running since 1999, it's known for staging the debut of many Israeli artists who have gone on to become famous.

CULTURE OF PEACE FESTIVAL

Tzavta Theater, 30 Ibn Gabirol St.; tel. 03/695-0156;
www.havatzelet.org.il under project; three days in
May; prices vary

The only festival of its kind in the Middle East, the annual Culture of Peace Festival includes Jewish, Muslim, and Christian traditional music.

Summer

OPERA IN THE PARK

HaYarkon Park; tel. 03/692-7782; www.israel-opera.
co.il under Special Events; from 9pm in July; free

The months of June through August are action-packed in Israel and Tel Aviv. The popular Opera in the Park showcases performances by the renowned Israeli Opera. Typical crowds to the opera performances are about 80,000 or more from all across Israel, so go early and take a taxi or bus.

TEL AVIV PRIDE PARADE

www.gaytelavivguide.com; early June

The famous Tel Aviv Pride Parade hosts more than 50 events throughout the weeklong festival (which is basically one big nonstop party), finishing with the Gay Pride Parade. The parade starts at Meir Park and usually finishes near or at Gordon Beach.

TEL AVIV-YAFO'S WHITE NIGHT

www.tel-aviv.gov.il; June

The annual Tel Aviv-Yafo's White Night festival is a celebration of UNESCO's 2003 recognition of Tel Aviv's Bauhaus White City as a World Heritage Site. The one-night festival features dozens of simultaneous indoor and outdoor events throughout the city, including music, art, dance, sports, workshops, and parades.

Fall

INTERNATIONAL PHOTOGRAPHY FESTIVAL

locations vary; www.photoisrael.org; Oct.; buy tickets
*by dialing *8780 from Israel or go to www.leaan.co.il;*
NIS39 and up

As the weather cools down, so do events. There are still some nice picks, including the International Photography Festival, a gathering of a couple hundred Israeli and international photographers for a week of workshops and events.

LOVING ART MAKING ART

www.tel-aviv.gov.il; Sept. just before Sukkot; free

An annual event that marks the opening of Tel Aviv's gallery season, the Loving Art Making Art festival is a three-day event that is part of Tel Aviv Art Year. Sixty galleries, museums, and exhibition spaces open to the public for free, leading Israeli artists join in street exhibits, and there are artists' workshops and alternative art spaces.

NIKE NIGHT RUN

start at Rabin Square, spectators and supporters
gather near the intersection of Ibn Gabirol St.
and Rokach Blvd.; www.tlvnightrun.co.il; run from
8pm-10:30pm; Oct.; NIS120-180

The Nike Night Run is a 10K night run from Rabin Square in Tel Aviv's City Center to Tel Aviv North Sportek. About 15,000-20,000 runners have participated in recent years.

Winter

TEL AVIV FASHION WEEK

HaTachana or First Station, main train platform-
performance area; http://fashionweektelaviv.com;
Nov.

Israel's official Tel Aviv Fashion Week includes receptions, parties, and fashion shows featuring some of the best Israeli designers from the country's lively fashion scene. An alternative fashion week also started running in recent years.

PIANO FESTIVAL

Various halls around Tel Aviv; tel. 03/762-6666;
http://pianofestival.co.il; Nov.

Piano Festival has programming completely in Hebrew but features some big names among Israeli pianists.

INTERNATIONAL EXPOSURE

Suzanne Dellal Center, 5 Yehieli St.; tel. 03/510-5656;
www.suzannedellal.org.il; Dec.; tickets vary

International Exposure showcases Israeli contemporary dance over the course of several days, with most performances at the Suzanne Dellal Center in Neve Tzedek.

JAZZ FESTIVAL

Tel Aviv Cinematheque; tel. 03/606-0800; tlv.
jazzfest@gmail.com; Feb.; prices vary

The annual Jazz Festival has been running for about 25 years and hosts jazz musicians from throughout Israel and the world.

Shopping

Shopping in Tel Aviv is all about what kind of shopping you want to do, because every option under the sun is available. Beyond the common souvenir shops, you can find everything from outdoor markets to the showrooms of Israeli designers.

SHOPPING DISTRICTS

North Tel Aviv

Connecting Ibn Gabirol and Dizengoff Streets is **Basel Street,** a popular shopping and hangout area. The heart of the area is **Basel Square,** where you will find some of Tel Aviv's coolest boutique clothing stores. Start at about 34 Basel Street and work your way up or down the block. The farther north you go on Dizengoff Street in North Tel Aviv, the more expensive and fancier the designer boutiques, wedding-gown stores, high-end clothing, jewelry, and shoe stores get.

PORT OF TEL AVIV

northernmost end of HaYarkon St.; tel. 03/544-1505;
www.namal.co.il

The retail stores at the Port of Tel Aviv are on the large side and are mostly chains, with a good selection of sporting goods items. The prices are on the high end, but they are also high-quality and include domestic name brands such as Fox, Shilav, and others. Aside from sports-related items, you can find smaller items like shoes and jewelry.

City Center

Parallel to Dizengoff Street is **Bugrashov Street,** which is known for its offbeat and trendy fashion stores and selection of cafés.

Adjacent to Carmel Market, just one street parallel to the east is **Nahalat Binyamin Street,** which has a stretch of cafés, shops, and bars that runs from Allenby Street south into the **Florentin** neighborhood. Florentin has a mixture of hip designer shops, cafés, and housewares stores.

South Tel Aviv

Unquestionably one of the best places in Tel Aviv for window-shopping is the old European-inspired neighborhood of **Neve Tzedek** (approx. Shabazi St. and north of Jaffa St. between Brant St. and Pines St.), with its high-end shops selling boutique jewelry, antiques, oriental rugs, clothing, and books.

Just a bit southeast of Neve Tzedek across the main drag of Jaffa Street is the neighborhood of **Florentin** (south of Jaffa St. and west of Hertsel St.), which was established in 1927 by Jews who emigrated from Greece. Today it is known as a hangout for hipsters and is full of upper-crust furniture and designer stores.

HATACHANA

between Neve Tzedek and the sea, parking entrance at HaMered St. at the corner of Kaufmann St.; www.hatachana.co.il; 10am-10pm Mon.-Sat., pubs, cafés, and restaurants open until midnight or last customer on Fri.

Due west from Florentin is the **Menashiya,** where you'll find the unique shopping experience of HaTachana, a hip shopping center with restaurants and cafés located at the Old Train Station Compound. The open space has incorporated elements from the original train station that opened in 1892. You can still see partial train tracks, cars, and freight terminals. You can find unique souvenirs at the **Made in TLV** (tel. 03/510-4333) emporium and boutiques. On Thursdays (7pm-midnight), it hosts Israeli designers and artists for an open-air trade show that includes DJ music.

OUTDOOR, OPEN-AIR, AND FARMERS MARKETS

North Tel Aviv

PORT MARKET

Tel Aviv Hangar 12 at the Port of Tel Aviv; tel. 03/544-1505; www.namal.co.il; 8am-8pm Mon.-Sat.

For a down-to-earth experience outdoors at the port, the Port Market features two levels of foodstuffs for sale. The emphasis is on the "slow food" movement, and options include organic cheese, handmade pasta, gelato, and more.

FARMERS MARKET

Port of Tel Aviv; 7am-3pm Fri.

Every Friday there is an open-air Farmers Market at the port, expanding the variety of delicious choices.

City Center

★ CARMEL MARKET

entrance to the market is on Allenby St.; www.shuktlv.co.il; 8am-dark Sun.-Thurs., 8am-2pm Fri.

Tel Aviv's most well-known open-air market is Carmel Market, named after its location on HaCarmel Street, between Magen David Square at the intersection of King George, Sheinkin, Nahalat Binyamin, and Allenby Streets, and also at HaKovshim Garden and the Carmelit bus terminal. It's an outstanding place to experience the local culture and buy fresh produce. Full of everything from spices to dry goods to clothing, the market is within walking distance of the beach. Vendors call out what they are selling by singing out unique songs, and you can buy everything from freshly squeezed juice to fresh-cut flowers.

There is a wide variety of things in the market to distract and amuse, including street musicians. But the best finds are farther inside the main entrances where there are tons of side alleys selling fresh fish, fruit, vegetables, and exotic spices and nuts.

Eastern Tel Aviv

LEVINSKI MARKET

Levinski St. in Florentin; tel. 054/226-8089; 8am-6pm Sun.-Thurs., 8am-4:30pm Fri.

The spices, nuts, and dried fruits of the Levinski Market make it a popular place for

1: pomegranates at Carmel Market **2:** *knafe* and baklava stall at Carmel Market **3:** antique shop in Old Jaffa

כנאפה חם
הכנה במקום

Knafeh is an Arab cuisine's
sweet pastry,
made from noodles
and goat cheese,
served hot

shopping for special treats. It's also the perfect place to do some last-minute souvenir shopping.

FLEA MARKETS
North Tel Aviv
ARTISTS' AND COLLECTORS' FAIR
Port of Tel Aviv, on the pier; 10am-6pm Sat.
The Artists' and Collectors' Fair is a weekly flea market overlooking the Mediterranean. It's a good place to find locally made arts and crafts including jewelry and small trinkets. When you're done perusing the market, enjoy the good selection of restaurants nearby.

Jaffa (Yafo)
JAFFA FLEA MARKET
east of the clock tower at the southern end of Old Jaffa, intersection of Olei Zion St. and Jerusalem Blvd.; 10am-6pm Sun.-Thurs., 10am-2pm Fri.
Probably the most fun you'd have shopping in Jaffa would be at the Jaffa Flea Market, with its combination of junk and unique finds, including copper, antiques, Persian tiles and rugs, and Judaica. Considered one of the major attractions of Old Jaffa, the flea market also has a number of cafés and pubs. During the summer, there's live music on Thursday evenings.

WEEKLY FAIRS AND TRADE MARKETS
City Center
DIZENGOFF CENTER FOOD FAIR
intersection of King George St. and Dizengoff St., North Building B, ground floor; tel. 03/621-2400, ext. 3003; www.dizengof-center.co.il/en; noon-8pm Thurs., 10am-4pm Fri.
On Thursdays and Fridays, Dizengoff Center hosts a popular international food fair for a chance to try a variety of dishes.

FASHIONABLY LATE
Dizengoff Square at intersection of Pinsker St. and Dizengoff St.; 4pm-11pm Thurs.; tel. 050/444-6861
Fashionably Late designer market is an open-air showcase of independent designers who put their work out in Dizengoff Square.

DIZENGOFF SQUARE VINTAGE AND ANTIQUES MARKET
next to Dizengoff Square at Dizengoff and Reines Sts.; noon-10pm Tues., 7am-4pm Fri.
Dizengoff Square Vintage and Antiques Market features vendors selling clothes, accessories, books, and arts and crafts.

A section of Nahalat Binyamin Street that runs parallel to Carmel Market is open to foot traffic only and has an outdoor **craft fair** (10am-5pm Tues. and Fri.). Vendors sell wooden toys, jewelry, Judaica, photography, and trinkets of all kinds amid street performers.

SHOPPING MALLS
City Center
DIZENGOFF CENTER
50 Dizengoff St., near the intersection with King George St.; tel. 03/621-2400; www.dizengof-center. co.il; 8am-10pm daily
With hundreds of stores, Dizengoff Center straddles two sides of Dizengoff Street and is connected by underground passageways and an overhead bridge. It is the oldest mall in town, and hosts an odd mixture of high-end stores, cafés, and lower-end bargain shops that sell cheap goods; it also has two cinemas. Some stores in the center are closed on Shabbat. It is a good place to visit if you need clothing, makeup, and computer supplies.

Eastern Tel Aviv
AZRIELI MALL
132 Menachem Begin Rd.; tel. 03/608-1179; 10am-10pm Sun.-Thurs., 10am-4pm Fri., and 8pm-midnight Sat.
Azrieli Mall is a huge, multilevel mall that includes a train station stop, a multiplex cinema, and every type of store you can imagine, from domestic chains such as Golf to international brands such as Gap. Convenient and well laid out, it includes coffee shop chains that are located throughout Israel (such as Aroma), cafés, and stands for manicures and pedicures. You can also easily travel from the mall by train or bus to and from other parts of the city.

The Heart of Israel's Fashion Industry

One of Israel's most surprising assets is its creative and daring fashion industry. Locally grown designers use creative tactics and approaches to create elegant and extremely well-made clothing, shoes, bags, and accessories. Though only a lucky few Israeli designers have managed to go international, the range of items available inside of Israel is incredible.

The hallmark of Israeli fashion is simple and chic designs that feature minimal trimmings or flourishes. The designers let the materials speak for themselves, whether it's a leather handbag or an evening dress. Israeli jewelry is also extremely unique and can be found throughout the country.

Some of the more well-known designers include Lia, Gazelle, D and A, Liat Ginzburg, Sasson Kedem, Yosef, and Zaya by Avital Coorsh. Israel's technological advances have led to the creation of cutting-edge ultrasonic bonding equipment that cuts and seals fabric pieces without sewing a stitch. The method, called seamless construction, has put Israel on the map in the intimate-apparel industry sector.

Boutique stores that sell almost exclusively Israeli designers can be found throughout the country, everywhere from trendy shopping districts to major shopping malls. Just ask shop owners selling more upscale clothing and accessories if they have any items by Israeli designers, and the answer will likely be yes. Many stores are extremely supportive and proud of local designers and will choose to sell their products over imported items.

Tel Aviv is Israel's fashion center, and every year it hosts two international fashion week shows in the fall (a result of an industry-splintered professional relationship). Tel Aviv Fashion Week and Gindi TLV Fashion Week are within one month of each other.

Local designer shops are changing constantly, but former fashion industry professional **Galit Reismann** (tel. 054/814-1499, www.tlvstyle.com, tour rates vary based on size of group and length) takes customers on half-day tours (3-5 hours) with personal introductions to designers and personalized shopping experiences.

GAN HA'IR

71 Ibn Gabirol St.; tel. 03/527-9111; most shops 9am-9pm Sun.-Thurs. and 9am-2pm Fri.

On the more exclusive side is Gan Ha'ir, a high-end mall centered around an open courtyard. Gan Ha'ir has a number of expensive stores that attract some of Tel Aviv's more sophisticated customers. You can find stores selling food, books, shoes, toys, and children's clothing. Inside the mall is a popular Hungarian café called Yehudith's and the rooftop Enav Cultural Center, where lectures, exhibits, concerts, and plays are often held.

Sports and Recreation

Tel Aviv's location on the sea and its sweltering summer days make it an incredibly active place after the sun goes down. Residents are known for showing a lot of skin, being somewhat image-conscious, and staying in shape, which makes for a lot of sporting options. For more low-key options like outdoor hangout space, you'll find some of the largest and most well-designed parks in the country.

PARKS

Dizengoff Square

intersection of Pinsker St. and Dizengoff St.; 24 hours daily; free

One of the most easily recognizable landmarks in Tel Aviv, Dizengoff Square is a broad, split-level plaza at the center of the White City with a distinct raised platform above street level and a multicolored fountain in the center. It's a great place to stroll, people watch, catch live street performers, and take in the overall atmosphere of this part of Tel Aviv. It's a great landmark to learn early on to help get your bearings.

Rabin Square

69 Ibn Gabirol St., south of City Hall; 24 hours daily; free

On November 4, 1995, Prime Minister Yitzhak Rabin was shot and killed by a Jewish assassin upon leaving a mass rally supporting the peace process. After his death, the location of the rally and assassination was renamed Rabin Square, and it still serves as a major staging ground for peace rallies, public music events, and annual book fairs. The **Yitzhak Rabin Memorial** (northeast corner on Ibn Gabirol St.) displays 16 basalt rocks from the Golan Heights sunk into the ground as a symbol of Rabin's roots and bond with Israel.

Meir Park

35 King George St.; 24 hours daily; free

Featuring a fishpond with floating flora, a dog run, and huge, old trees, Meir Park is a green sanctuary. It is also home to Tel Aviv's gay community center, which often hosts lectures, sports events, and potlucks. It's a popular spot for daytime group hangouts.

★ HaYarkon Park

Port of Tel Aviv and North Tel Aviv at Rokach Blvd.; tel. 03/642-2828 or 03/642-0541; www.park.co.il/en, www.parkfun.co.il; 24 hours daily; free

Among Tel Aviv's jewels, HaYarkon Park stretches about 1,000 acres (4 square km) west to east from the Port of Tel Aviv to the neighboring city of Ramat Gan. The eastern side of the park extends into a huge circular pattern and includes a large artificial lake, a 5-acre (20,000-square-meter) **tropical garden** with a microclimate and orchids, and a 10-acre (40,000-square-meter) enclosed **rock garden** (10am-2:30pm Sun.-Thurs., 10am-1:30pm Fri., 10am-3:30pm Sat.), a showcase of Israel's geology and 3,500 species of plants, including 6 acres (24,300 square meters) of cacti alone.

On the banks of the Yarkon, **Ten Mills** (east Yarkon promenade) is a group of old flour mills that operated for centuries, some of them as recently as the 1920s. The mills are situated on landscaped paths near a wooden bridge and an old dam. The Yarkon River cuts through the park to the Mediterranean, and it is divided into several sections.

An elongated section on the eastern side of the park is perfect for long walks, especially in the late evenings because it is well-lit and active. There are two connecting bridges (the Ibn Gabirol Bridge on the west and the Derech Namir Bridge on the east). Both sides of the river have bicycle and walking paths.

SPORTEK

Yarkon River north bank; tel. 03/699-0307; 6:30am-10pm daily; prices vary based on activity

In this section, on the north side of the river is Sportek, a sprawling collection of sports centers and playgrounds with tennis, volleyball, and basketball courts, baseball and soccer fields, inline skating courts (with equipment for rent), bungee and trampoline jumping, and an Olympic climbing wall.

ZAPARI

tel. 03/642-2888; call ahead for hours; NIS50

Near the lake is Zapari, a 7.5-acre (30,000-square-meter) oasis of tropical plant life, including banana trees. Zapari is home to a variety of exotic reptiles and birds from around the world, a swan lake with tropical fish and waterfalls, parrots, and a re-creation of a traditional African village.

The park hosts concerts and is home to two outdoor concert venues, **Wohl Amphitheater** (tel. 03/521-8210) and **Theater in the Park** (tel. 03/642-2828).

LUNA AMUSEMENT PARK

Merkaz Hayeridim, enter from southern Rokach Blvd. across from HaYarkon Park; tel. 03/642-7080; 10am-8pm Sat. and holidays; NIS80

Just on the edges of the park's eastern side is Luna Amusement Park, with a variety of rides for a wide range of ages.

MEYMADION WATER PARK

near Ramat Gan stadium on the eastern side of parking lot across from Luna Amusement Park; tel. 03/642-2777; www.meymadion.co.il; generally 9am-8pm daily but hours and open days vary, Apr.-early Oct.; NIS99, after 1pm NIS85

Spread out over 25 acres (102,000 square meters) is the popular and well-equipped Meymadion Water Park, which is the largest water park in Israel. Park features include water slides, pools for different ages, and a wave pool.

Hapisga (Summit) Park

Named for its location on the summit of Jaffa mound overlooking the sea, Hapisga Park (far southern end of promenade) is famed for its vista of Tel Aviv and the shoreline. In August the park's amphitheater hosts evening concerts, and the Zodiac Bridge is a place to make wishes according to your astrological sign.

Ha'atzmaut (Independence) Park

240 HaYarkon St.

The massive coastal Independence Park is just under half a mile (0.8 km) long and full of open spaces with breathtaking views of the sea, gay-community-friendly, and often used as a gathering spot. The southern end of the park abuts the Marina and is the access point for Nordau and Hilton Beaches.

Ramat Gan National Park

At almost 500 acres (2 square km), the Ramat Gan National Park (access through Ahad Ha'Am St.) is full of lawns, walking and riding paths, a lake with an artificial waterfall, and a Parisian-style garden.

SAFARI PARK AND ZOO

1 Ha'Tsvi Ave. in Ramat Gan National Park; tel. 03/630-5328, 03/630-5327, or 03/630-5326; www. safari.co.il; call ahead for hours; adult NIS59, senior NIS52, add NIS7 Safari bus fee for visitors without cars

At the center of Ramat Gan is the Safari Park and Zoo with about 1,600 animals from all over the world, including 68 species of mammals, 130 species of birds, and 25 species of reptiles. Check out Rotem the Sand Cat, a distinct regional species.

BEACHES

The beaches of Tel Aviv can be categorized by the types of crowds they attract and whether they are **official,** with lifeguards and changing facilities, or **unofficial,** without lifeguards or facilities and possibly with more dangerous currents or underwater conditions. Both types are free, but official beaches have some additional services such as lockers and equipment rental that cost money. Some of the prime beachfront is also taken up by outdoor seating for cafés, which will require you to buy something if you use one of their tables or chairs.

Hilton, Mezizim (Sheraton), Gordon, Frishman, Bugrashov, and Jerusalem Beaches all have sand courts available for **volleyball, beach handball,** and **soccer.** Aviv Beach has a designated area for surfing, kayaking, windsurfing, and kiteboarding.

North Tel Aviv
MEZIZIM BEACH

Unofficial; southern end of Nemal Tel Aviv St.

Located just near the Old City port, Mezizim Beach is known for its hip, trendy crowd of beautiful people and can be quite boisterous.

NORDAU BEACH

Official; off Nordau St. and HaYarkon Rd.

Nordau Beach is the city's only religious beach, with separate swimming areas for men and women. It's best to visit only if you are also religious or extremely conservative.

HILTON BEACH

Unofficial; at Jabotinsky St. and HaYarkon St.

In the middle of the service road between Mezizim Beach and the Marina is popular Hilton Beach, which is favored by hippies, surfers for its lights for night surfing, and dog owners and their pooches. It is also popular with Tel Aviv's gay community and has excellent access for people with physical disabilities. It is next to the Hilton Hotel.

★ City Center

A good place to start when visiting Tel Aviv beaches is the **City Center coastline** (tel. 03/724-0340), which runs roughly between Charles Clore Park and the Tel Aviv Marina. Along this stretch of coastline, there are about half a dozen beaches that are easy to access, free, quite clean, and safe.

GORDON BEACH

Official, at J.L. Gordon St. and Herbert Samuel St.

One of the best spots for a little bit of everything is Gordon Beach. Also known as Gordon-Frishman, it is extremely popular for its beach volleyball (even at night), hip beach bars, DJs, central location, and proximity to the Tel Aviv Marina. There are a large number of hotels nearby, shaded covers, public toilets and dressing rooms, sports facilities, cafés and restaurants, and a playground. You can rent lounge chairs and sunbathing beds starting at about NIS50, and there is a water sports area north of the sunbathing area for surfing, windsurfing, and kayaking.

BANANA BEACH

Official; 8 Herbert Samuel St.; tel. 03/510-7958; http://bananabeach.co.il

Hip and full of bustling activity, Banana Beach has options for playing in the sea and dining in style right on the shoreline. Options for refreshments and shade range from restaurants with deck seating to more casual setups with chairs and low tables under some shade right on the sandy beach.

FRISHMAN BEACH AND BUGRASHOV BEACH

Both unofficial; Frishman Beach: Frishman St. and Herbert Samuel St.; Bugrashov Beach: Bugrashov St. and Herbert Samuel St.

Easy to reach and within a four-minute walk of each other, Frishman Beach and Bugrashov Beach both have nearby public restrooms and are close to public transportation.

JERUSALEM BEACH

Official; just across from the Opera Tower at 1 Allenby St.

Close to places to eat and paid parking is Jerusalem Beach, where you can rent sunbathing chairs and lounge chairs. The nearby

one of the many beaches of Tel Aviv

geometric-shaped shopping center that used to be home to the Israel Opera and is built on the site of the first Israeli parliament across the street is a great place to get some air-conditioning if you need a break.

AVIV BEACH
Official; Herbert Samuel St. and Ezra HaSofer St.
Toward the southern end of the beach scene, Aviv Beach is close to the major transportation hub at the Carmelit bus station and paid parking. Aviv Beach is also known as Drummers' Beach for its popularity among drumming circles.

South Tel Aviv
CHARLES CLORE BEACH
Unofficial; at HaMered St. and Kaufman St.; tel. 03/724-0340
Relatively isolated on the southern end of the city is peaceful Charles Clore Beach, tucked into gorgeous, sprawling **Charles Clore Park** (12 Kaufmann St., from the south of the Dolphinarium Beach to Jaffa, http://clorefoundation.org.il) on the border of Jaffa. Popular with dog owners, the beach is near paid parking; a designated area for surfing, windsurfing, and kayaking; and a boardwalk with hotels, restaurants, and clubs. There is no lifeguard. The park has lush lawns, views of the Mediterranean, and access to Charles Clore Beach, and connects Tel Aviv and Jaffa with the promenade.

WATER SPORTS
Swimming
GORDON SWIMMING POOL
14 Eliezer Peri St. at the Tel Aviv Marina; tel. 03/762-3300; www.gordon-pool.co.il; 5am-7pm daily; weekdays NIS45, Sat. NIS50
The Gordon Swimming Pool is an unusual experience with its outdoor Olympic-size swimming pool filled with saltwater. It is heated and open year-round. You can get access to the pool and workout equipment on the beach for an additional fee.

Surfing, Diving, Boating, and Beach Sports
TOPSEA
165 HaYarkon St.; tel. 050/432-9001; www.topsea.co.il; 8am-sunset daily; NIS50 and up for rentals, NIS150 and up for lessons
Topsea is the oldest surfing center in Tel Aviv.

ISRAEL SURF CLUB
5 Herbert Samuel St.; tel. 03/510-3439; http://israelsurfclub.co.il; 8am-8pm daily; NIS100/hour for lessons
The Israel Surf Club near Charles Clore Beach also rents equipment and offers lessons.

DANIEL CENTER
2 Rokach Blvd.; tel. 03/699-0484; www.drc.org.il; 8am-8pm Sun.-Thurs., 8:30am-1pm Fri.
For boating, the Daniel Center in HaYarkon Park gives a free introductory **sea kayaking** lesson.

TEL AVIV DIVING CLUB
145 HaYarkon St.; tel. 054/662-7044; www.divetelaviv.com; 7am-8pm daily; NIS650 including gear rental
A popular water sport throughout Israel, diving has a number of good outfitters in Tel Aviv. The Tel Aviv Diving Club is the best place to start for dive lessons, custom dives, and advice.

ISRAEL SAILING ASSOCIATION
tel. 03/624-1112
For sailing information and recommendations, try the Israel Sailing Association.

BICYCLING
Tel Aviv is a very bicycle-friendly city, and with its miles of boardwalk and relatively flat landscape, it is also an easy place to cycle even if you're not in great shape.

TEL-O-FUN
www.tel-o-fun.co.il/en; NIS17 access fee, first 30 minutes free, and NIS75 for up to 3.5 hours
Aside from renting bikes from a specialty shop, a very simple and cost-effective

Tel Aviv Suburbs

The largely haphazard way that Tel Aviv was planned and grew (aside from the White City) created, by default, suburbs. These suburbs, which include cities such as Ramat Gan in the east, Holon in the south, and Ramat Aviv in the north, were less outgrowths of Tel Aviv and more something the sprawling city ran into as it grew.

Upon visiting Tel Aviv, there might be a museum or restaurant you want to check out in one of these areas. While they are not part of Tel Aviv proper, they are still very much connected to the city's thriving life and culture.

RAMAT AVIV

Ramat Aviv is home to several worthwhile museums, such as the **Yitzhak Rabin Center,** and its position at the north border of HaYarkon Park makes it a natural stop to include if your sightseeing takes you in that direction.

RAMAT GAN

There is enough to see between the Mediterranean Sea and the Ayalon Highway that you don't have to venture into Ramat Gan for fun. But if you happen to work your way to the far eastern side of HaYarkon Park, you'll find the 500-acre (2 square km) **Ramat Gan National Park** (Ramat Gan off Hwy. 4 near Tel Aviv, tel. 03/631-3964). Inside the park is Safari Park, home to approximately 1,600 animals from all over the world, including 68 species of mammals, 130 species of birds, and 25 species of reptiles.

Also close by is **Meymadion Water Park** (150 Rokach Ave., at Ganei Yehoshua Park, tel. 03/642-2777, NIS99).

---

option is the city's bicycle rental system, Tel-O-Fun. You can pick up and drop off a rented bike at any of the docking points throughout the city. The distinctive green bikes with large frames are easy to spot and comfortable for most body types. There is no law in Tel Aviv that requires bicyclists to wear a helmet.

TENNIS

The Tel Aviv system for tennis dictates that you reserve a court in advance.

THE NATIONAL SPORTS CENTER
6 Sheetrit St.; tel. 03/649-6464; http://nsc.org.il; tennis 6:30am-10pm Sun.-Thurs., 6:30am-8pm Fri.-Sat.; call for prices as they vary by day and time
There are several courts around town, including 18 courts at The National Sports Center. Contact the informal **Tennis Tel Aviv** (tel. 058/603-3370, tennis@tennis-telaviv.co.il) for specific information and recommendations.

SPECTATOR SPORTS
MENORA MIVTACHIM ARENA
51 Yigal Allon St.; www.sportpalace.co.il.; tel. 03/537-6376; NIS20-110
There are a couple of major sport arenas in Tel Aviv, including Menora Mivtachim Arena, home to Tel Aviv's Maccabi and Hapoel basketball teams.

BLOOMFIELD STADIUM
8 She'erit Israel St. in Jaffa; www.sportpalace.co.il/en/bloomfield; tel. 03/637-6000; NIS20-110
Bloomfield Stadium is the professional soccer arena and also hosts major international performers who draw huge crowds, such as Barbra Streisand.

HADAR YOSEF STADIUM
10 Sheetrit St.; www.nsc.org.il; tel. 03/649-7474; NIS20-110
The major sports stadium is Hadar Yosef Stadium, which hosts all kinds of sports, including soccer.

Food

You could try a different restaurant for every meal, every day in Tel Aviv and you wouldn't run out of options. The best picks range from high-end fine dining to casual fare fit for a picnic in the park. One of the hallmarks of Tel Aviv restaurants is that many (particularly the higher-end places) close between lunch and dinner. Lunch menus often have a special business menu, which indicates a lower price for an inclusive food-and-drink option. Most restaurants are open until very late, and some are 24 hours, 7 days a week, but fewer open very early in the morning. The majority of Tel Aviv restaurants are not kosher, so it is fairly easy to find options open during Shabbat. One thing to keep in mind about the hours that restaurants advertise is that they fluctuate slightly according to the level of business, particularly during the winter. If you plan to be early or late to an establishment, call in advance.

NORTH TEL AVIV
Mediterranean and European Fusion
WHITE PERGOLA
Yordei Hasira 1, Port of Tel Aviv Hangar 4; tel. 03/546-4747; www.hasuka-halevana.co.il; 10am-last customer daily; NIS110

Right on the water at the port, White Pergola, or *Hasukkah Halevana* in Hebrew, is an elegant and popular restaurant that specializes in a wide array of seafood dishes, but also serves beef and lamb. Some offerings include lobster, mussels, crab, and shrimp. There is seaside outdoor seating, and part of the restaurant's spacious interior has floor-to-ceiling blond-wood paneling that gives the feel of being inside the belly of a ship. The service can be quite slow, and the wine and alcohol menu is small, but well-selected.

★ SHALVATA RESTAURANT
Port of Tel Aviv Hangar 28; tel. 03/544-1279; www.shalvata.co.il; 5pm-11pm Sun.-Thurs., 9am-11pm Fri.-Sat.; NIS70

The unparalleled open seaside atmosphere of Shalvata Restaurant is a popular place for events. The 360-degree bar and restaurant, spread out over a wooden deck, face the sea, with shade from straw parasols. There are different sections with varied heights and types of seats, some directly on sand where you can kick off your shoes and dig your toes in. The menu is mainly pizza, pasta, chicken, and hamburgers, and there are varied options for alcohol, cocktails, and beer.

Italian
PIZZA FINO
169 Ben Yehuda St.; tel. 03/522-8165; noon-midnight Sun.-Thurs., noon-3pm Fri., about 6pm-midnight Sat.; NIS60

A kosher establishment that specializes in thin-crust pizza and calzones, Pizza Fino is a favorite among Tel Avivian pizza lovers. Its redbrick storefront is situated prominently at the intersection of Ben Yehuda and Jabotinsky Streets. The very casual atmosphere includes a window for walkup takeout, some indoor seating, and several outdoor sidewalk tables.

CITY CENTER
Middle Eastern
SHAKSHUKIA
94 Ben Yehuda St.; tel. 03/522-3433; 10am-10pm Sun.-Thurs., 10am-4pm Fri.; NIS60

The highly inventive Shakshukia offers many creative takes on *shakshuka* (a staple Middle Eastern egg-and-vegetable dish), including one option with turkey.

Meat and Seafood
HERBERT SAMUEL

6 Kaufmann St. at the Gaon House;
tel. 03/516-6516; http://herbertsamuel.co.il;
12:30pm-4pm and 6pm-midnight Sun.-Wed.,
12:30pm-midnight Thurs.-Sat.; NIS150

One of a group of three leading restaurants in Israel, Herbert Samuel is just across the street from the beach and promenade and specializes in meat and seafood dishes. Chef Yonatan Roshfeld is known for his reality TV show, which contributes to the huge buzz the restaurant enjoys as one of the best in Tel Aviv. Renowned for its outstanding service, the upscale and contemporary setting includes tables with window views of the sea and a bar. Specialty items on the menu include duck, shrimp lasagna, and an artichoke, chestnut, and truffle soup.

Mexican and South American
MEXICANA

7 Bugrashov St.; 03/527-9911;
www.mexicana.co.il;
noon-midnight daily; NIS60

If you're in the mood for deliciously satisfying and spicy, spicy, spicy, Mexicana has a Mexican menu that could quell most Americans' cravings for something familiar. The atmosphere is always bustling, especially on Shabbat, when it is one of the few places on its particular stretch of street that is open. The prices are not on the easily affordable end of Mexican restaurants, but one of the best items on the menu, and best priced, is the tortilla soup. The fajitas and chips are also excellent. There is a bit of outdoor sidewalk seating, and the indoor seating is brightly and cheerfully decorated. Overall, space is rather limited so you could end up getting cozy with other diners. The service is unfailingly friendly, upbeat, and accommodating, though you might have to make special requests a few times because they are so busy.

Thai
THAI HOUSE

8 Bugrashov St.; tel. 03/517-8568;
www.thai-house.co.il; noon-11pm daily; NIS75

Thai House serves up northwest Thai food and classics from the Bangkok and southern islands regions, including curry coconut dishes, street-stall dishes, organic green papaya salad, and farm-grown eggplant. Managed by a husband-wife team with roots in a long line of Thai restaurateurs, the restaurant also offers special fish dishes on request that are not listed on the menu. The somewhat shabby exterior belies the unique bamboo-walled interior that gives the feeling of being in a bamboo hut. Though small, just by reputation for its outstanding authentic Thai food, the restaurant attracts a large number of repeat customers. Reservations are recommended.

Cafés and Bistros
BAR GIORA

4 Bar Giora St., corner of 64 Dizengoff St.;
tel. 03/620-4880; 10am-last customer Sun.-Thurs.,
11am-last customer Fri.-Sat.; NIS55

Situated behind a customized tropical garden patio near Dizengoff Center, Bar Giora somehow combines a beach atmosphere with the comforts of a bistro. It's a favorite among locals, which adds to its reputation as a neighborhood institution. The multilevel establishment attracts a younger crowd and has live music in the evenings in the basement. The menu provides a wide range of salads, sandwiches, hamburgers, and Persian, Moroccan, and pasta dishes. There are also a variety of homemade pastries and desserts and a menu of specials.

CAFÉ METZADA

83 HaYarkon St., with entrance on the promenade;
tel. 03/510-3353; www.2eat.co.il/eng/cafe-metzada;
24 hours daily; NIS60

Known for its chicken schnitzel, great service, and excellent views of the sea, Café Metzada is just on the promenade and has a relaxed, calm atmosphere with indoor and outdoor seating. The menu and food preparation are simple, but the portions are large and there are a variety of items such as chicken wings, hamburgers, steak, salad, and dessert.

SOUTH TEL AVIV
Middle Eastern
★ ITZIK HAGADOL

3 Razi'el St.; tel. 057/943-8970; www.itzikhagadol. co.il/en; noon-midnight daily; NIS70

It doesn't have a fancy appearance inside or out, but Itzik HaGadol is legendary among generations of local Tel Avivians. Also known as Big Itzik, because of its extension on the other side of the narrow street, it has been in business for decades. Neither the interior nor the general atmosphere boasts warmth and relaxation, but it is impossible to dine here and leave hungry. With an emphasis on meat and *mezze* (Middle Eastern appetizers and hummus), you can order lamb chops, goose liver, kebab, grilled eggplant, and more to your heart's content. Be careful not to rack up a huge bill by ordering too much food, because it tends to accumulate quickly. You will start getting falafel, hummus, and *mezze* almost immediately after sitting down, so pace yourself and try one thing at a time.

Mediterranean and European Fusion
KIMMEL

6 HaShachar St.; tel. 03/510-5204; http://kimmelrest. co.il/en; noon-midnight daily; NIS125

Housed in a 129-year-old restored building that once belonged to a Turkish sheik, Kimmel uses its setting for its take on the "rustic" French country approach to food, drink, and atmosphere, largely succeeding. The arrangement of tables feels a bit like a cafeteria, but the overall warmth of the setting, down to the types of glasses used, overpowers the slightly utilitarian seating arrangements. Vegetables, wine bottles, and antique knickknacks adorn the walls and alcoves, and the dishes place emphasis on cheeses, meat, and fish in rich sauces, herbs, creams, and olive oil. Don't be shy about asking one of Kimmel's friendly waitstaff to explain certain menu items that border on exotic.

SUZANNA

9 Shabazi St.; tel. 057/944-3060; http://suzana. rest-e.co.il; 10am-1am daily; NIS70

A local favorite, Suzanna serves Greek and Mediterranean dishes that feature a wide variety of stuffed items. Housed in a distinctive yellow building in Neve Tzedek that includes a very inviting shaded terrace, Suzanna's menu includes traditional Moroccan soup, stuffed vegetables and fruits, stews, and grilled dishes. The outdoor bar is open nightly (7pm-1am).

Italian
PRONTO

4 Hertsel St.; tel. 03/566-0915; www.pronto.co.il; 12:30pm-3pm and 6:30pm-11:30pm daily; NIS90

Reputed to be one of the best Italian restaurants in Tel Aviv, Pronto has had more than 20 years to establish its stature in the local restaurant scene. A favorite place for doing business and entertaining clients, Pronto has a generous wine menu, and serves mostly pasta for main dishes with a few specialties, including braised duck and lamb chops. The spacious and modern interior includes a small bar and huge floor-to-ceiling windows that are right on street level.

Sushi
OKINAWA

46 Shabazi St.; tel. 03/510-1099; www.okinawatlv.co.il; noon-midnight Sun.-Fri., 5:30pm-midnight Sat.; NIS60

A rare find in the neighborhood, Okinawa seems to be the lone sushi bar and Japanese restaurant in the Neve Tzedek area. Serving a sashimi and sushi menu, the restaurant has a relaxed and friendly atmosphere with an accommodating staff, and they have a large cocktail menu to boot. It attracts mostly locals who enjoy sushi restaurants but haven't found a favorite yet.

Meat and Seafood
MANTA RAY

Alma Beach on the Tel Aviv Promenade, west of Charles Clore Park, near the Intercontinental David Hotel at 12 Kaufmann St.; tel. 03/517-4773; www. mantaray.co.il; 9am-midnight daily; NIS110

One of Tel Aviv's most famous restaurants, Manta Ray lives up to the hype. A place where Madonna and other stars are said to have eaten, this gourmet seafood restaurant serves items like mullet ceviche and baked blue bream. The breakfast menu, available until noon, is surprisingly affordable and very popular (make reservations). The building looks like a gray, cement hut on the beach, but the interior is spacious and welcoming, even though the clientele and staff tend to be on the yuppie side. It's a great place to have a bite and then hang out on the beach, though there is no swimming on this stretch of shoreline.

NG

6 Ahad Ha'Am St., corner of Yehuda Ha'hasid St., up the staircase; tel. 052/839-3119 and 03/516-7888; www.ngrestaurant.co.il/english; 6pm-1am Sun.-Thurs., 4pm-1am Fri., noon-1am Sat.; NIS110

Famed for its massive porterhouse steak that weighs in somewhere between 70-170 ounces (2-4.5 kg) and piglet in maple sauce and apples, NG was voted Best Meat Restaurant for three years in a row by *Time Out Israel*. Set in picturesque Neve Tzedek, the restaurant's atmosphere is quaint and romantic, with friendly, down-to-earth service (one of the owners might wait on you). There is a generous wine list and a selection of several beers from local breweries to round out the hefty food at this self-labeled "meat bar."

Mexican and South American
MEZCAL

2 Vital St.; tel. 03/518-7925; http://mezcal.rest.co.il; noon-2:30am daily; NIS50

Full of savory dishes, Mezcal specializes in Mexican street food and has a hip interior very reminiscent of Mexican restaurants in North America. The specialties include a variety of tacos, burritos, tostadas, and all the classic sides and starters ranging from guacamole to two varieties of nachos. Try the *bistec con papas*, a hefty amount of filet mignon steak served on a sizzling platter with potatoes and toasted corn. Mescal also has a fairly large alcohol menu with drinks ranging from beer in the bottle and on tap to mojitos and tequila-inspired beverages.

Wine and Tapas
★ VICKY & CRISTINA

HaTachana Bldg. 17 at 1 Kaufmann St.; tel. 03/736-7272 and 057/944-4144; http://vickycristina. rest.co.il; 5pm-last customer Sun.-Thurs., noon-last customer Fri.-Sat.; NIS90

Mentioned again and again by locals and tourists as a favorite, Vicky & Cristina is a Spanish tapas (Vicky) and wine (Cristina) bar, located in a spacious patio under an ancient rubber tree. The atmosphere is intimate and understated, with Latin background music. A wine bar with more than 120 selections (from 7pm daily) is on the back side of the patio with high barstools and a garden of mosaic-covered sculptures inspired by Barcelona's famous Park Güell.

EASTERN TEL AVIV
Mediterranean and European Fusion
★ MESSA

19 Ha'arbaa St.; tel. 03/685-6859; http://messa. rest.co.il; noon-2:30pm and 7pm-11:30pm daily, bar 7pm-last customer daily; NIS160

A very subdued, classy atmosphere that feels like dining in someone's home is a hallmark of Messa, a European-style restaurant known for its outstanding service and presentation. The entrance is hidden behind a large door on the corner of a building with a modern exterior. The interior's layout includes a huge, long community dining table and a bar. Known to attract customers from the upper echelons of society, Messa's food is based on French Provençal techniques and local ingredients. The restaurant emphasizes high-quality raw ingredients in their dishes.

CATIT

57 Nahlat Binyamin St.; tel. 03/510-7001; www.catit. co.il; 6:30pm-11pm daily; NIS180

A French gourmet meets Mediterranean fine dining experience and long considered one of Tel Aviv's best restaurants, Catit is a transplant from a small village where it earned a reputation as a must-visit restaurant. It is now one of the most highly regarded restaurants in Tel Aviv after almost a decade. Chef Meir Adoni is still known for his unique touch with food, including risotto in wine, veal fillet with Mediterranean olives and za'atar tapenade, and lamb with bulgur and spice seeds. Housed in a historical building with an upscale interior, the venue has an atmosphere that evokes elegant country. Due to its wide reputation, Catit attracts discerning locals and curious tourists alike.

Italian
RUSTICO

15 Rothschild Ave.; tel. 03/510-0039; www.rustico. co.il; noon-midnight daily; NIS60

Considered one of the best Italian restaurants in Tel Aviv, Rustico has another location (42 Basel St.) and has a selection of fresh pizzas and focaccia dishes that are baked in a large stone oven in view of patrons. They also serve homemade pasta, seafood, and risotto. The rustic Italian countryside interior includes a large bar in the center of the restaurant and windows with views of the avenue. Outdoor seating includes a beautiful wooden porch, but overall it is not the best place for an intimate meal, as it can get very loud and lively, with tables positioned relatively close together.

American
MOSES

35 Rothschild Blvd.; tel. 03/566-4949; http:// mosesrest.co.il; noon-4am daily; NIS65

Known and loved for its hamburgers (which some say are the best in Tel Aviv), Moses is a popular and trendy American-style eatery near the Tel Aviv Stock Exchange, Independence Hall, and a couple of smaller museums and galleries. The slightly pricey combination beef, lamb, and veal hamburger is recommended, but the service tends to be a bit slow in the afternoons. The interior is simple and fashioned after an American diner.

DIXIE

120 Igal Alon St., corner of 3 Totzeret Ha'aretz; tel. 03/696-6123; www.dixie.co.il; 24 hours daily; NIS65

The spacious layout, exposed brick, and huge

Dr. Shakshuka is a kosher Libyan restaurant.

bar give Dixie a very American (particularly New York City) vibe. Add the large portions of steak, chicken sandwiches, and hamburgers to the mix and you could almost forget you're in Israel. The menu changes three times a year, and a range of wines from leading Israeli and international wineries, beer, and cocktails are available. Known as the grandfather of the 24/7 restaurant concept in Israel, its clientele is very trendy and is a favorite of late-night clubbers. The restaurant also has delivery and takeout. Its main downside is the location, as it is a bit off the beaten path of sightseeing (unless you're hanging out with locals). It is close to HaShalom train station.

JAFFA (YAFO)
Middle Eastern
DR. SHAKSHUKA
3 Beit Eshel St.; tel. 057/944-4193; http://shakshuka. rest.co.il; 8am-midnight Sun.-Thurs.; NIS45

With a name like Dr. Shakshuka, there is bound to be a lot of hype. But as one of the few kosher Libyan restaurants in town that specializes in very large portions of the staple Middle Eastern egg-and-vegetable dish called *shakshuka*, Dr. Shakshuka has somewhat of a corner on the market in their location.

Skipping fancy presentation in both their food and decor, the restaurant's interior features old copper items like lamps hanging from the ceiling, exposed stone walls, and large palm plants. Popular with locals and tourists, the atmosphere is 100 percent Middle Eastern.

Cafés
BLACKOUT RESTAURANT
Retsif Haaliya Hashniya at Jaffa Port; tel. 03/633-0808; www.nalagaat.org.il; first sitting 6:30pm, second sitting 9pm Sun., Tues., Wed., and Thurs.; NIS120

The Nalaga'at Center's BlackOut Restaurant serves meals in complete darkness, employing waiters who are blind. The internationally acclaimed experience is well worth planning in advance for.

CAFÉ KAPISH
Retsif Haaliya Hashniya at Jaffa Port; tel. 03/633-0808; www.nalagaat.org.il; 6pm-11pm Sun.-Thurs.; NIS18

Also at the Nalaga'at Center, Café Kapish's deaf and hearing-impaired staff interact with customers using sign language. You can get coffee, beer, wine, and other drinks and snacks.

Bars and Nightlife

As soon as the sun goes down in Tel Aviv, residents come out in droves to party, eat, drink, and enjoy the beautiful evenings and wide array of entertainment. No matter what you are looking for, you will find it. Always carry some kind of ID and check the age range of the venue beforehand, as some places draw very young crowds or change the minimum age by the night. Have a backup plan, too, in case your destination is closed for that night or permanently.

Tel Aviv nightlife is among the liveliest in the world, with parties of all kinds that go well into the wee hours of the night. Bars, clubs,

pubs, and live music venues offer everything from beer and billiards to small venue rock concerts, and are great hangouts for a few drinks. The entire spectrum of nightlife is available, from a low-key time sipping drinks in a cavernous jazz club to dancing all night at a beachfront megaclub.

NORTH TEL AVIV
The seaside region just to the west of HaYarkon Park next to where the Yarkon River empties into the Mediterranean Sea has a nice variety of places for evening fun, many at or nearby the **Old Port of Tel Aviv**.

One of Tel Aviv's longest streets, Dizengoff Street runs from the north through the center of town and is full of great spots all along the way.

ROSA PARKS

265 Dizengoff St.; tel. 054/643-9958; https://rosaparksbar.co.il/en; 8pm-last customer daily; no cover

This is a laid-back bar that caters to a 25-plus, sophisticated, and upwardly mobile crowd. It has two levels with a pool table and a small upstairs bar with a view of the street. It's known for its wide variety of DJ music; the kitchen is also open all night.

SHABLUL JAZZ CLUB

Hangar 13 at the Port of Tel Aviv on Nemal St.; tel. 03/546-1891; www.shabluljazz.com; doors open 8pm, concerts start 9pm Sun.-Thurs., jam sessions 10:30pm, matinee shows 4pm Fri. and Sat. evenings after reopening from Shabbat; cover NIS50-150, NIS60 for food menu

For a relatively low-key evening and change of pace in an intimate, high-end setting, the Shablul Jazz Club features live music nightly, including famous domestic acts and international acts like the group Harp Concert Jazz. On Friday afternoons they offer a bistro menu with their matinee show and always serve top-shelf alcohol.

CITY CENTER

City Center has a huge concentration of nightlife spots. The area around **Allenby Street** has some popular local spots and very posh and trendy clubs (think dress code and VIP rooms) while central **Dizengoff Street** is home to many popular hangouts of all speeds. Get extra dressed-up if you want to try your luck at getting into some of the more exclusive spots, which have no qualms about turning customers away. One of the more artsy areas in Tel Aviv is near **King George Street** in close proximity to **Dizengoff Center.** On the upper side

of King George you can find some alternative cafés and bars that make for a nice start to the evening before the clubs get going around 11pm or later.

DIZZY FRISHDON

121 Dizengoff St.; tel. 03/523-4111; 8pm-4am daily

Along Dizengoff Street north of Dizengoff Center there is a nice variety of nightlife spots. On the northern end of the street is the bar-lounge Dizzy Frishdon, a popular hangout with a fun-loving crowd. It's an easy place to get into if you're willing to wait in line and make new friends. The cozy interior is dimly lit with a bar and a food menu.

MOLLY BLOOM'S

2 Mendele St., at the corner of HaYarkon St.; tel. 03/522-1558; www.molly-blooms.com; 4pm-last customer Sat.-Thurs., 2pm-last customer Fri.; NIS60

A popular Irish pub is Molly Bloom's, whose claim to fame is that it was the first Irish pub in Tel Aviv when it opened in 2000. Still a neighborhood favorite, it has a standard pub and sports-bar interior of wood, bar stools, and TVs. There's live Irish music every Monday starting around 9:30pm and open-microphone sessions on Fridays starting at 5pm.

BAR GIORA

4 Bar Giora St., at the corner of Dizengoff St.; tel. 03/620-4880; 9am-2am daily; NIS45

If you're in the mood for a place with a smoking room, a pool table, and more of a neighborhood vibe, go to Bar Giora with its café, bar, and live music, including a nightly "BBQ live music" from 9:30pm. There are multiple levels, and it is an old standard bar-coffee-shop-restaurant that has survived the frequent changes of the Tel Aviv nightlife scene. There is a two-for-one happy hour (5pm-9pm daily), a food menu with Middle Eastern and Persian dishes, and comfortable booths to sit in. The pool tables are not always open, so call ahead if you want to play.

SOUTH TEL AVIV

Just like the rest of the city, the southern part of Tel Aviv is hopping with a broad range of nightlife, including some spots popular with younger crowds that feature intense dance music and word-of-mouth-only underground parties that change locations weekly.

THE PRINCE

18 Nahalat Binyamin St.; tel. 058/606-1818; 5pm-1am Sun.-Thurs.; NIS30

The Prince is an artsy bar, bookstore, and coffee shop, with tons of books and wood paneling lining the walls. Not exactly a club or bar and not exactly a coffee shop or bookstore, it plays host to a hipster crowd that likes to hang out late. It is known for its central role in the young poetry revival movement and hosts writing salon groups and story slams (like poetry slams but with stories).

BEIT HA'AMUDIM

14 Rambam St.; tel. 03/510-9228; 11am-2am Sun.-Thurs., 10am-sunset Fri., from 7pm Sat.; NIS45

Off popular Allenby Street, Beit Ha'amudim, which means "house of columns," is a popular bar with jazz concerts, an intimate neighborhood crowd, and art exhibits. They are also known for their jazz brunches, and the food menu is all vegetarian.

EASTERN TEL AVIV

Just east of trendy Neve Tzedek near Allenby Street, there is a good selection of spots with more sophisticated, polished crowds. The surrounding streets have dance bars that come and go, and vary from slick and commercial to alternative. **Lilenblum Street** has a mixture of DJ clubs and bars. Tel Aviv's younger crowd (under 20) loves to hit the huge clubs and dance bars in the area near Ha'Masger to Ha'Rakevet Street.

RADIO E.P.G.B

7 Shadal St.; tel. 03/560-3636; radioepg@gmail.com; 9pm-6am daily; no cover, NIS20 for beer

Down a dark, unmarked alley is Radio E.P.G.B., a hipster dance club and music bar with a quirky atmosphere that includes a pinball machine and punk posters. Like many others, it attempts to lay claim to the best club/bar in the city, but in this case it might not be far off. The club features frequent live indie music performances, DJs spinning indie rock and electronic, and an overall extremely welcoming atmosphere for people of all types.

THE PENGUIN CLUB

43 Yehuda Halevi St.; tel. 03/566-1450; penguinclubtlv@gmail.com; midnight-6am daily; technically members only, NIS50

The Penguin Club is an underground haunt with electronic music and house DJs. It is a good spot to drop by on Wednesday and Thursday nights. The party doesn't really get going until about 2am or later, and goes strong until closing time at 6am. Officially it is a members-only club and is only for the 25-plus crowd, but there seems to be some leeway for determined tourists. Just go with a backup plan.

FRENCH 57

2 Brenner St.; tel. 02/638-2621; 6pm-3am daily; NIS60

A bit on the pricey side but worth it for the famed ability of its bartenders to make practically any drink a customer orders, popular cocktail bar French 57 has a chilled-out atmosphere reminiscent of a New Orleans bar. Background jazz music and a menu that features surprises such as Philly cheesesteak and ceviche add to the overall experience of being transported into a world far from Tel Aviv.

THE CAT AND THE DOG

23 Carlibach St.; tel. 03/561-5595 and 052/449-9188 for reservations; www.thecatandthedog.com; about midnight-7am daily; no cover weekdays, sometimes NIS60-80 weekends

A popular late-night hangout is The Cat and the Dog. Known as one of the most popular spots in the city for international DJs, it doesn't really get going until super-late, around 3am. The club features underground and electronic music and enjoys a long-standing popularity for the party atmosphere and dancing with a state-of-the-art light and sound system. It's a bit of a mixed scene as far as customers, so come prepared to experience local flavor.

THE BLOCK

157 Salame St., inside the Central Bus Station on the 4th Fl.; tel. 03/537-8002; www.block-club.com; doors open around 11pm daily; NIS80 and up for DJs

The Block has a high-quality analog sound system and a hefty lineup of international DJs. The urban atmosphere and on-trend customers help maintain its reputation as one of the coolest places in the city to party.

HAOMAN 17

88 Abarbanel St.; tel. 03/681-3636; open only on select nights, usually weekends and holidays; call ahead for hours; NIS60-100

A popular spot is Haoman 17, a megaclub that attracts top DJs from all over the world, and is also a favorite in the LGBQT community. It is one of the newer and certainly one of the biggest clubs in the city. There are multiple levels and three main dance areas.

JAFFA (YAFO)

TLV CLUB

Old Port at 26 Nemal Yafo St.; tel. 03/544-4194; midnight-6am Mon. and Fri.-Sat.; cover varies depending on performer

One of the oldest clubs in the city, the TLV Club is a large discotheque and live music venue that features Israeli rock and pop stars. The age of the crowd varies widely, and the line to get in is usually fairly long. TLV Club's atmosphere is all about partying hard.

GAY AND LESBIAN NIGHTLIFE

Tel Aviv is generally very gay- and lesbian-friendly. In addition, there is a nice selection of places that cater specifically to the gay and lesbian crowd.

DELI BAR

47 Allenby St.; tel. 03/642-5738 or 054/435-2834; deli 10am-8pm, bar until 2am daily; no cover

Popular among those who know it's there, Deli Bar is reached by passing through a sandwich shop to get to the back where the dancing is happening. Deli features hip-hop and electronica music by some of the city's best DJs and boasts a huge menu of cocktails and imported beers.

APOLO SEXY BAR

46 Allenby St.; tel. 03/774-1106; www.apolo.co.il; 10pm-5am daily; no cover, minimum one-drink purchase

Tel Aviv's lone men-only gay bar, Apolo Sexy Bar is for those looking for an especially intense experience. The basement area features a movie screen; there is a dark room, bar, and dance floor. Prior to midnight there is a reduced alcohol menu.

BOOTLEG

48 King George St.; tel. 052/805-4448; 8pm-7am daily; NIS50 for special DJs

Formerly the Maxim Club, Bootleg is a gay-friendly dance club with a relaxed atmosphere and house music. The crowd is generally comprised of people of all ages, and it has low light and loud music.

Accommodations

In Tel Aviv four- and five-star hotels abound, particularly along the coast where beach access is nearby. But there are various other options throughout the city for every budget, even near the sea. Some pitfalls of Tel Aviv hotels to watch out for include rooms that are extremely small but advertised as suitable for two people, accommodations that are not hostels but have shared bathrooms and showers, and places that might make you try to pay VAT, which is a tax only Israeli citizens or residents are required to pay. There are also often lower rates for tourists, and the best rates are usually found through online travel websites, which often offer discounts that aren't available when booking directly with the accommodations. Avoid phone reservations, as you might arrive and find your room has been given away. If you stay in Jaffa, keep in mind you might be awakened by singing coming from the loudspeakers of the local mosque, the sound of 4am calls to prayer. Parking is extremely hard to come by in Tel Aviv, so if you have a rental car, ask in advance about the parking options, as not every hotel offers space.

NORTH TEL AVIV
US$100-150
PORT HOTEL

*4 Yirmeyahu St.; tel. 03/544-5544; www.
porthoteltelaviv.com; US$149 d*

The small but accommodating Port Hotel is a newer, 21-room boutique hotel with free wireless Internet, refrigerators, and modern decor and interiors. The hotel has a rooftop lounge area with an outstanding view of the sea. The rooms are simple and very spare on trimmings, but with clean, modern lines. There are numerous nightlife options nearby, and it is just a five-minute walk to the Port of Tel Aviv.

US$150-200
ARMON HAYARKON

*268 HaYarkon St.; tel. 03/605-5271; www.
armon-hotel.com; US$165 d*

The Armon HaYarkon is a small hotel with an unremarkable exterior, but it has all the amenities you need, including breakfast, wireless Internet, TV, and refrigerator. It's also just a few minutes from the sea and the exciting Port of Tel Aviv with its bars, clubs, shopping, nightlife, and restaurants. It's also a short drive to Israel's domestic airport, Sde Dov, where you can catch flights to the popular southern tourist city of Eilat.

Over US$200
★ MELODY HOTEL

*220 HaYarkon St.; tel. 03/542-5555; www.atlas.co.il;
US$250 d*

Right on the edge of the massive Ha'atzmaut (Independence) Park, Melody Hotel is within easy walking distance of some of Tel Aviv's most popular beaches. A 2012 Travelers' Choice selection for Trendiest Hotel, this 55-room property has views of the sea and the park. The lobby lounge is open throughout the day, and Sunday to Thursday, it serves free snacks and drinks in the evening. During warmer months, the eighth-floor rooftop lounge is open. Amenities include LCD TV, wireless Internet, a safe, fridge, beach towels, bike and beach chair rental, and some discounts for sightseeing tickets and dessert and wine vouchers from the reception desk.

CITY CENTER
Under US$100
SUN AVIV HOTEL TEL AVIV

*9A Montefiori St.; tel. 03/517-4847; http://www.
sun-hotels.co.il; US$95 d*

Part of a small domestic chain, the Sun Aviv Hotel Tel Aviv has 20 tidy rooms and is located in between Carmel Market, Nahalat Binyamin outdoor mall, and trendy Shabazi Street in Neve Tzedek. A room includes continental breakfast, air-conditioning, minibar, satellite TV, laundry service, and car rental. The hotel is decorated in a very spare manner, with few trimmings or luxurious touches. There is a cafeteria on the ground floor and a 24-hour reception desk. During the day, cold and hot drinks can be ordered from room service.

US$150-200
ABRATEL SUITES HOTEL

*3 Geula St.; tel. 03/516-9966; www.
abratelsuiteshotel.com; US$200 d*

If you want to roll out of bed and into the Mediterranean Sea, Abratel Suites Hotel is a small but good option. With only 24 suites and six standard rooms, the hotel faces the sea and promenade; a room with a sea view costs extra. There are free parking and beach towels, and the entire hotel has central air-conditioning. Rates include breakfast and free coffee, tea, and cookies in the lobby.

CITY HOTEL

9 Mapu St.; tel. 03/542-5555; www.prima-hotels-israel.com; US$195 d

An extremely hip option that exudes Tel Aviv's modern style is the City Hotel. The hotel is known for its cozy but swank atmosphere and excellent restaurant. The 96-room hotel has a bright, modern interior, free wireless Internet throughout, an outdoor coffee shop on the terrace, room service, free parking, and event space. Guests can use a nearby gym for a fee, and several of the rooms feature a small balcony that can seat up to four. The hotel is a very short walk to the beach, and you can rent a bike or get beach towels from reception. Bed-and-breakfast options are also available for the spacious rooms that have a fridge, safe, and LCD TV.

DEBORAH HOTEL

87 Ben Yehuda St.; tel. 03/527-8282; www.arcadiahotels.co.il; US$175 d

Part of a regional group of hotels, the Deborah Hotel is a 69-room establishment just between lively Dizengoff Street and the sea. About two blocks from the sea promenade and the Tel Aviv Marina, Deborah Hotel is kosher and has a hotel synagogue and a Shabbat elevator. Wireless Internet, business traveler services, and a nearby gym at a discount are also available. The interior of the rooms is not spectacular but includes all the basic amenities. The height of the building also allows for some great views of Tel Aviv.

TLV88 SEA HOTEL

88 HaYarkon St.; tel. 03/620-4676; www.tlv88.com; US$180 d

Situated within a row of hotels just one block from the sea and promenade, TLV88 is a Bauhaus building from 1936 that gives the feeling of being right on the beach. Renovated

in 2012, TLV88 is one of the trendier options in the area and is self-described as "an intimate boutique hotel with a Monte Carlo style and a French Riviera flavor." The nautical decor of the rooms creates a sporty, seafaring atmosphere, and amenities include a 24-hour concierge service and free parking. Every room has a sea or city view and there is a seaside restaurant on the ground floor and a wide variety of other restaurants and entertainment venues nearby.

★ HOTEL DE LA MER

2 Ness Tsiyona St., corner of 62 HaYarkon St.; tel. 03/510-0011; www.delamer.co.il; US$189 d

Hotel De La Mer is an exclusive European-style boutique hotel. The exterior is restored historic Bauhaus and the interior has been arranged using feng shui techniques. Extremely close to the sea and beach, the nonsmoking rooms and suites have a range of options, including sea views and in-room whirlpool tubs. The range of services at De La Mer is huge, and includes wireless Internet, a coffee lounge where you can have breakfast, a sunbathing rooftop terrace, currency conversion, basic postal services, babysitting, clerical services, and 24/7 free coffee and tea service in the lobby. Some rooms have a balcony for an additional charge, and rooms have satellite TV, a writing desk, and a wardrobe closet. You can get adaptors, hair dryers, and irons at the front desk.

Over US$200
DIZENGOFF SUITES

39 Gordon St.; tel. 03/523-4363; www.dizengoffsuites.co.il; US$215 d

Even though it only has 21 rooms, Dizengoff Suites makes the most of its amazing location close to some of the highlights of Tel Aviv shopping and entertainment. The three available varieties of suite are recently renovated and include a fully equipped kitchenette, mini-fridge, air-conditioning, cable TV, and free wireless Internet. The elevator can only fit about two people at a time, and there is a card-key system for electricity in the rooms, some of which have a balcony or rooftop terrace. The overall feel is very homey, and the staff is friendly and accommodating. An excellent breakfast in the downstairs restaurant with a distinctly Parisian atmosphere, Café Marco, is included.

★ ARTPLUS HOTEL

35 Ben Yehuda St.; tel. 03/542-5555; www.atlas.co.il; US$210 d

A newer 62-room hotel dedicated to Israeli art, Artplus Hotel is like one big work of art from floor to ceiling and throughout the hotel. Murals on every floor were commissioned by five famous local artists, and the hotel's foyer and lobby feature works by two internationally renowned Israeli artists, Zadok Ben-David and Sigalit Landau. The overall design is retro modern. It is within easy walking distance to the beach. Amenities include tons of freebies, such as parking, bicycle rentals, breakfast, refreshments and snacks in the hotel's library every evening, a sun roof terrace, and coupons to local restaurants. Rooms include air-conditioning, a fridge and safe, an LCD TV, and hair dryer.

BELL BOUTIQUE HOTEL

50 HaYarkon St.; tel. 03/517-4291; www. thebellboutiquehoteltelaviv.com; US$209 d

The atmosphere, location, and price of the Bell Hotel are all right on the mark, even though there are some rustic touches. This seaside boutique hotel is near some of Tel Aviv's best nightlife and beach life. A double room includes free parking, wireless Internet, air-conditioning, fridge, coffee and tea service, and breakfast. The rooms are comfortably and artfully designed to reflect Tel Aviv's vibe of sand and sea, with a sandstone-based color scheme and some rooms with balcony seaside views and whirlpool tubs.

HOTEL METROPOLITAN AND METROPOLITAN SUITES

11-15 Trumpeldor St.; tel. 03/519-2727; www. hotelmetropolitan.co.il; US$229 d

With 227 rooms, the Hotel Metropolitan and Metropolitan Suites is big enough to give the experience of hotel luxury but still maintains a warm atmosphere. Some of the decor in the rooms is a bit dated, but the lobby bar and restaurant both have a modern feel and are open until the wee hours. It is right on the sea. Adjacent to the hotel are sister suites for longer-term stays. With services catered toward business travelers, the hotel has rooms with phones that allow for international calls, a business center (for an extra cost), laundry service, minibars, and car rental. There is also room service, and rooms are available for guests with disabilities. Guests have free access to a health club and to private parking for a fee. An outdoor pool is open April-October.

MARINA TEL AVIV

167 HaYarkon St.; tel. 03/521-1777; http://marina. telaviv-hotels.net/en; US$260 d

Conveniently located directly across from the Tel Aviv Marina and the Gordon Swimming Pool, the Marina Tel Aviv is a 160-room hotel with sea views and family-friendly rooms that caters to business travelers. Every room has air-conditioning, a bathtub, fridge, safe, and LCD TV. Hangout spaces include a lobby bar, a rooftop sundeck and swimming pool (in season), and a business lounge bar deck. Underground parking is available.

SOUTH TEL AVIV
Under US$100
FLORENTINE BACKPACKERS HOSTEL

10 Elifelet St.; tel. 03/518-7551; florentinehostel.com; US$60 d private room for two, US$25 one dorm bed

A home-style hostel in the trendy Florentin neighborhood, Florentine Backpackers Hostel has an unusual age restriction that only allows guests between the ages of 18 and 40. Private rooms have a double bed, air-conditioning, linens, and a shared bathroom and shower. There is also free wireless Internet, coffee and tea, a barbecue area, free parking, cell phone and bicycle rental, luggage storage, an indoor lounge, a fully equipped communal kitchen, and a rooftop terrace. It is within walking distance to Old Jaffa and the flea market, the beach and boardwalk, and the historic and hip Neve Tzedek neighborhood. Near the hostel there are numerous cafés, nightclubs, and pubs.

★ BEIT IMMANUEL CONGREGATION AND GUEST HOUSE

8 Auerbach St.; tel. 03/682-1459; www.beitimmanuel. org; US$92 d

Among the homier picks in Jaffa, the Beit Immanuel Congregation and Guest House is a good fit for all types of travelers on a budget and welcoming to couples and families with kids, as well as groups. The small 13-room guesthouse has simple and plain private rooms with bathrooms and dormitory rooms, all with coffee and tea service, air-conditioning and heat, and balconies in some rooms. Just next to the ancient Jaffa Port and some outstanding (and a bit less crowded) beaches, Beit Immanuel caters to special prayer tour groups or people traveling on short-term religious missions. There is free wireless Internet in the lobby and a quiet garden area on the ground floor. The included breakfast can be eaten in the garden between May and October. Luggage storage, free secure parking, conference facilities, and a prayer room are available, as well as a Hebrew-language worship service on Friday evenings with English translation.

JAFFA (YAFO)
Under US$100
OLD JAFFA HOSTEL AND GUESTHOUSE

13 Amiad St.; tel. 03/682-2370; www.telaviv-hostel. com; US$80 d

The Old Jaffa Hostel and Guesthouse is in an older building with touches that evoke a distinctly Middle Eastern flavor. Located across the street from the Jaffa flea market, a 10-minute walk from the Old City of Jaffa, and 15 minutes from the Jaffa Port, the hostel has a sizable rooftop garden and is close to several new cafés, wine bars, pubs, and restaurants. Housed in an old renovated building with high ceilings, colorful floor tiles, and balconies overlooking the flea market, the hostel is closed on national holidays. Amenities include free wireless Internet, a fee-based Internet station, a fully equipped kitchen, free coffee, tea, and cookies in the morning, and coin laundry service. There is also a storage safe and a code-locked entrance gate.

Over US$200
ANDROMEDA HILL

3 Andromeda Hill, Louis Pasteur St.; tel. 03/683-8448; www.andromeda.co.il; US$220 d

If you're planning on staying four nights or more in one place, Andromeda Hill includes a notably long list of amenities, such as a saltwater swimming pool and tremendous views of the sea. Just at the southern tip of Old Jaffa and close to numerous historical sites, beaches, and restaurants, the Andromeda Hill apartment-style stone complex is built on top of a buttress named for Greek mythology's Andromeda. The rooms are modern, simple, and functional, and some of the comforts include a lounge deck, free towel service, a fitness spa, a poolside café, an open promenade and gardens, en suite kitchenettes, a conference room, parking, and 24-hour security. Some rooms include a balcony. Massage services, a steam room and dry sauna, luggage storage, and wireless Internet are also available.

Information and Services

Tel Aviv caters to tourists and visitors from all over the world and presents information and services regularly in English, including at ATMs, post offices, and websites. It is also one of the most Wi-Fi-friendly cities in the world, so if you have a device like a tablet from a foreign country that works on a wireless network, it should also work in Tel Aviv.

INFORMATION

Tourist and Travel Information

There are three major tourist information centers in Tel Aviv.

HATACHANA TRAIN STATION COMPLEX TOURIST CENTER

HaTachana Bldg. 5; tel. 03/776-4005 or 03/516-6188, ext. 3; www.hatachana.co.il; 10am-8pm Sun.-Thurs., 9am-2pm Fri., closed on Jewish holidays

One of the most centrally located and easily accessible is HaTachana Train Station Complex Tourist Center. You can also have some fun shopping and eating at HaTachana.

HERBERT SAMUEL PROMENADE TOURIST CENTER

46 Herbert Samuel St.; tel. 03/516-6317, ext. 1; www.visit-tlv.co.il; 9:30am-6:30pm Sun.-Thurs., 9am-1pm Fri. Apr.-Oct., 9:30am-5:30pm Sun.-Thurs., 9am-1pm Fri. Nov.-Mar., closed on Jewish holidays

The Herbert Samuel Promenade Tourist Center is a reasonable stop to combine with going to the beach, as it is directly on the promenade and near swimming.

JAFFA CLOCK TOWER TOURIST CENTER

2 Marzuk at Azar St.; tel. 03/516-6188; jaffainfo11@bezeqint.net; 9:30am-6:30pm Sun.-Thurs., 9am-2pm Fri., 10am-4pm Sat. Apr.-Oct., 9:30am-5:30pm Sun.-Thurs., 9am-2pm Fri. Nov.-Mar., closed on Jewish holidays

Down in Old Jaffa is the Jaffa Clock Tower Tourist Center.

Maps and Guides

There are some useful online maps of Tel Aviv, including several very detailed options on the website for the **Israel Ministry of Tourism** (https://info.goisrael.com). They are especially helpful if you have access to a color printer.

Hospitals and Emergency Services

Very close to the center of Tel Aviv near Hamedim Square is **Ichilov Hospital** (6 Weitzman St., tel. 03/697-4444), which has some of the best facilities in Israel.

For emergencies 24 hours a day and transportation to the nearest emergency room, contact **Magen David Adom** (dial 101 or tel. 03/546-0111, www.mdais.com). Ambulance service is available by dialing 101.

For non-medical emergencies, contact the **Tourist Police** (tel. 03/516-5382, corner of Geula and Herbert Samuel Sts.) or dial 100 for the police in general. For a fire, dial 102 for the **fire department.**

Media

The home offices for most of Israel's domestic media companies are located in Tel Aviv, including the general news and interest **Ha'aretz** and **Yediot Ahronoth,** which have editions in English, as well as the English business publication **Globes.** Some publications only found here include **Time Out Tel Aviv.**

English-language radio can be found on 88FM.

SERVICES

Currency Services and Money Exchange

Banks and post offices will change money, but **post offices** (www.israelpost.co.il) charge no commission and have services that include buying foreign currency with a credit card (up to US$1,000), changing traveler's checks for the U.S. dollar and the euro, and changing cash. Some post office branches also have **Western Union** services.

There are also several money-changing locations in the center of the city. **Moneygram** (www.moneygram.com) is a popular company that has about three dozen locations throughout Tel Aviv. You can find exact addresses and contact information for Moneygram locations by visiting their website.

Banks and ATMs

All banks have branches or headquarters in Tel Aviv, the financial capital of the country. Most bank branches or buildings are on Allenby Street, Rothschild Boulevard, Herbert Samuel Street, and Yehuda Halevy Street. ATMs are also very easy to find in small shops and near commercial centers. Look for the green-and-white machines of **Israel Discount Bank** (27-31 Yehuda Halevi St., tel. 03/514-5555), which generally charge the lowest fee for withdrawing money from a foreign account. ATMs bearing the red, white, and black colors of **Bank Hapoalim** (50 Rothschild Blvd., tel. 03/567-3333) are also fairly easy to find.

For a specific listing of commercial bank addresses, go to the "Aliyahpedia" page on www.nbn.org.il and look under banking.

Postal Service

Post office locations can be found **online**

(www.israelpost.co.il). The **main post office** branch is at 132 Allenby Street, and there are some conveniently located but smaller branches around town (286 Dizengoff St., 61 HaYarkon St., 3 Zamenhoff St., 3 Mendele St., and 138 Yeffet St. in Jaffa).

Internet

More than five years ago, Tel Aviv began a free Wi-Fi hotspot program throughout the city, starting with Ben Gurion Boulevard. The hotspots don't allow visits to file-sharing websites and will block you if you try to download files that are too big. If you can't find a city hotspot, most cafés and coffee shops in Tel Aviv have free wireless access. The network now includes parks, city shores, main streets, and commercial centers.

Embassies

A branch office of the **American Embassy** (71 HaYarkon St., tel. 03/519-7475, https://il.usembassy.gov), the **Canadian Embassy** (3/5 Nirim St., tel. 03/636-3300, www.canadainternational.gc.ca), and the **Embassy of Australia** (Discount Bank Tower, Level 28, 23 Yehuda Halevi St., tel. 03/693-5000, www.israel.embassy.gov.au) are located in Tel Aviv, as are the **Embassy of South Africa** (12 Abba Hillel St., Ramat Gan, tel. 03/526-2566, www.safis.co.il/sites) and the **Embassy of the United Kingdom** (192 Hayarkon St., tel. 03/725-1222, www.gov.uk).

Transportation

It's very easy to get to Tel Aviv, travel within the city, and take short trips around the region. Tel Aviv itself is only about 20 square miles (52 square km), and is one hour from both Jerusalem and Haifa, the two other major urban centers of Israel. Public transportation does not run on Shabbat, and will stop about mid-afternoon on Friday and resume after dark on Saturday evening.

GETTING THERE

Air

BEN GURION INTERNATIONAL AIRPORT

Tel Aviv; www.iaa.gov.il; tel. 03/975-2386

Tel Aviv's Ben Gurion International Airport is about a 15-minute drive from the City Center. From the airport, you can get into the city by hotel shuttle, train, taxi, and bus.

The public transportation depot is on the second floor near Gates 21 and 23. Buses go from there to the **Egged** (www.egged.co.il, number 5, NIS26) station at nearby Airport City, and from there you can transfer to regular Egged bus lines. There are free passes to get from Airport City to the airport.

Train

Once on the **Israel Railways** train (www.rail.co.il, NIS20), you can be in Tel Aviv's City Center in 10 minutes from the airport, and in about 90 minutes from **Jerusalem.** There are several bus lines that leave about every 20-30 minutes from the airport and stop at four stations.

Tel Aviv's most southerly stop, **HaHagana,** will get you closest to Jaffa, Florentin, and Neve Tzedek in the south. The next stop, **HaShalom,** will drop you off at Azrieli Center, and get you near Dizengoff and some of the best beaches in the city. **Savidor Station** gets you in proximity of Jabotinsky Street and the Marina and Old Port. **University Station** is quite far north and actually gets you just outside of the city.

You can buy a daily or multi-journey ticket; kids under five travel for free.

Car

If you are driving into Tel Aviv, you are going to take Highway 1 from **Jerusalem** and Highway 2 from **Haifa.** You will run through the center of the city on Ayalon (North or South), also known as Highway 20. Ayalon has about half a dozen exits that lead to different parts of the city.

Bus

The green-and-white **Egged** (www.egged.co.il) buses travel into south Tel Aviv to the city's **Central Bus Station** (106 Levinski St.), just east of Neve Tzedek and Florentin. The station is a multilevel hub that looks a little bit like a low-end shopping mall. From here you can buy tickets and take buses that travel all over the country.

From **Jerusalem's Central Bus Station,** it is about an hour ride to Tel Aviv without traffic (number 220, NIS55). Try to avoid making the trip on a Friday afternoon, as the traffic is usually the worst at that time. Once in Tel Aviv, there are tons of taxis outside the front doors of the bus station.

Share Taxi

Sherut, or share taxis, also travel to and from Tel Aviv and are your best (and almost only) option during the weekend. A *sherut* from Jerusalem is about NIS35 or less, and leaves from City Center on Yafo Street, seven days a week. The end point for most *sherut* is the **Tel Aviv Central Bus Station.** If you are paying close attention and know where you are, you can call out to the *sherut* driver at certain points along the route to hop out after they have exited the freeway and are in Tel Aviv. If you are on the freeway and have some type of emergency and need to get off the bus, it's also acceptable to ask the driver to pull over and they will if there is a place to stop.

GETTING AROUND
Car

Tel Aviv is relatively easy to navigate by car, except that there is usually quite a bit of traffic. Since the western border of the city is the Mediterranean, and Ayalon Highway essentially forms the eastern border, you always have landmarks for orientation.

The **parking** system in Israel is universal: gray curbs are free parking, blue and white stripes are paid (look for the pay station and keep change on hand), and red and white stripes mean no parking. If you have a phone that operates inside Israel you can use the Payngo app to pay for parking.

Aside from renting a car at the airport, there is a group of car rental company offices on HaYarkon Street just north of Frishman Street. They include **Eldan** (114 HaYarkon St., tel. 03/527-1166, www.eldan.co.il), **Avis** (113 HaYarkon St., tel. 03/527-1752, http://avis.co.il), and **Shlomo Sixt** (122 HaYarkon St., tel. 03/524-4935, www.shlomo.co.il).

Bus

The city bus line, **Dan** (tel. 03/639-4444, www.dan.co.il/english) operates a series of very convenient lines throughout the city, and they have detailed information on their English-language website. The buses shut down for the weekend. A multi-trip Rav Kav Card offers a small discount per ride if you know you will be taking more than one ride. It can be purchased from the bus driver and works in both Tel Aviv and Jerusalem.

Taxis

Recommended by the Tel Aviv Tourism Bureau are **Gordon Taxi** (tel. 03/527-2999), **Habima Taxi** (tel. 03/528-3131), and **Kastel** (tel. 03/633-2253).

Rental Bikes

One of Tel Aviv's coolest features is **Tel-O-Fun** (www.tel-o-fun.co.il/en), a bicycle rental system. You can pick up and drop off a rented bike at any point throughout the city. There is no law in Tel Aviv that requires bicyclists to wear a helmet.

Shabbat and Holidays

For the most part, venues in Tel Aviv are open on Shabbat and holidays, but public transportation shuts down. You can find *sherut* (share taxis) at the Central Bus Station that will take you to a variety of places for a price, including to Jerusalem. They leave when the taxi is full, not on a set schedule.

Haifa and the North Coast

The north coast of Israel has a subtle, seductive charm, making it a place where you could easily lose track of time for days.

Whether you are in Haifa, Akko, Caesarea, Zichron Ya'akov, Nahariya, or Rosh Hanikra, there are options for indoor and outdoor activities and excursions, a surprising number of high-end boutique hotels, and some world-class wineries.

One of the best jumping-off places for exploring the region is Haifa, Israel's third largest city, situated on the coast a short drive north of Tel Aviv. The city is built up on the side of Mount Carmel and revolves around the massive, dominating Baha'i Gardens and Golden Dome socially, economically, and spiritually. Haifa is full of scenic vistas around

Highlights

Look for ★ to find recommended sights, activities, dining, and lodging.

★ **Baha'i Gardens and Golden Dome:**
Everyone talks about the Baha'i dome and gardens, but it's not until you see them that you understand why. A marvel of terraced landscaping and a reminder of the power of faith, they stand out among Haifa's sights (page 165).

★ **Louis Promenade:** There's no better place to get your first glimpse of Haifa than from the Louis Promenade. It's difficult to tear yourself away from the gorgeous vistas of the Port of Haifa and the lower city (page 172).

★ **Acre Old City:** If you make only one side trip on the north coast, go to the Old City in Akko (Acre). The centuries-old structures and odd, winding streets illuminate layers of history critical to understanding the region (page 182).

★ **Caesarea National Antiquities Park:**
Not far from Tel Aviv, you'll find surviving examples of Roman civilization, including an amphitheater, the hippodrome, and Hellenistic and Crusader ruins (page 191).

★ **Roman and Byzantine Aqueduct:**
The aqueduct outside of Caesarea is an excellent place to combine sightseeing with outdoor play. The ancient aqueduct creates a sort of barrier for the popular beach, which is an easy place to slow down to enjoy wading or swimming in the sea (page 192).

Haifa and the North Coast

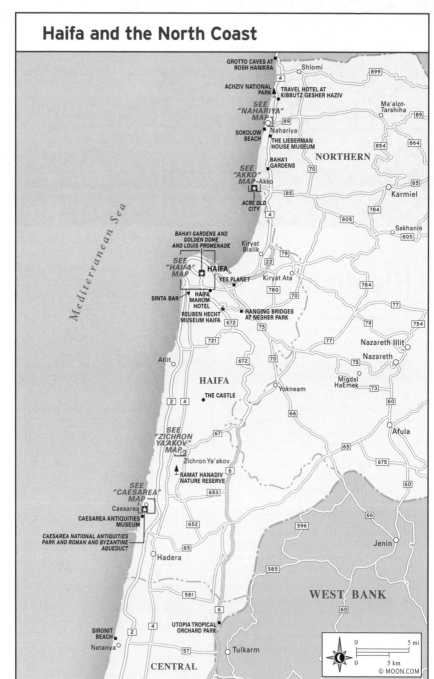

GROTTO CAVES AT
ROSH HANIKRA

Shlomi

899

4

ACHZIV NATIONAL
PARK

TRAVEL HOTEL AT
KIBBUTZ GESHER HAZIV

Ma'alot-
Tarshiha

89

*SEE
"NAHARIYA"
MAP*

89

Nahariya

SOKOLOW
BEACH

THE LIEBERMAN
HOUSE MUSEUM

854

864

NORTHERN

BAHA'I
GARDENS

70

*SEE
"AKKO"
MAP*

Akko

85

Karmiel

85

ACRE OLD
CITY

4

805

784

Sakhanin

805

Mediterranean Sea

BAHA'I GARDENS AND
GOLDEN DOME
AND LOUIS PROMENADE

Kiryat
Bialik

*SEE
"HAIFA"
MAP*

HAIFA

22

79

YES PLANET

Kiryat Ata

SINTA BAR

HAIFA
MAROM
HOTEL

780

70

784

REUBEN HECHT
MUSEUM HAIFA

672

HANGING BRIDGES
AT NESHER PARK

75

77

79

754

721

77

Nazareth Illit

Atlit

672

70

75

Nazareth

HAIFA

THE CASTLE

Yokneam

Migdal
HaEmek

73

60

66

Afula

*SEE
"ZICHRON
YA'AKOV"
MAP*

67

65

675

Zichron Ya'akov

6

RAMAT HANADIV
NATURE RESERVE

60

*SEE
"CAESAREA"
MAP*

653

Caesarea

66

596

CAESAREA ANTIQUITIES
MUSEUM

652

Jenin

CAESAREA NATIONAL ANTIQUITIES
PARK AND ROMAN AND BYZANTINE
AQUEDUCT

65

Hadera

585

581

WEST BANK

60

6

SIRONIT
BEACH

2

4

UTOPIA TROPICAL
ORCHARD PARK

Netanya

57

Tulkarm

CENTRAL

0   5 mi

0   5 km

© MOON.COM

every corner, excellent restaurants of all kinds, world-class museums, and a range of interesting activities such as long walks on the promenade by the beach. It is home to the "MIT of Israel," the Technion, and is known as a tolerant and inclusive place, where Arabs, Jews, and Christians live together peacefully.

Not far from Haifa are some of Israel's most memorable coastal spots, including Akko (a UNESCO World Heritage Site), Caesarea and the ruins of the Roman aqueduct, and the quaint, picturesque artist village of Zichron Ya'akov. A notable stopping point that is a bit off the beaten path is the little seaside town of Nahariya, where you'll find some of Israel's best surfing year-round and townspeople who will warm your heart with their hospitality.

Throughout the coastal region north of Tel Aviv, there is such a wide variety of things to see and do that you may find it hard to leave. Try to keep things open-ended. You might plan to spend just one night in Nahariya, but while riding a free bike rental from your hotel down the miles-long promenade by the beach, you may realize that plans change.

HISTORY

The earliest evidence of human settlements in the region of Haifa goes back to the 14th century BC. Haifa is mentioned in 3rd century BC Jewish Talmudic literature as a small fishing village and the home of several Jewish scholars. Haifa at that time is believed to have extended from the Jaffa Street Jewish cemetery to Rambam Hospital.

Its seaside position and port encouraged the capture and governance of Haifa by a variety of rulers throughout the ages, including Byzantines, Arabs, Crusaders, Mamluks, Ottomans, and Egyptians.

In 1909, around the same time Haifa was emerging as a major industrial port and center of population, the city became a sacred place for followers of the Baha'i faith when the remains of their religious leader, the Báb, were moved to

nearby Akko (Acre) and a shrine was built on Mount Carmel by 'Abdu'l-Bahá. Today, Haifa is a central site of worship, pilgrimage, and administration for the Baha'i religion.

After the Israeli War of Independence in 1948, Haifa became a gateway for waves of Jewish immigrants from all over the world coming to the newly established Jewish state. Several neighborhoods sprang up very quickly as a result to accommodate the new residents, and by 1970, Haifa's population was about 200,000. With the fall of the former Soviet Union, another huge influx of 35,000 more immigrants came to the city.

ORIENTATION

Haifa is Israel's third largest city and is about one hour directly north of Tel Aviv and about two hours northwest of Jerusalem. The city is built on and around Mount Carmel, and is full of winding, steep streets and main roads that sweep around the base of the mountain, following the shore of the sea.

Haifa is the gateway to the Galilee and Israel's north coast and makes an excellent base for excursions within an hour radius, including north to Akko, Rosh Hanikra, Nahariya; south to Zichron Ya'akov, Caesarea, and Tel Aviv; and east to Nazareth.

PLANNING YOUR TIME

Haifa is the perfect home base while exploring this region making day trips to the north coast. There are also some nice options for hotels in nearby areas, though they require a bit more of a sense of adventure to navigate. The best way to get around this region is by car; though regional bus lines are also quite accessible, they are not very frequent.

At least two nights are suggested for Haifa and nearby environs. Depending on how many trips you want to make to the surrounding areas, three nights and four days may be better. Anywhere between 2-5 days will give you a good but quick sampling of Haifa and its region.

Previous: the Baha'i Gardens in Haifa; detail of old city gates of Acre; Al-Jazzar Mosque in Akko.

Haifa's Topography and Neighborhoods

Haifa

The first time you enter Haifa it is easy to understand why it is known as "the San Francisco of Israel." The city's winding streets are extremely steep in places where the city climbs up Mount Carmel. There are three major tiers of the city.

WADI SALIB

The lowest is the old city center, **Wadi Salib,** which extends to **Wadi Nisnas** and is commonly called downtown. The area is the hub of Arab life and culture. In the same vicinity toward the **Port of Haifa** is the **German Colony** with its Templer-period buildings, visitors center, and restaurants.

HADAR

The next tier up is the **Hadar** neighborhood, which dates back to the 1900s and is about halfway up Mount Carmel. Hadar is home to a large Jewish synagogue and block after block of dense lower-end shops of all kinds. During Shabbat, part of a major street near the synagogue is closed to traffic, and the entire area shuts down from late Friday afternoon until well after dark on Saturday night.

CARMEL

One of the most prestigious areas in town that is also highest up on the mountainside is **Carmel,** which includes the French Carmel, Merkaz HaCarmel, Romema, Carmeliya, and more. Carmel is home to some of Haifa's finest restaurants and the most remarkable views.

The trick to seeing and experiencing a satisfying amount of Haifa is to plan your time according to which neighborhoods you are traversing. The neighborhoods and related sights are situated like steps up and down Mount Carmel.

A good approach is to plan a walking route that eventually leads to a resting place, such as following the Louis Promenade to the Baha'i Gardens as far down as you can go and ending up at the base of the gardens in the German Colony. You can also plan a route around the city's subway stops, making it easy to get in and out.

Itinerary Ideas

BEST OF HAIFA AND THE NORTH COAST

Day 1: Haifa

1 Start your trip in central Haifa with breakfast in the historic **German Colony.**

2 Then, walk 15 minutes south to visit the **Baha'i Gardens.** This is the headquarters of the Baha'i faith, so you're likely to run into pilgrims along the way. Take in the carefully cultivated gardens against the deep-blue backdrop of Haifa Bay and its fresh sea breeze air.

3 From the top entrance of the Baha'i Gardens, walk 5-7 minutes to **Louis Promenade** for a stunning vista of Haifa Bay.

4 From there, take a 15-minute stroll to one of the nearby restaurants, like the family-owned **Hanamal 24,** good for a glass of wine and some seafood in a relaxing atmosphere.

Day 2: Akko (Acre)

1 Get a rental car and set out from Haifa to **Acre Old City,** a UNESCO World Heritage Site comprised of a complex network of buildings, sites, and museums.

2 Spend the morning exploring and getting your bearings in the **Knight's Halls.**

3 Head back to where Acre's old and new city meet at **Al-Jazzar Mosque.**

4 Next to the mosque is the locally popular **Hummus Said,** which serves up generous helpings of hummus and pita, pickled *mezze* dishes, and other appetizers.

5 Use your energy from lunch to venture through **Templar's Tunnel.** Afterward, drive up to Nahariya, where you'll stay the night.

Day 3: Nahariya and Caesarea

1 Spend the morning exploring the natural **Grotto Caves at Rosh Hanikra,** at Israel's northernmost point at the border with Lebanon.

2 Back in Nahariya, the **Penguin** restaurant has a signature schnitzel dish, sandwiches, hearty Israeli options, and a solid wine and liquor selection.

3 If you're driving south to Tel Aviv, spend some time in the **Caesarea National Antiquities Park,** which includes archaeological remnants from the Hellenistic period (3rd century BC) to the Crusader period (12th century AD).

4 At Caesarea's old port area, **Helena** seafood restaurant serves up a gourmet menu designed by two of Israel's leading chefs.

Itinerary Ideas

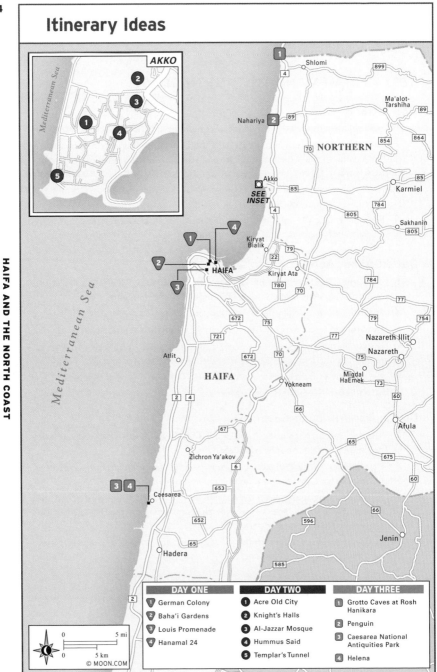

AKKO

Mediterranean Sea

Shlomi

Nahariya

NORTHERN

Ma'alot-Tarshiha

Akko
SEE INSET

Karmiel

Sakhanin

Kiryat Bialik

HAIFA

Kiryat Ata

Mediterranean Sea

Nazareth Illit

Nazareth

Atlit

HAIFA

Yokneam

Migdal HaEmek

Afula

Zichron Ya'akov

Caesarea

Jenin

Hadera

DAY ONE	DAY TWO	DAY THREE
1 German Colony	1 Acre Old City	1 Grotto Caves at Rosh Hanikara
2 Baha'i Gardens	2 Knight's Halls	2 Penguin
3 Louis Promenade	3 Al-Jazzar Mosque	3 Caesarea National Antiquities Park
4 Hanamal 24	4 Hummus Said	4 Helena
	5 Templar's Tunnel	

0   5 mi
0   5 km
© MOON.COM

Haifa

One of Haifa's main distinctions is its reputation as a model of peaceful coexistence among different faiths and ethnicities. You'll often hear Israelis remark on it, and in Haifa you can feel it. At the foot of the Baha'i Gardens and Golden Dome, you can hear the bells of a nearby Christian church and see Arabs and Jews eating in the same restaurants in the German Colony.

The life of the city revolves around several major points: the Baha'i Gardens and Golden Dome, the beaches, and the distinct neighborhoods on multiple ascending tiers from the seaside to the top of Mount Carmel. Many areas of Haifa remain open during the weekend (except for the Hadar district), so there are many things to do, see, and experience on Friday and Saturday.

SIGHTS

TOP EXPERIENCE

★ Baha'i Gardens and Golden Dome

Baha'i World Center; 80 Hatzionut Ave.; tel. 04/831-3131; www.ganbahai.org.il/en, inner gardens 9am-noon Tues.-Thurs., outer gardens 9am-7pm daily, closed Wed.; free entrance and free tours

Haifa's **Baha'i World Center** includes the golden Shrine of the Báb, terraced gardens, and administrative buildings covering the northern slope of Mount Carmel all the way to the foot of the mountain where it abuts the German Colony. The Baha'i faith is one of the youngest religions in the world, founded in the 19th century by Bahá'u'lláh in Iran. The Baha'i Gardens and Golden Dome are so massive and dominating that the center acts as the unofficial center of Haifa.

An extended staircase that goes up the side of Mount Carmel is divided into 19 terraces, and the golden Baha'i Shrine of the Bab is situated in a dominating position in the middle.

The golden-domed shrine marks the burial place of one of the two prophets of the Baha'i faith and can be seen from multiple points throughout the city.

The garden is an intricate work of art that exudes a calm and peaceful atmosphere. The outer gardens can be accessed from the top and bottom entrances, and free guided tours in English begin at noon from the top entrance.

The smaller but also very pretty and peaceful Baha'i Gardens in Akko are the resting place and former residence of the second prophet of the Baha'i faith, Báb.

Mané-Katz Museum

89 Yafe Nof St.; tel. 04/911-9372; www.mkm.org.il; 10am-4pm Sun.-Wed., 4pm-7pm Thurs., 10am-1pm Fri., 10am-3pm Sat.; adult NIS35, senior NIS17.5, child NIS23, combined Haifa museum ticket NIS60

In a small and distinguished house with views of the Bay of Haifa, the Mané-Katz Museum is tucked away at the southern end of Louis Promenade. The museum was the home of the artist Mané-Katz at the end of his life and features some of his work. Also on display are Jewish religious and ceremonial pieces and works by Marc Chagall.

Haifa Educational Zoo

124 HaTishbi St.; tel. 04/837-2390; www.haifazoo. co.il; 9am-4pm Sun.-Thurs., 9am-4pm Sat. and holidays fall and spring, 9am-1:30pm Fri. and holiday eves summer, 9am-6pm Sun.-Thurs., 9am-6pm Sat. and holidays, 9am-3pm Fri. and holiday eves winter; adult and child NIS35, senior NIS25

Situated high up enough in Haifa to afford gorgeous views of nearby mountains and on one of the Carmelit subway stops, the Haifa Educational Zoo is home to more than 100 types of animals, including bears, wolves, hyenas, and monkeys, spread out over some very hilly terrain. It is a great place for a family visit, especially with the carousel, sweet treats,

Haifa

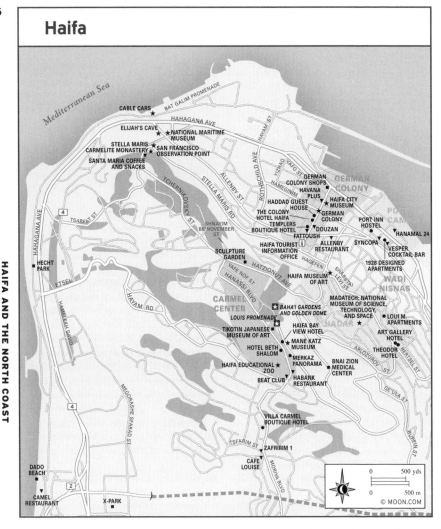

and playground just outside the zoo entrance, which is part of a popular park.

Haifa Museum of Art

26 Shabbetai Levi St.; tel. 04/911-5997; www.hma.org. il; 10am-4pm Sun.-Wed., 10am-7pm Thurs., 10am-1pm Fri., 10am-3pm Sat.; adult NIS45, senior NIS22.5, child NIS30, combined Haifa museum ticket NIS60

Among the three largest museums in Israel, the Haifa Museum of Art covers three floors and more than 37,000 square feet (3,500

square meters). The artwork ranges from Israeli to international contemporary permanent and changing exhibitions.

Haifa City Museum

11 Ben Gurion Ave.; tel. 04/911-5888; www.hcm.org. il; 10am-4pm Sun.-Wed., 4pm-7pm Thurs., 10am-1pm Fri., 10am-3pm Sat.; adult NIS35, senior NIS17.5, child NIS23, combined Haifa museum ticket NIS60

The Haifa City Museum is a good place to get some background on the history of Haifa.

Located in a former Templer school building in the historic German Colony, the museum has undergone renovations and additions over the years. The museum's changing exhibitions focus on topics of regional interest including architecture, history, and residents.

Stella Maris Carmelite Monastery

top of Stella Maris Rd., off Tchernikovsky St. and adjacent to the upper station of the Haifa cable car; tel. 04/833-7758; 6am-noon and 3pm-6pm daily; free

Whether you go to see the vistas or the Stella Maris Carmelite Monastery, heading to the top of Mount Carmel on Stella Maris Road is well worth it. The Carmelites are a religious order of the Catholic Church that took their name from Mount Carmel, where they originated. From about 1631 onward, the monastery was built and destroyed several times. The current structure was opened in 1836, and the interior is full of beautiful, detailed paintings that grace the small but exquisite interior's vaulted ceiling.

San Francisco Observation Point

across from Stella Maris Carmelite Monastery on Tchernikovsky St.; free audio guide at site

The blue dome cage of the San Francisco Observation Point provides a gorgeous view. A recording, in multiple languages, provides detailed background information on the area.

The National Maritime Museum

198 Allenby St.; tel. 04/853-6622; www.nmm.org. il; 10am-4pm Sun.-Thurs., 10am-1pm Fri., 10am-3pm Sat.; adult NIS35, senior NIS17.5, child NIS23, combined Haifa museum ticket NIS60

It can be a bit confusing to find, but The National Maritime Museum features a collection that covers 5,000 years of maritime history of the Mediterranean basin, the Red Sea, and the Nile. Note that it is just down the road from the more obscure **Clandestine Immigration and Naval Museum** (204

Allenby St.). Look for the large ships on display outside to lead you to the general area of the museums. The museum has three levels with permanent and changing exhibitions and is an interesting window into the region's maritime history.

Elijah's Cave

230 Allenby St.; tel. 04/852-7430; 8am-5pm Sun.-Thurs., 8:30am-12:45pm Fri.; free

Situated about midway up a mountainside is the humble religious and spiritual destination of Elijah's Cave. Expect to see people here praying, as it is an important site for followers of Christianity, Judaism, and Islam. It is widely believed to be a cave where the prophet Elijah lived, and ceremonies are sometimes held here on religious days. The site is accessible from the top of the mountain at Stella Maris Monastery, but much easier to reach from Allenby Street, and there are separate male and female entrances.

Cable Car

top entrance at Stella Maris Carmelite Monastery area at Tchernikovsky St. and bottom entrance at Bat Galim Promenade; tel. 04/833-5970; www. visit-haifa.org; 10am-6pm daily; NIS32 round-trip, NIS21 one-way

If you have no fear of heights, the cable car is one of the best ways to get great views of Haifa, Mount Carmel, and Haifa Port. The slightly rickety and globe-shaped cars dangle from cables that go up and down the mountainside on a regular basis during the day. The bottom car can be found nearby the Clandestine Immigration and Naval Museum and its huge outdoor ships. The lower cars drop you off at Bat Galim Beach and Promenade. The upper cars are a quick walk from the Stella Maris Carmelite Monastery. The top terminal has three restaurants with amazing views that are somewhat pricey but popular among locals.

German Colony

Good for simply strolling about and taking in a variety of scenery and restaurants, the German Colony is the area located roughly

The Influence of the German Templers

Throughout Haifa and the north coast, the influence of the German Templers can still be seen in the form of entire neighborhoods that exhibit graceful architectural design and exude an atmosphere of antique elegance.

German Templers of the late 19th century who settled in what was then Palestine are not the same thing as the Templar knights, a monastic military order of the 12th century that guarded European pilgrims in the Holy Land. Today, there are Templer neighborhoods in Jerusalem, Tel Aviv, and Haifa.

The German Templers' neighborhood in Haifa (called the German Colony, just like in Jerusalem) is not large, but its unique character has been carefully preserved and walking tours regularly explore it. It runs from the foot of the Baha'i Gardens roughly to the port between Rothschild and Ben Gurion Streets.

Haifa's German Colony has been recently restored in a major undertaking by the city and is one of the best places to have a relaxing meal (the businesses are open seven days a week), especially in combination with a visit to the Baha'i Gardens. It is also home to some of the city's best boutique hotels.

One odd aspect of the German Templers' history is that around the time of World War II, they were sympathetic to the Nazis and were ultimately expelled from Palestine.

between the base of the Baha'i Gardens and the port. Numerous buildings here were built during the 1800s by the German Templers, and the area provides a calm and charming respite from a day of more intense sightseeing. There are guided tours in multiple languages through the German Colony; check with the **information center** (48 Ben Gurion St., tel. 04/853-5606, www.visit-haifa.org, 9am-5pm Sun.-Thurs., 9am-1pm Fri., 10am-3pm Sat.).

Madatech: National Museum of Science, Technology, and Space

25 Shmariyahu Levine St.; tel. 04/861-4444; www. madatech.org.il; 10am-3pm Sun.-Wed., 10am-5pm Thurs., 10am-1pm Fri., 11am-6pm Sat.; adult NIS89, under 5 free

A good option if traveling with kids, Madatech: National Museum of Science, Technology, and Space is a massive, hands-on, experiential science museum geared toward enhancing science- and technology-based education. Housed in a restored historic 1912 building, the museum includes over a dozen interactive exhibits, a science park, and an interactive "edutainment" movie theater called Cinematrix.

Reuben Hecht Museum Haifa

University of Haifa, Mt. Carmel; tel. 04/825-7773; http://mushecht.haifa.ac.il; 10am-4pm Sun.-Mon. and Wed.-Thurs., 10am-7pm Tues., 10am-1pm Fri., 10am-2pm Sat.; guided tours for groups, free

A small but beautifully appointed museum on the University of Haifa campus, the Reuben Hecht Museum Haifa will satisfy the archaeologist in any traveler. Some of the exhibits create the experience of being in a town under siege by the Romans. The Canaanite mummies and remnants of an ancient ship that was discovered underwater in the 1980s are interesting touches, as is the exhibit of l'École de Paris artwork. The museum affords a wonderful vista of Haifa and a chance to wander about the university campus.

TOURS
Route of 1,000 Steps

If you are in good shape, adventurous, and good with maps, you can try the Route of 1,000 Steps, a self-guided tour that goes from the top of Mount Carmel down through

---

1: the dome interior of the Stella Maris Carmelite Monastery 2: exhibit at The National Maritime Museum 3: the entrance to the German Colony 4: Baha'i Gardens and Golden Dome

several major neighborhoods of the city, ending at the German Colony. The route starts from Savyonim Lookout Point near Yefe Nof Street. You want to be in the vicinity of the Crowne Plaza Hotel Haifa (124 Yefe Nof St.) to get started. There are four routes along the way that are marked by steps and color-coded.

Free Tours

Many hotels in Haifa offer free tours as a courtesy to their guests. Tour times and availability vary; when you check in, ask the front desk of your hotel if they have anything available and what the tour schedule is. It is worthwhile to try to book a hotel that offers free tours, as private tours are expensive. You can also stop into any hotel (there are several close to each other in the German Colony) and ask for information.

Private Tours

The **Haifa Tourist Board** (www.visit-haifa. org) offers some tours, but the schedules change and are often only on the weekend. If you are interested in arranging a private tour, stick with a licensed guide, which they can recommend.

ENTERTAINMENT AND EVENTS

Haifa is home to a multitude of things to do when the sun goes down, from wine tastings (oenophiles can enjoy a surprisingly wide variety of regional vintages) to live music, festivals, and the largest movie theater in Israel.

Cinema
YES PLANET
55 HaHistadrut St.; tel. 04/841-6898; http:// yesplanet.co.il; NIS59
Billed as one of the largest movie theaters in Israel, Yes Planet screens contemporary American and European movies. Films are shown in English with Hebrew subtitles, or in a foreign language other than Hebrew with English and/or Hebrew subtitles. Check in advance.

Live Music, Clubs, and Bars
BEAT CLUB
124 Hanassi Blvd.; tel. 04/866-2244 and 04/810-7107; 10am-midnight daily; cover varies
Part of the variety of options for day and night on Hanassi Boulevard, the Beat Club is a top live performance club in Haifa and the north, with live musical performances by leading domestic artists daily. Beat Club sometimes hosts international acts.

SYNCOPA
5 Khayat St.; tel. 054/614-2643; 8pm-last customer daily; NIS40
Recommended by locals who like to party (in typical laid-back Haifa style), Syncopa is a bar with a crowd that is generally over 25. Mostly playing funk music, the bar has a softly lit interior and is a popular spot for simply hanging out.

VESPER COCKTAIL BAR
9 Nahum Dovrum St.; tel. 05/656-0160; 8pm-last customer daily; NIS60
The perfect place to relax with a drink in downtown Haifa, Vesper Cocktail Bar is a popular local spot with a rich, woody upscale pub interior. The large selection of top-shelf alcohol and a variety of wines and beers is complemented by the food menu with a range of choices that includes everything from a burger to salmon carpaccio.

Festivals
FIRST FRUITS WINE AND CHEESE TASTING FESTIVAL
Haifa Auditorium Park near the Haifa Cinematheque in the Hacarmel neighborhood; tel. 04/853-5606; www.visit-haifa.org; 6pm-11pm daily; NIS120
Held annually around May or June, the First Fruits Wine and Cheese Tasting Festival showcases regional wineries, wines, and foodstuffs with an emphasis on Haifa and the north. In addition to wines from vineyards of all sizes, there are booths of boutique cheese makers, chocolatiers, olive oil, and wine accessories; workshops and lectures are also given.

BEER CITY FESTIVAL

Student's Beach; www.visit-haifa.org; last week of August; NIS80

During the last week of August, thousands of people gather in Haifa for the annual Beer City Festival, which includes beers from all over Israel and the world, as well as live music.

PUPPET FESTIVAL

Haifa Auditorium in Central Carmel; tel. 052/389-7487; yaeln@012.net.il; free

The end of August brings the completely free Puppet Festival, which includes children's performances, puppet shows, outdoor events, and an exhibition of masterpiece artistic puppets.

HAIFA INTERNATIONAL FILM FESTIVAL

multiple venues; tel. 04/801-3471; www.haifaff.co.il/eng; NIS60-120

Held in late September or early October annually, the Haifa International Film Festival has been operating for more than 30 years. It includes events, lectures, and awards.

FESTIVAL OF FESTIVALS

tel. 04/853-5606; www.visit-haifa.org; 9am-8pm Thurs.-Sat. in December; free

This popular December event is a multicultural food and folklore festival that bills itself as the only one of its kind in the Middle East. Also known as the Holiday of Holidays, the Festival of Festivals for several weekends throughout December makes use of the numerous religious holidays that occur among different faiths and cultures in the region during that month. The festival is held in the Wadi Nisnas neighborhood of Haifa, between the neighborhoods of Hadar and the downtown area around the German Colony. The main staging areas are on Khoury Street, Hatzionut Street, Shabbtai Levi Street, and HaWadi Street.

SHOPPING

Haifa has some great shopping, with specific shopping-dedicated districts.

GERMAN COLONY

Along Ben Gurion Boulevard near the waterfront in the German Colony are a variety of high-end shops, art galleries, souvenir shops, coffeehouses, and restaurants housed in historic 19th-century Templer buildings. Most of the shops are open by 10am and close around 8pm on weekdays, with some closed or operating on more limited hours on Friday and Saturday.

MERKAZ PANORAMA

109 Hanassi Blvd.; tel. 04/837-5011; 9am-8pm Sun.-Thurs., 9am-2pm Fri.

Conveniently located on Hanassi Boulevard within an easy walk to all the hotels in the area, Merkaz Panorama is a small, upscale shopping mall that offers a surprising variety of clothes, shoes, and coffee shops with sandwiches and salads.

SPORTS AND RECREATION

As a coastal city, Haifa is home to numerous parks, promenades, and outdoor activities. Its proximity to Mount Carmel also affords good hiking opportunities.

Parks, Gardens, and Beaches

DADO BEACH

You might want to take a car or taxi to get here, but Dado Beach (southwest Haifa coast) is the best place in town for enjoying the beach, whether or not you go in the water. The promenade is long, there are beach chairs with shade, and it has numerous options for eating. It's even pleasant in good winter weather.

SCULPTURE GARDEN

Mitzpor Shalom or Peace Park, upper section of Hatzionut Ave., corner of Shnayim Be'November St.; 8am-6pm daily; free

At the Sculpture Garden, 29 bronze sculptures by Israeli artist Ursula Malbin line the walkways and are scattered about the lawns. The garden has a sweeping view of Haifa, the Mediterranean Sea, and the hills of the Galilee and Lebanon on a clear day. It is a 10-minute walk to the midsection level of the Baha'i Gardens.

Israel's National Trail in Haifa

If you look closely, you will see signs in Haifa for the Israel National Trail (*Shevil Israel* in Hebrew, www.israelnationaltrail.com and www.israeltrail.net), a hiking footpath that runs 580-620 miles (930-997 km), depending on the routes, from the Red Sea in the south to the border with Lebanon in the north.

The trail, which takes about 45 days to complete, can be seen at various points in Haifa, where it can be identified by subtle trail markings of three stripes of white, blue, and orange. It is listed among National Geographic's World's Best Hikes.

The trail also passes through Jerusalem, Tel Aviv, Nazareth, the Negev, and the Sea of Galilee.

★ LOUIS PROMENADE

One of the best places in the city for a long walk full of incredible vistas of Haifa, the port, and the lower city, Louis Promenade (off Yefe Nof St. in the Carmel district) runs through the center of the Carmel district parallel to Yefe Nof Street. There are plenty of places to take photographs and enjoy the scenery. It is close to the main cluster of hotels on Hanassi Boulevard, which makes it an easy walk if you're staying in the area.

TIKOTIN MUSEUM OF JAPANESE ART

89 Hanassi St.; tel. 04/838-3554; www.tmja.org. il; 10am-7pm Sun.-Thurs., 10am-1pm Fri., 10am-3pm Sat.; adult NIS35, senior and child NIS23

Along Yefe Nof Street, just off the promenade, there are a couple of small but nice museums. One is the Tikotin Museum of Japanese Art, which showcases over 7,000 pieces of contemporary and traditional pieces of Japanese art. Founded in 1959, the museum is completely dedicated to the preservation and exhibition of Japanese culture. It is the only museum of its kind in the region.

MANÉ-KATZ MUSEUM

89 Yafe Nof St.; tel. 04/911-9372; www.mkm.org.il; 10am-4pm Sun.-Wed., 4pm-7pm Thurs., 10am-1pm Fri., 10am-3pm Sat.; adult NIS35, senior NIS17.5, child NIS23, combined Haifa museum ticket NIS60

Also along Yefe Nof Street is the Mané-Katz Museum, with its stunning location overlooking Haifa Bay. The museum opened in 1977 in the former home of Israeli artist Mané-Katz, a prominent member of a group of eastern and central European artists who trained in Paris during the two World Wars. The museum exhibits and displays Mané-Katz's work, including sculpture and paintings.

HECHT PARK

Ha'hagana St.; www.visit-haifa.org

The largest area of greenery inside Haifa city limits, Hecht Park is at the north end of Dado Beach and promenade and hugs the coast with continuous views of the sea. The park has a path for walking and running that spans an almost two-mile (3.2 km) perimeter.

X-PARK

southern entrance to Haifa in the Congress Center; tel. 04/788-3812; www.xpark.co.il; call for pricing as it depends on activity

Attracting every skill level, from families to professionals, the X-Park includes a skating park complex, an Olympic climbing wall, a rope park, paintball, and more. If you have extra time in the Haifa area or want to do something active on your way in or out of the city, this is a good option.

HANGING BRIDGES AT NESHER PARK

Carmel National Forest, arrive from Haruv St. in Nesher off Rte. 4; tel. 04/823-1452; www.parks.org.il; NIS38

If you have a car, the Hanging Bridges at Nesher Park can give you the experience of being up in

1: Sculpture Garden 2: a hanging bridge at Nesher Park 3: Louis Promenade

the trees. The bridges are suspended between canyons in the midst of the forest. There is a picnic and play area for kids, and it's about 25 minutes southeast of Haifa by car.

FOOD

Haifa's food scene offers two unique experiences: Druze cuisine and winery restaurants. Aside from that, it has a range of seafood restaurants, pubs, and standard Israeli fare of salads, toasted cheese sandwiches, and meat dishes. There is a decidedly Russian influence to some of the restaurants, including in the food preparation and the availability of meat dishes.

Mediterranean
ZAFRIRIM 1

1 Tsafririm St.; tel. 04/811-2235; www.zafririm1.co.il; noon-last customer daily; NIS60

The key word when describing Zafririm 1 is "cool." Everything from the atmosphere to the menu presentation and the unique preparation of dishes makes it a lively option for breakfast or lunch. Situated in the Carmel district, Zafririm 1 serves up dishes with a Mediterranean flair, such as Taboon chicken and Baladi eggplant. The restaurant's exposed-brick interior walls and black-lacquer tables with overhead lighting give it an overall feel of a New York spot you might find in SoHo.

Middle Eastern

Just next to the grittier Hadar district of Haifa is the mostly Arab section of town, Wadi Nisnas, home to several delicious options for falafel, hummus, shawarma, and the like. Around the area of Hanevi'im and Hehaluts Streets there is a nice selection of small falafel shops and stands, most of which are open from late morning (10am) to evening (about 9pm). They are excellent options for takeout or a quick, cheap bite to eat.

★ FATTOUSH

38 Ben Gurion St.; tel. 04/852-4930; 8am-1am daily; NIS70

One of the most popular spots in the German Colony for both food and atmosphere, Fattoush serves up a tasty variety of Middle Eastern food and the best cappuccino in town. The massive outdoor patio seating is situated in a grove of trees and decorated with tons of tiny touches, including colorful hanging beads, glass lamps, and brass finishes, similar to the cave-like interior of the restaurant. It all adds up to give an exotic feel that enhances the delicious food. A handwritten sign at the entrance states that all types of people of all backgrounds and beliefs are welcome. It is the type of place that you will want to go back to again and again.

DOUZAN

35 Ben Gurion St.; tel. 04/852-5444; http://douzan. rest.co.il; 9am-midnight daily; NIS60

At the family-run French-Arab fusion restaurant Douzan, the aim is to make customers feel at home and relaxed. Decorated with whimsical touches including old clocks, musical instruments, and velvety cushions, it is known for its surprising specialties, such as small meat pies with pine nuts (called *sfeeha*).

ALLENBY RESTAURANT

43 Allenby St.; tel. 04/852-9928; 7am-7pm Sat.-Thurs., 7am-5pm Fri.; NIS45

An excellent choice for Arab food in the midst of the German Colony, Allenby Restaurant is no-frills with fast, efficient service. With a plain storefront and a cafeteria-like interior, it caters to a more mature, working-class crowd, and is famous for its various presentations and side dishes accompanying its hummus, vegetable dishes, and Turkish coffee.

Bistro
SINTA BAR

127 Moriya Blvd.; tel. 04/834-1170; www.sinta-bar. co.il; noon-11pm daily; NIS 90

The open, split-level, loft-like floor plan of Sinta Bar gives this meat lover's paradise in Haifa's Ahuza district a cool and relaxed atmosphere. More than a decade old, the restaurant is one of Haifa's longer-running institutions and is a very short drive from the Carmel district. Serving up seafood and meat dishes with a nice selection of desserts made in-house, it is a low-key and classy option for dinner, especially if you're staying on the mountain.

Italian
HANAMAL 24

24 Hanamal St.; tel. 057/944-2262;
http://hanamal24.rest.co.il/en; noon-midnight
Mon.-Sat.; NIS120

Inspired by Tuscany, the upscale and renowned Hanamal 24 has several different rooms throughout the restaurant's space, including a lounge, piazza, and wine cellar. Touches of brick in the flooring and rich, warm wood tones throughout create a welcoming atmosphere. Some highlights of the gourmet dinner menu include salmon and drum fish ceviche, pork with white wine risotto, and other very inventive meat and seafood dishes. The extensive wine list includes choices from Israel and beyond.

Latin
HAVANA PLUS

25 Ben Gurion St.; tel. 053/809-4797; www.2eat.
co.il/havana-plus; 10am-3am daily; NIS80

You wouldn't expect to find Cuban-themed food in the German Colony in Haifa, but Havana Plus ably provides. With a richly decorated atmosphere that includes comfy pillows and hookahs, soft lighting and wood finishes, Havana is very relaxed and warm. Most of the menu items include meat and fish, with an occasional pasta dish, catering to Haifa's hipper and younger crowd. As long as you don't expect to find fried plantains and refried beans, you won't be disappointed.

Coffee Shops and Cafés
SANTA MARIA COFFEE AND SNACKS

entrance to Stella Maris Carmelite Monastery on
Tchernikovsky St.; tel. 04/859-7518; 8am-8pm daily;
NIS55

If you find yourself at the **Stella Maris Carmelite Monastery,** you won't miss the obviously positioned Santa Maria Coffee and Snacks at the entrance. Relaxed and casual in both its atmosphere and location, with a bright and airy feel, it's a terrific place to have a leisurely cup of coffee and enjoy a piece of famous apple strudel. They also have a nice selection of sandwiches, desserts, and breakfast items. The staff is incredibly friendly and upbeat, and there is a beautiful view of the open sky and sea.

Douzan restaurant in Haifa's German Colony

CAFÉ LOUISE

58 Moriya Blvd.; tel. 04/834-9950; www.cafelouise.
co.il; 10am-10pm Sun.-Thurs., 9am-3pm Fri.; NIS60

With its fresh, bright atmosphere and emphasis on the healthiest of dishes, including some gluten-free food options, Café Louise has another location in Haifa at the Grand Canyon Mall, and one in Tel Aviv. The seafood and meat dishes are punctuated with some vegan menu choices and whole wheat pasta. Catering to the health-conscious, it offers a nice alternative to standard café options.

★ HABANK RESTAURANT

119 Hanassi Blvd., Carmel Center; tel. 04/836-3363;
http://habank.rest.co.il; 8:30am-midnight
Sun.-Thurs., 8:30am-after midnight Sat.; NIS65

With their claim to fame as the first coffee shop/café in Haifa, HaBank Restaurant is a kosher restaurant that serves up standard but delicious fare including salads and meat dishes. Seating is creatively arranged with an outdoor patio, an indoor greenhouse-like area, and an inner area with a bar, flat-screen TVs, and fish tanks. They make their desserts in-house (try the banana crumble or the huge slice of unbaked cheesecake) and are known for their lamb pastry dish (NIS80). The crowd is very local and pretty subdued, and the staff is friendly and laid-back.

CAMEL RESTAURANT

Dado Beach; tel. 04/852-2990;
9am-2am daily; NIS55

One of many seaside cafés along the promenade at Dado Beach, Camel Restaurant is easy to spot, with its huge yellow sign that is reminiscent of a certain cigarette brand. Like many of the restaurants along the strip, its spacious, simple interior is suitable for sandy feet and wet towels. There is also tons of outdoor seating on the beach, with comfy, cushioned chairs and umbrellas, open even on nice winter days. It's a great place to get a large pizza to feed several people, and the staff is friendly and accommodating.

ACCOMMODATIONS

There are many hotel options in Haifa and the north coast, ranging from five-star luxury resort hotels to bed-and-breakfast options to very simple and affordable hostels. The only cautionary note is to beware booking a room in the Hadar district over the weekend. Though there are some affordable options there, the entire area shuts down from late Friday afternoon through late Saturday evening, and you'll be hard-pressed to even find a place to eat.

Under US$100

HAIFA MAROM HOTEL

51 Palmach St.; tel. 04/825-4355; marom.hotelasp.
com; US$95 d

With 50 rooms and a slightly removed position from the hustle of central Haifa, the Haifa Marom Hotel is situated in a peaceful location amid pine trees on top of Mount Carmel, with a sundeck surrounded by gardens. The plain but comfortably furnished rooms are air-conditioned and all include a bathroom, free wireless Internet, phone, and satellite TV. Deluxe rooms have a whirlpool bath. Other amenities include free covered parking and 24-hour room service. The hotel has dining rooms, large halls for conferences and events, a gym, and a spa. It is close to the Technion and Haifa University, the Horev Center, the Grand Canyon Shopping Center, and the city's sports hall.

PORT INN HOSTEL

34 Jaffa Rd.; tel. 04/852-4401; http://portinn.net;
US$99 d

Situated in a renovated Arabic-style building in downtown Haifa, the Port Inn Hostel is a cross between a hostel and a motel, with 18 vacation apartments, rooms, and dormitories to choose from. The central location is close to the Haifa Port passenger terminal, the Haifa Merkaz-Hasmona train station, and the Carmelit subway. It is also near the Baha'i Gardens, the German Colony, and numerous restaurants. The inn is decorated in a simple, homey manner, with a common lounge area with a multilingual satellite TV, a kitchen with free coffee and tea all day, and a lush tropical garden area for sitting and relaxing. There are coin-operated washing machines.

LOUI M. APARTMENTS

35 HeHaluts St.; tel. 054/837-1342; US$75 d

Near the National Museum of Science, the Hadar Shopping District, and the Carmelit subway, the Loui M. Apartments is a 14-room motel with a simple, boxy exterior and a plain interior with rooms and studios laid out with the feel of apartments. Rooms include an LCD TV, a small dining area, and a private bathroom. The building has a roof terrace and is about 10 minutes from Haifa Port.

US$100-150

HOTEL BETH-SHALOM

*110 Hanassi Blvd.; tel. 04/837-3480; www.
beth-shalom.co.il; US$110 d*

The family-run Hotel Beth-Shalom is a small 10-room hotel tucked away on busy Hanassi Boulevard that caters to pilgrims. It is near a number of sights, shopping, food, and an area of town that stays open during the weekend. The rooms are very small, but spotlessly clean, and every inch is well-utilized. The staff is extremely warm and accommodating, and there is some space at the front of the hotel for parking. Some rooms include a small balcony with a bit of canopy from the trees. Wireless Internet access can be purchased from the front desk for US$5.

★ ART GALLERY HOTEL

*61 Hertsel St.; tel. 04/861-6161; http://haifa.
hotelgallery.co.il; US$115 d*

The Art Gallery Hotel is a 40-room boutique hotel designed around the themes of art and scenery, with art galleries integrated into the interior. The Bauhaus building has a clean, modern interior, 24-hour concierge service, and parking. Two computers with Internet are available in the lobby, and there are free guided tours of the hotel art galleries. Though small by American standards, all of the rooms include free wireless Internet,

air-conditioning, LCD cable TV, and wooden floors, while suites feature a separate sleeping area, a balcony overlooking the city, and a spa bath. The 24-hour fitness center overlooks Haifa Bay, and the hotel offers free tour services. Slightly off the beaten path, the hotel is an excellent choice for a bit of luxury at an extremely affordable price, especially if you are traveling with a car. Beware of booking here over the weekend, though, as you'll be in an area that shuts down on Friday and Saturday.

1926 DESIGNED APARTMENTS

36 Moshe Aron; tel. 054/539-9040; http://1926.co.il; US$128 d

Situated in the bustling downtown Turkish market area, the 1926 Designed Apartments is a very small eight-room apartment suite that comes highly recommended by travelers for its location, modern atmosphere, and central location. The building is within easy walking distance from the Carmelit subway, direct buses throughout Haifa, Haifa Port, the Dagon Grain Museum, and the History of the City of Haifa Museum. The modern, bright, and pretty apartments in the renovated building include a sitting area with a sofa; a kitchen with a refrigerator, microwave, hot plate, electric kettle, cutlery, and dishes; air-conditioning; a 32-inch (81 cm) cable satellite TV; and free wireless Internet. Each studio apartment can accommodate two or three people.

THEODOR HOTEL

*63 Hertsel St.; tel. 04/867-7325; www.theodorhotel.
co.il; US$125 d*

The Theodor Hotel is a 98-room hotel in Haifa's Hadar neighborhood (the one that shuts down on the weekend). The hotel has free wireless Internet, small collections of books on all 11 floors, and a very comfortable, spacious lobby that feels more like a coffee shop. The modern, bright, and comfortably furnished rooms are geared toward couples and include cable TV, a kettle for tea and coffee, a safe, air-conditioning, and telephones for direct inbound calls. The hotel is slightly off the beaten path, but has views of the Carmel Mountains and Haifa Bay, and includes a lobby bar, restaurant, lobby TV, and laundry services. You can also buy postage and change money at the front desk. Hotel staff can assist with arranging for a doctor or babysitter, and there are on-site spa treatments.

HADDAD GUEST HOUSE

26 Ben Gurion St.; tel. 077/201-0618; www. haddadguesthouse.com; US$120 d

The small and rustic Haddad Guest House makes up in services what it lacks in flash. Some of the 13 rooms have a view of Mount Carmel, the Baha'i Gardens, or Haifa Bay. Rooms have a double or twin beds, a closet, private shower and toilet, a small, fully equipped kitchen, a small TV, hair dryer, and air-conditioning. An extra bed can be added to a room on request. Guest services include wireless Internet, laundry, and office services. Haddad's interior is extremely simple and a bit utilitarian, but it is located in the heart of the main street of the German Colony, the center of Haifa's nightlife, art gallery scene, shopping, museums, and cafés, and is 15 minutes by foot to the Baha'i Gardens. Ask the front desk for discount coupons for nearby restaurants.

US$150-200
HAIFA BAY VIEW HOTEL

101 Hanassi Blvd.; tel. 04/835-4311; www.nofhotel. co.il; US$165 d

Conveniently located just a 15-minute walk from the Baha'i Gardens in the center of the Carmel neighborhood and a few minutes from the Carmelit subway, the recently renovated and renamed Haifa Bay View Hotel has a sleek, modern decor, fantastic views of the water, and a late checkout. Most of the 91 rooms have outstanding views of Haifa Bay, the Baha'i Gardens, and the western Galilee. Parking is free and there are coffee shops, restaurants, and stores nearby. Inside the hotel is a cafeteria, a piano bar, and a kosher Chinese restaurant. Room amenities include cable TV, a hair dryer, a direct-dial phone,

air-conditioning, and a minibar. Lobby services include a coffee and tea corner, computers with Internet for free use, and personal safes at reception. The hotel can also assist with car rental, laundry services, and taxis.

THE COLONY HOTEL HAIFA

28 Ben Gurion St.; tel. 04/851-3344; www. colonyhaifa.com; US$195 d

The Colony Hotel Haifa, a 103-year-old restored boutique hotel in Haifa's historic German Colony, is known for its friendly staff. The building's lovely exterior is limestone with green shuttered windows, and inside there are 40 rooms and mini-suites with tiling accents and comfortable, modern furnishings that give an overall feel of historic luxury. The hotel's terrace overlooks the Baha'i Gardens, which are a straight 10-minute walk up Ben Gurion Street. The hotel has a 24-hour lobby bar, a spa room, gardens, and free wireless Internet in all the rooms. Concierge services help with reserving tours, laundry services, and takeout orders from nearby restaurants. The hotel is also near cafés, shopping, and Haifa Port.

★ TEMPLERS BOUTIQUE HOTEL

36 Ben Gurion Blvd.; tel. 077/500-3110; www. templers-haifa.com; US$189 d

There is something unforgettable about the Templers Boutique Hotel, set back a bit from the main street in the German Colony. The privately owned boutique hotel is perfectly located, with a huge private parking lot in the back and an indoor-outdoor café with a gorgeous patio and covered tables in the front. Some of the beautiful, classy, modern rooms feature massive freestanding bathtubs, whirlpool tubs, or huge showers, alongside luxurious and comfortable decor with sitting chairs and large, soft beds. Just at the foot of the Baha'i Gardens, the building dates back to 1870 and won first place in the German Colony's building renovation competition. Each room is designed in a different style, and the hotel offers last-minute deals and free Baha'i Gardens walking tours. It is near public transportation and all rooms have a kitchenette, a coffee and tea maker, a flat-screen satellite TV, free wireless Internet, and air-conditioning.

Over US$200
VILLA CARMEL BOUTIQUE HOTEL
1 Heinrich Heine St. off 30 Moriah Blvd.; tel. 04/837-5777; www.villacarmel.co.il; US$230 d

Villa Carmel Boutique Hotel is a 15-room boutique hotel with a modern, sleek interior that includes comfortable couches in the rooms and a pretty dining room. Situated in the middle of Haifa's prestigious Carmel district, the Villa was built as Haifa's most luxurious hotel in the 1940s and has been renovated with modern conveniences. Surrounded by a small glen of trees, the hotel was a regular choice of Israel's first prime minister, David Ben-Gurion, and his wife. The hotel is quite far off the beaten path, tucked away in a residential neighborhood, making it good for an immersive escape. Room amenities include Egyptian cotton linens, cozy beds, free wireless Internet, a desk and phone with conference call capability, and wide-screen HD TVs. Most rooms have a whirlpool bath or computerized jet shower. The hotel has a restaurant, lush garden, rooftop sundeck with a large whirlpool tub and sauna, and massages by appointment. There is also a fully equipped business center and private meeting space with screen and projector.

INFORMATION AND SERVICES

Haifa is a tourist destination for Israelis as well as tourists from abroad, and it is well-equipped for visitors.

Tourist Information
HAIFA TOURIST INFORMATION OFFICE
48 Ben Gurion St.; www.visit-haifa.org; 9am-5pm Sun.-Thurs., 9am-1pm Fri., 10am-3pm Sat.

You will see signs for it all over town, but there is only one Haifa Tourist Information Office, conveniently located in the German Colony. The office is full of flyers, maps, and information about the area. The real wealth of information, though, can be found in the staff working here: They will give you as many details as you can handle.

Online Resources

The most robust website for online resources about Haifa and the surrounding areas is the **Haifa Tourist Board** (www.visit-haifa.org). Don't worry about downloading their tourist

the Colony Hotel Haifa

guide, though. You will get offered the compact printed version at every turn once you are in Haifa.

Also useful is the **Haifa Aliya Website** (www1.haifa.muni.il/aliya) with tons of information on services, transportation, and the makeup of different neighborhoods for new residents of the area.

Hospitals and Emergency Services

Fairly centrally located and with an emergency room, the **Bnai Zion Medical Center** (47 Golomb St., tel. 04/837-1973, www.b-zion.org.il) is between the Hadar and Carmel districts.

You can also call **Magen David Adom** (tel. 04/851-2233) 24 hours a day for emergency services, including an ambulance to the nearest emergency room.

Police

The **tourist police** in nearby Tel Aviv can be reached by phone (tel. 03/516-5382) if the need arises, and they should be able to direct you to the appropriate location or service.

ATMs, Banks, and Currency Exchange

The most robust areas in town for ATMs, banks, and money-changing services are on Hanassi Boulevard near Yefe Nof Street and Ha'em Park, as well as on Ben Gurion Street in the center of the German Colony.

Inside the **Panorama Mall** (109 Hanassi Blvd., tel. 04/837-5011, 9am-8pm Sun.-Thurs., 9am-2pm Fri.) is a currency exchange desk.

GETTING THERE AND AROUND

Most visitors to Haifa arrive by car or the national Israeli intercity train. Egged buses that travel all over the country also go here. Once here, you can get around by city bus, taxi, or Israel's only underground subway, the Carmelit.

Car

Driving into Haifa is fairly simple, but once you get into the city you really need to have a GPS to navigate around Mount Carmel and through the winding, hilly streets. Take Highway 2 straight north from **Tel Aviv,** or Highway 1 to 2 or 6 from **Jerusalem.** Highway 2 is a very pretty drive along the coast in good weather, and you can even see some ancient ruins if you keep an eye out.

There are three car rental companies lined up next to each other at the northern entrance to the city. **Avis** (34 HaHistadrut St., tel. 04/861-0444, http://avis.co.il) is a familiar option, and if they cannot accommodate you, the competition is literally next door, including **Eldan** (164 HaHistadrut St., tel. 04/841-0910, www.eldan.co.il) and **Shlomo Sixt Car Rental** (48 HaHistadrut St., tel. 04/872-5525, en.shlomo.co.il).

Bus

There are buses leaving multiple times a day from **Jerusalem, Tel Aviv,** and elsewhere to get you into Haifa. Watch out: There are five stations within Haifa, and you could end up on the wrong side of town if you don't know where you're going. It's about a two-hour ride from Jerusalem and can be crowded on Thursdays and Fridays, especially in the late afternoon.

From Jerusalem or Tel Aviv, take an **Egged** bus (www.egged.co.il, NIS42 and up) from the **Central Bus Station.** Once in Haifa, there are more public Egged buses that run all over the city and even operate on the weekend, though not as frequently.

Boat

Some visitors to Haifa arrive and stay for a day or two due to a scheduled stop on their cruise ship or boat trip. The **Port of Haifa** (www.haifaport.co.il) is in the downtown area and about a 10-minute drive or 30-minute walk to the German Colony.

Train

The **Israel Railways** (www.rail.co.il, NIS20 roundtrip) train station is a 70-minute ride

Public Transportation Surprises

Haifa's cable cars

A pleasantly surprising aspect of Haifa, Israel's third largest city, is that it features some unique public transportation options that cannot be found anywhere else in Israel.

- The first surprise is that during **Shabbat** there is some public transportation running, something that not even Tel Aviv can claim. Public service on the green Egged buses still runs, though on a less frequent schedule.

- The second surprise is that Haifa is home to Israel's only subway, the **Carmelit.** Even though the Carmelit's range and distance is extremely limited (it goes in a straight line from the lower city to the upper city in just six stops), it's a convenient transportation option. The route goes directly through a major section of Haifa's tourist areas and is less intimidating for a first-time visitor than taking a bus or taxi.

- Haifa's final public transportation surprise is the **cable car** that traverses the side of Mount Carmel at a daring angle. It leaves every 15 minutes or less and has one stop at the top of the mountain and one at the bottom. It is yet another option for tourists looking for the quickest and least expensive route between some of the city's attractions, including Stella Maris Carmelite Monastery, San Francisco Observation Point, Elijah's Cave, and the National Maritime Museum.

from Tel Aviv and at least a three-hour ride from Jerusalem.

Cable Car

If you find yourself at Haifa's Bat Galim Promenade on the waterfront and want to get up the side of the mountain to see Stella Maris Carmelite Monastery, the **cable car** (top station on Tchernikovsky St. opposite the Stella Maris Carmelite Monastery, bottom station at the northern end of Bat Galim

Promenade, www.visit-haifa.org, 10am-6pm daily, NIS29 round-trip, NIS19 one-way) is the quickest and cheapest way to go. The ride only takes about seven minutes one way, but the dangling cars are slightly rickety and it is very high up.

Subway (Carmelit)

Haifa proudly boasts the only subway in Israel, the Carmelit (http://carmelithaifa.com, 6am-midnight Sun.-Thurs., 6am-3pm Fri., after sunset-midnight Sat., single ticket about NIS7, daily ticket NIS15), but the route it covers is very limited. It can be an easy way to experience various parts of the city, and there are restaurants along the way. It is most convenient if you're traveling in a straight line between the different stations at the lower city, Wadi Nisnas, and straight up the mountain to Hanassi Boulevard. In all, there are only six stations. You can buy a single, daily, or 10-ride ticket.

Akko (Acre)

Akko is full of mysterious, whispering nooks and crannies due to its well-preserved ancient architecture and its lengthy, rich history. Repeatedly conquered and occupied by different civilizations throughout the ages, the Old City of Akko (also called Acre) is a UNESCO World Heritage Site. To visit Akko's Old City and wander through the ancient halls of stone with their massive, arching ceilings is to step straight into the past.

Also a favorite locale to get world-class seafood (one of the region's most famous seafood chefs operates here) and within easy driving distance of Haifa, Akko is the perfect place to spend the afternoon sightseeing and then have a delicious meal.

SIGHTS

Baha'i Gardens

just off Hwy. 4 when entering Akko; tel. 04/831-3131; www.ganbahai.org.il/en/akko; inner gardens 9am-noon Fri.-Mon., outer gardens 9am-4pm daily; free

Smaller than its Haifa counterpart but similarly designed and landscaped, the Baha'i Gardens is the resting place of the founder of the Baha'i religion, and the location of the house where he lived during the last years of his life. The immaculate circular gardens create a peaceful cocoon of tranquility.

TOP EXPERIENCE

★ Acre Old City

1 Weizmann St. at southern end of HaHagana St.; www.akko.org.il/en; NIS15 and up for sites, combination ticket options available, ticket office at the Enchanted Garden

Akko's magnificent Acre Old City is a UNESCO World Heritage Site and comprised of a complex network of buildings, sites, and museums that would take about two days to tour completely. The Crusader city is a network of walls and fortresses, knights' halls, and beautiful, golden stone that seems to whisper stories from its past as you walk through the main complex of halls, buildings, and courtyards. There are some areas that recently underwent renovations, but the collective impact is akin to stepping straight into history.

HOSPITALLER'S FORTRESS

8:30am-6pm Sun.-Thurs., Sat., and holidays, 8:30am-5pm Fri. and holiday eves; NIS66 for part of combined ticket

The main buildings of the Old City, the Hospitaller's Fortress and its courtyard were the main fortress of a monastic military order that was established to treat the sick in the Holy Land. The order had its headquarters in Akko from 1191 to 1291.

UNDERGROUND PRISONER'S MUSEUM

tour reservations in advance at www.akko.org.il/ en; tel. 04/991-1375; 8:30am-4:30pm Sun.-Thurs., 8:30am-1:30pm Fri.; NIS25

Fascinating and a bit haunting, the Underground Prisoner's Museum features tons of life-size bronze statues of prisoners and other characters who played roles in the prison's history positioned throughout different rooms.

AL BASHA TURKISH BATH

8:30am-6pm Sun.-Thurs., Sat., and holidays, 9am-5pm Fri. and holiday eves; NIS25

The Al Basha Turkish Bath also features

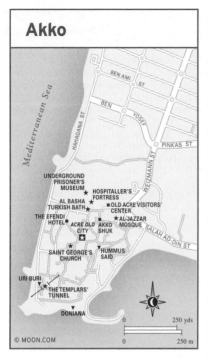

Akko

© MOON.COM

bronze, life-size statues of people going about their business in the bathhouse, including props and scenes of what life was like in the intact six rooms.

THE TEMPLARS' TUNNEL

9:30am-5:30pm Sun.-Thurs., Sat., and holidays,
9:30am-4:30pm Fri. and holiday eves; NIS15

It takes about 20 minutes walking through backstreets to reach The Templars' Tunnel, used by the monastic military order called Templars, which guarded European pilgrims visiting the Holy Land. The main fortress of the Templars was built at the western end of the tunnel, which extends 350 meters underground.

The route to reach the tunnel is not well-marked, making it necessary to ask for directions along the way. Set out by about 2pm to give yourself enough time to find the tunnel, explore it, and find your way back. You must have a ticket to enter, which you can purchase at the main ticket booth of the Old City.

Churches and Mosques

There are several ancient churches and mosques in Akko, most of which can be found on the very well-organized **website for the Old City** (www.akko.org.il/en).

SAINT GEORGE'S CHURCH

tel. 04/991-0563; call in advance for a visit

Considered one of the most beautiful churches in the Levant, Saint George's Church is a Greek Orthodox establishment that was likely Akko's first Christian house of worship built during the Turkish period.

AL-JAZZAR MOSQUE

tel. 04/991-3039; NIS15

Dominating and beautiful, the Al-Jazzar Mosque's brilliant green and white look stunning from a distance. The entrance to the mosque, the second largest in Israel, is up some steep steps at the beginning of the pathway that leads to the Templars' Tunnel. The mosque was inaugurated around 1781. The interior has beautiful pillars and arching below a second-floor open walkway, with inlaid inscriptions on the circumference of the inner building. There are no specific hours, but try to visit between 9am-4pm Saturday-Thursday, and avoid Fridays.

ENTERTAINMENT AND EVENTS

ACRE FRINGE THEATER FESTIVAL

Acre Old City; during the intermediate days of the Sukkot holiday in the fall; www.accofestival.co.il; NIS40-75

Renowned domestically and internationally, the Acre Fringe Theater Festival has been held every year since 1979 in the Old City. The festival's events include plays, street performances, booths, and fire demonstrations. The main events are held in the Hospitaller's Fortress.

SHOPPING

Akko's two main shopping areas can be found easily by looking for the green-and-white Al-Jazzar Mosque. Get to the far eastern side of

The World of Old Acre

In 2010, UNESCO declared the Old City of Acre (Akko) a World Heritage Site of outstanding universal value, and with good reason. The designation is international recognition of its history as home to a number of different cultures throughout the centuries, and guarantees a certain degree of protection and preservation for the sake of global humanity. Notable is the influence of the Templars, a military-monastic order that served the church in the Holy Land. Acre was a Templar stronghold from 1197-1291 AD.

Acre Old City is a historic, walled port city that has been populated—without interruption—since the time of the Phoenicians (about 1500-300 BC) until the modern day.

Acre Old City's position on a peninsula with a natural bay made it internationally important during the time of the Crusaders. Its strategic port became a center for international trade. In the 18th century, it was the regional capital of the Ottoman Empire after a long period of decline.

One of Acre Old City's most impressive monuments to its storied history is the remains of the Crusader City (AD 1104-1291) that have stayed almost completely intact above and below the modern street level. Since the 18th century, Acre Old City in its current state fits the characteristics of a fortified Ottoman city, with typical urban elements of a citadel, mosques, *khans* (roadside inns), and baths.

the Old City, and as you face the mosque, go to the left to find shops and stores that sell a variety of items like food and basic amenities. Go to the right (with the mosque on your left) and you'll pass through a small plaza that leads into the medium-sized *shuk* (outdoor market) that sells the typical regional wares that include dried fruit, spices, and pita.

FOOD
Middle Eastern
HUMMUS SAID

middle of the Old City market area, off Salah ad Din St.; tel. 04/991-3945; 6am-2:30pm Sun.-Fri.; NIS30

A good place to stop off for lunch, Hummus Said serves up piles of pita, pickled *mezze* dishes, and other appetizers, as well as hummus. It has a small, humble interior with just a few tables and is extremely popular among locals and tourists. Expect a crowd if you go during the height of mealtime.

Seafood
★ URI BURI

11 HaHagana St., waterfront; tel. 04/955-2212; www.2eat.co.il/eng/uriburi; noon-11pm daily; NIS115

Set up in an old Turkish house converted into a restaurant and facing the Mediterranean, Uri Buri specializes in unique and masterful seafood preparation and presentation thanks to its iconic chef-owner Uri Yurmias. The interior is set up with individual rooms and Arab decor for an intimate atmosphere with limited seating, so reservations are recommended for this widely acclaimed seafood restaurant destination. Outdoor terrace seating facing the sea is also available in good weather. The dishes are inventive—Creole shrimp with spicy sauce and mangoes, and fried calamari rings with three dips—and the half orders allow you to sample more.

DONIANA

6 HaHagana St., waterfront; tel. 04/991-0001; noon-2am daily; NIS70

Also on the waterfront and situated on the third floor of the building, Doniana is an Arab-style fish-and-meat restaurant with an atmosphere defined by its views of the sea and the city. The *mezze* selection is extensive and can be filling enough for a meal, especially for lunch.

1: Acre Old City **2:** the Underground Prisoner's Museum **3:** hummus and pita **4:** shopping at the *shuk*

ACCOMMODATIONS

Places to stay in Akko are very few and largely limited to luxury accommodations that might not be open in the low season. It is a very short drive from Akko to other nearby cities and towns such as Nahariya and Haifa that offer more options for places to stay at a larger range of prices.

Over US$200
THE EFENDI HOTEL

Louis XI St., P.O.B 2503, Acre Old City; tel.
074/729-9799; www.efendi-hotel.com; US$400 d

If you plan to spring for a night in Akko, try The Efendi Hotel, a five-star luxury boutique hotel with just 12 rooms in the historic Old City. The palatial hotel has views of the historic city walls and the Mediterranean Sea. Built from two ancient houses that were combined and restored over a period of eight years, the hotel has rooms spread out over three levels with different designs, and some feature illustrations, preserved wood, sea views, and views of the ancient city of Akko and the scenic mountains of the western Galilee. Hotel services include a spa room, a 400-year-old Turkish bath, a wine bar, and a cellar from the Crusader era. Rooms feature Egyptian cotton linens, goose-down pillows and blankets, robes and slippers, marble-lined bathrooms with large showers, freestanding bathtubs, and towel warmers. There is also free wireless Internet, a minibar, and an espresso machine.

INFORMATION AND SERVICES

Akko is a tourist destination, and once you get anywhere near the Old City and Al-Jazzar Mosque, it is well-equipped to meet your needs.

Old Acre Visitors' Center

1 Weizmann St.; tel. 04/995-6706; 8:30am-4pm
Sun.-Thurs. and Sat., 8:30am-3:30pm Fri. and holiday eves

Just to the right as you enter the Enchanted Garden, the Old Acre Visitors' Center has some useful maps and a seven-minute free introductory movie about Akko in English.

Online Resources

By far the best website about Akko, put up by the Old Acre Development Company, is www.akko.org.il/en. The website includes maps, site introductions, operating times, and background information.

ATMs and Money Exchange

The plaza in front of Al-Jazzar Mosque has a convenient combination of an ATM, a bank, and money exchange services.

Police and Emergency Services

Just around the corner from the Al-Jazzar Mosque you'll find the extremely friendly and accommodating volunteer **tourist police** (9am-5pm daily).

GETTING THERE AND AROUND

Akko is very easy to reach by car by way of Highway 4 (90 minutes from **Tel Aviv,** 30 minutes from **Haifa**) from either the north or the south. There is plenty of **parking** around town and plenty of signage in English to direct you to the Old City.

If you are taking a bus, **Egged** (www.egged.co.il) travels from **Haifa** (numbers 251 and 271) and the north (numbers 501 and 360). Once in the city, you can get from city center to the Old City on Egged bus numbers 61 and 62.

The **Israel Railways** (www.rail.co.il) Akko **train station** is an 80-minute ride from **Tel Aviv** and up to 3.5 hours from **Jerusalem;** from the station, it is a 15-minute walk to the Old City.

Nahariya

Nahariya is a surprisingly charming little town where everyone seems to know each other. It is brimming with sweet details, such as decorative lamps that line the streets. It's the perfect place to spend a low-key afternoon and evening while getting in some surfing, swimming, bike riding, or a long walk. Nahariya's city center is compact and quaint, with a nice selection of restaurants, shops, and scenery. The most enchanting aspect by day or night is the Ga'aton River that runs through the center of town and is bordered by graceful trees and a white railing. Burdened by its history as a nuclear waste dumping ground that has been in the process of getting cleaned up for years, Nahariya is small and quiet.

SIGHTS
Promenade

Pleasant even in the winter, Nahariya's long promenade (off HaMa'apalim St.) is very close to the town's center and has space for running, biking, and strolling. The buildings along the promenade are well maintained, and at some points there are restaurants and coffee shops. The promenade extends south for about five miles (8 km), almost to Akko.

Grotto Caves at Rosh Hanikra

Rte. 4 to the northernmost part of Israel; tel.
073/271-0100; www.rosh-hanikra.com; 9am-6pm
Sun.-Thurs., 9am-4pm Fri. and holiday eves, 9am-6pm
Sat. and holidays Apr.-Oct.; 9am-4pm Sun.-Fri.
and holiday eves, 9am-6pm Sat. and holidays
mid-Oct.-Mar.; adult NIS50, senior and child NIS37

A 10-minute drive from Nahariya are the gorgeous, sparkling blue Grotto Caves at Rosh Hanikra. About 220 yards (200 meters) of walking track lead down to the natural grottoes, which are lit. Located at Israel's northernmost point at the Lebanese border, the grottoes have a few other attractions, including a promenade, a cable car, and sea-view restaurants. The entire site is set up so you can experience both the grottoes and the sea through a network of paved

walkways and cable cars, though it's not particularly accessible to people with disabilities.

The Lieberman House Museum

21 Hagedud St.; tel. 04/982-1516; http://museum.
rutkin.info/en; 9am-1pm Sun., Tues., and Thurs.,
9am-1pm and 4pm-7pm Mon. and Wed., 9am-noon
Fri., 10am-2pm Sat.; free

Showcasing the history of the city of Nahariya and housed in the former home of one of the town's first settlers, The Lieberman House Museum includes an archive of photos, posters, announcements, and correspondence from Nahariya's past and the Lieberman house's past, dating from pre-1948 through today.

SHOPPING
NAHARIYA MALL

2 Irish St., Ein Sara; tel. 04/992-9977; www.
mall-nahariya.co.il; 10am-9:30pm Sun.-Thurs.,
9am-2:30pm Fri.

The small Nahariya Mall sells a variety of shoes, bags, and clothes and has a surf shop that sells equipment and might be willing to rent pieces out.

SPORTS AND RECREATION

There are several outdoor and recreational sports in and around Nahariya, including swimming, bicycling, surfing, and hiking.

Surfing

A popular pastime in Nahariya is surfing, particularly at **Sokolow (Sokolov) Beach** (Nahum Sokolow St. at the beach end of HaGa'aton Blvd.). The beaches are clean and easily accessible. On a day with good waves (even in the middle of a workday during the week), you can expect to see at least a dozen surfers in the water. Sokolow is considered a very consistent break, with waves that can get up to about seven feet (2 meters) or higher.

Nahariya

Swimming

Look for HaGa'aton Boulevard and follow it to the sea to find plenty of spots to swim. If you need a landmark on the shore, look for the large structure that resembles boat sails. Some of the beaches have a small fee (about NIS10) and others are free.

You'll likely see locals swimming in areas with warnings posted to not swim there, but don't be tempted to follow suit unless you're prepared. The undertow of the Mediterranean can be very strong, even in shallow water on a calm day. Stick to areas that are designated beaches with lifeguards. Try your luck at **Galei Galil Beach.**

Bicycling

A favorite pastime in Nahariya, biking is a good way to take in a lot of the seaside and hop into a café for lunch without tiring yourself out. Try the front desk at the centrally located **Shtarkman Erna Boutique Hotel** for **bicycle rentals** (29 Jabotinsky St., tel. 04/992-0170, www.sernahotel. co.il; NIS40 and free to hotel guests).

FOOD

Dining options in Nahariya are surprisingly plentiful and easy to access, and provide a variety of choices, even late at night.

American
SOGO SUSHI AND GRILL BAR

1 Jabotinsky St., corner of HaGa'aton Blvd.; tel. 04/900-0001; www.sogo-bar.co.il; 9am-3am daily; NIS55

The Sogo Sushi and Grill Bar is a restaurant by day and a dance bar by night. The interior is huge and spacious, with a massive bar and modern finishes on all of the decor. The food is a fairly standard fare of burgers, sandwiches, and salads. If you're looking for some nightlife, this is a good place to start.

Cafés
PENGUIN

21 HaGa'aton Blvd.; tel. 04/992-8855; 9am-midnight daily; NIS55

One of the oldest restaurants in town and always hopping, Penguin is easy to find with the life-size penguins at the front door. The interior is simple, spacious, clean, and classy, with tons of outdoor seating and a nice wine and liquor selection. Their signature dish is schnitzel, and they also serve a wide variety of sandwiches and do a typical hearty Israeli breakfast.

ACCOMMODATIONS

Nahariya has numerous accommodations that vary from cheap motels to upscale boutique hotels. There is no reason to settle for something you're unhappy with if you wind up staying here for a night or two. Most hotels are within very easy walking distance of the beach and promenade.

US$100-150
★ SHTARKMAN ERNA BOUTIQUE HOTEL

29 Jabotinsky St.; tel. 04/992-0170; www.sernahotel. co.il; US$150 d

Near the popular Galilee Beach and the train station, this is a classy, understated 26-room boutique hotel, originally opened in 1959 and run by multiple generations of a local family. All rooms are air-conditioned with free wireless Internet, cable TV, a telephone, and a small fridge, and some have a spa bath. Some of the rooms are on the small side, but every inch makes you feel perfectly at home, including the lavish breakfast that's included in your stay. Drinks are served in the private garden, and bicycles and parking are available for free. The owners know every possible detail about the surrounding area and can arrange excursions, discounts at local restaurants, and tickets to nearby historic Akko. In August, guests get free entrance to a private beach and country club with swimming pools and tennis courts.

TRAVEL HOTEL AT KIBBUTZ GESHER HAZIV

Kibbutz Gesher Haziv on HaOranim St., just north of Nahariya; tel. 04/995-8568; www.zimmeril.com; US$140 d

This bed-and-breakfast situated north of Nahariya near the cliffs of Rosh Hanikra is a short drive from Achziv Beach. Located on a communal Israeli settlement, or kibbutz, overlooking the Mediterranean, the atmosphere is pure Israel countryside. The 32 rooms are plainly decorated but warm, with private bathrooms, air-conditioning, televisions, refrigerators, microwaves, and free coffee and cookies. Several nearby nature reserves can be explored by foot, donkey, horseback, or jeep, and the location is also convenient for exploring Crusader castles at Montfort and Yechiam and Akko. The kibbutz offers discount coupons for all attractions and restaurants in the area, free wireless Internet in common areas, and free entrance to their pool, sports facilities, and children's playgrounds.

Camping
ACHZIV NATIONAL PARK

about three miles (4.8 km) north of Nahariya on the way to Rosh Hanikra; tel. 04/982-3263; www.parks. org.il; sign in and out for camping is by noon; adult NIS37, child NIS20

Just a bit north of Nahariya is the popular Achziv National Park, which has beautiful, secluded beaches. There is also a Crusader fortress in the area and the ruins of ancient Achziv.

INFORMATION AND SERVICES

As a small coastal town, Nahariya has all the basic services you might need. The residents are extremely friendly and most speak English. If you have questions, you should feel comfortable asking anyone you encounter on the street.

Online Resources

The best source of online information about Nahariya is the **Israel Ministry of Tourism** website (https://info.goisrael.com). Also full of useful information is the family-run **Shtarkman Erna Boutique Hotel's** website

Nahariya's promenade

(www.sernahotel.co.il), which has tons of tips and information about tourism in the area.

ATMs and Currency Exchange
Your best bet for an ATM and for changing money is the **Nahariya Mall** (2 Irish St., Ein Sara; tel. 04/992-9977; www.nahariya-mall.co.il; 10am-9:30pm Sun.-Thurs., 9am-2:30pm Fri.).

Police, Emergency, and Tourist Services
Dial 100 for the **police** and 101 for **emergency medical services** from any phone. Dial *3888 from any phone for tourism, the Israel Police, the Ministry of Interior services, the Airport Authority, and more.

GETTING THERE AND AROUND
Car
You can reach Nahariya very easily by taking Highway 4 north. It's about 40 minutes from **Haifa** and just over two hours from **Jerusalem.** Once here, it's a remarkably easy place to navigate, with tons of **free parking.** It's basically impossible to get lost with the Ga'aton River as a guidepost in the center of town.

Bus
From **Jerusalem,** the **Egged** bus (www.egged.co.il, number 960, NIS65 one-way) takes about three hours. From **Tel Aviv** (number 910, NIS73 one-way), it takes about 3.5 hours. Both have transfers in **Haifa.**

Once you are in Nahariya, several Egged bus lines operate throughout town.

Train
The **Israel Railways** (www.rail.co.il) train takes about three hours from **Jerusalem** (NIS65 one-way), and about 90 minutes from **Tel Aviv** (NIS48 one-way).

Netanya

A seaside resort spot that is known for its oddly 1970s-themed atmosphere and popularity among French visitors, Netanya is not a major destination for Israelis or overseas visitors. However, it is just about equidistant from Haifa and Tel Aviv, and is an option for exploring low-key places to eat, rest, or just relax on the beach without the crowds you find in Tel Aviv.

SPORTS AND RECREATION
Parks and Nature Reserves
Netanya has several natural attractions in its vicinity that the Tourist Information Office should be able to tell you more about.

UTOPIA TROPICAL ORCHARD PARK
Kibbutz Bahan; tel. 09/878-2191; www.utopiapark.co.il/ english; 8:30am-6pm Sun.-Thurs., 8:30am-3pm Fri., 8:30am-7pm Sat. and holidays summer, 8:30am-5pm Sun.-Thurs., 8:30am-3pm Fri., 8:30am-6pm Sat. and holidays winter; adult NIS59, senior NIS54, child NIS44

The Utopia Tropical Orchard Park is a good option because it can be reached by bus from the Netanya Central Bus station (#33 Native Express). Kibbutz Bahan, home of the park, is the last stop on the line. The park is an incredible, lush oasis near Netanya that boasts waterfalls, a massive indoor greenhouse with tropical plants, gardens of roses, carnivorous plants, herbs, a musical water fountain, and a deck area for eating and drinking. A late morning or afternoon visit to Utopia could be a welcome respite, especially during Israel's hot, muggy summer months.

Beaches
Netanya boasts eight beaches. The most central, **Sironit Beach** (base of Rishonim Promenade), has a **transparent elevator** down to the beach. Buffered by piers, the water is safe for swimming almost the entire

year. In the summer months, nearby restaurants provide entertainment, and there are sports tournaments and games on the beach.

Hiking

The **Israel National Trail** (www.israelnationaltrail.com, www.netanya.muni.il) passes through Netanya, winding through some scenic areas that include the urban **purple Iris reserve,** several of the area's beaches, and the cliffs next to the city. The entire trail is about 620 miles (998 km) from the Red Sea to the border with Lebanon.

INFORMATION AND SERVICES

TOURIST INFORMATION OFFICE

12 Ha'azmaut Sq.; tel. 09/882-7286; 8am-4pm Sun.-Thurs., 9am-2pm Fri.

The **Tourist Information Office** is right at the town center and offers information about Netanya and the surrounding area.

The **Netanya Board of Tourism** (www.gonetanya.com) has a great website that provides a lot of basic information for visitors.

GETTING THERE AND AROUND

Israel Railways (www.rail.co.il) has a **train station** in Netanya. The train ride is about 30 minutes from **Tel Aviv** (NIS16 one-way) and two hours from **Jerusalem** (NIS38 one-way).

Netanya is a 30-minute drive from Tel Aviv just off **Highway 2,** or 45 minutes off **Highway 4.**

From Jerusalem, the **Egged** bus (www.egged.co.il, number 947, NIS32 one-way) from the **Central Bus Station** takes about 90 minutes. From Tel Aviv, the Egged bus (number 641, NIS20 one-way) takes close to two hours.

Caesarea (Qesarya)

Caesarea is two towns: the ancient city and the modern, rural town that is a favorite place for the vacation homes of wealthy Israelis. The ruins of ancient Caesarea can be seen alongside the modern town. The main highlight is the massive Antiquities Park, with a few other smaller but notable attractions.

SIGHTS

TOP EXPERIENCE

★ Caesarea National Antiquities Park

off Hwy. 2 near Kibbutz Sdot Yam; tel. 04/626-7080; www.parks.org.il; 8am-6pm Sun.-Thurs., 8am-5pm Fri. Apr.-Sept., 8am-4pm Sun.-Thurs., 8am-3pm Fri. Oct.-Mar.; NIS40

The Caesarea National Antiquities Park is unique in its selection of buildings from different historical periods. Spanning about 2,300 years, the park covers an area of about 125 acres (50,600 square meters) and includes archaeological remnants from the Hellenistic period (the 3rd century BC) to the Crusader period (the 12th century AD), a time when Caesarea was a port city and Israel's capital.

Named for Augustus Caesar, who gave the city to King Herod, Caesarea was built up by Herod to include venues for entertainment, bathhouses, and places of worship. Touring through the Antiquities Park allows you to wander in between ancient buildings and ruins, including the **Hippodrome** and the still-used **Roman Amphitheater.**

Situated inside the national park, the **Caesarea Port** (tel. 04/626-8882, www.caesarea.com) is an intoxicating mixture of ancient and modern, including the ancient **Crusader City,** with ruins dating from 1291, when the area was destroyed. Aside from the ancient port itself, there is a beach, restaurants, galleries, and more. Here you can also find the multimedia exhibition **Travel Through Time** (long building next to the jetty, English presentation every 15 min.)

Caesarea (Qesarya)

that tells Caesarea's history in three stations: a short movie of the city's history from ancient times through today, a 3-D interactive presentation on the impact of different historical figures, and a computer-generated show that depicts the city's construction masterpieces throughout history from the time of Herod onward.

Caesarea Antiquities Museum

Kibbutz Sdot Yam; tel. 04/636-4367; www.parks.org. il; 10am-4pm Sun.-Thurs., 10am-1pm Fri.; NIS15

Just at the southern entrance of Caesarea is the Caesarea Antiquities Museum, home to a wealth of treasures from the Mediterranean Sea and the surrounding area, including ancient coins, late Roman sculptures, Roman and Byzantine gems and jewelry, and pottery. Many of the finds here were dug up from the ground in the surrounding area by residents on the kibbutz over the past several decades.

★ Roman and Byzantine Aqueduct

shore of the Mediterranean Sea, end point in Caesarea at Aqueduct Beach; 24 hours; free

More part of the scenery than a destination, the Roman and Byzantine Aqueduct is just a few miles east of modern Caesarea proper. It runs along the seashore in a stunning display of ancient engineering.

There are several portions of the aqueduct, some of which are underground. You can see another section along Highway 2 between Caesarea and Haifa. The portion nearest

Caesarea was built by the Romans in the 2nd century AD and was repaired many times, so portions of the still-remaining aqueduct are different ages.

The raised stone aqueduct was used to bring water to the old city of Caesarea, and a large portion of it is still intact. The incredible architecture and engineering of the aqueduct is apparent despite its somewhat crumbling façade, and is still incredibly beautiful, especially against the backdrop of the Mediterranean Sea. The part of the aqueduct that reached Caesarea has not survived.

If you're adventurous and in good shape, you can climb up on top of the aqueduct at Aqueduct Beach in Caesarea and walk along the top.

Birds Mosaic Floor

about 0.25 miles (0.4 km) from the Antiquities Park; free

Believed to be part of a large villa dating back to the 6th or 7th century BC, the Birds Mosaic Floor, with its detailed frescoes of regional flora and fauna, particularly birds, was likely part of a large open courtyard. Several other parts of the villa had mosaic floors and have also been discovered at the site. The area is open and easy to spot, and you can walk on the mosaic.

Tours
EGGED TOURS

www.eggedtours.com; Sun., Tues., and Fri.; US$125 from Jerusalem, US$120 from Tel Aviv

For a guided day trip to Caesarea plus a couple of other areas, Egged Tours has a one-day tour that also includes Akko and Rosh Hanikra. The tours depart from Jerusalem at 5:50am and from Tel Aviv at 7:15am.

ENTERTAINMENT AND EVENTS

Particularly in the summer, Caesarea is fun in the evenings, with its ambience of the ancient port and outdoor seating at cafés. It's not Tel Aviv, but it has a nice rhythm to it.

Concerts

During the summer months, the ancient **Roman Amphitheater** (Caesarea National Antiquities Park; tel. 04/626-7080; www.parks. org.il; NIS25-50) holds outdoor concerts in a magical, unforgettable setting. There is no official website for upcoming concerts, but you can try searching **Eventim** (www.eventim. co.il) close to the date you are interested in.

Festivals

Every year during the months of July and August on Tuesday nights, different events are held at the port near the art gallery market and food stands for **Caesarea Nights.** Events, which include movie screenings, are scattered throughout the port area.

SHOPPING

A great place to shop for gifts and souvenirs is the **Caesarea Port**, where you can find jewelry, ceramics, and Judaica items.

SPORTS AND RECREATION

Caesarea's main distinction for sports enthusiasts is its 18-hole international golf course, the only one of its kind in Israel. There are also some great places to go swimming and diving.

Beaches
AQUEDUCT BEACH

near Caesarea Center Country Club, just off Aqueduct St.

One of the best beaches to visit in the Caesarea area is Aqueduct Beach, which you will see signs for as you drive through town. There is free parking, but there are no restrooms or places to change.

Golf
CAESAREA GOLF CLUB AND PROFESSIONAL GOLF COURSE

Golf neighborhood; tel. 04/610-9600; golf@ caesarea.com; 6am-6:30pm Tues.-Sun. summer, 6am-5pm Tues.-Sun. winter; NIS480 for 18 holes

The Caesarea Golf Club and Professional Golf

Course was established in the 1960s by the Baron Edmond de Rothschild family and is the only international golf club in Israel. The grounds of the club include training ranges, a perfectly groomed course, a pro shop, and a gourmet restaurant. In 2009, the course was redesigned by internationally renowned golf course designer Pete Dye.

Diving
OLD CAESAREA DIVING CENTER

Caesarea National Antiquities Park main entrance; tel. 04/626-5898; www.caesarea-diving.com; NIS180 and up

The Old Caesarea Diving Center is in a unique location on the ancient ruins of Herod's now-submerged port. The center operates the **Underwater Archaeological Park** with preserved underwater treasures and marine flora and fauna. Both certified and inexperienced divers are welcome, and you can get guided and independent diving and snorkeling, lessons, and gear for rent.

FOOD
Seafood
HELENA

Old Town Caesarea Port; tel. 053/809-4915; www.2eat.co.il/eng/helena; noon-11pm daily; NIS110

In the heart of Caesarea's old town is the delightful Helena, a gourmet restaurant run by two leading chefs in Israel. The star of the restaurant's decor is the view of the sea and port from the massive outdoor deck that is mostly covered from the hot sun. The interior is extremely simple with hardwood floors and ceiling fans. The menu's Mediterranean style features mainly seafood dishes, including a rich bouillabaisse. They also do a nice fish fillet that is served on a bed of gnocchi with cream sauce, mushrooms, and spinach and offer an extensive wine and alcohol menu as well as a discounted business lunch.

1: the Roman and Byzantine Aqueduct 2: the Roman Amphitheater in Caesarea National Antiquities Park

Cafés
PORT CAFÉ

The Port; tel. 04/610-0221; www.portcafe.co.il; 8:30am-last customer daily; NIS75

Port Café has a great view and delectable dishes for any time of the day or night. It's a good bet for breakfast (omelets and other egg dishes), salads, tapas, pizza, and seafood entrées. The exterior has an ancient stone look, and the interior furniture gives the feeling of being on a ship, with heavy, worn wooden tables, deck, and railings. The café has an extensive wine and alcohol menu, including cocktails.

ACCOMMODATIONS

It is a tempting place to stay overnight, but Caesarea is strangely lacking choices for accommodations, particularly in the summer months. The only real hotel in the area is the extremely expensive Dan Caesarea.

Over US$200
DAN CAESAREA

1 Rothschild St.; tel. 04/626-9111; www.danhotels.com/caesareahotels; US$320 d

Luxury and location combine to make the Dan Caesarea an oasis-like experience. Surrounded by acres of private landscaped gardens, the hotel is just next door to Israel's only 18-hole golf course. The four-star hotel is less than a mile from the Mediterranean Sea and offers a large outdoor swimming pool, supervised activities for children, a spa, and sports courts. Many of the sleek, clean rooms in this 114-room hotel include views of the golf course and surrounding grounds and spacious private patios. The rooms are simply furnished and flooded with light, and every guest gets free wireless Internet, buffet breakfast, and parking. There are also four restaurants, 24-hour front desk, and town car service.

Two other great options if you want to stay in the area for a few nights are to go to nearby Zichron Ya'akov or to get a vacation rental through **Aloha Caesarea Vacation Rentals** (tel. 054/425-8045, www.aloha.co.il,

US$170 d and up), which can accommodate a variety of needs and groups. They also have accommodations in nearby areas.

INFORMATION AND SERVICES

The **Caesarea Development Corporation** (www.caesarea.com) has a useful website with plenty of photos and basic information about visiting the area.

GETTING THERE AND AROUND

It is very easy to get to Caesarea by car, but there is no direct train and the bus involves a transfer.

Car

Take Highway 2 about 30 minutes north of **Tel Aviv,** and follow the exit signs for Caesarea.

Follow the road until you see the anchor sculpture, turn right, and go to the end of the road to the visitors' parking lot.

Bus

From Jerusalem, take the **Egged** bus (www.egged.co.il, number 972, NIS32) from **Jerusalem** to **Hadera** (about an hour and 45 minutes), and then transfer to the **Nateev Express** (www.nateevexpress.com, number 76 or 77).

Train

From Jerusalem it is a 2.5-hour train ride on **Israel Railways** (www.rail.co.il) to the **Binyamina station** (NIS46 one-way). From Tel Aviv it is only 30 minutes (NIS27) to Binyamina. From the train station, take one of the waiting taxis to your destination (approx. NIS45). It's a 15-20-minute taxi ride.

Zichron Ya'akov

Situated on a mountainside overlooking the sea, Zichron Ya'akov is a sweet oasis in the hills just off the highway. It makes for a perfect place to stop for a meal or stay for a night. It has the feel of a village, and the town center's pedestrian mall has been carefully cultivated in a European style with a pedestrian restaurant and shopping area complete with live street performances during the warm summer months.

SIGHTS
Town Center

The main point of interest in town is the quaint, idyllic Town Center (Hameyasdim St.) that features carefully cultivated landscaping and neatly apportioned buildings. The overall atmosphere is artsy and welcoming in this area also known as the Midrahov. Once you're in Zichron Ya'akov, just follow the many signs to find the *Midrahov*, or ask anybody. The place is so small you can't get lost.

Once in Zichron Ya'akov, you can easily spend a leisurely afternoon or evening enjoying a meal and coffee, browsing through the many interesting shops for souvenirs, and listening to street musicians perform.

First Aliyah Museum

2 Hanadiv St.; tel. 04/629-4777; 9am-2pm Mon. and Wed.-Fri., 9am-3pm Tues.; NIS15

It is very small, but the First Aliyah Museum is interesting for a look at how early settlers dealt with life in Israel. Directly across the street from the gorgeous Gan Tiyyul (Strolling Garden), the museum tells stories of immigrants who came to then-Palestine, particularly Zichron Ya'akov, in the first wave of Jewish immigration that began in 1882. There are multimedia presentations, sculptures, photographs, and English descriptions of the exhibits on two floors in the tightly packed quarters.

Zichron Ya'akov

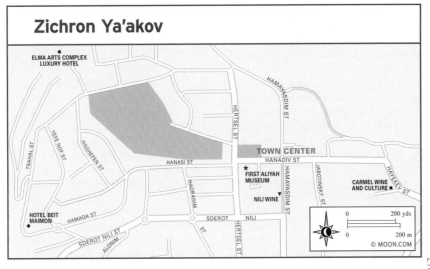

Carmel Wine and Culture

20 Derech Ha'Yayin/Winery St.; tel. 04/629-0977; www.
carmelwines.co.il; 9:30am-5pm Sun.-Thurs., 9am-2pm
Fri. and holiday eves; NIS25 and up for tastings

Housed in a wine cellar that was built in 1892 by Baron Edmond de Rothschild, the Carmel Wine and Culture is a must-see for any wine enthusiast. The complex includes a wine shop, a wine and culture center, a restaurant, two specialist tasting rooms, a small cinema, and a barrel room in one of Rothschild's historic underground cellars. A variety of wine workshops, winery tours, and tutored tastings are available, some of which require reservations.

SPORTS AND RECREATION
Parks and Beaches
RAMAT HANADIV NATURE RESERVE

Rte. 652 between Zichron Ya'akov and Binyamina; tel.
04/629-8111; www.ramat-hanadiv.org.il; 8am-4pm
Sun.-Thurs., 8am-2pm Fri., 8am-4pm Sat., crypt
closed on Sat.; free

At the southeastern entrance to Zichron Ya'akov is Ramat Hanadiv Nature Reserve, which includes a memorial garden and a nature reserve. It is also the final resting place of Baron Edmond de Rothschild and his wife.

The reserve has four circular routes with gorgeous vistas. There are also archaeological relics scattered throughout and the Ein Tzur spring. The park is home to a kosher dairy restaurant (tel. 04/844-9979) and a snack kiosk.

There are a few beaches nearby, but the closest authorized one is **Dor Beach** (just off Hwy. 4, NIS12), which is very clean and pretty, and has plenty of nice sand.

FOOD

Throw a rock in the town center and you'll hit a restaurant, coffee shop, pub, or café.

NILI WINE

43 HaMeyasdim St.; tel. 04/629-2899; www.
nilirestaurant.com; 8am-11pm Sun.-Thurs.,
8am-1:30pm Fri.; NIS70

The extremely popular Nili Wine serves kosher food with Italian, Japanese, and European touches, and an array of regional wines. The egg dishes have a decidedly French influence, while the various pasta dishes are reminiscent of Tuscany. Nili's Japanese offerings include seafood dishes and seaweed salad. A specialty is the cheese plate with five types of regional cheeses on a platter with raw vegetables, dips, and bread.

ACCOMMODATIONS
US$150-200
★ HOTEL BEIT MAIMON

4 Zahal St.; tel. 04/629-0390; www.maimon.com; US$195 d

Distinguished largely because of its charm but in part because of its lack of competition, the Hotel Beit Maimon is located in the hills of lovely and picturesque Zichron Ya'akov, just half an hour south of Haifa. The small 25-room hotel has an on-premises restaurant, room service for drinks, and some rooms with breathtaking views of the Mediterranean Sea. Every room has air-conditioning, a 32-inch (81 cm) LCD TV, direct-dial telephone, wireless Internet, a refrigerator, and bathroom with a shower, and some rooms have a connecting door and a large whirlpool bathtub overlooking the sea. There is also an outdoor whirlpool tub on the second floor.

Over US$200
THE CASTLE

Old Tel Aviv Haifa Rd. 4-10, Kerem Maharal; tel. 054/720-0661; US$350 d

About 20 minutes from Zichron Ya'akov, 30 minutes south of Haifa near the coast, The Castle is a 900-year-old Crusader fort transformed into a four-room hotel. The only structure in Israel from this period that is privately owned, The Castle was built as a home for the ruler of the area and has been painstakingly restored. Two suites have a balcony and two have a garden, each suite featuring massive stone bathtubs and paintings and artwork created by one of the owners. Free wireless Internet throughout (when it's working), free parking, 24-hour concierge service, a dining area, a fully equipped shared kitchen, and a balcony with an incredible view of the countryside. Excursions include horseback riding, bicycle rental, and picnic lunches.

ELMA ARTS COMPLEX LUXURY HOTEL

1 Yair St.; tel. 04/630-0111; www.elma-hotel.com; US$370 d

Part hotel and part arts hub is the Elma Arts Complex Luxury Hotel, a 95-room property that has many rooms divided into distinct buildings and cottages, each with its own style. The advance purchase rates directly through the hotel website offer significantly lower prices on rooms, and the modern, spacious interiors include many options with views of the sea. A stay here includes free wireless Internet, a pool with a poolside restaurant and bar, a spa, an espresso bar, and room service. Some of the rooms are used by artists for extended periods of creative work, and the hotel is home to the Elstein Gallery with 750 square meters of exhibition space.

INFORMATION AND SERVICES
GIDONIM TOURISM INFORMATION CENTRE

tel. 04/639-8811; gidonim@bezeqint.net; 8:30am-1pm Mon.-Thurs.

Just next to the Founder's Monument on Hameyasdim Street is the Gidonim Tourism Information Centre, where you can inquire—in advance—about arranging a tour in English.

The **Tourism Development Agency of Zichron Ya'akov** (www.zy1882.co.il) has some useful information.

Hanadiv Street pedestrian mall is the best place to find most services, including ATMs.

GETTING THERE AND AROUND

Zichron Ya'akov is relatively easy to reach and well known, so there is no problem asking for directions.

Car

If traveling by car, take Highway 2 to Route 70 and the exit for Zichron Ya'akov. It is about an hour from **Tel Aviv**. From **Jerusalem,** take Highway 6 to Route 70, which takes about 90 minutes.

Train

Binyamina Train Station is about a 12-minute drive from Zichron Ya'akov. The **Israel Railways** (www.rail.co.il) train takes 2.5 hours from Jerusalem (NIS85 round-trip) and 50 minutes from Tel Aviv (NIS40 round-trip).

Bus

From Jerusalem, the **Egged** bus (www.egged.co.il, NIS46 one-way) to Zichron Ya'akov transfers at Tel Aviv, stops at the **Binyamina Train Station,** and takes 2.5 hours. From Tel Aviv it is a 90-minute ride (NIS28 one-way) that also lands you at the train station. From there you will need to take a taxi.

The Galilee and the Golan Heights

Northern Israel has vast spaces of nothing but rolling green hills, punctuated by significant cultural and religious sites such as Nazareth, Tiberias, and Capernaum, to name a few.

This is one of the most beautiful parts of Israel and a perfect place to escape for an excursion into the countryside. Aside from religious attractions, northern Israel has beautiful scenery, world-class wine, archaeological and historical sites, outstanding sports and recreation, and interesting people.

East of Haifa is Nazareth, the town where Jesus lived for much of his life. Also built up the side of a mountain, upper Nazareth has some incredibly steep and narrow roads. The Old City of Nazareth is full of interesting sights including an outdoor market, but the main

Highlights

Look for ★ to find recommended sights, activities, dining, and lodging.

★ **Mount of Beatitudes:** The site where Jesus gave the Sermon on the Mount near Tiberias is one of the most peaceful spots in all of Israel (page 209).

★ **Capernaum:** The ruins and church at Capernaum, a city where Jesus once lived and taught, weave a magical web of mystery on the shores of the Sea of Galilee (page 209).

★ **Basilica of the Annunciation:** This cavernous, modern church in Nazareth yields a wealth of lovely details, including a huge collection of wall mosaics from all over the world depicting the Virgin Mary and Jesus (page 218).

★ **Beit She'an:** Tucked into a crevice between the borders with Jordan and the West Bank, magnificent Beit She'an has massive and remarkably well-preserved Roman columns (page 224).

★ **Gan Garoo Australia-Israel Park:** Animal lovers will enjoy the pure fun that awaits them at Gan Garoo, where kangaroos and other Australian animals live (page 225).

The Galilee and the Golan Heights

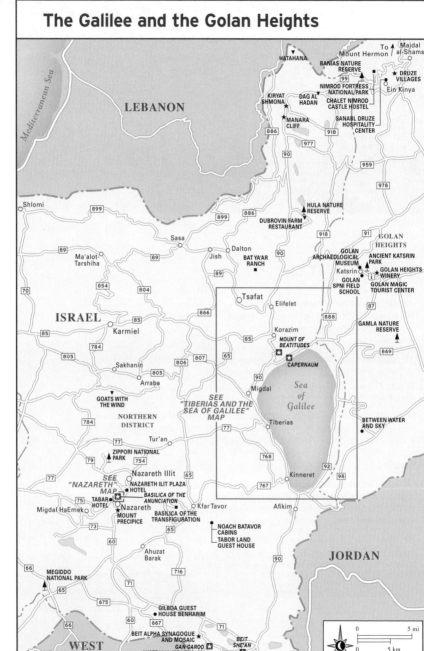

Mediterranean Sea

LEBANON

To Majdal al-Shams

Mount Hermon

HATAHANA

BANIAS NATURE RESERVE

99

DRUZE VILLAGES

NIMROD FORTRESS NATIONAL PARK

Ein Kinya

KIRYAT SHMONA

DAG AL HADAN

CHALET NIMROD CASTLE HOSTEL

MANARA CLIFF

886

918

SANABL DRUZE HOSPITALITY CENTER

977

959

90

978

Shlomi

899

899

886

HULA NATURE RESERVE

DUBROVIN FARM RESTAURANT

918

91

GOLAN HEIGHTS

Sasa

Dalton

90

GOLAN ARCHAEOLOGICAL MUSEUM

ANCIENT KATSRIN PARK

89

Ma'alot-Tarshiha

Jish

BAT YA'AR RANCH

Katsrin

GOLAN HEIGHTS WINERY

854

804

GOLAN SPNI FIELD SCHOOL

GOLAN MAGIC TOURIST CENTER

70

ISRAEL

866

Tsafat

Elifelet

888

87

85

Korazim

MOUNT OF BEATITUDES

GAMLA NATURE RESERVE

85

Karmiel

784

805

806

807

65

85

CAPERNAUM

869

Sakhanin

805

Arraba

90

Migdal

Sea of Galilee

GOATS WITH THE WIND

NORTHERN DISTRICT

SEE "TIBERIAS AND THE SEA OF GALILEE" MAP

784

77

Tiberias

BETWEEN WATER AND SKY

Tur'an

77

ZIPPORI NATIONAL PARK

754

768

92

98

79

SEE "NAZARETH" MAP

65

Nazareth Illit

NAZARETH ILIT PLAZA HOTEL

Kinneret

77

TABAR HOTEL

75

BASILICA OF THE ANUNCIATION

767

Afikim

Migdal HaEmek

Nazareth

MOUNT PRECIPICE

BASILICA OF THE TRANSFIGURATION

Kfar Tavor

73

65

NOACH BATAVOR CABINS

TABOR LAND GUEST HOUSE

60

Ahuzat Barak

90

JORDAN

66

MEGIDDO NATIONAL PARK

716

65

71

675

60

667

GILBOA GUEST HOUSE BENHARIM

71

66

BEIT ALPHA SYNAGOGUE AND MOSAIC

GAN GAROO AUSTRALIA-ISRAEL PARK

BEIT SHE'AN

WEST BANK

MOUNT GILBOA

669

0   5 mi

0   5 km

© MOON.COM

attraction is the Church of the Annunciation, a modern Catholic church built over the ruins of Byzantine and Crusader churches.

Though the Golan Heights (both upper and lower) and the Galilee are full of hiking, biking, camping, and swimming spots, the anchor of the region is the Sea of Galilee. The sea is the main water source for Israel and home to a number of significant sights, including the ancient town of Tiberias and the ruins at Capernaum, where Jesus once taught and lived. It was near Capernaum that Jesus gave the Sermon on the Mount and turned a few fish and loaves of bread into enough food to feed thousands. There are so many legends and so much history in the Golan and Galilee that after spending a few nights here, it's easy to slip into an introspective, philosophical state of mind.

HISTORY

Believed to be one of the earliest settlements dating back to the Early Bronze Age in the land known today as Israel, Tiberias was named in honor of the Roman emperor in AD 18. Following the destruction of the Second Temple in Jerusalem, many Jews fled to Tiberias, and the city eventually became an important center of religious Jewish learning. Tiberias is where the Mishnah, a commentary on the Torah, is believed to have been put together by powerful rabbis of the day. The Jewish Great Rabbinical Court was also located in Tiberias.

Key to the city's development is the nearby natural hot springs, renowned for their curative and therapeutic properties. Throughout the ages, Tiberias became known as one of Judaism's four holy cities.

The area around the Sea of Galilee is also deeply important to Christians. At a certain point in his life, Jesus is believed to have moved his base of activities to the northern shore of the Galilee, where several widely recognized miracles took place, including the multiplication of the bread and fish for the masses and walking on water. The significance of Jesus's activities here led to the establishment of many churches in the area after Christianity began to spread.

ORIENTATION

The Sea of Galilee (*Kinneret* in Hebrew) is home to one of the lowest-lying lakes in the world and is about 31 miles (50 km) around, with its eastern shore in the Golan Heights and its western shore in the Galilee. The area is full of religious history and legends, and numerous very well-preserved archaeological sites. Its two main cities are Nazareth, situated essentially in the middle of the region, and Tiberias, on the western shore of the sea.

Much of the region has year-round hiking trails, hot springs, and different types of ecotourism. A major baptismal site for pilgrims in the Jordan River is here, at Yardenit. The entire region seems vast on a map, but is actually relatively easy to navigate from one point to another by car, bus, and even by foot in some areas.

PLANNING YOUR TIME

Set aside about three days and nights to explore the Golan and the Galilee. A rental car is highly recommended in the interest of time and for the flexibility of seeing different sights, but you can also get to most areas by bus.

Immerse yourself in history and talk with the nuns at the **Mount of Beatitudes** near the shores of the Sea of Galilee, where Jesus is believed to have given the Sermon on the Mount. Drive to nearby Tiberias for a bit of souvenir shopping and lunch. Take in the captivating and dramatic ruins at **Capernaum** that include archaeological treasures: columns and an ancient synagogue. From there, plan to spend at least 2-3 hours exploring the trail along the Sea of Galilee that leads to numerous religious and archaeological sites, including **The Monastery of the Twelve Apostles.**

Plan to spend an afternoon exploring Nazareth's many charms, starting with the

Previous: Tiberias esplanade and the Sea of Galilee; ruins in Capernaum; market in the old city of Nazareth.

The Undefined Territory of the Golan Heights

landscape around Golan Heights

Depending on whom you ask about the status of the Golan Heights, you'll get a different answer; the geography alone can be confusing.

The area known as the Golan Heights runs from Mount Hermon in the north, at the intersection of the borders of Lebanon, Syria, and Israel, to the south at Hamat Gader and the intersection of the borders of Jordan, Israel, and the West Bank. The western side of the Golan Heights hugs the shoreline of the Sea of Galilee and the 1949 Israel-Syria armistice line. On the eastern edge of the Golan Heights is the complex, layered border of the 1974 ceasefire maintained by the United Nations Disengagement Observer Force, then as a DMZ buffer zone, and then the official border of Syria.

Israel considers the Golan Heights of significant strategic importance for three reasons: the presence of a defensible land border, a buffer for northern Israel from artillery fire, and access to the country's most significant water source in the Sea of Galilee. In 1981, Israel officially put the Golan Heights under Israeli law, jurisdiction, and administration, but its status as part of Israel is not universally accepted in the international community. There are some security considerations here, particularly with respect to bordering Syria.

Basilica of the Annunciation, where there are contemporary exhibitions of photography, sculpture, prints, paintings, and live concerts in the summer.

Good options for a base include Tiberias, which allows for a high degree of accessibility to nearby sites and towns. Ginosar is also a good lower-cost option. If you're feeling adventurous, it is feasible to hop across the Galilee and Golan by staying in Nazareth, Tiberias, Ginosar, and other small towns.

The most useful online information about Tiberias, the Golan, and the Sea of Galilee can be found on the website of the **Israel Ministry of Tourism** (https://info.goisrael.com). The independent, tourist-minded **Go Visit Israel** (www.govisitisrael.com) has tons of useful information in a simple format, but the website is a bit hard to navigate. The very useful **Zimmer Israel** (www.zimmeril.com) also has extremely helpful information from locals about a range of things, from accommodations to entertainment.

Tiberias and the Sea of Galilee

Tiberias is a medium-sized town of about 40,000 on the western shore of the Sea of Galilee and the largest town on the Galilee. It caters to domestic and international tourists, though some of its ancient sites are abandoned or not well preserved. It has been continuously occupied for thousands of years and encompasses historical and religious sites of Christian, Jewish, and Muslim origin in the town and nearby. The majority of the population is Jewish, and at more than 656 feet below sea level, it is the lowest city in Israel, making it extremely hot and humid in the summer.

The Sea of Galilee has a very narrow strip of land along most of the eastern shore that is on the Israeli side of the 1949 Israeli-Syrian armistice line. Most activities on the eastern shore center around water sports and outdoor adventures. Past the 1949 line toward Syria is the territory known as the Golan.

SIGHTS

Many of the more remarkable and interesting sights in Tiberias are just to the north, while the main attractions of the town are centered around the beautiful, long waterfront promenade with its many restaurants and cafés. Near the black basalt walls of the old city you'll see some ruins, abandoned and without any explanation of their history. Most of the sites in the area are Christian holy sites and burial sites of Jewish sages.

Tiberias
TOMB OF RABBI AKIVA
off Yohanan Ben Zakai St., on Trumpeldor St. north of town center; 24 hours daily; reception hours vary; free

Just up the mountainside behind the Kiryat Moshe neighborhood of Tiberias is the small, domed Tomb of Rabbi Akiva, a Jewish sage born in AD 50 who was killed for supporting the Bar Kochba revolt. The tomb has long been a pilgrimage site where devout believers pray for rain during drought years.

TOMB OF MAIMONIDES
off Yohanan Ben Zakai St., north of Tiberias town center; 24 hours daily; free

Near the Tomb of Rabbi Akiva is the final resting place of a popular sage and philosopher. The Tomb of Maimonides is known as a place to pray for good fortune, especially for a family. Also known as Ramban, Maimonides (mid-12th century) was employed in the court of the revered Muslim leader Saladin as his physician. The site features a symbolic walkway to the tomb with seven columns on each side with religious inscriptions and a stream of water next to them. There is a large metal structure covering the tomb complex that symbolizes a crown, a mark of respect in Jewish tradition.

MARINA AND OLD CITY
Along the shore of the Sea of Galilee in Tiberias is the lively and bustling marina and its wide selection of restaurants, shops, and beautiful views. The boats docked in the marina used to sell regular rides across the Sea of Galilee, but in recent years the tradition has declined and now it can be hard to hire a ride on the water, particularly in the low season, unless you are with a group.

The old city sits at the southern end of town and consists of a partial wall and a few buildings mixed in with the modern architecture. The end of the old city marks the beginning of the promenade.

DONA GRACIA HOTEL AND MUSEUM
3 Haprachim St.; tel. 04/671-7176; www.donagracia. com; 11am-5pm Sun.-Thurs., 11am-2pm Fri.; free

A former castle holds the Dona Gracia Hotel and Museum, dedicated to a Jewish woman named Dona Gracia, who used her

Tiberias and the Sea of Galilee

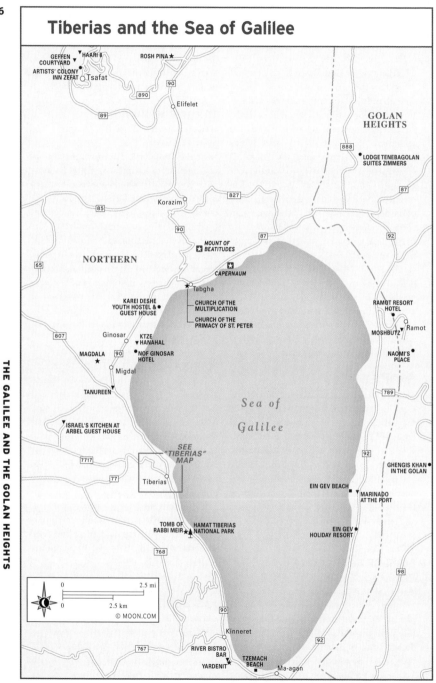

The Black Stones of Tiberias

black basalt wall in Tiberias

While visiting Tiberias and the surrounding region, you'll likely notice that many of the buildings are constructed with a distinctive black stone. The stone is volcanic black basalt, typical of the region and commonly found in Tiberias and nearby, particularly in older buildings.

The old tradition of using black basalt to construct buildings is fading away in modern times due to the need for structures to be more durable and less susceptible to damage during earthquakes. Though black basalt is beautiful and unique, it is not as safe or hard-wearing as modern building materials.

The old city of Tiberias is easy to distinguish from the newer areas by the clear demarcation of medieval black basalt walls and the contrasting white plaster in between the stones.

wealth to save many Jews from the Spanish Inquisition and establish a Jewish city in Tiberias. The different halls of the museum tell Gracia's story using scenery, visuals, and audio, and the main exhibit uses miniatures to depict different scenes. It is possible to request to dress in one of the hotel-museum's 16th-century-style costumes for a souvenir picture.

MONASTERY OF THE TWELVE APOSTLES

Rte. 87 at Kfar Nahum Junction; tel. 04/672-2282; capernaum1@gmail.com; 10am-5pm daily but call in advance because hours vary; free

The Greek Orthodox Monastery of the Twelve Apostles is easy to spot by its unusual pink-domed roof. The church isn't large, but its interior is remarkably detailed and ornate, and every inch of the walls seems to be adorned with paintings of the 12 apostles and scenes from their lives.

Around the Sea of Galilee
TOMB OF RABBI MEIR

south end of Tiberias near Ha'Marchatzaot Rd., just below the Tiberias hot springs; 8am-5pm Sun.-Thurs., 8am-2pm Fri.; free

The resting place of a well-known sage and one of Judaism's holiest sites is the Tomb of Rabbi Meir, a Sephardic tomb with a blue-domed roof that overlooks the Galilee. Meir's nickname Ba'al Haneis means "miracle worker," based on a legend that he saved his

Tiberias

GOLAN HOTEL
AHAD HAAM ST
HERTSEL ST
HAPALMACH ST
SHIMON DAHAN ST
BIALIK STREET
NEIBERG STREET
BERGER HOTEL
ASTORIA GALILEE HOTEL
YEHUDA HANASSI ST
OHEL YAAKOV ST
TABUR HAARETS ST
HAMEGINIM ST
GDUD BARAK RD
Sea of Galilee
TRUMPELDOR ST
BRENER ST
GOLANI ST
AL-HADIF ST
YOHANAN BEN ZAKAI ST
TOMB OF MAIMONIDES
DECKS RESTAURANT
YEHUDA YALEVI ST
DONA GRACIA YOSSI ST
SCOTS HOTEL
SHIRAT HAYAM BOUTIQUE HOTEL
TOMB OF RABBI AKIVA
HAYARDEN ST
DONA GRACIA HOTEL AND MUSEUM
HABANNIM ST
GALEI GIL RESTAURANT
YIGAL ALON PROMENADE
RESTAL HOTEL
HAGALIL ST
TIBERIAS OLD CITY
HAPRACHIM ST
LITTLE TIBERIAS
AVI'S RESTAURANT
HAKISHON ST
JESUS BOATS
EL RANCHO'S
TIBERIAS MARINA
MAMAN MANSION
ATZMON STREET
MAVOR ST
MONASTERY OF THE TWELVE APOSTLES
AVIV HOSTEL

0 250 yds
0 250 m
© MOON.COM

sister-in-law from the Romans with a single prayer. Jews around the world give charity in Rabbi Meir's name, and his tomb is a popular place for religious Jews to celebrate the first haircut of their three-year-old boys and pray for divine intervention. Every year, one month after Passover and four days before the holiday of Lag b'Omer, thousands of believers flock to the tomb and light huge bonfires.

TABGHA

Tabgha is a Greek word that means seven springs. In a cove on the northwestern shore of the Sea of Galilee is Tabgha (Rte. 87, Ginosar), known as the place where many miracles recorded in the Bible occurred, including the

miracle of Jesus multiplying three loaves of bread and two fish to feed 5,000.

CHURCH OF THE MULTIPLICATION

tel. 04/670-0180; 10am-5pm Sun., 8:30am-5pm Mon.-Sat.; free

The event of loaves and fish is marked by the Church of the Multiplication, a Christian church in Tabgha with a very simple interior that is a replica of a 4th-century basilica, with an outer courtyard and fishpond. The highlights of the church include a famed mosaic floor depicting a basket of bread flanked by two fish, and a rock underneath the church's main altar, which is believed to be the actual rock that Jesus blessed and broke the bread on.

CHURCH OF THE PRIMACY OF ST. PETER

tel. 04/672-4767; 8am-noon and 2pm-5pm daily; free

Also in Tabgha, from the Church of the Multiplication you can walk along a promenade about 200 yards (180 meters) to the very simple and boxy black basalt Church of the Primacy of St. Peter, the site where Jesus is said to have appeared to his disciples after his resurrection and forgiven Peter for denying him on the night of his trial. The church is built over a flat rock called the Table of Christ where it's believed a fire was lit for Jesus to have breakfast with his disciples. The church is also at the site where the miraculous catch of fish and multiplication of loaves of bread is said to have occurred, feeding thousands of people.

TOP EXPERIENCE

★ MOUNT OF BEATITUDES

Rte. 8177, off Rte. 90; tel. 04/679-0978; 8am-noon and 2:30pm-5pm daily Apr.-Sept., 8am-noon and 2:30pm-4pm daily Oct.-Mar.; NIS5 parking per car

Situated atop the Mount of Beatitudes, where Jesus is believed to have given the Sermon on the Mount, is a gray-domed **Roman-Catholic church,** surrounded by colonnaded walkways at the end of a garden.

The gardens are dotted with fountains and decorative tablets inscribed with excerpts from the sermon, and the hillside slopes down toward the Galilee, forming a natural amphitheater. There are plenty of benches and places to sit in the gardens, look out over the sea, and quietly contemplate the surroundings.

The interior of the church is small and simple and features a beautiful gold-ceilinged dome and a colonnaded portico that looks out over the Galilee. The site is run by warm and friendly nuns who are available to answer questions.

★ CAPERNAUM

Off Rte. 87 north of Tiberias; tel. 04/672-1059; 8:30am-11:30am and 3:30pm-4:45pm daily; NIS5

A large parking lot by the Galilee and a long path along the shoreline leads to Capernaum, one of the most astonishing sites in the area. Something about the ruins, which include remarkable foundations, colonnades, and even seats of an ancient synagogue, evokes a living feeling of the ancient past.

Not far from the foundation of the synagogue are the remains of a large limestone relief that used to be on the exterior of the synagogue. The detailed carved pictures on the stone include typical religious Jewish symbols and images of a synagogue.

Capernaum is the town where Jesus is said to have lived for three years and performed numerous miracles, including healing Peter's mother-in-law and raising the synagogue leader's daughter from the dead.

A modern church sits above the ruins of a church that was built on the site of Peter's house. You can see the ruins of the old church and its mosaic floor through a glass viewing floor. Throughout the site you can see small pieces of white paper with prayers written on them that have been folded up and placed in areas that are considered holy.

Capernaum is relatively small and easy to walk about; it includes an information desk and a snack shop. Modest dress is required: Keep your shoulders and legs covered.

YARDENIT

Kibbutz Kinneret off Rte. 90; tel. 04/675-9111; www. yardenit.com; 8am-6pm Sun.-Thurs., 8am-4pm Fri. Mar.-Nov., 8am-5pm Sun.-Thurs., 8am-4pm Fri. Dec.-Feb., last baptism one hour before closing, closed on Yom Kippur; free entrance, $10 robe rental

At the point where the Jordan River starts to flow out of the Sea of Galilee is the Yardenit baptismal site. A large limestone building marks the entrance, and baptisms can be performed in the river or in one of the 12 baptismal pools (though you should bring something to wear underneath if you plan on wearing a baptism robe because they are white and see-through when wet). There are changing facilities, a gift shop, and snacks onsite. The general atmosphere of Yardenit is a bit commercial and touristy, though scores of

pilgrims do visit every year to enter the waters. This is one location on the Jordan River that claims to be the site where Jesus was baptized by John, though there are other baptismal sites that are easy to reach.

MAGDALA

Migdal Junction on the western coast of the Sea of Galilee at Mt. Arbel; tel. 04/620-9900; www. magdala.org; 8am-6pm daily; NIS15, children under 12 free

Uncovered just a few years ago, the archaeological ruins at the site of Magdala include remains of a 1st-century synagogue and city. The oldest archaeological site excavated in the Galilee, and one of only seven 1st-century synagogues ever found in Israel, Magdala is believed to be a location where Jesus preached. The site includes an archaeological park, modern chapels, a visitors center, seaside chapel, and more facilities that are under construction.

ENTERTAINMENT AND EVENTS

There is not a lot to speak of when it comes to entertainment and events in and around Tiberias. It is a fairly low-key area, but one exception is the annual **Jacob's Ladder Festival** (Ginosar, tel. 04/685-0403, www. jlfestival.com, May, NIS225 and up), a three-day festival of food, wine, and live music in Ginosar, just a 15-minute drive up the Galilee shore from Tiberias.

SHOPPING

Tiberias is a good place to do a bit of shopping if you need clothes, shoes, or other basic items.

Once you get to the **Town Center** (you'll know it by the long outdoor chairs and counters under the covered sidewalk promenade), you can find a surprising variety of shops and stores at reasonable prices. Near the marina and promenade, the shopping is concentrated around the town's main streets, Hagalil and HaBannim. You can find everything from shoe stores to small grocery stores to national chain stores such as Fox and souvenir shops.

SPORTS AND RECREATION
Parks and Nature Reserves
HAMAT TIBERIAS NATIONAL PARK

Rte. 7677, 20 minutes south of Tiberias; tel. 04/672-5287; 8am-5pm daily Apr.-Sept., 8am-4pm daily Oct.-Mar., last entry one hour before closing; adult NIS18, child NIS10

Boasting 17 natural hot springs long renowned for their health benefits, Hamat Tiberias National Park is worth venturing out of Tiberias to see. Inside the park you will find a synagogue with a mosaic floor built between 286 and 337 BC, and the **Hammam Suleiman Museum** inside an ancient Turkish bathhouse at the entrance.

Beaches

There are two important things to note about the beaches on the Galilee. One is that even if you are a strong swimmer, stick to designated beaches that have lifeguards. Even though the Sea of Galilee just looks like a big lake, there is a notoriously strong undertow, and swimmers at unsupervised beaches have drowned. The other thing is that in recent years there has been a proliferation of privatized beaches, so many areas are completely restricted. Others charge for entrance. Wherever you are in the area, ask locals in the shops and restaurants for directions to the best beaches.

Noting the dangers and restrictions of beach access in the area, most swimming beaches are located on the eastern shore of the Galilee.

EIN GEV BEACH

Kibbutz Ein Gev on the eastern shore of the Sea of Galilee; tel. 04/665-800; 9am-5pm daily; adult NIS33, child NIS27

Among your options is the well-maintained Ein Gev Beach, adjacent to a restroom, lockers, and changing rooms.

1: Church on the Mount of Beatitudes **2:** Monastery of the Twelve Apostles **3:** Hamat Tiberias National Park **4:** Capernaum

TZEMACH BEACH

southern tip of the Sea of Galilee off Hwy. 90;
tel. 04/675-2440 and 052/303-3777; 9am-5pm
Sun.-Thurs. or call in advance for groups on
weekends; NIS55, NIS70 for night and day lodging

Another option just south of Tiberias is the very popular Tzemach Beach. There are tons of events here in the summer, beach umbrellas, and water sports galore, and it's an easy drive if you're staying in a hotel in Tiberias.

On the Water

In the past couple of years, it has become increasingly difficult to spontaneously hop on a boat in the Tiberias marina for a ride around the Sea of Galilee, especially in the low season. Your best bet is to inquire at one of the upscale hotels, such as the Scots Hotel, on the waterfront, about possible boat trips. Otherwise, you can try **Jesus Boats** (Tiberias Marina, tel. 057/775-8562, www.jesusboats.com, inquire for price).

Expeditions
JORDAN CARRIAGES

near the entrance to Kibbutz Kinneret off Rte. 90
south; tel. 052/370-1662; merkavot@nana.co.il;
year-round; adult NIS60, child NIS50, book in
advance

For a two-hour carriage ride adventure into the Galilean countryside, contact Jordan Carriages. The carriages are not plush, but the experience includes stops along the way in the Jordan Valley for things like baking pita bread, walks across rope bridges, and other activities.

BIKING

It gets hot and humid during the summer months, but riding a bicycle around town is highly recommended as a fun way to see the area. Some hotels rent out bicycles by the day; try the **Aviv Hotel and Hostel** (66 HaGalil St. in town center, tel. 04/672-3510, NIS45 and up). Just remember to start early and drink a lot of water.

There is a wide variety of other sporting and countryside adventures in the area of Tiberias

and the Sea of Galilee. A long list of possibilities can be found at www.zimmeril.com.

FOOD
Tiberias
★ LITTLE TIBERIAS

2 HaKishon St., Tiberias; tel. 04/679-2806; www.
littletiberias.com; noon-midnight daily; NIS85

A wide variety of customers from locals to tourists frequent Little Tiberias. Tucked into a building that forms part of the wall of the old city, it is just off the town's main street and next door to a score of other options. The interior is modern and has a homey feeling with tons of seating, and the staff is warm and friendly. Among the specialties is a beef Stroganoff. The types of dishes that are served here include standard favorites that can be found in Israeli kitchens: schnitzel, cucumber and tomato salad, pita, and more.

AVI'S RESTAURANT

4 HaKishon St., Tiberias; tel. 04/679-1797;
noon-midnight Sun.-Thurs., one hour after
sunset-midnight Sat.; NIS58

A family restaurant and one of the best known in town with an extremely loyal customer base, Avi's Restaurant serves Israeli-style meat and vegetarian dishes, and free *mezze* (appetizers). Their specialty is meat dishes, and the owner will probably send more food to your table than you can eat. The homey environment of Avi's (which is the name of the owner) includes arched windows, stone walls, stained glass windows, and a large aquarium.

DECKS RESTAURANT

Gdud Barak St. at the Lido Beach, Tiberias; tel.
04/672-1538; www.lido.co.il; noon-last customer
Sun.-Thurs., noon-1pm Fri., one hour after
sunset-after midnight Sat.; NIS100, reservations
needed

If you're looking for gourmet dining and romantic atmosphere at its very best while in Tiberias, Decks Restaurant should be your first stop. Their meticulous attention to detail includes grilling meat cooked over citrus, olive, and other kinds of wood. The restaurant's interior features a long deck that extends out over the Galilee; the deck is covered in the winter. It's an especially good place for a romantic meal, though it's easy to rack up a large bill.

GALEI GIL RESTAURANT

Old Promenade, Tiberias; tel. 04/672-0699;
11am-3pm Sun.-Thurs., 7pm-last customer Fri.-Sat.;
NIS60

Both family-run and family-friendly, Galei Gil Restaurant is one of the oldest seafood restaurants in Tiberias and known for its tilapia cooked over coals. Conveniently located in the town center on the shores of the Galilee with a view of the water, it has a welcoming and warm atmosphere. The menu is reasonably priced, and you should easily get your fill of food. They are only open for lunch during the week and only open for dinner on the weekend.

★ EL RANCHO'S

3 HaKishon St.; tel. 053/809-4609; www.2eat.co.il/
elrancho; noon-last evening customer Sun.-Thurs.,
noon-3pm Fri.; NIS85

Specializing in South American-style meats, the kosher El Rancho's claim to fame is that it serves the best steak in Israel, and everyone knows it. While the steak is very well done, it is typical by American standards. The friendly staff is accommodating and upbeat, and the interior is huge with exposed brick walls and wood touches, giving it a ranch house feeling. A nice touch to the interior is bottles of Israeli wine on display.

Around the Sea of Galilee
MARINADO AT THE PORT

Kibbutz Ein Gev; tel. 057/944-4106; www.marinado.
co.il; noon-last customer Sun.-Thurs., noon-one hour
before sunset Fri.; NIS95

Located on one of the oldest kibbutzim in the area, Kibbutz Ein Gev's restaurant Marinado at the Port has an incomparable view for outdoor dining. Not only are you sitting on the waterfront, you are in a semiprivate, idyllic setting. The restaurant itself is nothing fancy

in its interior and general presentation, and serves the typical seafood fare of the area, including whole St. Peter's fish, but it is perfect for a last-minute decision or a larger group. The only real problem with Marinado is that it's difficult to tear yourself away, especially if you go around sunset.

ISRAEL'S KITCHEN AT ARBEL GUEST HOUSE

Arbel Village just west of Tiberias on Rte. 7717; tel.
04/679-4919; 7:30pm-last customer daily; NIS120,
call in advance for reservation

A nice option just outside of Tiberias, Israel's Kitchen at Arbel Guest House is fine dining in a country farmhouse atmosphere, set in a small village. Known for their delicious meat dishes and fresh ingredients in an idyllic garden setting, Arbel mainly exists to feed their guests, but can accommodate outside customers who make advance reservations.

KTZE HANAHAL

Kibbutz Ginosar, off Rte. 90 north; tel. 04/671-7776;
9:30am-9:30pm Sun.-Thurs., 9:30am-midnight
Fri.-Sat.; NIS70

A Lebanese restaurant with friendly staff that caters to families, Ktze Hanahal is situated in the middle of a kibbutz about 15 minutes north of Tiberias. The restaurant's dishes blend local Galilee-style food with Lebanese home cooking. The food is served in large portions, which are best enjoyed family-style. The specialty of Ktze Hanahal is their kebab, put together while you watch. A fun feature of the restaurant is the playroom where weary parents can deposit their kids; the atmosphere is generally family-friendly and simple.

TANUREEN

off Rte. 90 north at Migdal Crossroads; tel.
04/671-2896; noon-midnight daily; NIS88

If you're heading out of Tiberias, just 15 minutes to the north is the Lebanese Tanureen, which serves seafood and meat prepared in a distinctively Middle Eastern style. Some of their specialties include grilled eggplant and Lebanese-style kebab. The restaurant's interior is spacious, modern, and upscale. It's not exactly what you'd expect to find off the beaten path and makes for a refreshing dining experience when you want to get off the road and relax.

RIVER BISTRO BAR

Yardenit, Kibbutz Kinneret; tel. 057/944-3619; onhadas@walla.co.il; 7pm-3am daily; NIS80

If you happen to have taken an afternoon to visit the baptismal site at Yardenit, stop off at the River Bistro Bar afterward for dinner. The combination of going to a riverside bar and grill after visiting the possible baptismal site of Jesus might seem odd, but it is one of the few decent options in the area. The interior has high, cabana-like ceilings, and tables are lined up against huge windows. The centerpiece is the bar, with its wide variety of alcoholic drinks and several types of beer on tap. The kitchen at the River Bistro Bar is obsessed with hamburgers, so your best bet here is probably a burger and a beer.

ACCOMMODATIONS

The town of Tiberias alone has about 30 different accommodations, from youth hostels to luxury hotels, with most options on or within easy walking distance to the beach or the promenade, restaurants, and shopping. Near Tiberias, around the shore of the Sea of Galilee, other options range from *zimmers* (private semi-luxury cabins to rent) to camping.

Tiberias

MAMAN MANSION

Atzmon St. in Schunat Achva Atzmon; tel. 04/679-2986; US$95 d

Located in the old city of Tiberias, Maman Mansion subscribes to the less-is-more philosophy, featuring a small sampling of choice amenities, including an outdoor pool, a great view of the Sea of Galilee, bike rentals, and free parking and wireless Internet. The small hotel houses 23 rooms in a 19th-century building. The rooms are bright with TV and air-conditioning. There is also a garden and chapel.

AVIV HOSTEL

66 Hagalil St.; tel. 04/671-2272; avivhotel@walla. com; US$75 d

It may be bare-bones when it comes to creature comforts, but Aviv Hostel fits the bill nicely for a clean, quiet, centrally located place to stay in Tiberias. The hotel/hostel shares restaurant facilities with its more upscale sister hotel next door, where your included breakfast is served from a massive, gourmet spread. The rooms offer a kitchen with a small fridge, private bathrooms, free parking, and balconies and views of the Sea of Galilee. It's a pretty good bang for your buck, especially if you're on a tight budget.

RESTAL HOTEL

Yehuda Halevi St.; tel. 04/679-0555; www.restal.co.il; US$145 d

For the price, the family-run Restal Hotel is a comfortable fit for a couple nights' stay in the center of Tiberias. The recently refurbished hotel has an outdoor swimming pool and modern decor with wood floors and flat-screen TVs in the rooms. The hotel is on the larger side, with 174 rooms, a bar, a 24-hour front desk, and a fitness center. There is free wireless Internet in all public areas.

BERGER HOTEL

27 Neiberg St.; tel. 04/671-5151; www.bergerhotel. co.il; US$125 d

On the hillside in central Tiberias and close to shops, restaurants, and 20 minutes by foot to the Sea of Galilee, the Berger Hotel is a medium-size hotel that features balconies with a view of the city in most rooms. Kitchenette rooms are available upon request, and rooms include cable TV with international channels, a private bathroom, and a telephone for incoming calls. There is also a restaurant, a 24-hour front desk, and free wireless Internet in public areas.

ASTORIA GALILEE HOTEL

13 Ohel Yaakov St.; tel. 04/672-2351/2; www.astoria. co.il; US$123 d

Overlooking Tiberias, the Astoria Galilee

Hotel is one of the oldest hotels in the city, and about 20 minutes by foot to the seashore. The hotel has 88 rooms, free wireless Internet, and modern updated decor. There is also an outdoor pool, table tennis, and a sauna. The location is convenient for exploring nearby sights and towns, including Safed and the Jordan River.

GOLAN HOTEL

14 Ahad Ha'Am St.; tel. 04/671-1555; www.golanhotel. co.il; US$190 d

With an outdoor pool overlooking the Sea of Galilee and a hot tub, the Golan Hotel is just at the northern end of Tiberias. There's also a fitness center with a gym and sauna where guests can book massages and other treatments. With almost 100 rooms, the Golan Hotel also has a 24-hour front desk, garden, and terrace.

★ THE SCOTS HOTEL

1 Gdud Barak Rd.; tel. 04/671-0710; www.scotshotels. co.il; US$475 d

One of the most prestigious and popular hotels in Tiberias, The Scots Hotel is situated just steps away from the promenade that runs along the Sea of Galilee. It is in a historic building that used to be a hospital and has been remade into a medium-size hotel with some rooms with views of the water. The hotel's restaurant serves gourmet food, and has a wine cellar and an art gallery on-site. You can also take advantage of the outdoor pool, in-room breakfast, currency exchange desk, and an ATM. Wireless Internet costs an extra US$18.

SHIRAT HAYAM BOUTIQUE HOTEL

Yigal Alon Promenade; tel. 04/672-1122; US$320 d

It only has 11 rooms, but the Shirat Hayam Boutique Hotel's pretty exterior and charming location on the Tiberias promenade make it a hot commodity. The rooms and suites all have an LCD cable TV, a fridge, and a tea kettle. The 19th-century building has been equipped to also allow for hot tubs and balconies in some suites, and there is room service and a 24-hour front desk. It is in a central location, so ask for a quieter room when booking if you need it.

Around the Sea of Galilee
KAREI DESHE YOUTH HOSTEL & GUEST HOUSE

D.N. Hevel Korazim; tel. 02/594-5633; www.iyha.org. il; US$125 d

Bookings fill up months in advance, but Karei Deshe Youth Hostel & Guest House is a great option if you want location and a low price. This youth hostel is situated on the western shore of the Galilee with a private beach, just about 20 minutes north of Tiberias. It has an inner courtyard, buffet breakfast, a basketball court, and wireless Internet. Rooms here book quickly year-round. It is also near the popular Yardenit baptismal site at the Jordan River and hot springs. The rooms come either as dormitories or private rooms with private bathrooms. There is a walking path nearby that leads through four major sites in the area: the Church of the Multiplication, the Mount of Beatitudes, Capernaum, and the Monastery of the Twelve Apostles.

NOF GINOSAR HOTEL

off Rte. 90 north just before Ginosar; tel. 04/670-0320; www.ginosar.co.il; US$200 d

The Nof Ginosar Hotel is a resort-style hotel on the western shore of the Galilee with a private beach and extensive grounds that are part of Kibbutz Ginosar. The arrangement is somewhat unusual with a 161-room hotel plus a holiday village nearby with 75 ground-floor rooms spread throughout the area and an outdoor pool. The complex also has basketball and tennis courts and a jogging track that runs along a river. The friendly, English-speaking staff can help arrange excursions into the surrounding area.

RAMOT RESORT HOTEL

eastern Sea of Galilee; tel. 04/673-2636; www. ramotresort.com; US$240 d

Ramot Resort Hotel is more like a resort compound of cabins than a hotel. Just at the foot of the Golan, the hotel has 123 rooms spread

out through cabins and chalets on grounds that overlook the Galilee through a canopy of palm trees. The rooms in the cabins are like small houses, with most of the amenities of home, including a kitchen, coffee service, a flat-screen TV, and huge, comfy beds. The area has hiking trails, and you can drive about 30 minutes south around the shore of the Galilee to reach Tiberias. The hotel sells out for the coming summer at least six months or more in advance.

EIN GEV HOLIDAY RESORT

Kibbutz Ein Gev; tel. 04/665-8035, tourist department tel. 04/665-8030; www.eingev.com; US$244 d

On the eastern shore of the Galilee, the Ein Gev Holiday Resort not only has extremely reasonable rates in an idyllic location, it can accommodate families and groups. Ein Gev, with a total of 166 rooms, is set up as a series of cabins spread over the grounds plus 40 rooms situated around the hotel's reception area in the main building. Ein Gev's specialty is organized tours for international visitors. Situated in the oldest kibbutz on the Galilee, their restaurant is famous for their St. Peter's fish. They offer free wireless Internet, comfortably furnished (though not fancy) rooms, and special offers throughout the year on their website. There is a game room, a playground, a spa treatment room, and beachfront access.

Beach Camping

The shores of the Sea of Galilee make a great place for camping if you are prepared with gear, especially during the summer months when the weather is extremely warm. Most campgrounds have some kind of entrance fee, which varies, but is generally about NIS22 per night and up for more luxury spots. It is best to call the campground in advance and verify their entrance fee and hours of operation.

Along the eastern shore of the Sea of Galilee, some campsites that include amenities like

---

1: Shirat Hayam Boutique Hotel 2: The Scots Hotel pool

running water, toilets, and showers are **Gofra Beach** (tel. 04/673-1942), **Halukim Beach** (tel. 04/673-2185), **Duga Beach** (tel. 04/673-1214), and **Sussita Beach** (tel. 04/665-8199).

At the northern end of the Sea of Galilee is **Amnon Beach** (northern tip of the Sea of Galilee near the Amnun 2000 Recreation Village, tel. 050/710-3420), and on the western shore is **Tamar Beach** (western shore of the Sea of Galilee, near Ginosar and 15 minutes north of Tiberias, tel. 04/679-0630 or 050/585-2101).

GETTING THERE AND AROUND
Car

Tiberias is located about two hours north of **Jerusalem** by car. Most of the drive is along Highway 6, which skirts the **West Bank.** It is about 90 minutes from **Tel Aviv,** also mostly along Highway 6.

Once you are in the area, Tiberias makes an excellent base to travel to other sites and towns along the shore of the **Sea of Galilee,** which has a circumference of only about 31 miles (50 km). With a car, you can easily leave your hotel in the late morning, see several sites at a leisurely pace, and be back in time for an early dinner. Tiberias itself is not that large and is very easy to navigate. If you are going to rent a car while visiting Israel, this region is the place to do so.

Bus

You can travel to Tiberias from **Jerusalem** by **Egged** bus (www.egged.co.il, number 963 or 962, NIS45 one-way) in about 2.5 hours. From **Tel Aviv** (number 835 or 841, NIS45 one-way), it is approximately a three-hour trip.

Once you are in Tiberias, there are city buses and some bus companies that operate exclusively in the north of Israel. In Tiberias call *6686 from a local phone, or check out a useful alternative (in English) for buses anywhere in the country, **Bus.Co.Il** (www.bus.co.il), which provides detailed transportation information and timetables for Tiberias and the surrounding areas.

Nazareth and Vicinity

Nazareth is an important city to both religious Christians and Arabs; the main draw for visitors is religious sites. Built up the side of a mountain, some of Nazareth's streets become increasingly steep and narrow the higher up you go, which can make it a bit difficult to navigate if you are driving. With a predominately Arab population, Nazareth is home to good Middle Eastern restaurants, an outdoor market, and an old city region.

SIGHTS
Nazareth
THE OLD CITY MARKET

In the course of visiting sites in Nazareth, you'll likely find yourself in the Old City, which includes a market (tel. 04/601-1072, board@nazarethboard.org, 9am-5pm Mon.-Fri., 9am-2pm Sat.) and a grouping of about 100 very impressive **Ottoman period homes.** You also might come upon the 18th-century **Saraya or Government House** (top of Aliyah Bet St.), built by a famous governor of the Galilee in 1740 as his summer home and currently undergoing renovations to become the Museum of Nazareth.

NAZARETH VILLAGE

5079 St. in the Old City, opposite the French Hospital; tel. 04/645-6042; www.nazarethvillage. com; 9am-5pm Mon.-Sat., last tour at 3pm; adult NIS55, senior NIS37, child NIS25

A careful recreation of life in Nazareth during biblical times, Nazareth Village is something similar to a living and breathing museum with guides in period dress who lead you through what life was like there 2,000 years ago.

★ BASILICA OF THE ANNUNCIATION

southwestern corner of the Old City; tel. 04/657-2501; www.basilicanazareth.org; 8am-5pm Mon.-Sat. Oct.-Mar., 8am-6pm daily Apr.-Sept.; modest dress; free

The Basilica of the Annunciation is one of the largest churches in the Middle East. It is a bit difficult to find it on your own, as it's located about halfway up the mountainside of very steep and narrow roads. It's best to reach it with a tour group or via a taxi.

The Catholic church was established in 1969 and built on the site of what is believed to be the Virgin Mary's original home. The cavernous, two-story church engulfs a cave and the remains of previous churches, including a stone wall behind the cave from a 12th-century Crusader church. There are two stories to the church, with the upper level overlooking the main worship area.

Among the most engaging and dynamic features in the church, on the walls and throughout the massive courtyard surrounding the building is an extensive collection of mosaic pictures from all over the world, each depicting scenes of the Virgin Mary with baby Jesus. There is also a small archaeological museum on-site that includes items from the Middle Bronze Age and Byzantine and Crusader times.

ST. GABRIEL'S CHURCH

Paulus VI St.; tel. 04/656-8488; www.nazarethinfo. org; 8am-noon and 2pm-5pm Mon.-Sat.; free

One of the loveliest among the many churches in town, the Greek Orthodox St. Gabriel's Church is just at the entrance to the city as you are coming from the north. This is the spot where, according to the Greek

Nazareth

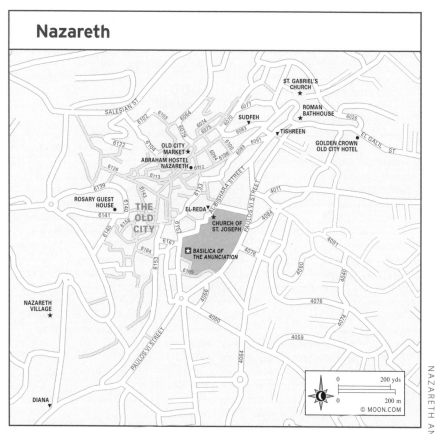

Orthodox tradition, Gabriel announced the future birth of Christ to the Virgin Mary. The church has a high, arched ceiling, and between the colonnades the ceiling is painted with religious images against a blue backdrop.

CHURCH OF SAINT JOSEPH

northwestern corner of the Old City near the Basilica of the Annunciation; tel. 04/657-2501; www.nazarethinfo.org; 8am-5pm Mon.-Sat. Oct.-Mar., 8am-6pm Mon.-Sat. Apr.-Sept.; free

The Church of Saint Joseph is said to be built over the carpentry workshop of Joseph, Jesus's father. The Franciscan church that is now on the site was established in 1914 over the ruins of older churches and the lower

level has an ancient water pit, mosaics, caves, and barns from ancient Nazareth of the 1st and 2nd centuries BC.

ROMAN BATHHOUSE

Mary's Well Square under the Cactus souvenir shop; tel. 04/657-8539; www.nazarethbathhouse.org; 9am-7pm Mon.-Sat.; NIS120 for private tours of up to four people, NIS28 pp up to four people at a time without tour

Breaking ground to build the Cactus souvenir shop in 1993 led to the discovery of the Roman Bathhouse, a 2,000-year-old bathhouse under the shop. Excavations have revealed underground heating tunnels, a hot room, and furnace. The tour fee includes refreshments.

Around Nazareth
MEGIDDO NATIONAL PARK

Megiddo and Yokne'am Junctions on Rte. 66; tel.
04/659-0316; www.parks.org.il; 8am-5pm daily
Apr.-Sept., 8am-4pm daily Oct.-Mar., last entry one
hour before closing; NIS27

One of Israel's several UNESCO World
Heritage Sites, Megiddo National Park surrounds the ancient ruins of the biblical town
Megiddo. A historically strategically important city conquered by ruler after ruler
throughout the ages, it is today a national
park that makes for a relatively easy hike.
Abandoned after the Persian period, Megiddo
is identified with Armageddon, the scene of
the battle of the End of Days according to
Revelation 16:14-21. The park includes a souvenir shop, a museum with an audiovisual
presentation, and guided tours by reservation.
The site is good for visits year-round; it takes
about one to two hours to tour it.

MOUNT PRECIPICE

Just about 1.5 miles outside of Nazareth is
Mount Precipice (second exit off Rte. 60 south
of Nazareth), also known as the Mount of the
Leap of the Lord, one of the city's highest
points. Mount Precipice is where the people
of Nazareth took Jesus to be thrown off the
cliff. There is a viewing platform to see the
landscape below, and at the same spot is the
Cave of the Leap, a 50,000-year-old cave
that has the remains of 13 human skeletons
and over 15,000 artifacts from the Stone Age.

ZIPPORI NATIONAL PARK

2.5 miles east of Hamovil junction on Rte. 79 between
Hamovil junction and Nazareth; tel. 04/656-8272;
www.parks.org.il; 8am-5pm daily Apr.-Sept.,
8am-4pm daily Oct.-Mar., last entry one hour before
closing; adult NIS30, child NIS17

About three miles west of Nazareth is the
well-laid-out Zippori National Park, which is
home to the ruins of a Crusader castle, foundations of a Byzantine church, and an excavated 4,500-seat Roman amphitheater. It is
also home to several mosaic floorings, including the Mona Lisa of the Galilee, a remarkable

depiction of a woman made from mosaic tiling. There is a visitors center at the entrance.
As you leave the park you can explore the
water channel and cistern.

FOOD
Nazareth
EL-REDA

21 Al-Bishara St., Old City Nazareth; tel.
04/608-4408; 7pm-2am Sun., 1pm-2am Mon.-Sat.;
NIS60

Just uphill from the Basilica of the
Annunciation, El-Reda is an Arab-style café
with a great view and an authentic atmosphere. Dishes prepared by the owner, Dehar
Zaidani, reflect his enthusiasm for regional
cuisine, which comes through in the range
of flavors and varied dishes, such as mushrooms with almonds and sweet potatoes,
various chicken dishes, a range of wines, and
hot apple cider. The bohemian atmosphere
of El-Reda, considered one of the best restaurants in Nazareth's lively restaurant scene, is
amplified from time to time with live music
and poetry.

TISHREEN

56 Al-Bishara St.; tel. 04/608-4666; noon-midnight
daily; NIS115

An upscale Middle Eastern restaurant in
Nazareth's Old City, Tishreen serves seafood,
vegetarian dishes, and some tasty Arab-style
pizza. Popular among locals for leisurely
lunches and dinners, Tishreen's interior is
muted and low-key with stone walls throughout, and a massive stone hearth oven.

SUDFEH

Al-Bishara St.; tel. 04/656-6611; noon-midnight
Mon.-Sat., 6pm-midnight Sun.; NIS80

A gorgeous, massive, stone-walled interior
is the first thing you notice upon entering
Sudfeh, which is inside a former stone Arab
house. The renovated lively restaurant-bar
stays busy, and it has a creative selection of

1: Basilica of the Annunciation **2:** view from Mount
Precipice

salads and local flavors in a European-style package. At just a 10-minute walk from the Basilica of the Annunciation, Sudfeh is an affordable, yet upscale, dining option that sometimes hosts live performances by local musicians.

DIANA

51 Paulos VI St.; tel. 04/657-2919; www.2eat.co.il/ eng/diana; noon-midnight daily; NIS70

When you're in the mood for a huge spread of Middle Eastern food, head to Diana, where you'll find unusual twists to common dishes, such as kebab on cinnamon sticks. Some of the ingredients used in the dishes are local to the Nazareth region. The lamb is particularly succulent and tender. Diana is a bit hard to find, so don't be shy about asking for directions; it is well known.

ACCOMMODATIONS

Nazareth

ABRAHAM HOSTEL NAZARETH

6091 Al-Bishara, Old City Nazareth; tel. 04/602-0469; www.abrahamhostels.com/nazareth; US$125 d

Abraham Hostel Nazareth, formerly known as Fauzi Azar Inn, is a small 10-room guesthouse in Old City Nazareth that exudes Arab charm because of its location and the architecture of arched outer colonnades and cave-like rooms. Housed in a 200-year-old Arab mansion, the inn has free wireless Internet, a common area terrace, and air-conditioning. Located near the *shuk,* vegetable market, restaurants and coffee shops, and the Basilica of the Annunciation, it works well as a base to explore Nazareth.

ROSARY GUEST HOUSE

6141/2 El-Dabas St.; rosarynaz@hotmail.com; tel. 04/655-4435; US$130 d

A bit off the beaten path but recently renovated, the Rosary Guest House is a restored monastery with 24 air-conditioned rooms that all have a balcony with garden views and a private bathroom. The Church of the Annunciation is a 10-minute walk away. The rooms are simply furnished, and there is free wireless Internet and a TV in the shared lounge. You can book tours directly at the guesthouse, and there is a chapel on-site.

GOLDEN CROWN OLD CITY HOTEL

16 Galilee St.; tel. 04/650-8000; www.goldencrown. co.il; US$160 d

The Golden Crown Old City Hotel is close to most major attractions in the Old City and has all the comforts of a midsize hotel, including gorgeous city-view rooms with satellite TV, a restaurant, a pool, and free private parking. The rooms are sleek, modern, and upscale with free wireless Internet, room service, and the option of having the included breakfast brought to your room.

Around Nazareth

TABAR HOTEL

5053 El Mutran St.; tel. 04/608-5400; www. tabarhotel.com; US$140 d

Tabar Hotel is a 90-room, five-floor hotel on a hillside of a largely residential area overlooking the city of Nazareth. The hotel has a modern, clean, simple interior, and every room has free wireless Internet, air-conditioning, and private balconies with views of the city and the Jezreel Valley. The hotel has a restaurant and coffee bar and is within walking distance to the Old City markets.

NAZARETH ILIT PLAZA HOTEL

2 Hermon St.; tel. 04/602-8200; US$240 d

Nazareth Ilit Plaza Hotel is a midsize luxury hotel with 184 rooms just on the outskirts of Nazareth. The hotel has a pastoral atmosphere amidst pine trees and gardens with views of the Jezreel Valley, Mount Tabor, and Gilboa Heights and is a 10-minute drive from Nazareth. The hotel's rooms are comfortably equipped with large, soft beds and updated, modern interiors, a safe, minibar, wireless Internet, and hair dryer. The hotel has a VIP lounge, gym, and assistance for tourism activities.

GETTING THERE AND AROUND

Car

Nazareth is just under two hours north of **Jerusalem** by car. Most of the drive is along Highway 6, which skirts the West Bank. It is about an hour and 20 minutes from **Tel Aviv,** also mostly along Highway 6.

Driving within Nazareth is an incomparable nightmare, unless you are accustomed to extremely steep, narrow streets that are sometimes not clearly marked as one-way. Using a GPS in Nazareth to navigate can make matters worse because certain parts of the city are so tightly packed. Nazareth Illit, or Upper Nazareth, and the Old City area have many of the more troublesome

streets but also many of the major sights. If you must drive to Nazareth, park near the entrance to the city and take cabs to your destinations.

Bus

Getting to the center of Nazareth, near the Basilica of the Annunciation, from Jerusalem by **Egged** bus (www.egged.co.il, number 955, NIS42 one-way) is just under 2.5 hours. From Tel Aviv, it takes three hours (number 702, NIS37.5 one-way).

Once you are in Nazareth, you can take city buses to get around. Visit **Bus.Co.Il** (www.bus.co.il) for information. But it is always best to ask for specific information at the front desk of any hotel in town.

The Galilee

There are numerous sites and things to do scattered throughout the Galilee, but the main attractions are outdoor activities, such as hiking.

SIGHTS

Tsfat (Safed) and Vicinity

off Rte. 89 west; tel. 04/692-4427; www.safed.co.il
Tsfat is an ancient town in the Upper Galilee 3,200 feet (975 meters) above sea level with commanding views of the Golan, the Hermon, Lebanon, and Syria. About 40 minutes north of Tiberias, Tsfat is a great place for short hikes to archaeological sites, such as **Montfort Castle** (24 hours daily), the Crusader fortress at the top of the town. Tsfat is also considered the center of Jewish mysticism and one of Judaism's holy cities.

Jish

A small town about 40 minutes northwest of Tiberias, Jish (from Tiberias, take Rte. 90 and then Rte. 89) sits near Dalton Lake and is a nice place to stretch your legs. There are a few archaeological sites, two historical

synagogues, and a unique mausoleum and burial caves within relatively easy distance of each other and marked with clear signage.

Rosh Pina

A 120-year-old *moshav* (an Israeli cooperative of community farms) situated on the northeastern slope of Mount Canaan overlooking the Hula Valley and the Golan, Rosh Pina (Rte. 90 about 30 minutes northeast of Tiberias) has a well-developed tourism industry that caters to high-end customers. It has a variety of restaurants and hotels. Farmers started the *moshav* in the late 1800s with the support of Baron Edmond de Rothschild. The town makes a good base for touring the upper Galilee and the Golan. Its historic **town center** has some spots worth exploring, including an audiovisual presentation about the town's history at the **House of Officials** (center of Rosh Pina, HaChalutzim St., also known as the Old Rosh Pina Office, tel. 04/693-6603, 8:30am-5pm Sun.-Thurs. and 8:30am-1pm Fri.-Sat., NIS20).

The Jesus Trail

Throughout the Galilee, there are scores of sights that were significant in the course of the life and teachings of Jesus. Even sights that have more obscure connections to Jesus are advertised as places where relatives of Jesus lived, worked, or were born. Some of the most significant points are Nazareth, Cana, Migdal, Tabgha, Magdala, and Capernaum.

It is possible to have a guided experience along what has become known as the Jesus Trail (http://jesustrail.com) and literally walk in the footsteps of where Jesus is historically recorded to have lived, traveled, and spread his teachings. The 40-mile (64 km) trail connects Nazareth to Capernaum. There are a variety of accommodations along the trail, and portions can be explored by bicycle.

The Jesus Trail website provides a significant amount of information about hiking routes between biblical sites significant to Jesus and his activities in the Galilee region. A combination of ecotourism and religious tourism, the Jesus Trail covers several significant points between Nazareth and Capernaum. You can also take a self-guided tour that includes hiking guidance and prearranged accommodations along the way for six days and five nights.

hikers along the Jesus Trail

Kiryat Shmona
SCENIC CABLE CAR

Kibbutz Manara, Rte. 90, Kiryat Shmona; tel. 04/690-5830; 9:30am-5pm daily Mar.-July and Sept.-Oct., 9:30am-7pm daily Aug., 11am-4pm daily Nov.-Feb.; NIS59 weekdays and NIS69 weekends, last car is half an hour before closing

In the heart of the Hula Valley, Kiryat Shmona's (take Rte. 90 north, one hour from Tiberias) main attraction is the **scenic cable car.** It is the longest cable car in Israel, going from Kiryat Shmona up to the cliffs of Kibbutz Manara. At the observation point at the top of the cable car is a restaurant, hiking path, and sports center.

★ Beit She'an

off Shaul HaMelech St., Afula; tel. 04/658-7189; www.parks.org.il, https://info.goisrael.com; 8am-5pm Sat.-Thurs. Apr.-Sept., 8am-4pm Sun.-Fri., 8am-5pm Sat. Oct.-Mar.; NIS27

Just at the southern edge of the Galilee where it meets the West Bank is 6,000-year-old Beit She'an, home to **ancient ruins** that are scattered throughout the modern city and **Beit She'an National Park.**

Another of Israel's UNESCO World Heritage Sites, Beit She'an is one of the oldest cities of the Ancient Near East and sits at the crossroads to the Fertile Crescent. Incredibly, about 20 layers of settlement have been found at Beit She'an that go as far back as the 5th millennium BC. Beit She'an rose to its height under the Romans and the Byzantines before being destroyed by an earthquake in AD 749.

You can pick up a free map at the entrance and tour around this remarkable archaeological site that was known as Scythopolis during the late Roman and Byzantine periods (2nd-6th centuries AD). Excavations that started here in the 1960s revealed a **Roman Amphitheater.** More recent work to uncover the city has exposed a beautiful **downtown,** with colonnaded main streets, a central plaza, fountain, a Byzantine bathhouse, and more.

In the evenings, a few hours after the park closes, the park hosts a multimedia **night show** for an extra fee. The night show comes with the added benefit of enjoying the park when the sun and the temperature, which can get up to over 100°F (38°C) in the summer, have gone down.

Beit Alpha Synagogue and Mosaic

Kibbutz Heftziba, Rte. 669; tel. 04/653-2004; 8am-4pm daily and until 5pm in the summer; adult NIS18, child NIS9

The 6th-century Beit Alpha Synagogue and Mosaic features a magnificent mosaic floor. It is considered simplistic compared to other mosaics in the region, but it is one of Israel's great archaeological treasures. One of the first archaeological discoveries in modern Israel, the mosaic has images from the zodiac arranged in reverse order, which do not correspond to the region's seasons.

★ Gan Garoo Australia-Israel Park

Kibbutz Nir David, off Rte. 669 at Gan Ha-Shlosha; tel. 04/648-8080; www.nirtours.co.il; 9am-4pm Mon.-Fri., 9am-5pm Sat.; NIS45

One of the more unusual places you'll find in Israel is the four-acre Gan Garoo Australia-Israel Park in Beit She'an Valley. Created by importing kangaroos from Australia, the park is home to a variety of other Australian animals including flying foxes, cassowaries, koalas, and more.

In typical Israeli fashion, the operation isn't too tightly controlled, which makes it possible to mingle a bit with the animals and get a close look at wildlife that you might never see otherwise. You can hand-feed the kangaroos and pet the goats. The park is a nice change of pace from the ancient ruins, parks, and religious sites that dominate the area. It is also great fun for kids, though you might want to closely supervise any children with you.

ENTERTAINMENT AND EVENTS

SHE'AN NIGHTS FESTIVAL

Beit She'an Foundation for Culture and Tourism; tel. 04/658-8892; https://info.goisrael.com; prices vary

The annual She'an Nights Festival is not to be confused with the She'an Nights multimedia show that runs in the evenings on a regular basis in Beit She'an National Park. The festival is held annually, usually around the time of the Jewish autumn festival of Sukkot (Oct.) and includes food, wine, street performers, and music.

SPORTS AND RECREATION

Parks, Nature Reserves, and Mountains

MOUNT GILBOA

Full of different outdoor pursuits from hiking to paragliding, Mount Gilboa is at the southernmost part of the Lower Galilee. Some of its features include the **Gilboa Iris Nature Reserve** (Mar.-Apr.), **hiking trails,** and a **scenic road** (Rte. 667) that includes places to stop and look at the vista.

HULA NATURE RESERVE

Upper Galilee; tel. 04/681-7137 and 04/693-7069; www.agamon-hula.co.il; 9am-4pm Sun.-Thurs., 6:30am-4pm Fri.-Sat.; depending on activity NIS23 and up

Hula Nature Reserve is a world-class site for observing nesting and migrating birds in a natural habitat. The reserve is right in the heart of the Hula Valley and offers a wide range of activities for nature lovers, including guided night tours.

BASILICA OF THE TRANSFIGURATION

tel. 04/673-2283; https://info.goisrael.com

Noted for its exceptionally breathtaking view, **Mount Tabor** is about 30 minutes east of Nazareth and said to be the place of Jesus's transfiguration. On the mountaintop is the Basilica of the Transfiguration, a complex that includes a Greek Orthodox church and

a gorgeous Franciscan church with a colon-naded interior of white stone and high ceilings. There are also Crusader and Byzantine ruins on the mountaintop.

MANARA CLIFF

Rte. 90, Kiryat Shmona; tel. 04/690-5830; www.cliff. co.il; 10am-4pm Mon.-Thurs.; call in advance because prices and hours of operation vary

More than just a nice, long cable car ride over the hills, Manara Cliff is like a huge indoor-outdoor playground that also offers mountain slides, scenic trains, rock climbing, archery, hiking, bungee trampolines, zipline rides, and extreme mountain biking. Situated in the Upper Galilee with a view of the Hula Valley, a restaurant, and a sports center, Manara Cliff also offers a guided hiking tour of the area.

BAT YA'AR RANCH

Amuka; tel. 04/692-1788; www.batyaar.co.il

Offering a variety of ranch-themed activities, Bat Ya'ar Ranch has short horseback rides, family activities, and a ranch-house-style restaurant. It is conveniently located just about 10 minutes from Safed.

FOOD
Mediterranean
GOATS WITH THE WIND

near Moshav Yodfat, Har Hashabi; tel. 050/532-7387; www.goatswiththewind.com; 10:30am-3pm daily; call one day in advance for reservations; NIS90

If you're in the mood for an expedition that ends with a unique dining experience, try Goats with the Wind, an organic cheese and goat farm and restaurant in the heartland of the Upper Galilee. The restaurant is at the end of a dirt track. It is privately owned and operated, so you get a truly unique Israeli experience. The goat cheese comes from goat milk on the farm and is presented elegantly. All seating is on private verandas where you can feast on dishes like tomato and eggplant

salad, *labaneh,* fried eggplant, cabbage salad, and other Mediterranean delights.

Steak and Seafood
DAG AL HADAN

Tel Dan in Kiryat Shmona; tel. 04/695-0225; www. dagaldan.co.il; noon-last customer daily Sept.-June, 9am-last customer daily July-Aug.; NIS95

In the middle of the pastoral Galilean countryside is Dag al HaDan, a kosher dairy restaurant next to the Dan River known throughout Israel. The restaurant's emphasis is on fish, especially trout, which is fitting because its name means fish on the Dan River. You can also get *mezze,* sandwiches, and other standard Mediterranean café fare, and the layout is housed in a rustic, barnlike structure with plenty of seating.

HATAHANA

1 HaRishonim St., Metula town center; tel. 04/694-4810; 1pm-10:30pm Mon.-Thurs., 1pm-midnight Sat.-Sun.; NIS90

With a reputation as an outstanding place to get a steak, Hatahana, which means "the mill," raises its own cattle and serves up a variety of scrumptious meat dishes including T-bone steaks, lamb chops, and hamburgers. It tends to get packed with meat lovers, so reservations are recommended.

Cafés
★ GEFFEN COURTYARD

55 Alkabetz St., Safed; tel. 050/881-8104; 10am-6:30pm Sun.-Thurs., 10am-3pm Fri.; NIS50

The steady stream of tourists to Tsfat ensures that there are several options for places to eat, but none are quite as charming as the Geffen Courtyard. Replete with a winery, a vineyard, an art museum, and a scenic view, Geffen is overflowing with entrancing details. Considered a must-stop location in the region, they serve a lovely selection of wines, regionally made cheeses, and fresh breads. The stone interior is accented by a nice setup of wooden tables and a breathtaking view.

1: street in Rosh Pina **2:** ancient ruins at Beit She'an **3:** Gan Garoo Australia-Israel Park **4:** footpath and an observation tower in the Hula Nature Reserve

HAARI 8

8 Haari St., Safed; tel. 04/692-0033; noon-10pm Sun.-Thurs.; NIS45

The always popular Haari 8 is a standout for its unusually accommodating service and generous portions that include options even for vegans. This kosher restaurant is just at the edge of Safed's Old City, making it a convenient stop for an American-style hamburger for lunch after a morning of touring. The menu has a variety of other meat options, including "Moroccan cigars," a lamb-filled dish in the shape of a cigar.

ACCOMMODATIONS
US$100-150
TABOR LAND GUEST HOUSE

Kfar Kisch; tel. 050/544-1972; www.taborland.com; US$120 d

The Tabor Land Guest House boasts views of the Jordanian Gilead Mountains to the east and Mount Tabor to the west. The accommodations are clean and extremely simple with four rooms (some dormitory-style), and there is free wireless Internet throughout the premises. The location is a good jumping-off point for hikes in the Lower Galilee. Guests can use the kitchen, garden, terrace, and living room with a TV and DVD player.

US$150-200
GILBOA GUEST HOUSE BENHARIM

Harod Spring Nature Reserve, Gid'ona; tel. 050/336-0061; www.benharim.com; US$190 d

Situated in a quaint village, Gilboa Guest House Benharim is a very simple, eight-room establishment with free wireless Internet, an outdoor area equipped for barbecues, and an on-site spa and wellness center. The simply decorated rooms have views of the Gilboa Mountains and include a TV. Some rooms are dormitory-style with a shared bathroom, and there is a fully equipped common kitchen and reading area. The guesthouse is near numerous outdoor attractions, including the Harod Spring Nature Reserve and Beit She'an National Park.

Over US$200
NOACH BATAVOR CABINS

Kfar Kisch; tel. 052/283-7397; www.zimmeril.com; US$245 d

Country luxury is the specialty of Noach Batavor Cabins, at the Kfar Kisch *moshav*, where they cater to couples. Three luxury wooden cabins include hot tubs, panoramic views of Mount Tabor, free wireless Internet, and an LCD TV and DVD player. Every cabin has a kitchenette and luxury amenities like robes and slippers. The *moshav* has an olive oil plant with guided tours and tastings. Nearby attractions include the church on top of Mount Tabor and the Nahal Tabor Nature Reserve. It is a great area for outdoor sports including canoeing, hiking, biking, and horseback riding.

ARTISTS' COLONY INN ZEFAT

9 Simtat Yud Zayin, Safed; tel. 04/604-1101; www.artcol.co.il; US$230 d

With only four rooms, booking well in advance at the extremely popular Artists' Colony Inn Zefat is a must. The bed-and-breakfast is in a fully renovated stone villa with rooms that have been converted into comfortable, modern suites that include free wireless Internet, a large breakfast, and espresso. Located in the artist colony district of the ancient city of Safed, the villa has a garden and terrace with views. All custom-designed suites have a flat-screen TV, and there is free coffee and snacks in the lobby. The International Centre for Tzfat Kabbalah is a five-minute walk away, and it is 25 minutes by car to the Sea of Galilee.

GETTING THERE AND AROUND
Car

The Upper and Lower Galilee make up a broad swath of land that is relatively easy to cross by car, and many of the roads and highways between towns and cities have been recently or are in the process of being widened and improved. It takes about 90 minutes to get to the Lower Galilee from **Jerusalem** and a little over an hour from **Tel Aviv.**

Once you are in the Galilee, because of the empty expanses between towns and cities, you might encounter people **hitchhiking** by pointing their index finger toward the ground or just standing near a bus stop and trying to catch your eye as you pass. It is legal to hitchhike in Israel and frequently used for transportation in more deserted areas, but the typical cautionary notes about hitchhiking or picking up hitchhikers still apply.

Bus

As in the rest of the country, the easiest and most convenient bus service around the Galilee is **Egged** (www.egged.co.il), which lists schedules, bus numbers, and times in English. You can also check **Bus.Co.II** (www.bus.co.il).

There are **bus stops** near some major sights, but you will need to plan ahead and communicate with your driver about where you need to go.

Taxis and Share Taxis

You can order a taxi in this region by going through any hotel or hostel, and often local businesses will know drivers in the area. Share taxis are also a popular mode of transportation. It is imperative to tell your driver at the outset where you want to go.

The Golan Heights

The Golan is situated in the northernmost region of Israel and shares borders with Lebanon and Syria. It is a popular domestic weekend getaway spot and also a favored spot for hiking and other outdoor pursuits. The Golan Heights is home to fine wineries and apple and cherry orchards and the source of much of the beef and dairy in the region.

SIGHTS
Druze Villages

Throughout the internationally disputed territory of the Golan there are several Druze villages inhabited by a total of about 20,000 Druze, an Arab people of Syrian descent who have Israeli citizenship. The Druze are known by reputation as warm and willing hosts to visitors. They make up about half of the sparsely populated Golan.

Druze villages include **Ein Kinya** (near Mt. Hermon next to the Sahar River), which is the smallest but the most popular among tourists. The other villages are **Majdal al-Shams** (near intersection of Rte. 98 north and Hwy. 989 north), **Bukata,** and **Misada.** You can freely enter any of the villages, which are safe and welcoming to visitors.

Katsrin

The capital of the Golan Heights, Katsrin (take Rte. 87 north to Hwy. 9088 west), or Qatsrin, was founded in 1977 and is considered the tourism center of the region.

GOLAN ARCHAEOLOGICAL MUSEUM

Rte. 87, Merom Golan; tel. 04/696-2412; http://katsrin.com/en/golan-archaeological-museum; 8am-5pm Sun.-Thurs., 8am-3pm Fri., 10am-4pm Sat.; NIS27 with the Ancient Katsrin Park

The town's features include the Golan Archaeological Museum. The modern, well-maintained museum is small but laid out well. It has a short film and exhibit about the Golan. You can also learn about the destruction of Gamla, a stronghold during the First Revolt against Rome that the Romans destroyed in AD 67.

ANCIENT KATSRIN PARK

Rte. 87, Merom Golan; tel. 04/696-2412; 9am-4pm Sun.-Thurs., 9am-2pm Fri. Sept.-May; 9am-6pm Sun.-Thurs., 9am-4pm Fri., 10am-4pm Sat. June-Aug.; NIS27 with the Golan Archaeological Museum

In the immediate vicinity is the Ancient Katsrin Park. The park features the remains of

The Mysterious Druze

the Druze village of Majdal al-Shams

The people of the Golan Heights, in particular the Druze, are just as complex as the division of borders and land. Previously Syrian residents, the Druze in the Golan follow a mystical religion that is largely secret and has its own courts, laws in personal matters, and leadership.

The approximately 20,000 Druze in the Golan (the majority population in the region) have a unique status as a minority group and have been serving in the Israeli military and border police since 1948, even though their passports read "undefined" as their nationality. The Druze culture is Arab, but they don't follow mainstream Arab culture, and have held high-level positions in the political, public, and military life of Israel.

The Druze religion allows for women to attain high positions, and its major aspects are considered secret, though they will allow that they believe in reincarnation.

Druze villages are renowned for their warm hospitality, and are located mainly in the Galilee and the Golan. The largest Druze village in Israel is in Daliyat el-Carmel, on Mount Carmel in the heart of the Carmel National Park, just southeast of Haifa. In the Golan, the center of Druze life is the village of Majdal al-Shams, with a population of 8,000 at the foot of Mount Hermon. Misada, Bukata, and Ein Kinya are also important Druze villages in the Golan.

a 3rd-century Jewish village, including an ancient synagogue. Two reconstructed houses are set up with props of common objects that might have been used when the village, which was likely struck by an earthquake, was inhabited.

Golan Heights Winery

Rte. 87, south of Katsrin; tel. 04/683-8435; www.golanwines.co.il; 8:30am-5:30pm Sun., 8:30am-6:30pm Mon.-Thurs., 8:30am-1:30pm Fri. and holiday eves; NIS20

The producer of several popular domestic brands, the world-famous Golan Heights Winery is less than two miles from Katsrin. It features a visitors center that offers tours (book in advance) and a gift shop with the full range of wines and wine accessories.

Dolmens (Prehistoric Megalith Tombs)

As you are traveling about the Golan, you will likely see dolmens, or prehistoric megalith tombs, that date to about 30 BC and are believed to have been used for burial by nomadic tribes, and then possibly reused for secondary burial long later. The dolmens look like flat rocks stacked on top of each other in partially freestanding formations; they appear in the middle of desolate areas.

SPORTS AND RECREATION
Parks and Nature Reserves
BANIAS NATURE RESERVE
east of Kibbutz Snir on Rte. 99; tel. 04/690-2577 for spring, tel. 04/695-0272 for waterfall; 8am-5pm Sat.-Thurs., 8am-4pm Fri. and holidays Apr.-Sept., 8am-4pm Sat.-Thurs., 8am-3pm Fri. and holidays Oct.-Mar.; adult NIS30, child NIS15, combination tickets available for Nimrod Fortress and Banias for adult NIS40, child NIS20

At the foot of Mount Hermon is the Banias Spring that leads through a canyon to the magnificent Banias Waterfall. It's all part of Banias Nature Reserve. The reserve has some very scenic trails that are highlighted with archaeological ruins.

Within the reserve there are several sites to visit, depending on which route you take. Once called Caesarea Philippi, you can take a 45-minute trail to go through **Roman and Crusader ruins,** including a Roman bridge. Farther along is the **waterfall,** and a backtrack route will take you toward **Agrippas' Palace.**

NIMROD FORTRESS NATIONAL PARK
Rte. 989 between Kiryat Shmona and Mt. Hermon; tel. 04/694-9277; 8am-5pm Sat.-Thurs., 8am-4pm Fri. and holidays Apr.-Sept., 8am-4pm Sat.-Thurs., 8am-3pm Fri. and holidays Oct.-Mar.; adult NIS22, child NIS10, combination tickets available for Nimrod Fortress and Banias for adult NIS40, child NIS20

The relatively easy two-hour hike in Nimrod Fortress National Park leads to unique offerings such as a vulture nesting site and a secret passageway at Nimrod Fortress. Situated above Banias Spring on the slopes of Mount Hermon, the 13th-century fortress was gradually built up over time and the hiking path passes by a huge gate, an ancient toilet, guard towers, and cisterns.

MOUNT HERMON
off Rte. 98; www.skihermon.co.il; 8am-4pm daily; adult NIS55, child NIS45

Not what you'd expect to find in the Middle East, but when in season, Mount Hermon has a functioning ski resort complete with a ski lift. If you don't ski, you can play on snow sleds, ride the cable car, or hang out in the restaurant. In the summer, the area has gorgeous vistas of Syria, Lebanon, the Galilee, and the Hula Valley, and you can take guided tours, ride mountain sleds, and tool around the mountain bike park.

GAMLA NATURE RESERVE
Rte. 869 from Gamla Junction to Daliyot Junction on the eastern side of the Sea of Galilee; tel. 04/682-2282/3; 8am-5pm Sat.-Thurs., 8am-4pm Fri. and holidays Apr.-Sept., 8am-4pm Sat.-Thurs., 8am-3pm Fri. and holidays Oct.-Mar.; adult NIS30, child NIS16

Gamla Nature Reserve has relatively easy hikes that run 1-4 hours. The site includes observation plazas, a snack bar, and binoculars for rent. The reserve is famed for its griffon vulture observation point and views of an ancient city and the remains of a Byzantine church. It is also home to one of the most ancient synagogues in Israel.

FOOD
Farm Restaurants
DUBROVIN FARM RESTAURANT
Rte. 90, Merom Golan, grounds of Dubrovin Farm; tel. 04/693-7371; dubrovinfarm@bezeqint.net; call in advance for reservations as hours vary; NIS125

The Dubrovin Farm Restaurant is located on the grounds of a reconstructed farm founded in 1909 near the Hula Nature Reserve. There is a complete farmhouse and a small museum with interactive exhibits and activities for kids (tel. 04/693-7371, NIS12). The restaurant serves a prix fixe menu featuring meat dishes and nondairy ice cream for dessert. It is best enjoyed by groups.

Israel's Wine Country

The history of wine in Israel is a long one. For thousands of years, Jews have been using wine for mostly sacramental purposes. The development of wine and the wine industry today has reached the point that some wines made in Israel are recognized internationally and even win international awards. There is the added element in Israel of a wide variety of kosher wines.

Israeli wine country is concentrated in a few areas: in the foothills of Jerusalem and the surrounding areas, the Negev Desert, the Golan, and the Galilee. Unfortunately, the industry is still young enough that wine-related tourism hasn't developed to the point where you can take a wine tour of any regions. But you can make arrangements through a tour guide, by request, to visit different wineries. Many wineries have visiting centers and offer the chance to take a tour and have tastings for about NIS40.

In the Golan Heights, the center of tourism, Katsrin, is also the center of the regional wine industry, led by the Golan Heights Winery (www.golanwines.co.il), which is considered by many to be the grandfather of Israel's modern-day wine industry. The visitors center offers a variety of tours and tastings in multiple languages and has a gift shop.

In the Upper Galilee, particularly in the area of Carmel Mountain, there are a variety of wineries of all sizes. An excellent website that gives an overview of Israel's wine country is Israeli Wines (www.winesisrael.com/en), where you can get current news and information about the industry as well as product information.

Middle Eastern Fusion
UNDEFINED

Majdal al-Shams main road; tel. 050/764-1699; 11am-10pm Wed.-Mon.; NIS55

If you get as far north as Majdal al-Shams near the Syrian border, check out the local, sophisticated Undefined, named for the description that most Syrian Druze have on their IDs under the identifying factor for nationality. Serving an interesting mix of Asian and Middle Eastern dishes, steaks, and fresh fruit desserts, the café setting has a friendly atmosphere that sometimes hosts live acoustic performances.

Moshav Dining
MOSHBUTZ

third turn inside Moshav Ramot, eastern shore of the Galilee; tel. 04/679-5095; 6pm-last customer daily; NIS80

Conveniently located and with a simple, warm atmosphere and very extensive regional wine menu, Moshbutz takes its name from the combination of the words *moshav* and *kibbutz*, reflecting its roots in connection with the moshav. Try to get a seat near the windows and

enjoy the view of the eastern shore of the Sea of Galilee. They do serve dishes such as hamburgers, but the beef is in the aged style and may not appeal to an American palate. A better bet is the beef stew in wine stock or the pork spareribs (a rare find in this part of the world).

ACCOMMODATIONS
US$100-150
GHENGIS KHAN IN THE GOLAN

Givat Yoav, Neot Golan; tel. 052/371-5687; www.gkhan.co.il; US$132 d

One of the more unique experiences available for accommodations, Ghengis Khan in the Golan is a popular specialty lodging spot with just five rooms (or tents, rather) along the Golan Trail. Family-run with handmade tents and free wireless Internet, it is something of a contradiction. It provides an area to cook out, a garden with seating, and a shared kitchen with an option to buy food supplies. The tents are equipped with mattresses, pillows, and private or shared bathrooms nearby. Nearby excursions include horseback riding, hiking, and jeep trips for hire. The Galilee is just 15 minutes by car, and buses to and from Tel Aviv and Jerusalem stop nearby.

1: Banias Waterfall **2:** the ruins of Nimrod Fortress

GOLAN SPNI FIELD SCHOOL

Katsrin; tel. 04/696-1234, field school reservations hotline tel. 03/638-8688; www.teva.org.il; US$141 d

The Society for the Protection of Nature in Israel (SPNI) has field schools throughout Israel and the Golan, and they make a great option if you are looking for something affordable and conveniently located, and only need the most basic in amenities and comfort. Even in the high season of summer, the Golan SPNI Field School is reasonable. The simple, ground-floor accommodations are surrounded by trees, and it caters to groups of travelers, including touring and Birthright groups, so you might have a lively crowd of young people there with you. Every room is air-conditioned and can hold about six people. Breakfast is included in the price.

US$150-200
BETWEEN WATER AND SKY

Neot Golan; tel. 054/488-2299; www.a-hotel.com/israel/neot-golan; US$200 d

The mystical grounds of Between Water and Sky cater to couples looking for a romantic getaway and offer three cabin suites that come with a hot tub, a flat-screen TV with satellite, a furnished balcony with views of the Sea of Galilee, free wireless Internet, a minibar with free nonalcoholic drinks, and a DVD library. Basically every element of pampering is covered, including flowers, chocolate, wine, and cookies when you arrive. There is an olive press on the property that can be toured to see how olive oil is made, and it is just five minutes from the Sea of Galilee.

CHALET NIMROD CASTLE HOSTEL

Nachal Nimrod; tel. 04/698-4218; www.bikta.net; US$179 d

Situated on the side of Mount Hermon is the Chalet Nimrod Castle Hostel with varied types of cabins that were built by owners Guy and Lilach. The independent cabins are void of technology and surround a central lodge where you can get breakfast (for an extra fee) and maps and travel guides to the surrounding area. The whole vibe of the chalet is peace and calm, and its location on the Golan Trail makes for easy access to hiking. The cabins are air-conditioned and include a kitchenette, and there is a restaurant on-site. Additional amenities can be found nearby.

Over US$200
SANABL DRUZE HOSPITALITY CENTER

Ein Kinya, Golan Heights, Nimrod; tel. 050/577-8850; www.zimmeril.com; US$275 d

Best for families and couples, the Sanabl Druze Hospitality Center is a small religious property in the Druze village of Ein Kinya in the Golan Heights with a selection of suites and villas. A stay here includes access to a Druze restaurant (ask for the stew) and options for suites and villas that all have a TV and DVD player, a hot tub, a balcony, and modern, luxurious furnishings. There are also cooking facilities, and a traditional Druze buffet breakfast is included. There is free parking and wireless Internet, and you can arrange for horseback riding, hiking, and jeep excursions through the center. If there's snow, it's a five-minute drive to skiing on Mount Hermon. It's also near Banias Nature Reserve and Nimrod Fortress National Park.

LODGE TENEBAGOLAN SUITES ZIMMERS

293 Gan Hashiqmim, Had Nes; tel. 04/697-0027; US$275 d

To the north of the Galilee with just four suites, Tenebagolan Suites Zimmers is a luxury experience that caters to people who want a rustic experience with individualized pampering. Every suite has a hot tub, a terrace view of the Golan Heights, and a flat-screen TV. You can borrow a bicycle for free, and there is also free wireless Internet. A common kitchen is open for use, and a prepared Israeli breakfast is included. It is five minutes to the Galilee and about 30 minutes from Tiberias.

NAOMI'S PLACE

Kochal, Moshav Ramot; tel. 04/673-2157; www. zimmeril.com; US$250

One of several luxury accommodations on the Ramot Moshav, Naomi's Place is a bed-and-breakfast in the midst of a date plantation. The four wood cabins are set on spacious grounds that include a swimming pool, playground, and an area to cook out. About five minutes from the Galilee and 20 minutes from the holy city of Safed, it is very close to hiking trails. Every cabin has a cozy, warm interior with soft lighting and large, luxurious beds, a private garden, hammock, a kitchenette, and fireplace. Though breakfast is provided, there are also restaurants nearby.

VILLA GOLAN

Inbar St. on the outskirts of Katsrin; tel. 050/957-5758; www.zimmeril.com; US$230 d

Conveniently located near a bus stop and just five minutes from the Golan Heights Winery, Villa Golan is a very small luxury bed-and-breakfast in the sweet little town of Katsrin. The four suites all have a fully loaded kitchenette, a huge bed, a TV-DVD player, and free wireless Internet. You get a free bottle of wine on arrival and breakfast is included. There is an option for a room with a hot tub. The town's country club gives guests of Villa Golan a discount, and it's a short drive to the Galilee.

INFORMATION AND SERVICES

GOLAN MAGIC TOURIST CENTER

Katzrin Shopping Center; tel. 04/696-3625 or 052/289-4029, ext. 3; www.magic-golan.co.il; 9am-5pm Sun.-Thurs., 9am-4pm Fri., closed on Jewish holidays

Conveniently located in the Katzrin Shopping Center, the **Golan Magic Tourist Center** can help you get going in the right direction.

GETTING THERE AND AROUND

Car

If you can manage it, the best way to get around the Golan Heights is by car. Any other independent mode of transportation might prove a bit tricky. One option is to rent a car in Tiberias from **Eldan Car Rental** (1 HaBannim St., tel. 04/672-2831, www.eldan.co.il), the largest domestic car rental company in Israel.

Bus

Egged buses (www.egged.co.il) do travel into the Golan, and a trip to **Katsrin (Qatsrin)**, a city about 40 minutes north of Tiberias, is possible. To Katsrin from **Tel Aviv** is about 3.5 hours (number 843, NIS46 one-way), and from **Jerusalem** it is closer to 4 hours (number 966, NIS46 one-way). Once you are in the Golan, there are Egged routes that traverse between the towns on a regular basis.

The West Bank

Despite the complicated legal, political, and human rights situation in the West Bank, it remains home to some important archaeological and spiritual sites—holy to Muslims, Jews, and Christians.

Situated between Israel and the border with Jordan, the West Bank is an area of about 2,200 square miles (3,540 square kilometers). The West Bank encompasses significant ancient biblical cities such as Jericho, Bethlehem, Hebron, and Nablus, alongside more modern cities like Ramallah and Ariel. Many people also refer to the area collectively as **Palestine** or as **Judea** and **Samaria.** The separation barrier constructed by Israel running along much of the highway is a physical

Highlights

Look for ★ to find recommended sights, activities, dining, and lodging.

★ **Church of the Nativity:** This ancient church in Bethlehem, believed to be the birthplace of Jesus, has an atmosphere of mystery and wonder (page 242).

★ **Jacob's Well:** Way off the beaten path, Jacob's Well is where Jesus is said to have once stopped for a drink of water. It is housed deep under a massive church that's set amid vast, lushly landscaped grounds (page 251).

★ **Mount of Temptation Monastery:** High above Jericho is the place where Jesus is said to have been tempted by Satan. This spot is now home to a monastery, which you can reach by a cable car that travels over the biblical-era ruins of Jericho (page 253).

★ **Hisham's Palace:** A mosque, massive mosaic floors, decorative touches, and fountains are the highlights of these ruins near Jericho, still in the process of being restored and preserved (page 253).

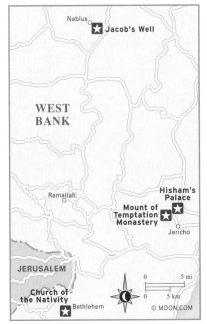

The West Bank

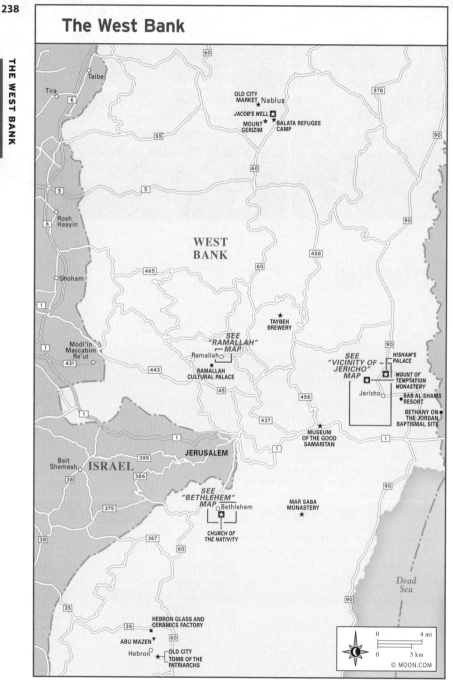

Taibe

Tira

60

578

OLD CITY
MARKET · Nablus

JACOB'S WELL ★
MOUNT ★ ★ BALATA REFUGEE
GERIZIM CAMP

55

90

60

Rosh
Haayin

WEST
BANK

458

90

Shoham

465

60

5

1

TAYBEH ★
BREWERY

SEE
"RAMALLAH"
MAP

SEE
"VICINITY OF
JERICHO"
MAP

HISHAM'S
PALACE

90

Modi'in
Maccabim
Re'ut

431

Ramallah

RAMALLAH
CULTURAL PALACE

443

45

458

437

1

MOUNT OF
TEMPTATION
MONASTERY

Jericho

BAB AL SHAMS
RESORT

BETHANY ON
THE JORDAN
BAPTISMAL SITE

MUSEUM ★
OF THE GOOD
SAMARITAN

1

Beit
Shemesh

395

JERUSALEM

ISRAEL

38

386

375

SEE
"BETHLEHEM"
MAP

Bethlehem

MAR SABA
MONASTERY ★

90

38

367

CHURCH OF
THE NATIVITY

60

35

Dead
Sea

90

HEBRON GLASS AND
CERAMICS FACTORY

35

ABU MAZEN ▼

Hebron

OLD CITY
TOMB OF THE
PATRIARCHS

0   4 mi

0   5 km

© MOON.COM

border that continues to be extended, while the legal border is based on the 1949 Armistice Agreement Line.

The actual landscape of the West Bank is a patchwork of olive and lemon tree groves, Arab villages and cities, and Jewish settlements, with the occasional checkpoint or fence with concertina wire. While the West Bank is not part of Israel proper, different interpretations of borders, the increasing presence of Jewish settlements, and the decreasing holdings of Arab villages have seriously complicated its status both regionally and internationally. Israel maintains a strong military presence in many areas of the West Bank, particularly in areas where there are Jewish settlements.

Complications and special considerations aside, the West Bank is one of the most fascinating areas of the region. It is a bit on the wild side and evokes a feeling of being in untamed territory. But it's also an easy place to connect with a rich historical past. Looking out over the rugged, sparsely populated landscape with its patchwork of gray-green olive trees and minarets, it is easy to see why so many people of different faiths want to maintain a connection to this part of the land.

HISTORY

The recent history of the West Bank is the most relevant for the purpose of travel. The current border of the West Bank was created in a 1949 armistice agreement that divided the newly created Jewish state from the other parts of the Mandatory Palestine.

In the 1948 War of Independence, Israel took control of the western part of Jerusalem, and Jordan took control of the eastern part, including the Old City, home to dozens of sites that are deeply important to the Christian, Jewish, and Muslim faiths. Until 1967, the West Bank was ruled by Jordan. In 1967, the Six Day War between Israel, Egypt, Jordan, and Syria led to Israel's capture of the eastern side of Jerusalem. The result of that war is essentially the reason for today's existence of East and West Jerusalem. According to international law, East Jerusalem is part of the West Bank, and situated inside of the 1949 armistice lines. According to Israeli practice, East Jerusalem is under the control and governance of the Jerusalem Municipality and the Israeli government. The complexity of this background is why border police patrol the area around and inside of Jerusalem's Old City; it is technically situated on a border zone.

The West Bank (except for Jerusalem) of today is divided into three zones: Palestinian Authority-controlled (Area A); joint Palestinian Authority and Israeli-controlled (Area B); and Israeli-controlled (Area C). The status of both Jerusalem and the West Bank is one of the most contentious issues impeding progress toward a peace agreement between the Palestinian Authority and Israel.

KNOW BEFORE YOU GO

Areas

If you looked at a map of the West Bank, you would see a complex division of shaded zones indicating territory and control. Some parts of the West Bank are completely under Palestinian control, some are under shared control with Israel, and some are completely under Israeli control; these are known as **Areas A, B, and C,** respectively. The divisions are part of the reason that while traveling through the West Bank you will find checkpoints, fences, and gates in certain areas. It's important to understand whether you are in Area A, B, or C, as it will impact how you move about and what the generally accepted customs are.

- **Area A:** Palestinian Authority-controlled. Nablus is in the very center of a large Area A section.

Previous: cable cars going from Jericho to the Mount of Temptation Monastery; rugs for sale in Bethlehem; pickled vegetables for sale in Hebron's *shuk*.

The West Bank vs. Palestine

The language used to describe the land to the east of Jerusalem commonly referred to as either the West Bank or Palestine tends to be vague.

The "west" in the name refers to its western proximity to the Jordan River, as it used to be part of the Hashemite Kingdom of Jordan. A reference to the area as Palestine is more of a political statement than a formal name. The hope for many is that this will change, however.

In November 2012, the United Nations granted Palestine non-member observer status, while still urging efforts for a formal, two-state solution between Israel and the Palestinians. At the time of publication, no such solution had been reached.

The most neutral way to refer to the region is to call it the West Bank.

- **Area B:** Palestinian Authority and Israeli military joint-controlled.

- **Area C:** Israeli military-controlled (Area C). The city of Ariel (which started as a small settlement) is in an Area C section. Most of the West Bank is Area C, and every major Arab town in the region, even if it is in Area A or B, is surrounded on almost every side by Area C territory.

An easy way to remember who is in control where goes something like this: the Palestinian Authority (PA) has an A in its acronym, and controls Area A. Both the PA and Israel control area B and the word "both" starts with B. By process of elimination, Area C is fully Israeli controlled.

There are some special cases, such as Hebron, which is an occupied city under Israeli military control. Some Arab villages and Jewish settlements are in more than one area, or in an area that is not controlled by their respective government.

Also keep in mind that some areas of the West Bank are extremely religiously conservative and have significant security concerns (such as Hebron), and other areas are tricky to navigate unless you connect with a group of some kind (such as Nablus).

Checkpoints

There are checkpoints posted in various locations between Israel and the West Bank and inside the West Bank at the edge of Israel-controlled territory. Most checkpoints consist of guard huts manned by soldiers who may or may not stop vehicles. If you're driving, it's good to know where the trunk release is located, in case you're asked to open the trunk. Taxis are often stopped. It is always wise to have your passport handy for inspection, and be prepared with a very clear, simple answer about the purpose of your visit.

Safety

It is important to take into account safety precautions before you go to any area in the West Bank. The general rule of thumb is to always err on the side of caution in all things. Also, keep any electronics or camera equipment out of sight and close by.

Money and Business Hours

Using Israeli currency is recommended, though U.S. currency is also taken (but you will likely get hugely overcharged).

Keep in mind that the Muslim holy day of the week is Friday, so most businesses and services are shut down for at least part or all of that day.

Language and Dress

The major languages spoken in the West Bank are Arabic and Hebrew; English is less common. It is advisable to learn a few key phrases in Arabic before traveling to the region, including common greetings and pleasantries. It will help break the ice and make it easier to communicate about more complicated topics.

The Settlement Issue

One of the most confusing and complicated issues in the West Bank is the settlements: groups of Jews who have settled in homes throughout the region. The population of Jewish settlers in the West Bank is well over 350,000 and growing all the time. That number does not include about 300,000 Jews who live in East Jerusalem and developments around the Jerusalem area.

The presence of settlements in some parts of the West Bank is illegal according to international law. The continued support (and in some cases encouragement) of settlements by the Israeli government is interpreted by many as an act of bad faith in the peace process with the Palestinian Authority and has been a major stumbling block in that process. The Israeli government has forcibly removed settlements when they are on land controlled fully by the Palestinian Authority and also forcibly removed Palestinians from their homes in other areas. Some settlers live peacefully next to their Arab neighbors, whose villages often surround them, but there have been many cases of violence from both sides.

The range of settlements is enormous. They can be anything from a small group of 10 families living on a hilltop in fairly makeshift accommodations to well-established cities with a full infrastructure and municipal government services. In areas that are not fully under Israeli military control, the government provides armed soldiers for protection, supplies basic services such as electricity, and builds roads.

The issue of settlements is extremely contentious both domestically and internationally. The unsatisfactory resolution of the situation and continued building of new settlements are regarded as a major impediment to peace between Arabs and Jews in the region. The very existence of Jewish settlements throughout the West Bank creates a serious problem in the question of the formal establishment of a Palestinian state. If the armistice line that demarcates the West Bank were to become the legal border of a Palestinian state, a quarter of a million Jews would find themselves living in a foreign country.

Several excellent books have been written on the topic; one of the best is called *Lords of the Land* by Idith Zertal and Akiva Eldar.

When traveling in the region, it is important to wear conservative clothing (especially for women), which generally means nothing too tight or revealing, and it's best to keep arms and legs covered.

Resources

While tourism is being promoted more heavily in the West Bank in recent years, it is nowhere near as established as in Israel. There are some good online resources and a governmental agency to visit for more information.

An excellent online guide for all things in the West Bank is **Visit Palestine** (www.visitpalestine.ps/en). The **Official Tourism Site** (http://travelpalestine.ps) for the region is less robust, but also has some good tips and information.

There are three major Arabic dailies in the region: *Al Quds, Al Ayyam,* and *Al Hayyat* newspapers. Many shops and markets also sell foreign English newspapers and magazines. A popular English periodical, *This Week in Palestine* (www.thisweekinpalestine.com), has listings of major events, happenings, and tourism services and can be found throughout the region for free.

Guide Services

Offering a wide variety of tourism services, **BeinHarim Tourism Services Ltd.** (tel. 03/542-2000, www.beinharimtours.com) has an online chat service and arranges tours to most areas in the West Bank. **Explore West Bank** (tel. 059/824-4150, zzzaa_2009@hotmail.com) can also provide tour services in Ramallah and elsewhere.

ORIENTATION

The West Bank is the area to the west of the Jordan River and east of Israel. To enter or exit the West Bank, you will have to pass through checkpoints. Under normal circumstances, the checkpoints are cursory and you are not stopped. The West Bank extends just to the north of Jenin and covers much of the Dead Sea. Its southernmost point is just 25 minutes from Be'er Sheva, the largest city in the Negev. The border between Israel and the West Bank north of Jerusalem is roughly along Highway 6, which runs north to south, and circles around Nablus just south of Afula. South of Jerusalem, the West Bank border extends south between Highway 35 and Highway 60 until it circles east before reaching the city of Be'er Sheva.

PLANNING YOUR TIME

It is worth spending a couple of days in the West Bank exploring the more notable places. There are also some fantastic day hikes in the region.

If you plan to stay in the West Bank for a couple of nights, a good place to base yourself is Bethlehem or Ramallah. Both places have a range of options.

The best way to get around the region is by car or share taxi. Many parts of the West Bank are much better experienced as part of an organized tour group or with a hired private tour guide who speaks Arabic and can drive. Hire a guide in Jerusalem; the odds of getting ripped off are high if you hire someone in Bethlehem.

Bethlehem

Bethlehem is a city of about 75,000 people that depends largely on tourists and pilgrims who are attracted by its religious and historical sites, chief among them the place where Jesus was born. It is 15 minutes from Jerusalem and completely controlled by the Palestinian Authority. It is illegal for Israelis to enter Bethlehem.

SAFETY

Bethlehem is 15 minutes from Jerusalem's city center, and the entrance is through a fairly strict checkpoint. You must bring your passport with you and be prepared for a wait when leaving the city. Though it is basically safe, tensions can run high there from time to time, so check your embassy website before going.

Once in Bethlehem, you will notice a number of heavily armed Palestinian Authority troops standing on the street. Though they may look intimidating, they are actually extremely friendly to tourists and are a great resource for information.

Despite the paranoia some people have about visiting Bethlehem, it is a generally safe and friendly city, though if you are driving you might get lost, even with a GPS.

SIGHTS
Manger Square

The heart of Bethlehem's Old City and the jumping-off point for the town's most popular attractions and events is Manger Square (center of Bethlehem off Manger St.). A large number of hotels and places to eat are also located here.

TOP EXPERIENCE

★ CHURCH OF THE NATIVITY

Manger Sq.; tel. 02/274-2440; church hours 6:30am-7:30pm Mon.-Sat. Apr.-Sept., 5:30am-5pm Mon.-Sat. Oct.-Mar.; grotto hours 6am-noon and 2pm-7:30pm Mon.-Sat. Apr.-Sept., 5am-noon and 2pm-5pm Mon.-Sat. Oct.-Mar.; on Sun. church is open for holy mass and grotto is open only in afternoon; free

Not overly impressive from the outside, the Church of the Nativity is imposing and affecting once you duck through the low main entrance door. Basically at the center of

Bethlehem

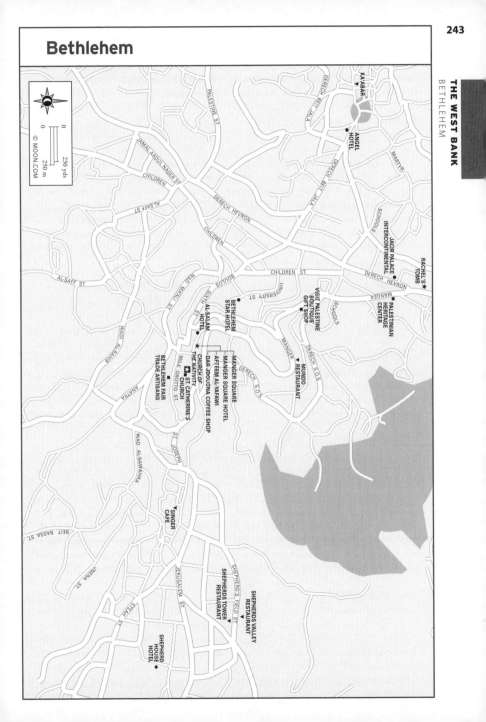

© MOON.COM

0   250 yds
0   250 m

KA'ABAR

ANGEL HOTEL

DERECH BEIT JALA

PALESTINE ST.

JAMAL ABDUL NASER ST.

CHILDREN

AL-SAFF ST.

DERECH HEVRON

CHILDREN

DERECH BEIT JALA

MARTYR

SCHOOLS

JACIR PALACE INTERCONTINENTAL

RACHEL'S TOMB

CHILDREN ST.

DERECH HEVRON

DERECH MANGER

PALESTINIAN HERITAGE CENTER

AL-SAFF ST.

WADI MA'ALI ST.

SIXTH

BOULOS

UNIVERSITY ST.

VISIT PALESTINE BOUTIQUE GIFT SHOP

SCHOOLS

BETHLEHEM STAR HOTEL

AL-SALAM HOTEL

SIXTH ST.

MANGER

MANGER SQUARE

MANGER SQUARE HOTEL

AFTEEM AL-YAFAWI

DAR JDOUNA COFFEE SHOP

DERECH S.O.S.

MUNDO RESTAURANT

WADI AL-KHIR

CHURCH OF THE NATIVITY

ST. CATHERINE'S CHURCH

MILK GROTTO ST.

BETHLEHEM FAIR TRADE ARTISANS

ANATRA

ST. JOSEPH

WAD AL-SAW AHRA

SINGER CAFÉ

BEIT BASSA ST.

JNENA ST.

JERUSALEM ST.

STEAH ST.

SHEPHERD'S FIELD ST.

SHEPHERDS TOWER RESTAURANT

SHEPHERDS VALLEY RESTAURANT

SHEPHERD HOUSE HOTEL

Bethlehem in the Old City, it is one of the oldest working churches in the world, having been constructed by the Roman emperor Constantine in the 4th century AD. The modern church is under the control and guardianship of the Greek Orthodox Church, the Roman Catholics, and the Armenians.

The church building is over the grotto where Mary is believed to have given birth to Jesus. The pillared interior is dark, with shafts of light streaming through the high windows and low-hanging ceremonial lamps. The entire atmosphere is quite solemn and mysterious.

Due to its popularity among tourists and pilgrims, you might run into people selling their tour guide services just outside the entrance of the church. They charge NIS80 or more. If you hire a guide, it's best to make arrangements in advance and go with them to the site.

To get to the grotto, you need to go down some stairs where you'll see a 14-pointed silver star with the inscription *Hic de Virgin Maria Jesus Christus Natus Est* (Here Jesus Christ was born to the Virgin Mary). Nearby is the **cloister of St. Jerome,** who is known for translating the Bible into Latin.

ST. CATHERINE'S CHURCH

Manger Sq. in the Old City; 6am-noon and 2pm-7pm daily Apr.-Sept., 5:30am-5:30pm daily Oct.-Mar.; free
The location of the annual Catholic midnight Christmas mass that is broadcast on television globally is the Roman Catholic St. Catherine's Church, attached to the Church of the Nativity. The late-19th-century church was built by Franciscans and has a series of grottoes that were once used as places to live.

Rachel's Tomb

Jerusalem-Hebron Rd. near the entrance to Bethlehem; 7:30am-4pm Sun.-Thurs., 7:30am-3:30pm Fri.; free
The third holiest site to the Jewish religion, Rachel's Tomb is the burial site of Rachel, wife of Jacob, who died giving birth to his second son. Over the years, the domed structure of

the tomb has been gradually enclosed in a walled compound due to the deteriorating security situation in the area. Access to the tomb, essentially a place of prayer, is divided into men and women.

Mar Saba Monastery

about 9 miles (15 km) from Bethlehem; tel. 02/277-3135; 8am-5pm daily; free
Only men are allowed to enter, but the 5th-century Greek Orthodox Mar Saba Monastery is a beautiful building that has existed in its current state for 1,500 years and overlooks the Kidron Valley. There is no electricity or running water in the monastery, and it is full of passages, alcoves, cells, and stairs that add to its ambience.

ENTERTAINMENT AND EVENTS

CHRISTMAS EVE

One of the main events in Bethlehem is Christmas Eve, which includes a midnight mass in St. Catherine's Church, visiting the birthplace of Jesus in the Church of the Nativity, and celebrations and live music in Manger Square, around the stage and enormous Christmas tree that are set up for the event.

SHOPPING

There is a solid amount of shopping in Bethlehem, but the main draw is undoubtedly in the area surrounding **Manger Square.** There are several shops that cater to pilgrims and sell postcards and handmade trinkets, boxes, and nativity-scene pieces made from olive wood, many with inlaid mother-of-pearl. Shop owners will bargain in some cases.

Just off Manger Square is a pedestrian street full of shops selling all kinds of goods, from handwoven rugs to soda. The shopkeepers try to sell products for a price that is based on the product's status as an antique. If you

---

1: the Church of the Nativity grotto 2: atrium at St. Catherine's Church 3: Mar Saba Monastery

plan on shopping here, do not pay the first price you're offered; instead, be willing to walk away to get the lowest possible bid from the vendor.

VISIT PALESTINE BOUTIQUE GIFT SHOP

Opposite central bus station on Manger St.; tel. 02/277-1992; www.visitpalestine.ps; 9am-6pm Mon.-Sat.

Take time to visit the Visit Palestine Boutique Gift Shop even if you are not in the mood for shopping. The Visit Palestine operation extends far beyond staff who speak impeccable English and sell one-of-a-kind, locally made and fair-trade products in their Bethlehem shop with its indoor-outdoor balcony coffee shop and restaurant with free Internet. Visit Palestine is one of the leading West Bank tourism outfits in Bethlehem and throughout Jerusalem and the West Bank.

PALESTINIAN HERITAGE CENTER

Maha Saca, Manger St.; tel. 02/274-2381; www.phc.ps; 10am-8pm Mon.-Sat., call ahead to confirm if open

Well worth a stop is the Palestinian Heritage Center, which sells embroidery and other handcrafted products. The center employs women from refugee camps in the West Bank and aims to preserve Palestinian heritage through the display and sale of authentic dresses, jewelry, furniture, and more. They also sell a range of embroidered items and house a permanent exhibition on Palestinian cultural heritage.

BETHLEHEM FAIR TRADE ARTISANS

Milk Grotto St.; tel. 02/275-0365; www. bethlehemfairtrade.org; 10am-5pm Mon.-Sat.

A great place to shop for locally made products, including ceramics, blown glass, and olive-based products like soap and wood, is the Bethlehem Fair Trade Artisans. Contact them for more information about their tour guide services and educational programs about their products and the area.

FOOD

If you visit Bethlehem for one day, the easiest place to get something to eat is near Manger Square, where choices range from hot, fresh, and cheap falafel and pita to more upscale hotel dining.

Middle Eastern

AFTEEM AL-YAFAWI

Manger Sq. in the Old City; tel. 02/274-7940; afteemrestaurant@yahoo.com; 8am-9pm Mon.-Sat.; NIS60

Known for its very consistent and delicious falafel, Afteem Al-Yafawi is a family-owned restaurant that has been in business since 1948. The restaurant is in an old Arab-style building of stone, and they serve generous helpings of hummus, falafel, and other traditional Middle Eastern foods.

SHEPHERDS VALLEY RESTAURANT

Shepherds Field St., Beit Sahour; tel. 02/277-3875; 11am-5pm Mon.-Sat.; NIS55

You can experience Bedouin hospitality at Shepherds Valley Restaurant. You can lunch inside a huge Bedouin tent on *mezze* (appetizers) and grilled meat and vegetables, with a view of the area that, according to tradition, is where the shepherds saw the star above Bethlehem that led them to baby Jesus.

SHEPHERDS TOWER RESTAURANT

Shepherds Field St., Beit Sahour; tel. 02/277-3222; 10am-11pm daily; NIS45

A popular spot on the border of Bethlehem and Beit Sahour is Shepherds Tower Restaurant. There's spacious seating in a Bedouin-style atmosphere that includes popular barbecue dishes, generous portions, and after-meal water pipes.

KA'ABAR

Beit Jala St., near Municipality Bldg., Beit Jala; tel. 02/274-1419; 11am-9pm Mon.-Sat.; NIS40

For an experience that will get you some interaction with locals, Ka'abar is in the village just west of Bethlehem called Beit Jala. Ka'abar grills chicken outdoors, but it has no menu.

When you order, you get a prix fixe menu with meat and five side dishes and mint tea to finish. It's just a taxi ride from Manger Square.

Italian
MUNDO RESTAURANT

Manger St.; tel. 02/274-2299; 11am-11pm daily; NIS55

For some really delicious pizza made with high-quality ingredients, Mundo Restaurant is family-friendly and a popular spot for both tourists and locals. They serve all kinds of other Italian food, mostly pasta dishes, and the interior of the restaurant is lined with floor-to-ceiling wood. An entire wall is comprised of huge windows that afford a fantastic view of the area.

Cafés and Coffee Shops
DAR JDOUDNA COFFEE SHOP

Manger Sq. in the Old City; tel. 02/274-3212; 9am-8pm Mon.-Sat.; NIS40

The sweet little Dar Jdoudna Coffee Shop is housed in an old textile factory building with an olive oil press. It's a good place to have a coffee with something sweet. Dar Jdoudna means "our grandfather's house," which is symbolic of the Palestinian expression of returning to their ancestral homes.

★ SINGER CAFE

Old City St., Beit Sahour; tel. 59/992-9989; www. singercafe.com; 8am-9pm Mon.-Sat.; NIS42

Always popular with locals, foreign correspondents, and expats alike, Singer Cafe is cozy to the extreme—it feels more like someone's house than what it really is: a singular experience that will make a stop to the Bethlehem area memorable. The food menu includes regional favorites like *shakshouka* and other egg and vegetarian dishes. They also serve a range of coffee, tea, and beer.

ACCOMMODATIONS

Bethlehem is highly accustomed to international visitors, including pilgrims and tourists of all kinds, and set up with a range of accommodation options from five-star hotels to hostels and guesthouses.

Under US$100
AL-SALAM HOTEL

Manger St., opposite the Church of the Nativity; tel. 02/276-4083/4; samhotel@p-ol.com; US$70 d

If you are on a budget but still want to be close to the action, Al-Salam Hotel has the location and price that outweigh the very sparse setup. Every room has a bathroom, shower, TV, and phone. The hotel is on the small side with only about two dozen rooms and very plain, spare furnishings. It is a good option if you are making a last-minute booking and want a budget price.

ANGEL HOTEL

184 Al-Sahel St., Beit Jala; tel. 02/276-6880; www. angelhotel.ps; US$95 d

With a great atmosphere and an affordable price, the Angel Hotel is one of Bethlehem's more well-known and popular places to stay. It is a bit off the beaten path in nearby Beit Jala, but the hotel has a rooftop restaurant with incredible views, free wireless Internet, a breakfast buffet, and a bar with an outdoor terrace. The rooms are decorated very simply with tile flooring and have basic amenities.

BETHLEHEM STAR HOTEL

Freres St.; tel. 02/274-3249; www. bethlehemstarhotel.com; US$85 d

The Bethlehem Star Hotel is on the plain side and known as a favorite spot for foreign journalists to stay. Close to Bethlehem's city center, the midsize hotel has a fantastic view of the city from its breakfast room, and there is also a rooftop restaurant and free wireless Internet. Every double room comes with a minibar, hair dryer, direct dial phone, and an LCD TV. The hotel has a lobby coffee shop and the rooftop restaurant has views of Shepherd's Field and other sites around the city. There is live music once a week.

US$100-150
SHEPHERD HOUSE HOTEL

Shepherds Field St.; tel. 02/274-0656, 02/274-0657, or 02/274-0658; www.shepherdbethlehem.com; US$135 d

The midsize Shepherd House Hotel is in

a pastoral setting and a short drive to the Church of the Nativity and other Christian sites. Billed as "the only four-star hotel in Bethlehem," the hotel has a 24-hour front desk, dry cleaning and laundry service, and free wireless Internet. Some of the more than 100 rooms have a balcony with a view of the lovely mountain landscape that surrounds Bethlehem. The exterior of the building is simple, but the rooms are comfortably furnished and spacious, and the elegant lobby is full of comfortable chairs and nice corners for sitting.

US$150-200

★ JACIR PALACE INTERCONTINENTAL

Jerusalem-Hebron Rd.; tel. 02/276-6777; www.jacirpalace.ps; US$160 d

The Jacir Palace Intercontinental gets its name from its former status as a palace. The perfectly beautiful, classy hotel has a soothing atmosphere and is full of elegant touches. Even if you're not a guest here, it's worthwhile to have a cappuccino in the lobby coffee shop amid the massive stone pillars and skylight atrium. All of the 250 rooms at the Jacir are decorated in a warm yet elegant fashion with comfortable touches like loveseats and coffee tables, bathtubs, balconies overlooking the hotel grounds, and a sitting area with satellite TV. The hotel has a restaurant, gym, bar, a massive lobby that doubles as a coffee shop, and a pool. Make reservations as far in advance as possible; it is far and away the nicest place in town and books early, especially during December. It is a short drive to the Church of the Nativity.

MANGER SQUARE HOTEL

Manger St.; tel. 02/277-8888; http://mangersquarehotel.com; US$160 d

About as close as you can get to the main action in town is Manger Square Hotel, an upscale hotel with 220 rooms that caters to international visitors. The hotel has a spacious lobby and dining room that serves buffet-style meals, free wireless Internet throughout, and

modern rooms with wooden furniture, satellite TV, and minibar. Though it is just steps from the main tourist attractions of Bethlehem, the hotel may entice you to stay inside and relax at the bar or get room service.

INFORMATION AND SERVICES

Tour Guides

Visiting Bethlehem with a tour guide is a good way to experience the city and avoid many of the hassles you might encounter on your own.

(JOHN) HANNA AWWAD

PO Box 51340, Jerusalem, 91513; tel. 02/289-9305 or 054/445-2824; awwadhanna@yahoo.com; NIS200 and up

(John) Hanna Awwad is based in Jerusalem, which is best because you would not want to go to Bethlehem and then try to hire a guide. John is so well-known and connected in Jerusalem that if he happens to not be available, he will be able to recommend an alternative.

VISIT PALESTINE TOURS

Opposite central bus station on Manger St.; tel. 02/277-1992; www.visitpalestine.ps; 9am-6pm Mon.-Sat.; NIS60 and up pp

Regardless of the type of experience you're looking for, Visit Palestine Tours will likely be able to help. The company is also an excellent resource for information and can point you in the right direction.

GETTING THERE AND AROUND

There are several ways to get into Bethlehem, and all of them involve going through a checkpoint.

Checkpoint

The main checkpoint entrance to Bethlehem is 15 minutes from Jerusalem city center at the end of Hebron Road. Going into the city is easier than getting out because the guards check the cars going into Jerusalem a bit more closely.

Alternative Tours

In recent years, there has been a proliferation of alternative tour companies offering options other than the standard tour guide or group. Many of the alternative tours emphasize a participatory experience, such as helping to pick olives during the harvest, or have a political agenda or slant. Either way, they can give you a fresh perspective on the West Bank.

GREEN OLIVE TOURS

One of the most popular and well-known social-enterprise alternative tour companies is Green Olive Tours (tel. 03/721-9540 in Israel, U.S. tel. 612/276-2077, www.toursinenglish.com). The company gives tours that deal with the culture, history, and political geography of the West Bank for groups and individuals. The work the company does also aims to support the local population in the areas it tours by working with local tour guides, setting up overnight host-family stays, and encouraging the purchase of local crafts.

ALTERNATIVE TOURISM GROUP (ATG)

Another option is the well-established and reputable Alternative Tourism Group (74 Star St. in Beit Sahour, tel. 02/277-2151, www.atg.ps), a Palestinian NGO that specializes in taking a critical look at the historical, cultural, and political situation in the West Bank. The company is based in Beit Sahour, near Bethlehem. They also launched a smartphone app called Palestine and Palestinians, available in the Google Play store, which provides comprehensive information on the region and its people.

Though Green Olive Tours and ATG are separate companies, they sometimes work in cooperation with one another.

Taxis

Taking a taxi into Bethlehem might prove difficult. The easiest thing to do is take a taxi to the checkpoint, walk through, and find another taxi on the other side. It is a bit confusing where the checkpoint is exactly because of the lack of signs into or out of the city. Just follow the general flow of traffic, or keep asking until you get the right directions.

Share Taxis

If you go to **Damascus Gate** in Jerusalem near the Old City, you should be able to find a bus or *sherut* (share taxi) that will take you to Bethlehem. Just be confident about what you're doing, and don't get tricked into being driven for a fixed price by a taxi. Insist that they use the meter; it's the law.

Buses

You can also take a **Jerusalem city bus** straight down Hebron Road (bus numbers 71, 72, 73, or 74) to the end, walk through the checkpoint, and pick up a taxi on the other side. Bus routes change, so check in advance what bus number goes in the right direction.

Nablus and Vicinity

Mentioned many times in the Bible by the name Shechem, and often a flashpoint of violence, over the past decade-plus Nablus has been steadily growing and stabilizing, though it still sometimes experiences violence. There is also a sizable outdoor market, An-Najah National University, and plenty of opportunities to try the regional treat, *knafe,* for which Nablus is famous.

Situated at the center of the Palestinian-controlled area of the West Bank, Nablus is avoided by most Israelis, and in times of regional unrest, scheduled tours to the area are often canceled. If you can manage the trip, Nablus has a unique charm and very warm residents. But check your embassy's website for any travel warnings before going.

SIGHTS

There are very few sights in Nablus, unless you are interested in a political tour, with an overview of the current situation and some modern history about the Second Intifada

and its aftermath. Nablus, however, is a fun place to stroll, buy some souvenirs for a great price, and try *knafe.*

Old City

The center of Nablus is home to the Old City, which serves as a destination for shopping, eating, and sightseeing. There are six quarters to the very densely populated Old City: Yasmina, Gharb, Qaryun, Aqaba, Qaysariyya, and Habala. You can find Turkish baths here and a few historic monuments. Note the fading posters plastered about the area and remembrance plaques of people who died during the fighting with Israeli forces, including a few bullet holes in walls and unrepaired windows.

Give yourself a few hours to shop, eat, and people-watch in the passages of the indoor-outdoor **Nablus Old City Market.** Enjoy a rich, dark cup of Arabic coffee and eat the traditional Arabic sweet cheese-custard treat, *knafe,* in its birthplace at one of the stalls in the market.

grounds of the Bir Ya'qub monastery, the site of Jacob's Well

Refugee Camps

Since the establishment of the state of Israel, various regional wars and conflicts and disputes over land have forced displaced Arab residents into refugee camps. In many cases, the people in the refugee camps exist in a situation of instability and dire poverty.

According to the United Nations, the West Bank is home to 775,000 registered refugees, and about a quarter of them live in refugee camps.

One of the largest, Balata Refugee Camp, is just outside Nablus. It was established in 1950 and persists through this day, with a population of about 25,000 and an unemployment rate of 25 percent. Balata's population is larger than most towns in the region. Balata's civil society is extremely active. Its landscape consists of small, rough alleys between tightly packed stone buildings with piles of rubble instead of a simple playground or park.

Much of the support for residents of refugee camps comes from international bodies such as the United Nations, nonprofits, and nongovernmental organizations.

Mount Gerizim

Overlooking Nablus is Mount Gerizim, home to the last remaining community of Samaritans, who are guardians of some of the region's strictest and most ancient religious traditions. They believe that the earth of the mountain they live on was used by God to create Adam, and thus it is extremely holy to them. The area has numerous archaeological ruins. It is possible to visit the area, including the Samaritan community that lives here, but you should arrange for a guide familiar with the area to take you. On Passover, you can see a traditional lamb sacrifice at the community center.

★ Jacob's Well

off Rte. 5487 at the entrance to Nablus; tel.
09/237-5123; 9am-noon and 2pm-4pm daily, until
5pm in the summer; free

Well worth the side trip of about 10 minutes by car from Nablus city center, Jacob's Well is said to be the same well from which a Samaritan woman gave Jesus a drink of water during a long journey 2,000 years ago. The well (also known as the Well of Sychar) is an object of pilgrimage, housed deep inside the caverns of a massive Eastern Orthodox Church on the grounds of Bir Ya'qub monastery, built over and around a 4th-century church.

Beneath the high altar at the center of the church is the crypt that houses the well. You can descend into the cavernous crypt and draw a drink of cool, clear water from the same well Jesus drank from. The well has been measured as about 130 feet (40 meters) deep, adding to its reputation as one of the more authentic sites in the Holy Land because it would have been almost impossible to move.

Even though it is immediately off a main road, the gate and high stone wall keep the area protected and give the very pretty grounds of the church the atmosphere of a calm oasis.

The church, grounds, and well are closely guarded. You should call in advance of a visit to make sure it is open. Only call if you are certain you will visit, as they might open it especially for you and await your arrival.

Balata Refugee Camp

The Balata Refugee Camp Community Center is the largest refugee camp in the West Bank and home to about 25,000 people. You can ask a local taxi to take you to the center, where you can learn about the refugees' living situation. They also sell a number of nice, handmade items that are small, lightweight, and easy to pack for a return trip. The profit from the sale of the goods goes to support the community center and women artisans in the community.

Knafe

Whatever else you eat, go in search of *knafe* (pronounced ka-nah-feh), a flat Arab cheese-and-biscuit-type creation cooked up on large, shallow pans and served fresh out of the oven. There are several shops in the Old City that sell it; ask anybody to point you in the direction of the nearest *knafe* shop. A happy warning: The variation on *knafe* served in Nablus is considered the best of the best, so once you have it here, you will likely be ruined for eating it anywhere else.

FOOD

For a wide variety of things to eat in Nablus, just head anywhere near the Old City, where you will find everything from restaurants to snacks and sweets.

ZEIT OU ZAATAR

Al Yasmeen Hotel, City Center; tel. 09/233-3555; 9am-9pm daily; NIS55

A very nice spot to sit for some light food and tea or coffee is Zeit Ou Zaatar. The furniture and appointments in the sitting area are mixed antique and modern pieces, and the atmosphere is very Middle Eastern with old lamps and mirrors. It is the perfect spot for an intimate discussion, and the impeccable service is on par with a four-star hotel.

AL SARAYA

Hiteen St., just east of the Nablus Mall; tel. 09/233-5444; http://visitpalestine.ps; 11am-9pm daily; NIS55

Partly charming for its atmosphere and partly for its food, Al Saraya serves up delightful Palestinian dishes, such as *mansaf* (lamb in fermented dried yogurt) and *musakhan* (roasted chicken cooked with onions, sumac, allspice, and saffron), in the setting of a 150-year-old house. Old copper lights and oriental window frames add to the ambience of this favorite neighborhood spot. It is just on the outskirts of the Old City, making it an easy stop after an afternoon of sightseeing.

ACCOMMODATIONS

There isn't much reason to stay overnight in Nablus, but if you do need a hotel, it would be advisable to gravitate toward an area where foreigners gather.

INTERNATIONAL FRIENDS' GUEST HOUSE

Annajah Al Qadeem St.; tel. 09/238-1064; ifriends. house@gmail.com; US$55 d

The International Friends' Guest House can provide both an affordable place to stay and historical and current information about the political situation in the region. The guesthouse offers a variety of resources for researchers and those who want to make a trip to the Old City of Nablus and nearby refugee camps. There are also activities and seminars on a weekly basis. The building is a lovely, older stone house with some nice gardens and not far from the center of the city.

INFORMATION AND SERVICES

Two very useful websites about Nablus are www.nablusguide.com and http://visitpalestine.ps.

GETTING THERE AND AROUND

The two best ways to get to Nablus are by hired **taxi** or **share taxi.** Don't be surprised when your hired taxi stops along the way to pass you off to another taxi at a large taxi parking lot just outside the city limits. It is related to the security situation in the region. Most Israelis will not go to Nablus, nor do they want to, but it is a safe place for a foreign visitor. Keep in mind that it is a conservative, mostly Muslim town. You should always check your embassy website in advance.

From **Jericho,** Nablus is an approximately two-hour, olive-grove-filled drive.

The easiest, cheapest, and safest way to get around Nablus is by hired taxi.

Checkpoints

The checkpoint situation surrounding Nablus changes according to the severity of the security situation. You will go through at least one checkpoint, maybe more, before arriving. Be prepared with a very clear, simple answer about the purpose of your visit and keep your passport handy.

Jericho

The ancient and low-lying city of Jericho is situated at about 853 feet (260 meters) below sea level. There are some amazing archaeological and biblical sites here, reflecting its thousands of years of history as a continuously inhabited city.

Jericho has been conquered repeatedly over the millennia, first by the Israelites after 40 years of desert wandering when, according to the Bible, Joshua made the walls come tumbling down. It was also conquered by the Babylonians, Romans, Byzantines, Crusaders, and Christians. Modern-day Jericho is in the West Bank, in Area A, and is controlled by the Palestinians.

SIGHTS

★ Mount of Temptation Monastery

Outskirts of Jericho on the slopes of Mount of Temptation; 8am-1pm and 3pm-4pm Mon.-Fri., one hour later in the summer, 8am-2pm Sat.; free

Perched about 1,140 feet (350 meters) above Jericho and seemingly etched into the side of a cliff is the Greek Orthodox Mount of Temptation Monastery, also called Jabel Quruntul, which dates back to the 12th century. The Crusaders originally built one church in a cave partway up the cliff and another church on the summit.

The current monastery dates back to the 19th century. The mountain is believed to be the place where Jesus was tempted by Satan. If you take the cable car ride, you will pass over excavations of biblical-era Jericho.

CABLE CAR

Entrance to Mount of Temptation Monastery area; tel. 02/232-1590; 8:30am-6:30pm Mon.-Sat.; adult NIS40, child NIS22

You can take the 30-minute hike up the mountainside or ride the cable car to reach the monastery in about five minutes, but the view from below can also satisfy.

Museum of the Good Samaritan

off Hwy. 1 at Kfar Adumim Junction; www.parks.org.il; 9am-5pm Sun.-Thurs.; NIS20

Situated on the main highway between Jerusalem and Jericho, the Museum of the Good Samaritan offers a chance to see some detailed mosaics from around Israel and the West Bank. Also on display indoors and alongside the mosaics that range from quite small to massive are stones with ancient engravings. The museum offers a chance to learn a bit of the history of the Samaritans and their contributions to the region.

TOP EXPERIENCE

★ Hisham's Palace

about 2 miles (3 km) off Qasr Hisham St., follow guidepost signs; tel. 09/232-2522; 8am-5pm daily Oct.-Mar., 8am-6pm daily Apr.-Sept.; NIS15

The gorgeous ruins of Hisham's Palace are a major archaeological site in Jericho. The palace was built in the 8th century, possibly as a seasonal retreat of some kind.

It's just a mile (1.5 km) north of Jericho proper, and the excavated site shows the

Vicinity of Jericho

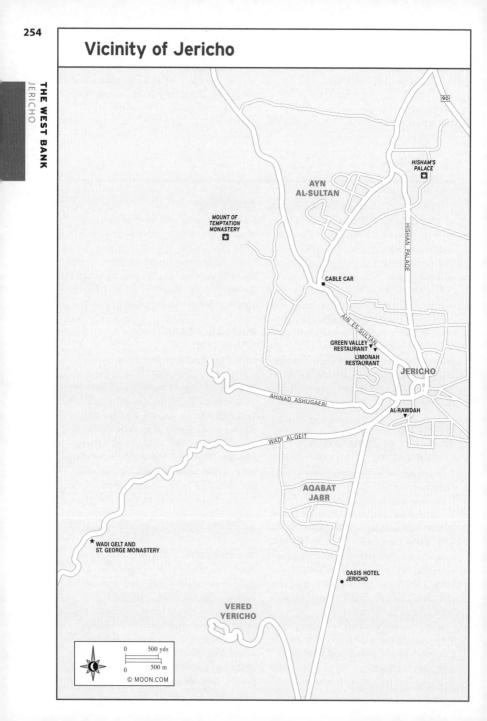

AYN AL-SULTAN

HISHAM'S PALACE ★

MOUNT OF TEMPTATION MONASTERY ★

HISHAN PALACE

CABLE CAR

AIN ES-SULTAN

GREEN VALLEY RESTAURANT ▼

LIMONAH RESTAURANT

JERICHO

AHINAD ASHUGAERI

AL-RAWDAH ▼

WADI AL-QEIT

AQABAT JABR

★ WADI QELT AND ST. GEORGE MONASTERY

OASIS HOTEL JERICHO

VERED YERICHO

0   500 yds
0   500 m

© MOON.COM

remains of buildings that were destroyed in an earthquake in AD 747. Among the site's treasures are a mosque, water fountains, enormous mosaic floors, and decorative accents like the often-photographed carved six-pointed-star window.

Restoration and preservation work have been carried out with the cooperation and support of the Italian government, UNESCO, the Palestinian Department of Antiquities, and the Franciscan Archaeological Institute. There is a small museum just to the right of the entrance that has a collection of pottery found at the site. You can see a short video about the site with a ticket at the visitors center.

Bethany Beyond the Jordan Baptism Site

off Hwy. 90; www.parks.org.il; Sun.-Fri. 9am-dusk; free

Situated about 6 miles (9 km) north of the Dead Sea, the Bethany on the Jordan Baptismal Site is an easy-to-reach baptismal site. It may not offer all the trappings of more touristy baptism sites, but its spiritual foundations remain intact. The site has stairs with rails to go into the Jordan River and is patrolled by Israeli soldiers. Just a stone's throw away across the water is Jordan and another baptismal site with Jordanian soldiers. It is an easy stop on the road between the Dead Sea and Jerusalem.

Wadi Qelt

If you are up for a 90-minute hike through a canyon that has year-round flowing water fed by three streams, pass through Wadi Qelt (at Kosiba), where there are plenty of shady spots to stop and even swim to cool off.

St. George Monastery

Wadi Qelt Rd. in Kosiba; tel. 05/025-9949; 8am-11am and 3pm-5pm Mon.-Fri., 9am-noon Sat., 9am-5pm Sun., but hours can change so call in advance; free

The ruins of the Greek Orthodox St. George Monastery, which you can also get to by car if you choose not to hike, date back to AD 420.

The current structure is a 19th-century restoration completed by the Greek Orthodox Church. The upper floor of the monastery, which looks like it is clinging to the side of a cliff, is an ancient cave with three churches and a bell tower built around it. The building is about three miles (5 km) from Jericho.

FOOD

★ LIMONAH RESTAURANT

Muntazhat St.; tel. 02/231-2977; call for hours as they vary; NIS55

On a main road, Limonah Restaurant serves up a wide variety of food ranging from hummus to pizza and is known for ridiculously large portions. The staff is helpful and friendly, and it's spotlessly clean.

AL-RAWDAH

Ketf Al-Wad St.; tel. 02/232-2555; 8am-8pm daily; NIS50

Time-tested and popular, Al-Rawdah is the oldest restaurant in Jericho, serving barbecue and boasting beautiful views of the city.

GREEN VALLEY RESTAURANT

Ein Al-Sultan St.; tel. 02/232-2349; noon-9pm daily; NIS60

An easy stop is Green Valley Park, an indoor-outdoor restaurant owned by a respected local family and partially supported by international charity. They serve up Middle Eastern dishes, *mezze*, and meat grilled outdoors.

ACCOMMODATIONS

If you want to stay a night in Jericho, there are a variety of options, but the lower-end accommodations tend to come and go. The safest bet is something on the higher end with international connections.

US$150-200
BAB AL SHAMS RESORT

Al-Maghtas Rd.; tel. 02/231-3733; US$180 d

The Bab Al Shams Resort is not quite a resort, but this smaller hotel does have an outdoor pool on pretty grounds encircled by palm trees and a bar. The rooms are very basic,

with simple beds and very few furnishings or creature comforts, but with private bathrooms. The well-kept rooms also have air-conditioning, a mini-fridge, and a flat-screen TV. The hotel offers a breakfast buffet and a space to barbecue on hotel grounds.

Over US$200
OASIS HOTEL JERICHO
Jericho-Jerusalem Rd.; tel. 02/231-1200; US$240 d
The Oasis Hotel Jericho offers every amenity typical of a luxury hotel, including a variety of options for dining, beautifully landscaped grounds, a Dead Sea water pool, a full-service spa, and outdoor tennis courts. Set on the outskirts of Jericho, it is 30 minutes from the Dead Sea and an hour from Jerusalem. It also has a full suite of business services. The 181 rooms are modern with nice furnishings, desks, TVs, and comfortable, large beds. Room service and free continental breakfast are also available.

INFORMATION AND SERVICES
The **Alternative Tourism Group** (www.atg.ps) has an app for smartphones and a website, both with useful information about non-mainstream tours, such as political explainer groups and solidarity-based activities, like olive picking.

GETTING THERE AND AROUND
As with everywhere else in the West Bank, keep your passport handy in case you need it at **checkpoints.** The easiest way to get to Jericho if you don't have a rental car is to go from Ramallah via **buses,** which depart several times throughout the day. The schedules are fairly informal, so you might need to ask around once you are in Ramallah. From **Nablus,** Jericho is an approximately two-hour, olive-grove-filled drive.

Hebron

Known as the City of the Patriarchs, Hebron is thousands of years old and full of historical and religious significance and tension. Situated on four hills at an elevation of about 3,000 feet (900 meters), it is holy to Muslims, Christians, and Jews alike because it is home to the tomb of Abraham and other patriarchs and matriarchs.

More than a dozen Jewish settlements surround the city, and several hundred Jewish settlers live in the city, which is within the jurisdiction of the Palestinian Authority but under Israeli military control. The settlers who live in the city are accompanied by armed Israeli military guards.

VISITING HEBRON
It is recommended you visit Hebron with a tour guide or with a tour group, as it will take all of the guesswork out of where to go and what to do, and give you smoother access to the sites amid the complicated security situation.

Tours
A centrally located local tour company called **Explore West Bank** (base of street at the Tomb of the Patriarchs; tel. 059/824-4150; zzzaa_2009@hotmail.com; $150 per day or $75 half day) can ferry you around the city and the region very easily.

Other good tour companies are **Green Olive Tours** (tel. 03/721-9540 in Israel; U.S. tel. 612/276-2077; www.toursinenglish.com; NIS220 and up) and **Abraham Tours** (67 Hanevi'im St. in Jerusalem; tel. 02/566-0045; http://abrahamtours.com; NIS200 and up).

1: Bethany on the Jordan Baptismal Site 2: Hisham's Palace 3: Mount of Temptation Monastery 4: St. George Monastery

SIGHTS
Old City

One of the oldest of its kind in the West Bank, Hebron's Old City includes a large *shuk* with gorgeous arched ceilings. Hebron is one of the only Islamic cities that has maintained its original urban layout, which is dominated by the Mamluk architectural style.

Tomb of the Patriarchs (Cave of Machpelah) and Ibrahimi Mosque

end of the street in the Old City; tel. 052/429-5554 or 052/431-7055; 4am-8pm Sun.-Thurs.; dress modestly, including head covering for women; free

The traditional burial site of Abraham and other patriarchs and matriarchs, the Tomb of the Patriarchs is one of the most sacred sites in Judaism, Islam, and Christianity. The Ibrahimi Mosque, second only to Jerusalem's Al Aqsa Mosque in terms of regional significance to Muslims, is located here.

The mosque was built after the tombs were enclosed by Herod the Great, who built a huge wall around the burial sites and the cave. The structure was later turned into a church and then a mosque, with four Mamluk minarets on the corners of the building (only two remain). The current structure includes prayer halls, inner and outer areas, and extremely steep stairs, which lead to the rooftop area where domes mark the burial sites.

In 1994, there was a shooting of Muslims at prayer in the mosque. Since then, there has been ongoing tension and violence in Hebron, and the site, as well as the city, is tightly guarded and controlled. The visiting hours of the cave and the mosque vary, especially during religious holidays, so it is best to call in advance. If you visit during a time when regional tensions are flaring, it might also be difficult to gain entrance; be sure to take your passport.

SHOPPING

Hebron is known for its grapes, leatherwork, glassblowing, colorful and attractive ceramics, and carpets. The *shuk* is unfortunately a bit of a touchy area because it is adjacent to a part of town under tight control, but you can find a great deal of local handiwork here.

Shuk

Boasting arched rooftops and vast alleys, Hebron's *shuk* (in the town center,

the Tomb of the Patriarchs

10am-6pm daily) is a site to explore for treats, souvenirs, or just for the fun of it. Things on sale include fresh and dried fruit, olive-wood items, pottery, glass craftwork, and leather products.

Glassblowing

Hebron is famed throughout Israel and the West Bank for ceramics and glassblowing. The major glassblowing workshops of Hebron are near the northern entrance to the city in the direction of Bethlehem.

HEBRON GLASS AND CERAMICS FACTORY

Ras al Jora St., in the northern part of Hebron; tel. 02/222-8502; hebronglass@yahoo.com; 10am-5pm Mon.-Fri.

One of the major glassblowing workshops, the Hebron Glass and Ceramics Factory sells beautiful, original pieces that range from multicolored goblets to dishes and decorative boxes. You can take photographs, watch glassblowers using ancient techniques (probably imported to the area by Venetians), and buy products.

FOOD

The *shuk* is always a good place to pick up snacks, and you can usually find dishes like falafel there. If that isn't enough to satisfy your appetite, Hebron has a few other quick and inexpensive options, particularly on and around Nimra Street.

Middle Eastern

★ ABU MAZEN

Nimra St.; tel. 02/222-6168; 11am-9pm daily; NIS30

The very popular Abu Mazen has a great reputation and is a good option for a delicious, affordable meal. It gets very crowded at lunchtime as it serves up salads, fresh bread, Middle Eastern lamb dishes, and vegetarian choices, including soup. The atmosphere is that of a fairly typical home-style restaurant, with simple furnishings and a lot of regulars.

INFORMATION AND SERVICES
Online Resources

There are a couple of websites with information about Hebron, the **Hebron Municipality** site (www.hebron-city.ps) and the site of the **Jewish Community of Hebron** (http://en.hebron.org.il).

Safety and Security

Hebron's central Shuhada Street was closed years ago because of violence in the area. The street, which used to be a main thoroughfare and full of shops, now has restricted access, despite the fact that it leads to the Tomb of the Patriarchs and Ibrahimi Mosque. International visitors can walk and drive down it, but be aware that there are sometimes clashes in this area.

GETTING THERE AND AROUND

From Jerusalem, take the bus from next to **Damascus Gate** at the Old City to Abu Dis, and make sure to tell the bus driver you are going to Khalil (Arabic for Hebron). From Be'er Sheva's **central bus station,** there are several options for buses, but make sure you don't get a ride on the bus that's going to the nearby settlement of Kiryat Arba. From Ramallah and Bethlehem, take a *sherut* **(share taxi)** from the town centers.

Once you're in Hebron, you will need to choose different transportation routes for either the Palestinian Authority-controlled side or Israel-controlled side. For the Palestinian Authority-controlled side (which is most of the city), go from the **bus station** by Damascus Gate in Jerusalem (bus number 21, NIS15). You will transfer at the Bethlehem bus station and switch to a *sherut* (NIS15). The Israeli-controlled side, including the Tomb of the Patriarchs, requires bus number 160 from the **Jerusalem Central Bus station** (NIS12).

The simplest thing to do is to take a *sherut* from Jerusalem to Bethlehem, and then ask your driver where to find another *sherut* to Hebron.

Ramallah and Al Bireh

Ramallah (and its twin city Al Bireh) is just a 15-minute drive from Jerusalem and known as a Palestinian cultural and arts hub, rather than a hot spot for archaeological or religious sightseeing. There are also a number of excellent restaurants in this area and some good hotels. Although Ramallah might seem like a good alternative place to stay if you are planning on sightseeing in Jerusalem, be aware that you will have to go back and forth through a checkpoint.

SIGHTS
Taybeh Brewery
1 Taybeh Rd., Taybeh, just outside Ramallah; tel. 02/289-8868; www.taybehbeer.com; 8am-4pm Mon.-Sat., 30-minute tours 9am-2:30pm Mon.-Sat.; free

A truly original stop on a trip to the Middle East is Taybeh Brewery, the only Palestinian brewery in existence. Taybeh, a town of about 1,500 people, is the only majority-Christian Palestinian community in the Holy Land. The driving force behind the family-run brewery is a father-daughter team, and they

are the main sponsors and advocates of Taybeh's annual Oktoberfest.

ARTS AND CULTURE CENTERS

Ramallah is home to several arts and culture centers that are NGOs and operate with international assistance. The centers put on all kinds of arts-related events throughout the year.

THE POPULAR ART CENTRE (PAC)
Al Bireh; tel. 02/240-3891; www.popularartcentre.org

Most notable among these centers is The Popular Art Centre (PAC), which is also home of the renowned Palestine International Festival. PAC runs a number of arts programs for children, has a cinémathèque, and promotes traditional music and dance.

AL-KASABA THEATRE AND CINÉMATHÈQUE
Hospital St. in Ramallah; tel. 02/296-5292/3; www.alkasaba.org

Established originally in 1970 in Jerusalem,

Downtown Ramallah's busy streets make for good shopping.

Ramallah

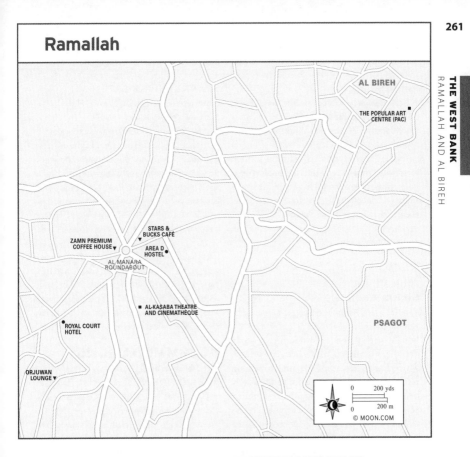

the Al-Kasaba Theatre and Cinémathèque works on a local and international level in arts promotion, including a past international film festival, theater productions, and hosting international artists.

RAMALLAH CULTURAL PALACE

Industrial Zone; tel. 02/298-4704; http://culture.ramallah.ps

Established in 2005, the Ramallah Cultural Palace executes a mission similar to the other centers in the area in its promotion and support of arts, poetry, and music programs in the community.

ENTERTAINMENT AND EVENTS

TAYBEH OKTOBERFEST

Taybeh, just outside of Ramallah; www.visitpalestine.ps; first Sat.-Sun. in Oct.

Yes, there is a beer festival in the West Bank, even though it only has one brewery. The annual Oktoberfest features an interesting mix of local folk musicians, hip-hop and brass bands, and local dishes throughout the two-day event.

PALESTINE INTERNATIONAL FESTIVAL

various locations; www.popularartcentre.org; tickets vary

Founded in 1993 to host and showcase international arts in the West Bank, the Palestine

International Festival includes a wide array of music, poetry, and performance events in surrounding Arab villages and refugee camps.

PALFEST

Ramallah and various locations in East Jerusalem and the West Bank; http://palfest.org; free

The Palestine Festival of Literature, known as PalFest, was founded in 2008 and showcases the Middle Eastern love for the written word with domestic and international writers, poets, and songwriters. They facilitate workshops and put on musical performances. Some events are in English, and the festival is held in various locations throughout the West Bank and East Jerusalem.

FOOD
Fine Dining
ORJUWAN LOUNGE

Hope St., central Ramallah; tel. 02/297-6870; 10:30am-midnight daily; NIS75

Locally grown food and handmade pasta are the highlights of Orjuwan Lounge, which has a classy, upscale atmosphere on par with something you'd find in Tel Aviv or Jerusalem. It was among the restaurants chosen to participate in the annual French Culinary Week in Palestine sponsored by the French government. Serving a range of dishes that includes everything from arugula salad to lamb and chicken dishes, Orjuwan is decidedly Western food with an Asian flair. Their main offerings are soups and appetizers, salads, risottos, seafood, and favorite Italian dishes such as ravioli, prepared inventively with local flavors and ingredients, but they also have a surprising range of creative main dishes. They are known for their weekend brunch and an experimental tasting menu of 12 dishes that requires a reservation 24 hours in advance.

Cafés and Coffee Shops
ZAMN PREMIUM COFFEE HOUSE

Al Teereh St. roundabout; tel. 02/295-0600; 24 hours daily; NIS45

ZAMN Premium Coffee House is one branch of a very successful local chain of upper-end coffee shops. It is a popular gathering place and serves up excellent coffee and sweets.

STARS & BUCKS CAFÉ

City Center; tel. 02/297-5674; 9am-midnight Sat.-Thurs., 3pm-midnight Fri.; NIS75

Just for the novelty and bizarre experience of it, try Stars & Bucks Café right in the center of Ramallah. You'll find yourself marveling at how they have managed to get away with such blatant spoofing of an international brand. Many tourists visit just to buy souvenir evidence to show people back home. It's a fairly large place (and a regional chain) that has decent coffee on the second floor of a building at the center of the first major roundabout in town. They serve a wide variety of main dishes in addition to their coffee offerings, including noodle dishes, sandwiches, and Chinese food. It operates as both a coffee shop and a hookah lounge, so you can also smoke a water pipe while you're here.

ACCOMMODATIONS
Under US$100
AREA D HOSTEL

Maliki Bldg., top floor, Jamal Abdel Nasser St.; tel. 056/934-9042; http://ramallahhostel.com; US$65 d

The Area D Hostel is a youth hostel that caters to independent backpackers who want a good base in the region to do some exploring. The hostel features private and dorm rooms with shared bathrooms and private apartments with private bathrooms, free wireless Internet, a 24-hour front desk, and a snack desk. The rooms are simply furnished with tile floors. It is situated in a central location near the bus to Jerusalem, and tours can be arranged through the front desk.

US$100-150
ROYAL COURT SUITE HOTEL

24 Jaffa St.; tel. 02/296-4040; www.rcshotel.com; US$150 d

A very nice option that includes semi-luxury accommodations and rooms with balconies big enough to dine on, the Royal Court Suite Hotel is a small hotel with suites in Ramallah's business district, across from the city park and near the new city center. There is a rooftop restaurant, whirlpool tubs and kitchenettes in the comfortably furnished suites, balconies with views of the city, and a complimentary buffet breakfast. There are many restaurants nearby, but you can also dine at the hotel's bar with outdoor seating, which is frequented by both locals and tourists.

INFORMATION AND SERVICES
Online Resources
The **Municipality of Ramallah** (www.ramallah.ps) has a multilingual website, but the functions are a bit limited; it basically provides you with some background information and a few pictures.

Safety and Security
Violence sometimes erupts in Ramallah, particularly near the Qalandia Checkpoint. It is always best to check with your embassy in advance of a visit.

GETTING THERE AND AROUND
Checkpoints
Ramallah's main drawback for visitors coming from Jerusalem is going through the infamous **Qalandia Checkpoint,** which involves a complex series of checks, especially in times of unrest. By far the easiest thing to do is get to the checkpoint, walk through, and take a taxi on the other side.

There are alternative routes that are longer and more circuitous, but unless you are riding in a *sherut* (share taxi) or a bus, just go through Qalandia.

Taxis and Share Taxis
Many taxis from Jerusalem won't go through the Qalandia Checkpoint because of the trouble getting back through it. If you take a taxi, insist that the driver set the meter. The driver might insist on receiving a large sum of money upon delivering you to Ramallah with the reasoning that they have to go back through the checkpoint. Your best bet is to take a taxi to the checkpoint, walk through, and catch another taxi on the other side.

Bus
Ramallah is just 15 minutes from Jerusalem, so you can always find a bus at **Damascus Gate** that is going there, though the ride might be longer as they go around Qalandia to avoid the lines.

Eilat and the Negev

The southern half of Israel is home to the vast

Negev Desert, a sparsely populated region filled with myriad archaeological sites, desert hikes, and various camping options.

The Negev is the largest desert in Israel, and accounts for more than half of Israel's land. It is home to the ancient city of Be'er Sheva, Bedouin tribes, and some of Israel's most popular ecotourism destinations.

Despite being sparsely populated, the Negev has numerous outstanding options for a range of activities such as desert hikes, camping, and guided off-road adventures. Some of the region's more notable ecotourism experiences include accommodations like environmentally friendly, custom-designed desert huts and camel rides.

At the northeastern side of the Negev is the Dead Sea, the lowest

Highlights

Look for ★ to find recommended sights, activities, dining, and lodging.

★ **Masada National Park:** Arguably the most dramatic vista in the region is from this hilltop fortress of Herod the Great that served as the last stand for a band of rebel Jews facing off against the Roman army (page 269).

★ **Ein Avdat National Park:** The always-flowing stream at this park is a highlight of easy-to-navigate desert trails engineered to protect the natural environment. It is a prime ecotourism site (page 277).

★ **Avdat National Park:** Adjacent to Ein Avdat, Avdat National Park is home to one of the most famous Nabataean cities, situated along the ancient incense route (page 277).

★ **Mitzpe Ramon Observatory and Ramon Crater:** Mitzpe Ramon is the site of the largest of three massive geological craters in the Negev, as well as numerous hiking routes (page 279).

★ **Coral World Underwater Observatory:** See scores of rare, colorful tropical fish at this underwater world just a few miles outside of Eilat (page 287).

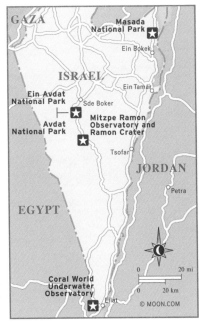

Eilat and the Negev

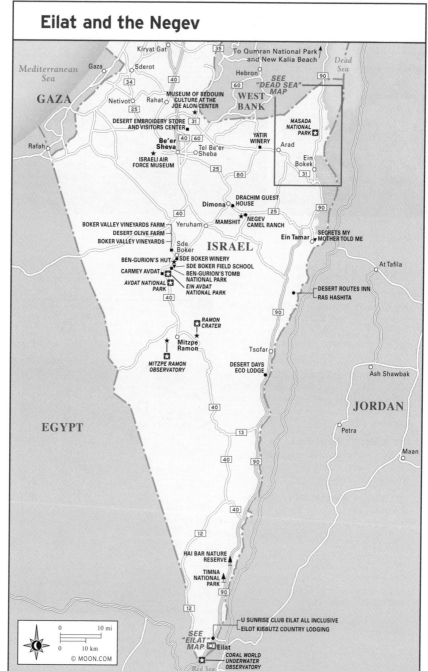

point on Earth, famed for its therapeutic waters and warm air. The Dead Sea is beloved for its mud, which you can take directly out of the sea and spread on your body. The tourism demand in the Dead Sea region means that there is a wealth of hotels, many of them luxury, that cater to guests looking to do nothing but relax and unwind. It is also a fairly easy drive from Jerusalem, making it the perfect side trip if that is your base.

Along the western shore of the Dead Sea are the stunning ruins of Masada, believed to be a former mountaintop fortress of Herod the Great, where a group of rebel Jews took their last stand against Roman soldiers. On a clear day, you can see much of the expanse of the Dead Sea far below.

At the southernmost tip of the Negev is Eilat, famed for its resort-like atmosphere and water recreation sports, particularly diving. It is one of the most popular vacation destinations in Israel and also one of the hottest places in the country, especially in the summer. Shopping in Eilat includes a tax-free bonus status. It is the only place in Israel without the standard Value Added Tax (VAT) on goods and services. It is also the easiest overland gateway to Petra, Jordan, across the border.

If you have the time, energy, money, and willingness, there are many sights to see and adventures to be had around the south and Eilat.

PLANNING YOUR TIME

The south is full of vast spaces of desert, punctuated by a few major destinations, including the Dead Sea, Be'er Sheva, and Eilat. The minimum amount of time you should plan to spend in the south is three days, which should give you just long enough to experience the best of what the region has to offer.

Be cautious when you make any travel plans during the summer months (especially July-September). The temperature can be brutally high at times (above 105°F, 40° C), and combined with the humidity in the area of the Dead Sea, it can make even the most exciting trip miserable, especially if you're not accustomed to the climate. It can also be dangerous if you don't drink enough water or avoid the sun.

You should allow at least two days for Eilat, as it is very far south, and most activities involve water sports. It is also the most logical place to jump off for a side trip to nearby Petra, Jordan's famed archaeological site, for which you should allow at least an overnight stay.

The Dead Sea

The lowest point on Earth, the Dead Sea draws tourists from all over the world to indulge in its rich mud and relax in its spas. The high salinity of the waters of the Dead Sea means it is barren of sea life, but makes it possible to easily float on the water. Surrounding the sea are a few smaller towns and clusters of hotels and restaurants, with one large strip of mostly luxury hotels and restaurants that cater to tourists.

ORIENTATION

Once one complete body of water, the Dead Sea is now split into northern and southern basins because of the sea's sinking water level. Some believe it is due to resource exploitation for popular health and beauty products, and others believe it is due to state exploitation of water resources. Most of the larger northern basin is within the West Bank on the western shore and within Jordan on the eastern

---

Previous: Ein Gedi Nature Reserve; Nubian ibex in Ein Gedi; salt deposits on the shore of the Dead Sea.

Dead Sea

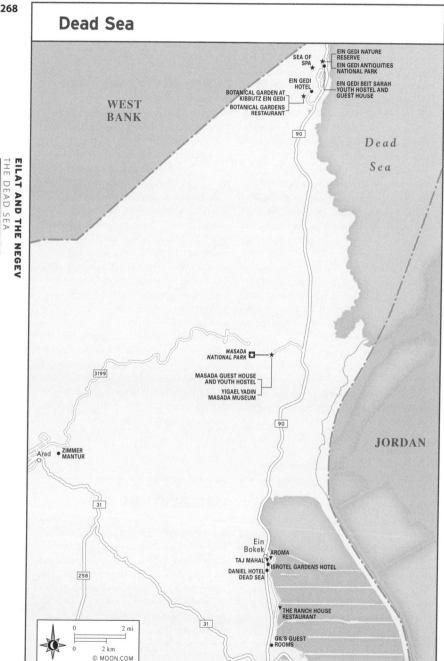

WEST
BANK

SEA OF
SPA

EIN GEDI NATURE
RESERVE
EIN GEDI ANTIQUITIES
NATIONAL PARK

EIN GEDI
HOTEL

EIN GEDI BEIT SARAH
YOUTH HOSTEL AND
GUEST HOUSE

BOTANICAL GARDEN AT
KIBBUTZ EIN GEDI
BOTANICAL GARDENS
RESTAURANT

90

Dead

Sea

MASADA
NATIONAL PARK

MASADA GUEST HOUSE
AND YOUTH HOSTEL
YIGAEL YADIN
MASADA MUSEUM

3199

90

JORDAN

Arad
ZIMMER
MANTUR

31

258

Ein
Bokek

AROMA
TAJ MAHAL
DANIEL HOTEL
DEAD SEA
ISROTEL GARDENS HOTEL

THE RANCH HOUSE
RESTAURANT

GIL'S GUEST
ROOMS

31

90

0   2 mi
0   2 km
© MOON.COM

shore. Look across the Dead Sea and you will see Jordan not far off.

The declining water level of the Dead Sea has led to a proliferation of dangerous sinkholes, which has led to the closure of some popular free beaches. There are still plenty of options for beaches and sinkholes are closely monitored, but the area is changing.

The first destination just across the West Bank border is Ein Gedi, home to an ancient spring and waterfalls and a couple of accommodation options. The southern half of the Dead Sea is where you'll find the major grouping of hotels and activities catering to tourists in Ein Bokek and just to the south. Between Ein Gedi and Ein Bokek are various beaches and spas.

SIGHTS

TOP EXPERIENCE

★ Masada National Park

approximately one hour south of Jerusalem via Rtes. 1 and 90; tel. 03/539-6700 and 08/658-4207/8, reservation center for sound and light show tel. 08/995-9333; www.parks.org.il; 8am-5pm daily Apr.-Sept., 8am-4pm daily Oct.-Mar., last entry one hour before closing and one hour earlier on Fri. and holiday eves; NIS35-80 depending on cable car ticket choice

There are many mysteries surrounding Masada National Park. Chief among them is what exactly happened to the Jewish inhabitants who were surrounded by the Roman army, besieged for months, and ultimately committed suicide to avoid capture.

One of Israel's several UNESCO World Heritage Sites, Masada is famed for its view of the Dead Sea and the impossibly steep ascent that you can make by cable car or on foot. The entrance fee to the park also includes camping fees.

Masada sits at the top of a high peak above the Dead Sea. What is left today are remnants of the once-magnificent court that was originally built by King Herod. You can rent an audio guide to the site, which seems like

nothing more than dusty, hot archaeological remains on top of a huge hill unless you look closely and take your time to explore. The best way to get into the spirit of Masada is with a tour guide (inquire in advance) who can walk you through the various points and answer questions.

On a clear day, the view of the Dead Sea from Masada is incredible, and you can see it from the top of Masada or from the cable cars that take you up and down from the visitor's center. You can walk up via the path on the side of the mountain, but that can be a dangerous endeavor in hot weather: People do get heat exhaustion and dehydration while on the trail. Whether you go up by cable car or trail, take water and drink continuously.

YIGAEL YADIN MASADA MUSEUM

tel. 08/658-4207/8 and 08/658-4464; museum.m@npa.org.il,;8am-4pm Sun.-Thurs.; NIS25 or combined ticket with park entry

Don't miss the inventive and informative Yigael Yadin Masada Museum just past the very classy gift shop. Entrance to the museum is included with the price of your ticket, and you'll get an automatically activated audio guide to accompany you through the choice, well-displayed artifacts and life-size recreations of people in scenes related to Masada. It brings the entire experience to life and is one of the coolest museums you'll see in Israel, even if it's a bit small.

Ein Gedi Nature Reserve

off Rte. 90; tel. 08/658-4285; www.parks.org.il; 8am-5pm daily Apr.-Sept., 8am-4pm daily Oct.-Mar., with additional entrance restrictions; adult NIS35, child NIS20

About 20 minutes down the road from Masada in the direction of Jerusalem is Ein Gedi Nature Reserve, a charming, conveniently located reserve brimming with the deer-like ibex, small hyrax, and natural pools filled by water that has been flowing for about 2,000 years.

There are three main trails in, and it's a short, relatively easy hike from the park entrance straight up to the second natural pool for a refreshing swim under the waterfall. It's not deep enough for a serious swim, but it seems like heaven on a hot day. Go early in the morning before huge groups descend on the popular trails from around noon onward.

You can also see the remains of an ancient irrigation system, and there is a snack bar and souvenir shop at the entrance. But be aware that rangers patrol the area for people eating inside the reserve; you could get fined if caught eating food here.

EIN GEDI ANTIQUITIES NATIONAL PARK

off Rte. 90; tel. 08/658-4285; www.parks.org.il; 8am-4pm Sat.-Thurs., 8am-3pm Fri.; included with admission to the nature reserve

Inside of the Ein Gedi Nature Reserve, just north of the main parking area, is the Ein Gedi Antiquities National Park with its 1,200-year-old mosaic floor left over from an ancient Jewish synagogue from the 3rd century AD. The complex is shaded and has places to sit. The mosaic floor has mysterious inscriptions that include a warning to not reveal the local secret (likely a reference to the production of a local persimmon perfume).

Qumran National Park

13 miles east of Jerusalem via Hwy. 1 to Rte. 90; tel. 02/994-2235 or 02/654-1255 for guided tours; www.parks.org.il; 8am-5pm daily Apr.-Sept., 8am-4pm daily Oct.-Mar., last entry one hour before closing; adult NIS25, child NIS12

In 1947, a Bedouin goat herder discovered the first seven scrolls of what became known as the Dead Sea Scrolls in a cave inside of what is now Qumran National Park. In the 1950s, 10 more caves with manuscripts were discovered. Though it took time to understand what the scrolls were, the findings rocked the worlds of archaeology, anthropology, and religion. Made by Jews between 200 BC and AD 70, the scrolls fill in important details about ancient scribal practices, traditions, and techniques of biblical interpretation.

Today you can tour the Qumran complex, the remains of an ancient city of a strict religious sect called the Qumrans, including the nearby 11 caves and underground tunnels.

Botanical Garden at Kibbutz Ein Gedi

off Hwy. 90 alongside the Dead Sea at Tamar Regional Council; tel. 08/659-4726; www.ein-gedi.co.il; dawn to dusk daily; free

Just inside Kibbutz Ein Gedi is the Botanical Garden, which makes for incredible nighttime tours with its diverse plant life and selection of flowers that bloom after sunset. It shelters more than 1,000 varieties of flora from all over the world. People from the kibbutz actually live within the garden, and they give tours to groups and individuals.

ENTERTAINMENT AND EVENTS

Festivals

TAMAR FESTIVAL

multiple venues; www.tamarfestival.com; Oct.; NIS180-250

Every year the Tamar Festival lasts for several days in October during the Sukkot holiday and features performances by local and international artists. Events during the day include hikes, tours, and children's activities. The festival is known for its choice lineup of activities and music featured in various venues in the south of Israel, including the Botanical Garden at Ein Gedi, the Kikar Sdom villages, and Masada. If you plan ahead and pay a bit extra, you can camp in the midst of the event.

Sports Challenges

VEOLIA DESERT CHALLENGE

tel. 050/883-3004; info@desertchallenge.co.il; Dec.; NIS80-140

With a lineup that includes a mountain bike marathon and a moonlit run, the two-day Veolia Desert Challenge is for extreme sports lovers who also love the desert. The event also

---

1: Cable car in Masada National Park **2:** caves in Qumran National Park **3:** Botanical Garden at Kibbutz Ein Gedi **4:** David's waterfall at Ein Gedi Nature Reserve

includes family activities, camping accommodations, and a general atmosphere of enjoying the desert through experiencing extreme sports.

DEAD SEA HALF-MARATHON RACE

www.eingedi-run.co.il; Feb.; NIS110-340

The Dead Sea Half-Marathon Race has been going strong for more than three decades. The run takes place near Ein Gedi in February, when the local temperature is more bearable, and includes gorgeous views of the Dead Sea along the way.

SHOPPING

Anywhere near the beaches of the Dead Sea, gift stores and shops abound, mostly selling Dead Sea-related beauty and skin products, revered for their unique qualities and health benefits. The most extensive network of shopping, though, is in the area of **Ein Bokek,** just off Route 90.

The dark side of Dead Sea products is the lack of regulations surrounding the removal and use of natural resources from the Dead Sea. The exploitation of resources from the Dead Sea has been connected to environmental problems in the area and there are lingering questions over legal claims to the land.

SPORTS AND RECREATION

The main attraction in the Dead Sea region is undoubtedly the Dead Sea itself. The lowest point on Earth and filled with extremely salty, fish-free waters, the Dead Sea is renowned for its rich mineral deposits and health benefits.

There is a great deal of controversy surrounding the use of materials from the Dead Sea and other issues with development and exploitation of resources in the area. The sea is slowly disappearing, revealing a major swath of exposed land in its center, splitting the sea into northern and southern basins.

At many points in the sea, you can enter the waters and rub the reputedly therapeutic

mud on your body and face. Take care if you have any open wounds, as the salty waters can cause intense stinging pain. Do not put your head under the water or rub the water in your eyes. If you do get water in your eyes, flush it out right away with clear water.

The major beaches of the Dead Sea are well equipped with showers, changing rooms, snack bars, lounge chairs, and shade. The less-used beaches still often have showers, but might be lacking the famed therapeutic Dead Sea mud.

Beaches

NEW KALIA BEACH

outskirts of Jerusalem; tel. 02/994-2391; www. dead-sea.org.il; 8am-6pm daily Apr.-Sept., 8am-5pm daily Oct.-Mar.; adult NIS40, child NIS30

The northernmost of the Dead Sea beaches that is closest to Jerusalem, about a 40-minute drive, is New Kalia Beach. The beach has a covered snack and drink bar, which plays loud music, changing rooms, showers, beach chairs, and umbrellas. It is slightly disconcerting to see the minefield warnings just a stone's throw from the beach, but there is plenty of mud and the general atmosphere is very mellow. A Bedouin tent area, camping facilities, and a Dead Sea products gift shop are also on hand.

Spas and Health Resorts

Famed for its health benefits, the Dead Sea region has a wide range of spas, stretching from the Kibbutz Ein Gedi area all the way to Ein Bokek.

SEA OF SPA

Kibbutz Ein Gedi; tel. 08/659-4934; www. eingediseaofspa.co.il; 8am-5pm daily Oct.-Mar. and 8am-6pm Sun.-Thurs., 8am-5pm Fri. Apr.-Sept.

Any hotel in the area will know of nearby spas and their reputation, but you can also try Ein Gedi Sea of Spa, with its natural hot springs, sweet water pool, natural cosmetic mud, beach, and body treatments center.

FOOD

The Dead Sea area is marked by long stretches of road where there is nothing to eat, punctuated by groupings of restaurants.

Ein Gedi
BOTANICAL GARDENS RESTAURANT

Kibbutz Ein Gedi; tel. 08/659-4221; www.ein-gedi. co.il/en; 7am-10am and 6:30pm-8:30pm daily; NIS75

There are very few food options in the Ein Gedi area, but the Botanical Gardens Restaurant is a fairly nice restaurant with a huge amount of space. It feels a bit like a cafeteria and an all-you-can-eat buffet. The setting is gorgeous, though, amid the Kibbutz Ein Gedi Botanical Garden, and it is just off the hotel's lobby, where there is also a small bar and lounge area. The restaurant is kosher, but they do serve dinner on Friday night with a huge buffet.

Ein Bokek

If you find yourself in the Ein Bokek area, your best bet for decent food will probably be at one of the large hotels or one of the shopping centers. If you want something on the beach, the generic beach restaurants and snack stands are easy to find.

AROMA

Petra Shopping Center, circular shopping center in the middle of Ein Bokek; tel. 08/995-4021; www. aroma.co.il; 8am-11pm daily; NIS45

For simple coffee, sandwiches, and salads, you can go to the local branch of Aroma. There isn't much atmosphere, but it is open daily and a relatively predictable experience with free wireless Internet to boot. Once you are at the shopping center, there are other options as well.

TAJ MAHAL

Leonardo Hotel Inn at 3-4 Kamen St. on North Shore; tel. 053/809-4823; www.taj-mahal.co.il; noon-2am daily; NIS70

At the Leonardo Hotel Inn is the Bedouin tent restaurant and bar Taj Mahal, where you can sit on cushions and puff on a hookah. The restaurant has a fairly limited food menu, with mostly simple steak and chicken dishes and salads, but they do have an extensive beer, wine, and alcohol list. Their schedule varies despite their published hours, especially in the off-season, so call before going to make sure they are open and serving food.

THE RANCH HOUSE RESTAURANT

Isrotel Hotel Dead Sea, off Rte. 90; tel. 08/668-9666; 7pm-11pm Sun.-Thurs., 6:30pm-11pm Sat.; NIS110

In the lobby of the Isrotel Hotel is The Ranch House Restaurant, an upscale establishment that serves American-style dishes, and is open mainly for dinner. The atmosphere is spacious, modern, and relaxing and their specialty is serving cuts of meat by weight.

South Dead Sea
SECRETS MY MOTHER TOLD ME

off Rte. 90 at Sodom Sq.; tel. 052/899-1199

At the very southern end of the Dead Sea are a few options for food in an area called Neot HaKikar, but most of these venues require reservations. One of them is Secrets My Mother Told Me, which serves breakfast, lunch, and dinner, but you must call in advance for reservations. They offer buffet-style spreads and are best for groups of four or more.

ACCOMMODATIONS

There is a variety of accommodations in and around the Dead Sea region, ranging from camping to five-star hotels. The fanciest hotels are grouped in and around Ein Bokek, on the southern end of the waters. This area is built up with restaurants, shops, and spas. At night, it looks a bit like Las Vegas. There are also a number of options in the area of Ein Gedi and Masada, which have about 20 minutes of road in between them. Other options are at Almog, Kalya, and Arad, which are not as close to the beaches, but still keep you in the vicinity.

Under US$100
MASADA GUEST HOUSE AND YOUTH HOSTEL

Masada at Ein Bokek; tel. 08/995-3222; www.iyha. org.il; US$98 d

The Masada Guest House and Youth Hostel is a relatively large building for a hostel that looks like it was carved out of the hillside. It has a private swimming pool (in season) and is near the entrance to Masada National Park. All 88 rooms have a private shower and bathroom, air-conditioning, and a minibar. There is also a large dining room and an Internet station available, and breakfast is included.

US$100-150
ZIMMER MANTUR

Mivtza Lot 30, Arad; tel. 054/766-9308; US$125 d

A villa that has been converted into three separate units, Zimmer Mantur has a guest garden and cookout facilities, and the rooms have balconies with views of the garden or the nearby valley. Free wireless Internet and a flat-screen TV come with the room, and there's easy access to nearby jeep excursions in the Negev and Judean Deserts.

US$150-200
NOF TAMAR

Ein Tamar; tel. 052/886-8632; www.noftamar.co.il; US$158 d

At the very southern end of the Dead Sea just next to the salt pools is Nof Tamar. The very tiny three-room property has views of the Negev Desert from air-conditioned log cabin chalets that have world-class amenities including satellite TV, whirlpool bathtubs, verandas, and kitchenettes. It is about 30 minutes from Masada and an hour from Be'er Sheva.

GIL'S GUEST ROOMS

Neve Zohar village, Ein Bokek 107; tel. 052/270-2502; www.gils-guest-rooms.de; US$175 d

Simple but cozy, Gil's Guest Rooms is a viable option for accommodations if you want to be in the Ein Bokek area but want to pay a little less. There's free wireless Internet and satellite TV, and you can get breakfast and dinner on-site. It's not fancy, but the rooms are a good size and the staff is helpful in navigating around the Dead Sea area.

ISROTEL GARDENS HOTEL

Ein Bokek; tel. 08/668-9090; www.gardenshotels. com; US$195 d

Just a two-minute walk from the beach, Isrotel Gardens Hotel is a 200-room hotel with a massive, sprawling layout, spa treatments, two indoor swimming pools, an outdoor pool, and a children's pool. All of the rooms overlook the Dead Sea. The breakfast buffet is included.

Over US$200
EIN GEDI HOTEL

Kibbutz Ein Gedi; tel. 08/659-4222; www.ein-gedi. co.il; US$245 d

The Ein Gedi Hotel is set within a kibbutz that boasts a botanical garden and a huge outdoor swimming pool with changing rooms and showers. The hotel also has a private beach, and there is a nearby spa with mineral pools. It is a 10-minute drive from the Ein Gedi Nature Reserve and 15 minutes from Masada. All of the rooms have tea and coffee service and satellite TV. The on-site restaurant serves a huge buffet dinner on Friday night, and there is a small bar and information center in the hotel's main lobby.

DANIEL DEAD SEA HOTEL

off Rte. 90, Ein Bokek; tel. 08/668-9999; www. tamareshotels.co.il; US$312 d

Daniel Dead Sea Hotel is a full-fledged luxury hotel with all the trimmings in its 302 rooms, including desert and Dead Sea views. The hotel also has swimming pools, a conference center, and a health club with a gym, sauna, whirlpool, and steam room. The rooms have clean, modern interiors with balconies and views of the water. Free wireless Internet is included.

GETTING THERE AND AROUND

The Dead Sea area is remarkably easy to get to by car or bus from Jerusalem or Bethlehem. Once in the area, you can traverse the entire shore of the sea along Route 90 in about 80 minutes. It is about 45 minutes from Jerusalem to the northernmost area, Kalya, and another 30 minutes to Ein Gedi Nature Reserve, and yet another 25 minutes to the major hotel and restaurant area of Ein Bokek. From Ein Bokek you can get to the very southern end of the Dead Sea at Neot HaKikar in another 30 minutes.

Car

From **Jerusalem,** take Highway 1 east to Route 90 and follow the signs to the Dead Sea. You will drive for about an hour, part of the way in the West Bank, until you get to Ein Gedi, which is just over the border from the West Bank on the Israeli side. From **Tel Aviv,** take the same route, except add a bit more time along Highway 1. It's approximately a two-hour drive, give or take, depending on traffic.

Once you are in the area, it is very easy to get around by car. There is only one main road (Rte. 90) and everything is clearly signposted or obvious from a distance. For example, it is impossible to miss the massive grouping of hotels at Ein Bokek.

Bus

Buses go to the Dead Sea on a very regular basis from **Jerusalem. Egged** buses (www. egged.co.il, bus numbers 421, 486, or 487, NIS42) is the vendor, and it takes about 90 minutes to reach Ein Gedi. The bus stops are situated along Route 90, and a good one to begin with is at the **Ein Gedi Beit Sarah Youth Hostel and Guest House** because it is immediately adjacent to Ein Gedi National Park.

From Tel Aviv, take off from the **Arlozorov Terminal** (bus number 421, NIS50) for the trip, which takes about 2.5 hours. Watch out for other routes from Tel Aviv that require transfers.

Once you get off the bus, you'll be very close to the Ein Gedi Nature Reserve and it will be easy to get back on the bus and continue southward. Be aware that the Ein Gedi Beit Sarah Youth Hostel and Guest House won't let you past their gate if you are not a registered guest, though.

The Negev

At a glance it might seem barren, but the Negev is full of the possibility of close encounters with all kinds of wildlife, which is part of what makes it a popular destination for nature-related hikes and other activities. It is also the gateway to Eilat, the southernmost city in Israel.

ORIENTATION

The largest city in the Negev, Be'er Sheva is ancient: It was founded over 3,700 years ago. Developed into a more modern city by the Ottomans and then the British, the Be'er Sheva of today is a mixed city of immigrants—Jews, Arabs, and Bedouins—from dozens of countries. Home to the University of the Negev, it also makes a logical base for starting adventures in the region, particularly to Arad or Dimona (both about 40 minutes away).

Also about 40 minutes due south from Be'er Sheva is the historic Kibbutz Sde Boker, former home of Israel's first prime minister David Ben-Gurion. The kibbutz and nearby Midreshet Sde Boker are centers for ecotourism in the region, and are a good stop on the way to see Mitzpe Ramon, Ein Avdat National Park, and the ancient Nabataean city of Avdat.

The People of the Negev

One of the most unique characteristics of the Negev is the people who live there and have lived there throughout history. In ancient times, Nabataean traders developed several cities along their profitable regional routes. Abraham made his home in the very ancient city of Be'er Sheva. Others who have lived in the vast desert region throughout the ages include Arab nomads, Canaanites, Philistines, Edomites, Byzantines, Ottomans, and Jews. The ancient economy of the Negev was based largely on sheepherding, agriculture, and trade.

The modern Jewish habitation of the Negev started a century ago with about a dozen settlements. Israel's first prime minister, David Ben-Gurion, was a major advocate of settling in the Negev after moving to Kibbutz Sde Boker.

Among the current residents of the Negev are Arab Bedouins. As you travel through the Negev and the south of Israel, you'll notice quite a number of semi-permanent Bedouin encampments or clusters of makeshift homes dotting the desert landscape. The Bedouin were once a nomadic people who have largely settled down and integrated into modern culture, but some of their nomadic tendencies endure.

SIGHTS

Be'er Sheva

Modern Be'er Sheva is not the most remarkable-looking place, but it has a few interesting stops, including a couple of good museums.

NEGEV MUSEUM OF ART

60 HaAtsmaut St.; tel. 08/699-3535; www.negev-museum.org.il; 10am-4pm Mon.-Tues. and Thurs., noon-7pm Wed., 10am-2pm Fri.-Sat.; NIS15

One such museum is the Negev Museum of Art in Be'er Sheva's Old City, a 1906 building that was home to the Turkish governor. The renovated structure has two galleries with contemporary exhibitions of photography, sculpture, prints, and paintings, and hosts live concerts in the summer.

TEL BEER SHEBA

off the Be'er Sheva-Shoket junction on Rte. 60 just south of Omer; tel. 08/646-7286; www.parks.org.il; 8am-5pm daily Apr.-Sept., 8am-4pm daily Oct.-Mar.; adult NIS15, child NIS7

Tel Beer Sheba is the site of an ancient city that dates back to the 10th century BC. You can walk around what is left of the ancient streets and buildings; the layout is extremely visible, making it easy to imagine what it was like to live there. The Tel is considered to be of unparalleled importance for the study of biblical-period urban planning and biblical history and, as such, is designated a UNESCO World Heritage Site. If you are here in the summer months, go as early in the morning as possible and take a hat and water. There is no shade, except for the observation tower, which you can climb up.

ISRAELI AIR FORCE MUSEUM

Hatzerim Air Force Base, Rte. 2357, about 5 miles southwest of Beer Sheva; tel. 08/990-6853; www.iaf.org.il; 8am-5pm Sun.-Thurs., 8am-1pm Sun.; NIS30

The Israeli Air Force Museum exhibits Israeli aviation history, including over 140 aircraft and antiaircraft installations, among them missile launchers.

MUSEUM OF BEDOUIN CULTURE AT THE JOE ALON CENTER

Rte. 40 to Dvira Junction, then follow signs for Joe Alon Center; www.joealon.org.il; tel. 08/991-3322; 9am-4pm Sun.-Thurs.; NIS20

One of a kind, the Museum of Bedouin Culture at the Joe Alon Center documents the unique aspects of Bedouin culture as it transitioned from a nomadic to modern lifestyle. It is situated in the Lahav Forest near Kibbutz Lahav, about 12 miles north of Be'er Sheva. The museum is the central focus of the Joe Alon Center, inside a round building that resembles a tent. The Bedouins' story of transition is told through a series of life-size mannequins, and admission includes a cup of coffee in a Bedouin tent.

Sde Boker and Ein Avdat

Kibbutz Sde Boker and ecotourism and historical sites close by make for an interesting stop as you traverse the Negev.

BEN-GURION'S HUT

Kibbutz Sde Boker; tel. 08/656-0469; www.bgh. org.il; 8:30am-4pm Sun.-Thurs., 8:30am-2pm Fri., 10am-4pm Sat. and holiday eves, last entry 30 minutes before closing; NIS10

The kibbutz has a winery and gift shop, but the main attraction is Ben-Gurion's Hut, the home of Israel's first prime minister David Ben-Gurion and his wife, Paula, left just as it was when he died in 1973. The house is referred to as a hut because of its modest appearance. Ben-Gurion, who idealized the Negev as the frontier land of Israel, lived in the house with his wife when Sde Boker was just a young kibbutz. A building next to his house has an exhibit—a short historical animated film—about Ben-Gurion's connection to the Negev.

BEN-GURION'S TOMB NATIONAL PARK

off Rte. 40 near Ben-Gurion College; tel. 08/655-5684; www.parks.org.il; always open; free

The final resting place of the prime minister and his wife can be found at Ben-Gurion's Tomb National Park. Their gravesites overlook a stunning desert view that includes the Tzin Canyon and the Avdat highlands right in the midst of the Negev.

★ EIN AVDAT NATIONAL PARK

off Rte. 40; tel. 08/655-5684; www.parks.org.il; 8am-5pm daily Apr.-Sept., 8am-4pm daily Oct.-Mar., last entrance one hour before closing; adult NIS29, child NIS15, combination ticket with Avdat National Park adult NIS46, child NIS24

The gorgeous Ein Avdat National Park features the Nakhal Zin canyons, springs, waterfalls, and various native plants and animals.

Ein Avdat is also home to the mysteriously ever-flowing waters of the Avdat Spring that have cut a deep, narrow canyon through the rock. For the adventurous traveler, it is an excellent place to wade on a hot day or even take a swim.

The park features a well-designed trail that protects the natural habitat, and you can see all kinds of wildlife if you take your time and stay relatively quiet. The most commonly seen animal is the ibex, a mountain goat that is endlessly fascinating as it scales the steep desert cliffs with ease. The park is about a 30-minute drive north of Mitzpe Ramon and roughly 45 minutes south of Be'er Sheva.

★ AVDAT NATIONAL PARK

off Rte. 40; tel. 08/655-1511; www.parks.org.il; 8am-5pm daily Apr.-Sept., 8am-4pm daily Oct.-Mar., last entrance one hour before closing on Fri. and holiday eves; adult NIS27, child NIS14, combination ticket with Ein Avdat National Park adult NIS46, child NIS24

Avdat National Park is home to one of the most famous Nabataean cities along the incense route that the expert traders used to transport incense, spices, perfumes, and other goods.

Avdat flourished around 30-9 BC, and it was subsequently destroyed and rebuilt, rising and falling until the Arab conquest in the 7th century AD.

Some of the most remarkable aspects of the ruins include the restored gateway on the acropolis, the Roman bathhouse and watchtower, the 4th-century churches, and caves that served as burial places, storage, and cisterns.

Avdat has a visitors center with more information about the site, including a short film about the incense route and related spices. The site is a key stop for travelers interested in understanding more about how the ancient spice route worked, its social and economic functions, and its significance regionally and globally.

The Ancient Incense Route

For seven centuries, the mysterious Nabataeans established and worked their incense trade over a network of routes that totaled more than 1,200 miles (1,900 km). The Nabataean incense trade route, which extended from Yemen and Oman in the Arabian Peninsula to the Mediterranean, operated from the 3rd century BC to the 4th century AD. The main trade route was from Petra, the capital city of the mighty Nabataeans in Jordan, just across the border of modern-day Israel.

The portion of the route in the Negev Desert included the four Nabataean towns of Halutsa, Mamshit, Avdat, and Shivta. The ruins of fortresses, agricultural landscapes, and advanced irrigation systems that remain are evidence of the incredible profits that were made in the trade of frankincense and other valuable incense and spices.

The water collection and irrigation systems of cisterns, reservoirs, dams, and channeling made large-scale agriculture possible in the towns along the incense route that were supported by the wealth of the incense trade. The most outstanding evidence of the water systems can be found in the vicinity of Avdat and the central Negev.

The incense route is a UNESCO World Heritage Site and considered a testimony to ancient technology and innovation used to successfully settle and support human life in the extremely harsh desert setting.

TOP EXPERIENCE

★ MITZPE RAMON OBSERVATORY AND RAMON CRATER

Rte. 40; tel. 08/658-8691; www.parks.org.il; 8am-4pm Sat.-Thurs., 8am-3pm Fri. and holiday eves, one hour later in the summer; NIS44

Most incredible at sunset or sunrise is the Mitzpe Ramon Observatory and Ramon Crater, where the largest of three massive geological craters in the Negev can be seen. The surrounding Ramon Crater Nature Reserve (Makhtesh Ramon Nature Reserve) is part of a complex that includes the observatory as well as a visitors center with a bookstore and hiking information.

In the nature reserve are a variety of hiking trails, the more advanced trails of which can take up to three days to traverse. You can arrange hiking expeditions of all kinds through the nature reserve, and even experience Bedouin tents, rappelling, and more.

The visitors center is a good place to learn about the area and put questions to the Israel Nature Reserves Authority staff working there, as well as ask about hiring guide services. There are also slide and film shows and

a museum with exhibits about the area's natural habitat. Make sure to keep a map with you at all times when hiking in the area, as well as water and a hat. The museum's film about the crater is partially dedicated to the memory of Israel's first astronaut.

The observatory is about 1.5 hours south of Be'er Sheva on Rte. 40.

Bedouin Tents and *Khans*

Throughout the Negev you'll see extensive groups of humble, semipermanent Bedouin dwellings dotting the landscape. You can have a closer encounter with Bedouin culture by visiting a Bedouin tent and *khan* (roadside inn) in Sefinat Hamidbar, Khan Hashayarot, and Khan Beerotayim. The tents and *khans* (which can be good for overnight camping or a rest stop) can be found at the Mashabei Sadeh junction, near the ancient city of Avdat and the village of Ezuz. It's best to visit 10am-4pm daily. There's no formal fee, but you will be encouraged to buy either food or crafts, and should come prepared to spend at least NIS30-40.

Along the Incense Route

Near the modern city of Dimona are the highlights of the 1,500-mile (1,900 km) **Ancient Incense Route** that was used by merchants

1: the Ramon Crater visitor's center **2:** Museum of Bedouin Culture at the Joe Alon Center **3:** Avdat National Park **4:** canyon in Ein Avdat National Park

The Powerful and Mysterious Nabataeans

Much has been written and said about the empire of the ancient Nabataeans, but they, and their former capital city in Petra, Jordan, remain shrouded in mystery.

The Nabataeans were master traders, builders, and experts of ancient technology for creating ingenious water systems to support and sustain desert life. Bolstered by the wealth they earned over 700 years of their hugely profitably incense trade route, they established a society and culture in the harsh desert.

Natural disasters wiped out part of the Nabataean history in their capital city of Petra, limiting definitive information about certain aspects of their culture. One thing that is known is that their traders traveled in caravans across vast distances in the deserts, transporting spices, incense, and perfumes, which were shipped out of the port at Gaza. As time passed, the way stations that grew out of their passage back and forth through the Negev Desert grew into cities where terraced agriculture and sophisticated irrigation practices helped them thrive.

The remains of the four Nabataean cities of Halutsa, Mamshit, Avdat, and Shivta are significant archaeological sites, but the most remarkable and breathtaking remnant of the Nabataeans is the ancient city of Petra in Jordan.

The Roman Empire attempted more than once to conquer the Nabataeans, and in AD 106, they finally succeeded. The caravan cities, particularly Avdat, fell into decline after the Roman conquest.

and traders in ancient times. A section of about 100 miles (160 km) cuts through what is today known as Israel and ends at the Port of Gaza. You can visit some of the stops on the route, declared UNESCO World Heritage Sites in 2005.

MAMSHIT

Rte. 25, about 5 miles southeast of Dimona; tel. 08/655-6478; www.parks.org.il; 8am-4pm daily Apr.-Sept., 8am-4pm daily Oct.-Mar., last entry one hour before closing; adult NIS22, child NIS10

At Mamshit there is a reconstructed city with streets, arched structures, mosaics, a large house, and ruins of an inn, churches, a bathhouse, rainwater collecting pools, and other structures. Mamshit was the site of the discovery of a trove of almost 11,000 silver coins. Beyond visiting the park, you can camp here overnight.

Beyond Mamshit are the sites of **Avdat,** which include the ruins of a fortress, churches, homes, a bathhouse, and a workshop. Then there is **Shivta** (tel. 08/655-5684, www.parks. org.il) and the northernmost stop of **Halutsa,** where you can find the ruins of a theater and a church.

Wineries

It might seem surprising to hear of wineries that exist in a vast, harsh desert, but the pioneering spirit that is such a defining characteristic of the Negev and its people has made it possible.

SDE BOKER WINERY

Visitors Center next to Ben Gurion's House at Sde Boker; tel. 050/757-9212; www.sde-boker.org. il; 8:30am-4pm Sun.-Thurs., 8:30am-2pm Fri., 10am-4pm Sat., tastings by appointment; prices for tastings vary

One of the more well-established wineries in the Negev and the first to open there, this winery is run out of Kibbutz Sde Boker, where Israel's first prime minister and advocate of desert life, David Ben-Gurion, lived with his wife. Winery tastings should be arranged in advance by calling.

CARMEY AVDAT

Off Hwy. 40 next to Ein Avdat National Park; tel. 052/270-5328; www.carmeyavdat.com; 9am-6pm daily, tastings and tours by appointment; prices vary

This winery has its vineyards in the ancient, already-existing terraces that are part of the ruins of an agricultural settlement that is about 1,500 years old. They use the annual flash floods to irrigate, and the entire family takes part in every step of the wine-making process. The winery harvested their first yield in 2002.

YATIR WINERY

Tel Arad, tel. 054/645-8871; www.yatirwinery.com; visits by appointment only, call ahead; prices vary

Situated at the southern tip of the Judean Desert near the Dead Sea at the foot of archaeological site Tel Arad Fort, this winery's vineyards are in the largest planted forest in Israel, the Yatir. Their wines are sold at the exclusive London department store Selfridges, and they are known for their white wines.

BOKER VALLEY VINEYARDS

Rt. 40 at Tlalim Junction near Sde Boker; tel. 052/682-2930; www.bokerfarm.com; wine shop open 10am-4pm daily; visits and tastings by appointment only, call ahead; prices vary

Planted in 1999, Boker Valley Vineyards grows its grapes on ancient terraces and the winery grounds include bed-and-breakfast accommodations. Boker Valley is part of a network of Israeli wineries in the area, and they grow and bottle both red and white wines.

ENTERTAINMENT AND EVENTS
Festivals
ZORBA THE BUDDHA FESTIVAL

tel. 08/632-6508; www.zorba.co.il; late Mar.-Apr.; NIS110

In the spring, the big show in the south is the Zorba the Buddha Festival, which runs for four or five days and has a strong spiritual, Buddhist slant. The festival takes advantage of the desert landscape to showcase musical performances, theater, movement exhibitions, meditation, and dance. Imagine sipping a cup of chai in a desert setting: complete mellowness in the heart of the desert.

IN-D-NEGEV

Mitzpe Gvulot, Rte. 234 to Ze'elim Junction; http:// indnegev.co.il; Oct.; NIS90-220

For fans of indie rock music and camping in the desert, In-D-Negev is three days of music, camping, and celebrating with a general spirit of togetherness and inclusion. The festival organizers even make allowances for kids, with activities and a play area. There is usually a crowd of about 4,000 people.

SHOPPING

The best and the majority of shopping in the Negev outside of Eilat is in Be'er Sheva.

BE'ER SHEVA BEDOUIN MARKET

south of the David Hacham Blvd. and HaMelacha St. intersection, southwest of the Old City in Be'er Sheva; 8am-4pm Thurs.

The most unique aspect you'll likely encounter at the Be'er Sheva Bedouin Market is Bedouin women completely covered in black. The majority of items for sale are racks and racks of discount clothing, as well as a few stalls for items like water pipes, toys, and candy. If you take your time, you can find some Bedouin craft items for sale, and it can be a great place to mingle with locals.

As the major metropolis for many smaller towns in the south, Be'er Sheva has several strip malls that include outlet stores and a little bit of everything. There are several strip malls around town, but the biggest is collectively referred to by locals as "the big strip mall"; it's just on the outskirts of town.

DESERT EMBROIDERY STORE AND VISITORS CENTER

Lakiya, off Rte. 31 north from Be'er Sheva; tel. 08/651-3208; www.desert-embroidery.org; 9:30am-1:30pm Sun.-Thurs., 10am-4pm Sat., closed on Muslim holidays; call in advance

About 20 minutes northwest of Be'er Sheva is the Desert Embroidery Store and Visitors Center, where you can buy colorful and attractive hand-embroidered items like bags, wallets, and the like. The store is run by the Association for the Improvement of Women's Status Lakiya branch. The visitors center specializes in traditional Bedouin hospitality, where you can sit on woven cushions and have a light lunch. Call in advance to alert them you are coming, especially if you have a large group or are planning on eating lunch here.

SPORTS AND RECREATION
National Parks and Nature Reserves
TIMNA NATIONAL PARK

about 17 miles north of Eilat off Rte. 90; tel. 08/631-6756; www.parktimna.co.il; 8am-4pm Sat.-Thurs., 8am-3pm Fri. and holiday eves Sept.-June, 8am-1pm Sun.-Mon. and Wed.-Sat., 8am-1pm and 5pm-8pm Tues. with guided sunset tours by reservation July-Aug.; adult NIS44, child NIS39

More than a park, Timna National Park is an entire experience that includes hot air balloons and famed touring routes, including the incredible natural rock formations of Solomon's Pillars. There are also family activities by the lake, a restaurant and souvenir shop, and sunset and night tours.

HAI BAR NATURE RESERVE

20 miles north of Eilat on Rte. 90; tel. 08/637-6018; www.parks.org.il; 8:30am-5pm Sun.-Thurs., 8:30am-4pm Fri.-Sat.; NIS39, Predators Center only NIS25

The Hai Bar Nature Reserve includes a small petting zoo, an African village, and a play archaeology dig for kids. It is just under 5 square miles (8 square km), and if you have a rental car, you can rent a tour CD and drive through the park, dodging friendly ostriches as you go. The adjacent **Predators Center** is about 7.5 square miles (12 square km) and home to local birds and animals of prey, including the only remaining lappet-face vultures in Israel.

Bike and Jeep Tours
DESERT ECO TOURS

office in Eilat; tel. 052/276-5753; www.desertecotours.com

The Negev is an excellent area for sporty adventures like biking tours, which can be booked through a company like Desert Eco Tours. You can tour major sites in the region by bicycle on one- or two-day trips. The company also offers jeep tours, which are an excellent way to see the area, especially if you aren't used to hiking in the heat and if you can handle the bumpy ride.

Solomon's Pillars in Timna National Park

Desert Ecotourism

One of the most interesting and attractive parts of touring the south of Israel is experiencing what is known as desert ecotourism. In a general sense, desert ecotourism includes options for accommodations that employ sustainable practices and in many cases are built by hand to blend with the desert environment. Accommodations might also be rough, on par with camping, including staying in tents with outhouses and minimal creature comforts, as well as staying in Bedouin tent encampments.

Other aspects of desert ecotourism include farms and animal reserves that allow visitors to see desert animals up close; Bedouin arts and crafts tours; archery; and bicycling. Most aspects of desert ecotourism emphasize minimal impact on the environment but maximum exposure and experience.

A very useful website for desert ecotourism information in the south and throughout Israel is Ecotourism Israel (www.ecotourism-israel.com). If you are looking for guided tour options, try Desert Eco Tours (tel. 052/276-5753, www.desertecotours.com).

Archery
DESERT ARCHERY PARK
Mitzpe Ramon; tel. 050/534-4598; www. desertarchery.co.il; prices vary

If you're up for learning something new while traveling, the Desert Archery Park might be of interest. You can take a hike through the desert while shooting a bow and arrow and taking in the scenery.

FOOD
Be'er Sheva
SABA GIABETTO
28 Rager St., Rasco Center; tel. 08/627-2829; 10am-9pm Sun.-Thurs.; NIS45

A favorite standby among locals, Saba Giabetto is known for its homey atmosphere (*saba* means grandfather in Hebrew), tasty sandwiches, and sassy menu with fun facts and information about the restaurant.

★ ARABICA
12 Hertsel St.; tel. 08/627-7801; http://arabica-rest. co.il; 11:30am-last customer Sun.-Thurs., 11:30am-an hour before sunset Fri., hour after sunset-last customer Sat.; NIS80

Serving up Middle Eastern fusion cuisine in a central location, Arabica has a modern, upscale atmosphere. The menu is arranged under price categories that start at NIS69 and go up to NIS125, and include meat and seafood dishes. It is very popular, and you might be in for a long wait unless you make reservations.

CASA DO BRASIL
1 Montefiore; tel. 08/627-3330; www.casadobrasil. co.il; noon-midnight Sun.-Thurs., noon-4pm Fri., 30 minutes after sunset-last customer Sat.; NIS60

Situated close to city center and hotels, Casa do Brasil is all about serving up nice, big cuts of beef in a casual, party-like atmosphere. A domestic chain with three locations, the Be'er Sheva branch has a very spacious, simple interior and outdoor seating.

METAH MIDBAR
Mercuz-HaNegev Building off Yitzhak St.; tel. 054/633-6020; noon-midnight Sun.-Fri., 1pm-midnight Sat.; NIS35

The cheap prices at Metah Midbar don't come easy: a sometimes-rowdy crowd of students from the nearby Ben-Gurion University campus can make for a loud atmosphere. The best menu items include standbys like the hamburger and the chicken salad. They also have wireless Internet and outlets behind the bar, so it's a great place to stop if you want to check email or other things online.

Dimona
Dimona is a smaller town near the ancient Nabataean city of Mamshit that offers a

few very simple options for food, including the typical national chains of CaféCafé and Aroma, both in Peretz Center.

PIZZA BACHCHAN

3 Herzl Blvd.; tel. 08/657-0550; www.piza-pazzaz.
co.il; Sun.-Thurs. 9:30am-10pm, Fri. until 3pm, Sat.
until 11 pm; NIS80

A bit of a change of pace from hummus and pita, Pizza Bachchan serves up gourmet pizza with hearty amounts of toppings. It is part of a domestic chain of pizzerias. They will deliver if you are staying at a nearby hotel. The price varies according to what kind of toppings you get, but you can generally expect to pay about NIS80 for a two-topping pizza.

Mitzpe Ramon

A solid bet in the Negev for a range of dining options is Mitzpe Ramon, home of the must-see Ramon Crater.

★ HAKATZE

2 Har Ardon St.; tel. 08/659-5273 or 050/756-5063;
noon-8pm Mon. and Wed.-Fri.; NIS40

Hakatze is a simple restaurant that makes home-style Israeli food with an emphasis on grilled meats and typical Middle Eastern side dishes, including pita bread. An unusual nice touch is the English magazines that can be read in the back of the restaurant.

HADASA'AR

6 Har Boker St.; tel. 08/940-8473; 8am-8pm
Sun.-Thurs., 8am-4pm Fri.; NIS40

A combination coffee shop and gift shop, Hadasa'ar also sells organic groceries and operates as a semi-cooperative. It's a good place to stop off if you just want something quick and light, and maybe a souvenir for the road.

★ RAMON INN RESTAURANT

1 Ein Akev; tel. 08/658-8822; breakfast 7am-9am and
dinner 7:30pm-9:30pm daily; NIS120 fixed price

Situated inside the Ramon Inn, the Ramon Inn Restaurant has a huge buffet that varies by the day and includes a wide variety of dishes with local flavor (meaning spicy in

some cases). There's a bit of a rush for food when the dining room doors open. You need to have a reservation if you are not a guest at the hotel, but it is guaranteed to be filling. They also serve a buffet breakfast.

Sde Boker

Situated in a fairly isolated spot, the area around Sde Boker has some phenomenal sites to visit, but very few options for restaurants. It's a good area to carry some food to go with you from Mitzpe Ramon or wherever you are coming from.

SDE BOKER FIELD SCHOOL

Midreshet Ben-Gurion; www.boker.org.il/english

In an area where there are very few choices for something simple, the Sde Boker Field School has a decent option: a snack shop with shaded outdoor seating with an incredible view of the Negev Desert. Right next door to Kibbutz Sde Boker and not far from the Ramon Crater, it's situated in the perfect spot to just stop, have a quick bite, and move on. If you've brought snacks with you and just want a place with outdoor picnic tables and free parking, it's also convenient for that. Don't miss the view from the observation deck about 100 yards (90 meters) away from the picnic tables.

ACCOMMODATIONS

The Negev is the perfect place to take advantage of some of Israel's most unique overnight stays, including desert camping and Bedouin lodging.

Under US$100

RAS HASHITA

Meshek 85, Hatzeva; tel. 052/366-5927; US$30 d

Situated near the ancient incense route, Ras Hashita is a very rustic and inexpensive stay in the midst of the Arava Desert. Guests are put up in tents in the middle of a small complex with space for 16 different accommodations, which share an outdoor bathroom. There is also a public tent for hanging out on mats and swinging in hammocks. There is a shared kitchen, and you're allowed to cook out on the premises. Hiking trips in the desert and other excursions can be arranged from here.

NEGEV CAMEL RANCH

Rte. 25, southeast of Dimona; tel. 08/655-2829; www.cameland.co.il; US$56 d

Offering a truly unique place to stay, Negev Camel Ranch is a working farm that raises camels for riding. It's the perfect place to experience a camel desert ride and excursion into the desert. Near Mamshit, the ranch has very simple desert huts for sleeping and shared bathrooms, with towels and bedding provided. Dinner, which is only served until 7pm and is an extra US$15, is a traditional vegetarian meal that includes lentils, rice, and bread with dates and tea for dessert. You can also visit the farm and the camels for free if you're not game to stay here.

MITZPE RAMON YOUTH HOSTEL

4 Nahal Nikrot, Mitzpe Ramon; tel. 08/658-8443; www.iyha.org.il; US$98 d

Set on the northern ridge of the Ramon Crater, Mitzpe Ramon Youth Hostel is a typical, plainly decorated but clean hostel with a good number of rooms (almost 50), which is handy in the busy summer season when most hostels book months in advance. There are private bathrooms with showers available, and breakfast is included. If you're heading out to do some hiking, the hostel can help arrange for lunch to take, and can also assist with jeep and camel tours.

GREEN BACKPACKERS

10/6 Nahal Sirpad; tel. 08/653-2319; www. thegreenbackpackers.com; US$71 d, cash payments for in-person payment and no breakfast included with online booking

Set in Mitzpe Ramon, the very tiny Green Backpackers is an ecotourism hostel that caters to backpackers and is run by guides. The hostel only takes adult guests, and has free wireless Internet in common areas, a shared kitchen, and a shared TV-DVD and computer station. Near the Ramon Crater and the Israel National Trail, the hostel is convenient

to public transportation. You can get travel advice and maps, and rent gear here.

US$100-150

DESERT DAYS ECO LODGE

off the Arava Rd. near Zukim village; tel. 052/617-0028; US$139 d, often has 2-night weekend minimum during high season

You'll be hard-pressed to find something as unique as the Desert Days Eco Lodge. Designed by Tel Aviv transplants who built the place themselves, the nine "eco-huts" in the Arava Desert look like they sprang straight up from the desert itself. Every hut mirrors and blends with the desert environment; they have solar-panel-generated electricity, and used water is recycled into the desert. Huts include free wireless Internet and there is an outdoor swimming pool and a communal *khan* (roadside inn) for guests to mingle with each other and learn about the area.

DESERT ROUTES INN

Moshav Hatzeva; tel. 052/366-5927; www. shvilimbamidbar.co.il; US$134 d

Right in the middle of Moshav Hatzeva, Desert Routes Inn is a small inn with less than a dozen rooms near the border with Jordan in the Arava Desert. The inn is the perfect combination of desert hospitality blended with modern conveniences. The cozy rooms have small but comfortable beds, and the common areas of the inn are designed with exotic but simple touches that include woven sitting mats around huge tables, hammocks, and semi-covered outdoor patio seating. The rustic desert experience is buffered by amenities like free wireless Internet, a hot tub, private patios with desert views, a swimming pool on the moshav, and shuttle service to and from Hatzeva Junction, where buses going to Jerusalem and Tel Aviv stop.

DRACHIM GUEST HOUSE

1 Hanasi Blvd., Dimona; tel. 08/655-6540; www. drachim.org; US$128 d

The Drachim Guest House is a spacious property with 59 rooms that is something between a hotel and a hostel and just 30 minutes from the Dead Sea. Drachim's perks include a semi-Olympic indoor swimming pool, a spa, gardens, free wireless Internet, and a cafeteria where the included breakfast is served. The rooms are simple but homey, and the whole place is set up for the traveler who wants a taste of comfort and luxury without going broke.

DESERT OLIVE FARM

Ramat Negev, Sde Boker; tel. 052/558-3065; www.zimmeril.com; US$144 d

The Desert Olive Farm achieves the perfect combination of a desert experience with all the luxury touches that Israeli *zimmers* are known for, including whirlpool bathtubs. You can stay in a cabin, tent, or suite; note that if you stay in a tent, all of your bathroom facilities are under the stars. The farm is 20 minutes from Mitzpe Ramon, 40 minutes from Be'er Sheva, and is absolutely gorgeous and enchanting.

RAMON SUITES HOTEL

8 Nahal Meishar St., Mitzpe Ramon; tel. 08/658-8884; www.ramonhotel.co.il; US$149 d

The midsize Ramon Suites Hotel is basic, nice, and modern, offering suites with kitchenettes. The three-floor hotel has 34 rooms with free wireless Internet and use of a laptop for no extra charge, tea and coffee service, and spacious rooms. The highlight of Ramon Suites' location is that it's at the doorstep of the Ramon Crater Nature Reserve, and the hotel will give you a free bike to take a ride there.

US$150-200

BOKER VALLEY VINEYARDS FARM

Rte. 40 between Tlallim and Sde Boker; tel. 08/657-3483; www.bokerfarm.com; US$182 d

Don't let the hot tub and nice wine selection fool you: Boker Valley Vineyards Farm is pure rustic Negev Desert accommodations. The five sweet cabins are set around the property of Negev Farms, a working wine producer with vineyards and organic olive trees. Each cabin has a refrigerator, as well as coffee and

tea service, and there is a cookout area. You can eat dinner at the farm if you arrange it in advance; it's near Avdat National Park. Neve Midbar thermal baths give discounts to guests.

Over US$200

DESERT HOME

70 Ein Shaviv St., Mitzpe Ramon; tel. 052/322-9496; www.baitbamidbar.com; US$225 d

A little piece of luxury in a desert setting, Desert Home is known for its designer interior that includes bleached wood floors and carefully designed rooms painted in beautiful, calming colors. You might not need the fireplace, but the five rooms all also come with free wireless Internet, furnished balconies, a kitchenette, a satellite TV, and daily room service of the included breakfast. One last perk is the garden hot tub.

Camping

There are a variety of camping options in the Negev. If you brought gear, stick to designated camping areas and pay the entrance fee or you might get fined by a park ranger. The most useful website for camping information is the **Israel Nature and Parks Authority** site (www.parks.org.il). You can search parks by region, and the listings all include camping information.

GETTING THERE AND AROUND

The area of the Negev is vast and spread out, with large distances in between sights and places to eat and sleep. It's possible to get around by bus and train, but there is generally very little traffic, and it also makes for fairly easy and enjoyable driving if you have a car.

Car

The main city of the Negev, Be'er Sheva, is about a two-hour drive from **Jerusalem,** mostly along Highway 6. Though it looks circuitous on a map, the best and fastest road out of Jerusalem is immediately west and then south, rather than straight south, which will add about 20 minutes to your drive time.

From **Tel Aviv,** you can reach Be'er Sheva in less than 90 minutes, mostly along Highway 6.

Train

The **Israel Railways** (www.rail.co.il) traverses several points in the Negev, including Be'er Sheva. The trains between the south at Be'er Sheva and **Jerusalem** take about 2.5 hours (NIS42 one-way). From **Tel Aviv,** it is about 80 minutes to Be'er Sheva (NIS32 one-way).

Bus

By far the most convenient way to get to the Negev and to travel around in the area is by **Egged** bus (www.egged.co.il). From **Jerusalem** it is about two hours (bus numbers 446 and 470, NIS33 one-way) to Be'er Sheva and from **Tel Aviv** it is about 90 minutes (bus number 370, NIS20 one-way). Once in the area, **Metrodan** buses get you around locally. They do not have a website in English, but you can find related information on a **compilation website** (www.bus.co.il).

Eilat

As far south as you can go in Israel is the resort town and diving destination of Eilat. Summer temperatures in Eilat reach well over 100°F (80°C), but in the midst of winter and early spring it is very pleasant.

Eilat has grown up around the axis of the Red Sea. Most major destinations, activities, restaurants, accommodations, and sites in Eilat are somewhere on or near the shore of the Red Sea.

If you're driving, it is almost impossible to get lost in Eilat, and it's full of massive roundabouts that make driving in a foreign country less intimidating.

SIGHTS

Eilat's main draw is its world-class diving, its beaches, and the many opulent hotel and spa options. There are a few standout places to have fun, especially if traveling with kids.

Dolphin Reef Diving Center

Metsarim St. on South Beach; tel. 08/630-0100; www.dolphinreef.co.il; 9am-5pm Sun.-Thurs., 9am-4:30pm Fri.-Sat. and holidays; adult NIS66, child NIS44

The Dolphin Reef Diving Center is Israel's version of swimming with the dolphins. At the center, bottlenose dolphins can be visited from the floating piers and observation points. Guided swims are also available. Included with the entrance fee is a full day's access to the park and observation points, including beach access, but there is no lifeguard. There's an extra charge for access to the snorkeling and diving center, relaxation pools, the children's activity center, and the underwater photography center. The center also has a restaurant, and there is a bar on the beach.

TOP EXPERIENCE

★ Coral World Underwater Observatory

Rte. 90; tel. 08/636-4200; www.coralworld.co.il/ en; 8:30am-5pm Sat.-Thurs., 8:30am-4pm Fri. and holidays; NIS99, including Oceanarium, child NIS89

Hours of pure fun and enjoyment are just five miles (8 km) from Eilat's city center at the Coral World Underwater Observatory, distinguishable by the structure pointing into the sky.

Throughout the complex, which includes a cafeteria, you can look through a dozen different windows to see bright, rare fish, including a dark room for viewing glow-in-the-dark sea life and phosphorescent fish. For an extra

Eilat

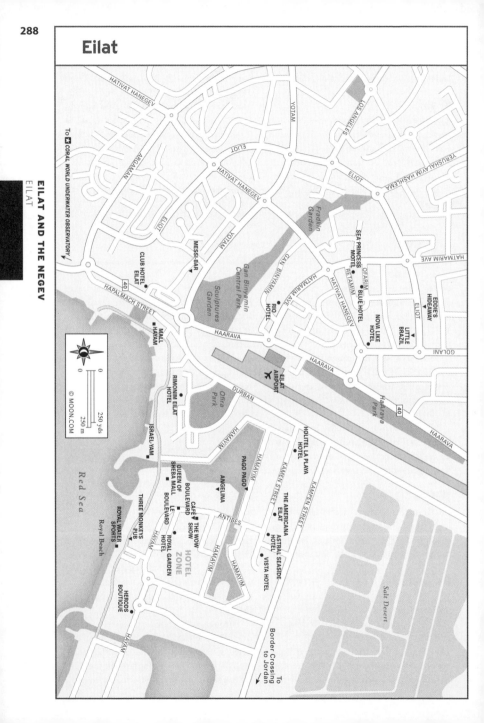

HATIVAT HANEGEV

To 🐠 CORAL WORLD UNDERWATER OBSERVATORY

YOTAM

LOS ANGELES

ELIOT

ELIOT

YERUSHALAYIM HASHLEMA

HATIVAT HANEGEV

ARGAMAN

ELIOT

HATIVAT HANEGEV

Fradkin Garden

ELIOT

YOTAM

HATMARIM AVE

MESSI BAR

Gan Binyamin Central Park

GAN BINYAMIN

SEA PRINCESS MOTEL

OFARIM
RETAMIM

BLUE HOTEL

EDDIE'S HIDEAWAY

CLUB HOTEL EILAT

Sculptures Garden

HATMARIM AVE

HATIVAT HANEGEV

NOVA LIKE HOTEL

ELIOT

GOLANI

HAPALMACH STREET

40

RIO HOTEL

LITTLE BRAZIL

HAARAVA

HAARAVA

MALL HAYAM

EILAT AIRPORT

HaArava Park

40

HAARAVA

RIMONIM EILAT HOTEL

Ofira Park

DURBAN

Red Sea

ISRAEL YAM

HAMAYIM

HOTEL LA PLAYA HOTEL

Salt Desert

QUEEN OF SHEBA MALL

PAGO PAGO

KAMEN STREET

BOULEVARD

ANGELINA

THE AMERICANA EILAT

KAMEN STREET

Royal Beach

THREE MONKEY'S PUB

ROYAL WATER SPORTS

LE BOULEVARD

CAFÉ THE WOW SHOW

ROYAL GARDEN HOTEL

ANTIBES

ASTRAL SEASIDE HOTEL

VISTA HOTEL

HAYAM

HOTEL ZONE

HAMAYIM

HAMAYIM

HERODS BOUTIQUE

HAYAM

Border Crossing to

To Jordan

© MOON.COM

0   250 yds
0   250 m

N

charge, you can go for an underwater dive in a 100-ton (90,000-kg) yellow submarine.

It's easy to spend half a day at the Observatory and Oceanarium, especially if you time your visit around daily events, like the 11am shark feeding and the 3pm Amazon animal feeding, in addition to a trip to the Oceanarium's simulated-motion theater, a trip up to the observatory tower where you can see the neighboring countries of Jordan and Egypt, and a visit to the café.

ENTERTAINMENT AND EVENTS

Festivals and Shows

RED SEA WINTER JAZZ FESTIVAL

various venues around Eilat; http://en.redseajazz.co.il; Jan.; NIS40-150

If you are in Eilat in the dead of winter, the Red Sea Winter Jazz Festival is a combination of music, culture, and events. It spans several days and is considered one of the best festivals of its kind in all of Israel, attracting international acts and the best domestic artists. Concerts are held in three venues, one of which overlooks the Red Sea. Package deals on hotels, flights, and shows can be found on the festival website.

THE WOW SHOW

Royal Garden Hotel, 1 Kampen St., North Shore; tel. 08/638-6701; www.isrotel.co.il; shows run 11am-8:30pm Mon.-Sat.; NIS75-110

For a performance full of acrobatics, dance, and lighting effects all to a soundtrack, The WOW Show is a fun way to spend some time. The thematic performance changes every year and sometimes includes dancing, comedians, and other performing artists.

Bars, Pubs, and Clubs

THREE MONKEYS PUB

23 Pa'amei HaShalom St., Royal Beach Promenade; tel. 08/636-8888 or 053/809-4596; www. threemonkeyspub.co.il; 9pm-late night daily; no cover

The Three Monkeys Pub is Eilat's oldest and most well-known sports bar and live performance venue with beach seating and

a laid-back atmosphere. There's a lengthy cocktail, beer, and alcohol menu and light food options.

MESSI-BAR

1 Yotam, middle floor; tel. 052/351-7336; 9:30pm-late night Tues.-Sun.; minimum age 25 years; no cover

Popular with both locals and tourists, Messi-Bar features all kinds of rock music in both English and Hebrew. The extremely casual atmosphere plays on the town's beach vibe, with sturdy, tall wooden tables and room for dancing.

SHOPPING

Eilat's special offering to shoppers is that there is no Value Added Tax (VAT) on items in stores. The selection of stores is similar to what you'll find in the rest of Israel, but they are geared toward drawing customers in for deals with special late-night sessions and an extra-soothing level of air-conditioning to escape the heat.

MALL HAYAM

1 HaPalmach, North Shore; tel. 08/634-0006; 9:30am-11:30pm Sun.-Thurs., 9am-one hour before sunset Fri.

For everything you could possibly want to buy, Mall Hayam is Eilat's biggest mall. The mall has everything from a game center to international and domestic clothing chains to food and a fantastic view of the Red Sea.

QUEEN OF SHEBA MALL

North Beach promenade near the Hilton; 10am-midnight daily

In close proximity to a number of hotels, the Queen of Sheba Mall is 43,000 square feet (4,000 square meters) of commerce with a view of the Eilat marina and places to grab a quick bite to eat.

LA BOULEVARD

5 Antiv, North Shore; tel. 08/638-6666; 9am-11pm daily

Eilat's version of Rodeo Drive or a Parisian avenue is La Boulevard, a shopping center that comes with street lamps, wood benches, air-conditioning, and cover from the sun. The products are high-end, international brands of jewelry, fashion, sporting goods, and a French-inspired bakery.

SPORTS AND RECREATION

The main sporting attraction and a major draw to the area in general is diving. Other popular water-related activities in Eilat include glass-bottom boats and the many beaches in the area.

Beaches

There are a variety of beaches in Eilat that offer something for everyone, including water sports, parties, restaurants, and nightclubs. At **HaShchafim (or Herod's) Beach** (north Eilat near Herod's Hotel) you can see movie screenings. **HaZahav Beach** (near the hotel promenade between the Isrotel Royal Beach Hotel and Dan Hotel) is synonymous with romance and has great atmosphere for just kicking back. **Dolphin Reef** (on Eilat-Taba Rd. after the Dead Sea Works potash plant) is the place to swim with dolphins. **Royal Beach** (in front of the Royal Beach Hotel off Pa'amei HaShalom St.) is the best bet if you want to dine on the sand.

Diving and Water Sports

CORAL BEACH NATURE RESERVE

Coral Beach opposite the Eilat Field School; tel. 07/637-6829; www.parks.org.il; 9am-5pm daily; adult NIS35, child NIS18

Over 100 types of stony coral and 650 species of tropical fish grace the Coral Beach Nature Reserve at the southern end of Eilat. The centerpiece of the reserve is a 13,000-square-foot (1,200-meter-long), densely populated coral reef that runs parallel to the beach.

ROYAL WATER SPORTS

Shvil Hayam St.; tel. 08/646-6881; www.eilat-city. net; 8:30am-7:30pm daily; NIS240 and up per day pp

Royal Water Sports is a sports club on Royal Beach with banana boats, tubing, Jet Skiing, kayaking, and paddleboats.

AQUA SPORT

Mitsrayim Way; tel. 08/633-4404; www.aqua-sport. com; 9am-4pm daily; NIS280 and up per day

One of the best diving schools in the country, Aqua Sport has been in business for nearly five decades and can accommodate divers of every level. They also rent equipment and have showers, bathroom facilities, and Bedouin tents. Introductory dives for people ages 8-88 are offered daily.

DIVER'S VILLAGE

Mitsrayim Way; tel. 08/637-2268; www.diversvillage. co.il; 10am-5pm daily; NIS280 and up

Opposite the Coral Beach Nature Reserve is Diver's Village, which has been operating for 20 years, rents diving and snorkeling equipment, and gives lessons. Introductory and refresher lessons are available, and there are showers and toilets, a snack bar, and three guest rooms. Introductory dives are available to kids as young as seven.

Glass-Bottom Boats

ISRAEL-YAM

North Shore at the marina between Caesar Hotel and Sheraton Moriah Hotel; tel. 08/633-2325; www. israel-yam.co.il; boats depart from the marina at 10:30am, 1pm, and 3:30pm; prices vary

For a glimpse into the underwater world of the Red Sea without putting a toe in the water, you can ride on one of the Israel-Yam 72-foot (22-meter) yachts. The boats include a sundeck, a dance floor for private parties, and a snack bar. The lowest level has a long, rectangular window in the floor for underwater viewing. A two-hour ride includes a tour past the coral reef and the Japanese Gardens along the Israeli-Jordanian border, and dolphin-watching on the Israeli-Egyptian border at Taba.

1: Coral World Underwater Observatory **2:** Red Sea corals **3:** Dolphin Reef Diving Center **4:** kayaks on a beach in Eilat

FOOD
Italian
ANGELINA

3 Antibes on King Solomon Promenade; tel.
053/809-4348 or 08/636-3439; http://eilat.city/en;
7pm-11pm Sun.-Thurs., 8pm-11pm Sat.; NIS55

With a simple atmosphere and an open kitchen, Angelina specializes in all manner of pizza and pasta, including a delectable zucchini, sweet potato, and feta cheese pizza pie and a spinach and gorgonzola pasta dish. The general atmosphere definitely feels like a pizzeria, but it's a nice option for a hearty Italian meal at a very affordable price, and it is right by the water with promenade seating.

Seafood
THE LAST REFUGE

Turkiz St. near the Coral World Underwater
Observatory; tel. 08/637-2437; 12:30pm-11pm daily;
NIS130

Preceded by its sterling, decades-long reputation as one of the best seafood places in town, The Last Refuge has colorful nautical interior decor and boasts a gorgeous view of the Red Sea. Some menu highlights include fish, mussels in garlic and cream, grilled lobsters, and seafood platters.

★ PAGO PAGO

99 HaMayim; tel. 08/637-6660 or 08/633-7747; www.
pagopagorest.com; 12:30pm-11:30pm daily; NIS75

A popular spot to kick back and enjoy some atmosphere is Pago Pago, situated right on the beach with a view of the Red Sea in a very sleek, modern building. The menu includes steak and seafood dishes as well as custom desserts. Try the shrimp calamari Marseille or Spanish mackerel with yogurt. The restaurant is not huge, but the dual-level layout includes a long bar and a warm atmosphere with wood flooring.

EDDIE'S HIDEAWAY

8 Eilot St.; tel. 08/637-1137; 6pm-11:30pm Mon.-Fri.,
2pm-10:30pm Sat.; NIS65

Tucked away in a discreet location is the aptly named Eddie's Hideaway, a well-known local spot that has been in business since 1979. Serving a variety of seafood and meat dishes done in the French culinary style, such as shrimp, steak, and shellfish, Eddie's has a modest exterior and simple, understated interior. It makes for an excellent intimate, romantic dinner for two.

South American
★ LITTLE BRAZIL

3 Eilot St.; tel. 08/637-2018; www.littlebrazil.co.il;
12:30pm-11pm daily; NIS120

If you make it a bit off the beaten path of the city center in search of a hearty meat meal, go to Little Brazil, an all-you-can-eat, South American Churrasco-style meat restaurant. The atmosphere is warm and friendly, and because of the location there's a mix of locals and tourists. There's also meat from the roaming waiter, called a *pasador*.

Cafés and Coffee Shops
CAFÉ BOULEVARD

5 Antibes; tel. 08/638-6699; 8am-11pm daily; NIS45

In the heart of the high-end Royal Garden Hotel shops avenue, Café Boulevard is set up as a classic café with items on display in a case and a massive, spacious interior with small tables and sofas. Known for the quirky pictures they create in customers' latte foam, Boulevard usually features a Friday night live performance and has a decent alcohol menu.

ACCOMMODATIONS

Eilat's status as a major domestic and international tourist destination means that there is a plethora of upper-end hotels and hotel chains. Many of the nicer hotels require a two-night minimum stay when booking on the weekend, and the fairly standard feature of Israeli hotels to include breakfast isn't universal in Eilat. Check in advance about included breakfast, as it might be by request only. Most hotels are grouped around the beaches and diving areas.

Under US$100

SEA PRINCESS MOTEL

136 Retamim St.; tel. 08/910-2330; www.seaprincess. co.il; US$95 d

One of the most affordable places to stay in pricey Eilat is the Sea Princess Motel, next to the Eilat Bus Station and 10 minutes to major shopping destinations, including Mall Hayam. With about three dozen private rooms and dorm rooms that all have a TV, a fridge, and a microwave, the Sea Princess has free wireless Internet in common areas, a TV in the lobby, and a garden. The front desk is 24 hours, and you can go by foot to the nearest beach, which is about 15 minutes away.

US$100-150

BLUE HOTEL

123 Ofarim St.; tel. 08/632-6601; http://bluehotel. co.il; US$130 d

Still affordable and with a few extra perks, the Blue Hotel has a 24-hour front desk, newspaper service, and rooms with a terrace. As a guest you also have access to rental bicycles and a tour desk, and wireless Internet is free throughout the hotel. Recent renovations add to the general ambience of the hotel, which is very breezy and tropical. It's possible to book a package stay at the hotel for diving.

HOLITEL LA PLAYA HOTEL

3 Simtat Shfifon, off Kamen St., tel. 08/939-4555; US$145 d

One of the coolest features of Holitel La Playa Hotel is the palm-tree-encircled outdoor swimming pool. The hotel, which is near Eilat Airport, is decorated in Moroccan style, and all the rooms have a TV, sofa, and coffee and tea service. Near city center and the beach, La Playa is a larger hotel with over 200 rooms, a spa, a cinema, a library, pool tables, video games, and a mini market. When you're tired of the beach, you can order food and drinks poolside or hang out in the hotel's bar for a drink. If you book on the weekend, there is a two-night minimum stay.

THE AMERICANA EILAT

7 Kamen St. at North Beach; tel. 08/630-3777; www. americanahotel.co.il; US$135 d

The layout of The Americana Eilat is slightly motel-ish with three stories and rooms that open directly to the outside, but the amenities and price make it a worthwhile stay. There are a variety of types among the 140 rooms that include some with balconies and a view of the pool, kitchenettes, connecting rooms, and extra-large family rooms. The rooms are bright with comfortable, modern furnishings and include free wireless Internet, a fridge, a hair dryer, and cable TV. There is also a sauna and hot tub, a shaded children's pool, a supermarket, a spa club, and a restaurant and nightclub at the hotel. Not far away is the promenade and waterfront.

RIO HOTEL

9 Hatmarim Ave.; tel. 08/630-1111; US$129 d

Tucked right into the middle of central Eilat, the Rio Hotel is a boutique establishment with a trendy, upscale interior that includes a bar, restaurant, and small pool. Very close to the airport and bus station, guests here get access to the neighborhood disco at Hotel Mega and a free glass of wine with dinner at the hotel restaurant.

US$150-200

PRIMA MUSIC HOTEL

Turkiz St. at Almog Beach; tel. 08/638-8555; www. prima-hotels-israel.com; US$170 d

Truly just a hop, skip, and a jump from beachfront access, Prima Music Hotel is just five minutes from Coral Beach. The hotel's bright, tropical interior is designed on a musical theme complete with a music room with vintage records that guests can play, giving it a quirky touch. Other features include a common area sea view terrace and some rooms with a sea view, cable TV, and CD sound systems. A stay here includes a huge buffet breakfast, bicycle rentals, and the option of a dinner buffet. It's also close to scores of restaurants at Almog Beach Marina. The Olympic-size swimming pool has a view of the Red Sea and there are tennis and volleyball courts on the hotel grounds.

NOVA LIKE HOTEL

6 Hativat Hanegev St.; tel. 08/638-2444 reception, tel. 03/542-5555 reservations; www.atlas.co.il; US$158 d

Trendy and very family-friendly, the Nova Like Hotel is a recently renovated larger hotel. The rooms surround a pool and many include a balcony with a pool view. The suites with two larger hotel rooms and large studios all have a kitchenette. There's also a kids' pool, sundeck, lobby lounge and bar, bicycle rental, and live entertainment during the high season. About 10-15 minutes by foot gets you to the main Eilat beaches. Rooms include free wireless Internet and direct-dial telephones.

★ ASTRAL SEASIDE HOTEL

6 Durban St.; tel. 08/636-7444; www.astralhotels. co.il; US$190 d weekdays, US$228 d weekends, hotel requires two-night stay on weekends

Boasting one of the best poolside views of the Red Sea in town, the Astral Seaside Hotel has a massive wooden poolside sundeck and lounge chairs. The spacious rooms are beautiful, bright, and modern and some include floor-to-ceiling windows with a terrace and sea views. The medium-size hotel also has a children's club, evening shows in high season, and in-room Swedish massages by request. There's free lobby wireless access, a synagogue, spa, and lobby bar, and it's just minutes away from the sea.

HERODS BOUTIQUE

23 Pa'amei HaShalom St., North Shore; tel. 08/638-0010 or 03/511-0000; www.herods-hotels. com; US$193 d

The multistory Herods Boutique has views of the lagoon and the Edom Mountains. Home to a wide variety of activities geared toward kids, the hotel's rooms include a special channel on the TV for kids, minibars, coffee and tea service, and an option for connecting doors. The interior design has slightly opulent touches, and many of the rooms have a balcony with a

view. The hotel also boasts the largest conference center in Eilat as well as a swimming pool. The hotel is at the end of the promenade. Be careful when booking, as there are several hotels in Eilat with the word Herod in their name.

VISTA HOTEL

17 Kamen St., North Shore; tel. 08/630-3030; www. vistaeilat.co.il; US$160 d

Equipped with its own marina, the Vista Hotel, also near Aqaba City Center Shopping Mall, has an outdoor pool with a bar, free wireless Internet in public areas, a fitness center, a restaurant, and an indoor bar. The hotel is smallish, with about 84 rooms, but the interior layout has a very spacious, modern, clean feeling. The rooms are on the smaller side, but most of them have a cityscape or water view, and include a TV, free newspapers, a fridge, and free wireless Internet. The front desk can help with tickets and tours, business services, and currency exchange. Some cool touches are the waterfall in the pool and the arcade for kids.

EILOT KIBBUTZ COUNTRY LODGING

Kibbutz Eilot, about three miles north of Eilat; tel. 08/635-8816; www.eilot.co.il/en; US$165 d

An option for a more pastoral experience is Eilot Kibbutz Country Lodging, which allows you to be near the action of Eilat but with some peace and quiet. The hotel is small, with only 40 rooms, but offers an indoor and an outdoor pool, a garden with facilities for cookouts, rooms with balconies, and a petting zoo for kids.

Over US$200
U SUNRISE CLUB EILAT ALL INCLUSIVE

Kibbutz Eilot; tel. 03/511-0098 or 08/630-5333; www.fattal-hotels.com; US$220 d

Luxury accommodations in Eilat are big business, and the U Sunrise Club Eilat All Inclusive is a prime example of the all-inclusive options that are available. Near North Beach, Dolphin Reef, and Aqaba City Center Shopping Mall, this large hotel includes everything but free wireless Internet. There are a range of dining options, from coffee to a full restaurant, concierge service, and a 24-hour front desk. Rooms have minibars, safes, satellite TV, balconies, and direct-dial phones, and some ground-floor rooms open to a broad lawn. The interior design is quite spare but very nicely done with a Spanish theme, and the rooms are very spacious. Almost everything you could need is at this hotel.

CLUB HOTEL EILAT

2 Kheil HaHandasa Blvd. off of Hubaz St.; tel. 08/636-1666; www.clubhotels-israel.com; US$315 d

Expensive but worth every penny, the Club Hotel Eilat is more like an oasis compound of luxury than a hotel. The main attraction is the massive outdoor pool that includes waterslides, waterfalls, and the shade of palm trees. The hotel also has a synagogue, spa and sauna, restaurant, arcade, gym, and 40 acres (162,000 square meters) of grounds. The nautical interior design of the massive 700-room hotel almost gives the feel of being in cabins on a cruise ship. When you get tired of playing at the hotel, the beach and lagoon are within easy walking distance.

RIMONIM EILAT HOTEL

Tarshish St., North Shore; tel. 08/636-9369; http:// english.rimonim.com; US$408 d

Famed for its high-quality guest service, the Rimonim Eilat Hotel is literally one minute away from the Red Sea beach and right in the middle of Eilat's main shopping district. Every room has a balcony that overlooks the sea and the hotel's large outdoor pool. There is a lobby bar, restaurant, gym, and spa. The rooms are modern and designed with bright colors and extra touches like a dining bar, a large-screen TV, and sliding glass doors that lead to the balcony.

ROYAL GARDEN HOTEL

1 Kampen St., North Shore; tel. 08/633-7010; www. isrotel.com; US$360 d

Home to the well-known nightly WOW Show, the Royal Garden Hotel caters to people on family vacations with roomy suites decorated with wood accents and cozy interiors that feel more like home than a hotel room. The gorgeous, lagoon-like outdoor pool and water park has a snack bar, and the hotel is near the boardwalk and beach. Be warned that the hotel does not provide pool towels or have a restaurant, but every room has a kitchenette complete with utensils and a dining area.

U CORAL BEACH CLUB RESORT

Almog Beach; tel. 08/635-0000; www.fattal-hotels. com; US$330 d

The U Coral Beach Club Resort is an all-inclusive option that has its own beach, swimming pool, and spa center. The hotel features include a bar with the option for lounging on the outdoor deck with a drink and on-site live stage performances. This 281-room hotel offers a free shuttle bus, a gift shop, a poolside bar, and rooms with all the amenities you could possibly need, decorated in a simple, modern, upscale style. Dry cleaning and laundry service, room service, babysitting, and a hair salon are also available.

INFORMATION AND SERVICES

The tourism and information services in Eilat are some of the best in Israel since it is such a popular destination.

The well-equipped and helpful **Municipal Tourism Corporation Eilat** (2 Yotam St.; tel. 08/636-7890; rstourism@eilat.muni.il; 8am-5pm Sun.-Thurs.) is an operation of the City of Eilat and caters to international tourists, with a large amount of information in English. The **city's official tourism website** (www. redseaeilat.com) is very well done with anything and everything you could want to know about Eilat. It includes listings of every kind of service imaginable.

Eilat City (www.eilat-city.net) is run by locals and a useful and easy-to-use website.

In an emergency, contact the **Eilat Tourist Police** (tel. 08/636-7209 or 106) or emergency medical services **Magen David Adom** (tel. 08/637-2333 or 101).

There are about half a dozen currency exchange locations around town, including **Money Gold** (Mall HaYam; tel. 08/634-0049; open during mall hours) and **Nawi Money Exchange** (8 Antibes St., North Beach promenade near the Hilton and the Queen of Sheba mall; tel. 050/388-3111; 10am-midnight Sun.-Thurs., 10am-4pm Fri.).

GETTING THERE AND AROUND

Getting to Eilat seems daunting if you are starting from Tel Aviv or Jerusalem, but once you're on the way, it's a fairly straight and uneventful (though lengthy) trip by car or bus.

Car

From **Jerusalem,** it is a minimum four-hour drive to Eilat. Late at night there is very little traffic and you don't have the burden of the hot sun beating down on your vehicle or fighting with the air-conditioning. The roads are not lit for most of the way, and there is a great deal of blackness as you drive through the mountainous areas near the Dead Sea and through the Negev Desert. However, every turn along the road is very clearly marked, especially in the areas where it is a two-lane highway.

From Jerusalem, follow Route 90 south as far as you can go until you reach Eilat. If you drive during the day, it's a good idea to take the whole day and incorporate a stop or two along the way at the Dead Sea.

From **Tel Aviv,** take Highway 6 to Route 40 south for about four hours. The route from Tel Aviv takes you past the incredible crater at Mitzpe Ramon and cuts straight through the desert with long stretches of nothing but a gas station every now and then.

Once you're in Eilat and driving about, you'll easily get the hang of navigating the plethora of enormous roundabouts that control traffic. The city is well signposted, and there is plenty of parking.

Bus

The bus trip from **Jerusalem** to Eilat is just under five hours on an **Egged** bus (www.egged. co.il, bus number 444, NIS80 one-way). From **Tel Aviv** to Eilat, it takes well over five hours (bus numbers 390 and 394, NIS80 one-way).

Once you're in Eilat, the only public transportation service in town is Egged.

Air

It is possible to reach Eilat by plane. The **Eilat Domestic Airport** (tel. 08/636-3800, www. iaa.gov.il) takes flights from **Arkia, El Al, Israir,** and **Sun Dor** airlines. The airport is small and convenient, and flying is a good option if you plan to also take a trip to **Petra, Jordan,** while you're in the area. Most tour companies will pick you up directly from the airport if you arrive on a morning flight.

Petra, Jordan

A few hours across the border from Israel's southernmost point of Eilat is the ancient Nabataean city of Petra. Its distinctive massive colonnaded buildings are carved directly from the stone faces of mountains. The inexpressibly exquisite architecture holds an abundance of undiscovered history.

Petra is the ancient capital of the Nabataeans, a once-powerful civilization of highly successful traders, water conservation engineers, and architects who were nomadic until they settled in what is now southern Israel to southern Jordan around the 6th century BC. Inhabited initially by another civilization, Petra is sometimes called "the lost city" for a period when most outsiders were forbidden. In 1812 the Swiss traveler, geographer, and academic Johann Ludwig Burckhardt posed

Highlights

Look for ★ to find recommended sights, activities, dining, and lodging.

★ **Wadi Rum:** This expanse of desert in Jordan is full of unusual rock formations. Mountains of sandstone and granite rise as high as 5,500 feet (1,675 meters) (page 303).

★ **Roman Theater:** This Roman-style theater is a wonder of ancient architecture (page 306).

★ **Byzantine Church:** Built on top of other ruins, the Byzantine Church in Petra has 230 square feet (70 square meters) of mosaic floors (page 306).

★ **Great Temple:** Petra's largest freestanding structure, the Great Temple underwent extensive excavation work carried out by students from the Joukowsky Institute at Brown University (page 308).

★ **Al-Deir Monastery:** Up 800 rock-cut steps above Petra's amphitheater is this monastery and its unique, massive urn (page 309).

To
AL-DEIR MONASTERY

Great Temple

Byzantine Church

PETRA

Roman Theater

0   100 yds
0   100 m

To
WADI RUM

© MOON.COM

as an Arab man from India on pilgrimage to sneak into a closely guarded holy site. It was his trickery that led to the Western rediscovery of the ruins of Petra.

In 1985, UNESCO declared Petra a World Heritage Site, and in a global popular vote of more than 100 million people in 2007, it was honored as one of the New Seven Wonders of the World. Much of Petra's history has been lost in the sands of time, meaning that generally accepted modern facts should be taken with a grain of salt instead.

HISTORY

Dating back to prehistoric times, Petra was at one time situated at a key crossroads between Arabia, Egypt, and Syria-Phoenicia. It is widely believed to have been built and inhabited by the powerful Nabataean incense route traders, who used it as their capital city. The Byzantines, Romans, and Crusaders were also residents, contributing to the construction of different buildings and the city layout.

The structures of Petra are part constructions, part carvings made from rose-colored rock in the midst of a series of cavernous gorges and rocky mountain peaks. The color of the stone gives Petra the nickname "the rose city."

It is one of the most famous archaeological sites in the world and an outstanding example of a blending of Hellenistic architecture and Eastern traditions. Unfortunately, Petra is in a part of the world prone to earthquakes, putting the structures at risk of damage or destruction.

One of the most fascinating aspects of Petra's history is how much of it remains a mystery. On a guided trip through the area, you may hear your guide refer to this uncertainty with the standard line, "85 percent of Petra's history is unknown." Though the unknown is a bit frustrating as a visitor, the mystery makes it all the more enchanting and exciting, not to mention

inspiring—particularly for writers and artists. In fact, the area has a wide range of accommodations that such visitors can find something to suit their tastes if they make a visit. It's a place where your imagination about the ancient world can run wild.

ORIENTATION

Petra is between the Dead Sea and the Red Sea in Jordan. If you set out from Petra from the southernmost border entry on the Israel side at Eilat (there are three border entries), you will find yourself in Aqaba, Jordan. From Aqaba, you can take a taxi, bus, or tour bus to Petra. It takes about two hours including one or two short stops.

About halfway along the way to Petra from the south, you will pass by **Wadi Rum,** a desert landscape that has been immortalized in Western films and is a popular ecotourism destination.

In Wadi Rum and along the way to Petra you will see very unusual rock formations, including bright bands of colorful mineral deposits etched into the stone landscape in beautiful colors.

Once you arrive, you will find yourself in an Arab village called **Wadi Musa,** immediately adjacent to the archaeological site of Petra. Wadi Musa is home to about 99 percent of Petra's restaurants, accommodations, and services. The large Jordanian city of Amman is about 3.5 hours to the north.

PLANNING YOUR TIME

Most people will say you need several days to see Petra. If you have come over from Israel and are on a tight schedule, try to allow for at least an overnight stay. It is possible to get a feel for Petra in one day, but you will be rushed. If you cross into Jordan at Aqaba, most of the day will be spent getting through the border checkpoint, traveling to the site, walking in, walking around a bit, getting back out, and then returning to the border.

Previous: the Al-Deir Monastery; bedouin rugs; detail of the Treasury.

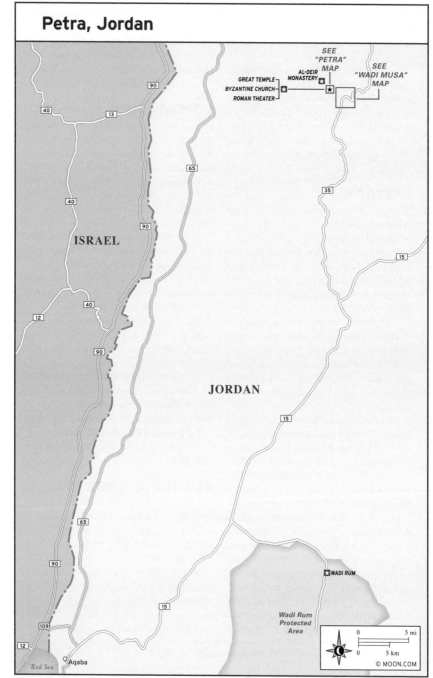

Petra, Jordan

SEE "PETRA" MAP

SEE "WADI MUSA" MAP

AL-DEIR MONASTERY

GREAT TEMPLE
BYZANTINE CHURCH
ROMAN THEATER

90

40

13

40

65

90

35

15

ISRAEL

40

12

90

JORDAN

15

65

90

15

109

12

WADI RUM

Wadi Rum
Protected
Area

Red Sea

Aqaba

0   5 mi
0   5 km

© MOON.COM

The whole process takes about 12 hours and is the quickest possible version of a trip to Petra if you are coming directly from Eilat on the Israeli side.

There are plenty of very affordable accommodations in the immediate area within walking distance to Petra. In addition, a two-day entry ticket to Petra costs only about US$7 more than the rather expensive single-entry ticket.

KNOW BEFORE YOU GO
Visas, Passports, and Entrance Fees

There are three land border crossings from Israel into Jordan in the north, center, and south of the country. The two most convenient and relevant for travelers to Petra are the Allenby/King Hussein Bridge Border Crossing and the border crossing at Eilat-Aqaba. Visas are issued on the spot at the Eilat crossing, and you don't need to provide photographs.

If you cross at the **Allenby/King Hussein Bridge,** you need to pay for your visa (about JD20) in advance at the Jordanian embassy in Tel Aviv. You will need two photographs, and you'll get the visa within 24 hours.

If you enter Jordan by **air,** you will need to pay for a single-entry Jordanian visa (about JD22), which you can do at the airport, usually in the same place where you change money.

If you cross from Eilat to **Aqaba** by sea or land, through the port or at the crossing from Israel, your visa should be free for one month for most nationalities, including Americans and Canadians. The only fee you might be charged is an exit fee of JD5 for overland exits back into Israel. Aqaba is a Special Economic Zone Area (SEZA) set up for free trade, which is why the visa requirements are different.

When heading to Aqaba, do not pay tour guides on the Israeli side of the border who tell you to give them cash for a visa, as they may simply pocket the money.

Make sure that your **passport** is valid for at least six months past the date you plan to leave Jordan.

Money

The official currency of Jordan is the **Jordanian dinar** (JD), and it is divided into 10 dirham, 100 qirsh (or piasters), and 1,000 fils. Half-dinar and one-dinar coins are most common, and bills come in denominations of 1 dinar, 5 dinars, 10 dinars, 20 dinars, and 50 dinars. JD1 is typically worth about US$1.40 or NIS5.50.

If you are coming from Israel, change your shekels to dinars before crossing the border, or at one of the money-changing desks that are along the way as you pass through the many stops that you need to make at the border (formally named the Wadi Araba Crossing/South Border). If you are trying to pay in shekels after entering Jordan, it will really put a damper on your trip, as most people will have no idea what to charge you.

You can also get by very easily in Wadi Musa and Petra with U.S. currency, but don't expect change and keep the conversion rates in mind when getting prices.

Itinerary Ideas

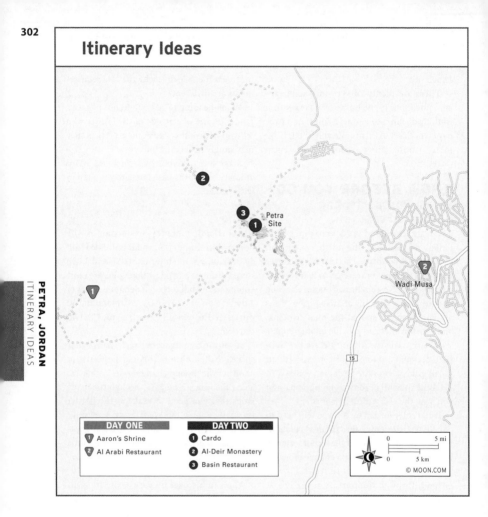

DAY ONE	DAY TWO
1 Aaron's Shrine	1 Cardo
2 Al Arabi Restaurant	2 Al-Deir Monastery
	3 Basin Restaurant

Petra Site

Wadi Musa

15

0   5 mi
0   5 km

© MOON.COM

Itinerary Ideas

PETRA IN TWO DAYS

Day 1

1 Start your time with a two-hour hike to Petra's highest point at the top of Mount Aaron, **Aaron's Shrine,** renovated by an Egyptian sultan in the 13th century AD.

2 After you've hiked back and had a rest at your hotel, head to the centrally located Shaheed roundabout **Al Arabi** restaurant for some traditional maglubeh and fatteh.

Day 2

1 A popular destination for **desert hiking,** the main thoroughfare of Petra's **cardo** leads to a **long hike** of 800 steps up the side of the rock face.

2 At the end of the 90-minute climb is the **Al-Deir Monastery,** a towering structure with a crowning urn that allows for an unimpeded, 360-degree view of Petra and the surrounding area.

3 After you've hiked back down, stop off at **Basin Restaurant** for their buffet and dessert.

Sights

The road from the border of Egypt at Aqaba, which most tour groups and guides use as a rally point for excursions to Petra, is marked by the starkness of almost nothing but desert for about two hours, except for Wadi Rum. Once you get to Wadi Musa, the main site is Petra.

★ WADI RUM

Rte. 15 between Aqaba and Petra; www.aqaba.jo; JD5, under 12 free

On the way to Petra is the singular landscape of Wadi Rum Protected Area, the filming location for much of the 1962 classic *Lawrence of Arabia*. *Transformers II* and part of one of the *Star Wars* movies were also filmed here.

Wadi Rum is a 450-square-mile (720-square-kilometer) expanse of desert filled with unusual rock formations and mountains of sandstone and granite that rise as high as 5,500 feet (1,520 meters) and are often compared to the surface of the moon. Visiting Wadi Rum is strictly controlled. The safest and easiest thing to do is hire a travel guide through a hotel in Aqaba who can take you there.

Another option is to go to Wadi Rum's **Visitors Center** (one hour northeast of Aqaba on Rte. 15, turn right at sign, tel. 03/203-5360; 10am-5pm daily), which has posted prices for hiring a local Bedouin guide who can escort you in a 4x4 vehicle or by camel. It's also possible to hire a guide for a campout in a Bedouin tent. Don't forget water, a hat with a brim, and sunscreen. Research

the related environmental and ethical issues you might wonder about before your trip, as standards always differ by region, country, and culture.

The Visitors Centre is part of a complex of buildings that includes an interpretation center, crafts shops, a ticket office, and a restaurant. Within Wadi Rum there are multiple natural sites to see, including ancient rock paintings, historical points of interest, and dramatic sunrise and sunset vantage points from atop desert sand dunes.

PETRA

www.visitpetra.jo; 6am-6pm daily Apr.-Oct., 6am-4pm daily Nov.-Mar., 7am-4pm daily during the month of Ramadan; JD55-95 for one day, JD60 for two days

The ancient site of Petra is next to the Arab village of Wadi Musa. The **Visitors Center** can sell you tickets, arrange for guides, and give you background information. It is located at the end of a row of small shops just before the entrance to Petra and downhill from the tourist bus parking lots. The entry ticket is relatively expensive at JD55-95 if you are not staying overnight in Petra.

Ticket prices can also differ based on whether you are a foreigner or a local, the length of your stay, and the number of planned entries. It is almost impossible to see the site adequately in one day. It is expensive to enter Petra, but quite affordable to add an extra day or two to the base ticket price for multiple entries.

Petra

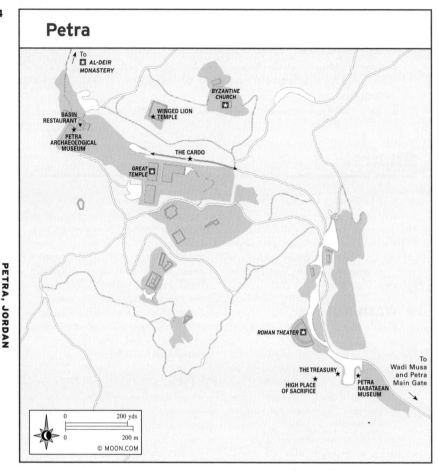

AL-DEIR MONASTERY

BYZANTINE CHURCH

WINGED LION TEMPLE

BASIN RESTAURANT

PETRA ARCHAEOLOGICAL MUSEUM

THE CARDO

GREAT TEMPLE

ROMAN THEATER

THE TREASURY

HIGH PLACE OF SACRIFICE

PETRA NABATAEAN MUSEUM

To Wadi Musa and Petra Main Gate

0   200 yds
0   200 m

© MOON.COM

Wear the most comfortable shoes you own, and be prepared for a mini-hike in and out of the site, which takes at least one hour each way. Once inside, you will have plenty of opportunities to climb up into buildings and explore different ruins. Aside from walking, there are few other options for getting in and out. There are horse-drawn carriages and donkey-drawn carts that take people in and out of the first main canyon, but it's strongly recommended that you walk on your own. If mobility is an issue, it's advisable to research the use of animals at Petra online before you arrive, and if you decide using one is

necessary, closely check the care and condition of any animal you hire.

Obelisk Tomb

Just between the *siq* (main passage, or literally "cleft") and the main entrance to Petra is the mysterious Obelisk Tomb, situated next to huge rocks with strange curves. The beautifully intricate tomb is Egyptian with Nabataean and Egyptian inscriptions.

The *Siq*

The main passage into Petra is the *siq*, an almost 4,000-foot-long (1220-meter-long)

Wadi Musa

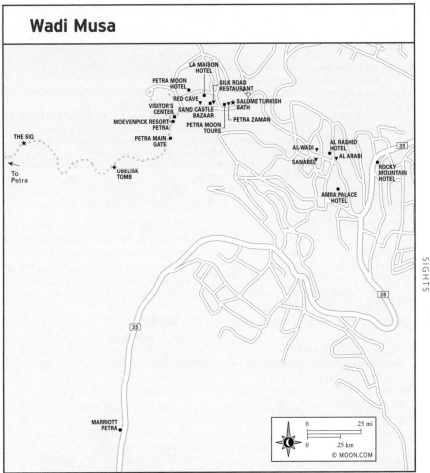

LA MAISON HOTEL
PETRA MOON HOTEL
SILK ROAD RESTAURANT
RED CAVE
VISITOR'S CENTER
SAND CASTLE BAZAAR
SALOME TURKISH BATH
MOEVENPICK RESORT PETRA
PETRA MOON TOURS
PETRA ZAMAN
THE SIQ
PETRA MAIN GATE
To Petra
UBELISK TOMB
AL-WADI
AL RASHID HOTEL
AL ARABI
SANABEL
ROCKY MOUNTAIN HOTEL
35
AMRA PALACE HOTEL
35
35
MARRIOTT PETRA

0   .25 mi
0   .25 km
© MOON.COM

canyon that slices through the mountains that lead to that breathtaking first view of Petra.

Along the way, there are all kinds of details worth stopping to take in, including notches for votives that might have been ceremonial, paving stones, and the waterway system that lines both sides of the floor of the *siq*. This is where Harrison Ford rode his horse in a memorable scene in *Indiana Jones and the Last Crusade*.

The Treasury (Al-Khazneh)

Among the countless dramatic views in Petra is the breathtaking Treasury. It's both impossible to miss and difficult to drag yourself away from. Known to locals as Al-Khazneh, its colonnaded facade is a towering 130 feet (40 meters), with depictions of mythological figures carved into the stone.

The most famous and most photographed of Petra's many sites, the treasury is thought to house something valuable, money perhaps, in the urn at the top of the structure. Though people have been trying to dislodge it for years to see if it really contains riches, nobody has succeeded.

The Shrine of Aaron

At the very top of Mount Aaron (Jabal Haroun) in Petra is the modest, white-domed Shrine of Aaron. The shrine commemorates the death of Aaron, the elder brother of Moses, and was constructed by the Egyptian Mamluk Sultan in the 13th century.

The highest point in Petra, the shrine is perched on part of the Sharah mountain range. According to tradition, the location of the shrine is the place where Aaron died.

Since antiquity, other religious structures have been built here. According to tradition, a 10-year-old Muhammad visited Aaron's shrine. The site was closely guarded by Bedouins to keep away non-Muslims for a long time, but is now open to and a site of pilgrimage for Jews and Christians as well as Muslims. Aaron is considered a prophet in all three religions.

It is a long hike up a rugged mountain to the site. If you go, plan ahead, set out early in the morning, and take water and protection from the sun.

★ Roman Theater

With an estimated capacity of 3,000-7,000 people, the Roman Theater is a focal point for many visitors in both ancient and modern times.

The theater dates back to around 9 BC-AD 40 and was restored in the past decade. Built during the reign of King Aretas IV, its capacity is believed to indicate that at one time the population of Petra was about 24,000 people, based on the Roman-style building practices of making one seat for every family.

You can climb up and get a view into the amphitheater from close up, where you'll also get a better perspective of the semicircular structure and the strange feature in the back of some previously existing tombs cut into during construction of the theater. It makes a great spot for a perspective-check photograph by a travel companion, as you'll appear dwarfed by your surroundings.

Royal Tombs

There are several hundred elaborate, cave-like tombs with intricate rock carvings throughout Petra. Many are empty and you can walk inside them. Just opposite the amphitheater, you'll see the Royal Tombs above ground level with columns cut into the rock wall face. A Byzantine inscription states that one of the tombs was the final resting place of King Malichus II until it was converted into a church in AD 447.

In the immediate vicinity is the ceremonial Palace Tomb, likely used as a place to hold funerals or feasts, and the Tomb of Sextus Florentinus, the Roman governor of Arabia who loved the desert region so much that he wanted to be buried here.

The Cardo

Though devastated by a major earthquake in AD 363, Petra's main street (originally Nabataean but reconstructed by the Romans around the early 1st century BC when the city was a Roman outpost) still has some of its original marble stones and inscriptions. One inscription from AD 114 attests to the restoration of the cardo after Rome annexed the Nabataean Kingdom.

The Roman cardo, or main thoroughfare, a typical feature of cities conquered by Rome, served as the major street for commerce and ceremonial processions.

★ Byzantine Church

Probably built over earlier ruins of Petra is the Byzantine Church, notable for its remarkably intact 30 square feet (70 square meters) of mosaic floors. Pictures in the mosaics include depictions of mythological figures and the four seasons. The church and the mosaics

1: sandstone formation in the Wadi Rum desert
2: mosaic floor in the Byzantine Church 3: the Obelisk Tomb 4: Roman Theater

are still in the process of being excavated and preserved.

In 1993, the famed Petra Scrolls were discovered in the Byzantine Church. The collection of 152 papyrus scrolls dates back to the 6th century AD, confounding experts because this was after Petra is believed to have already started to decline.

The scrolls represent the largest collection of written material from antiquity ever found in Jordan. Studied by teams from the United States and Finland, they contain a great deal of information about the region in the Byzantine era, including agricultural practices, property and estate practices, tax records, and details about how residents of Petra lived in tight proximity to one another.

TOP EXPERIENCE

★ Great Temple

So much is unknown about the Nabataeans, and this includes who exactly they worshipped. The Great Temple is a perfect example of this. The largest freestanding structure in Petra, it underwent extensive excavation at the hands of students from the Joukowsky Institute at Brown University. The institute has a detailed, extensive, and interactive map of the excavation on its website (www.brown.edu/Departments/Joukowsky_Institute/Petra).

The temple is also known as the Temple of Dushara, after the god who some believe was worshipped here. It is generally agreed that it was probably the main place of worship in Nabataean Petra. Complete with its own theater, the entire site is about 92 by 131 feet (28 by 40 meters) and features crafted limestone and a complex system of tunnels. Important to the Nabataeans during the 1st century BC, it was probably also used by the Byzantines.

The massive, complex structure sits on a slightly elevated position with stairs leading up to it and is rectangular in shape with major upper and lower sections. It is one of the most important archaeological and architectural structures in Petra. The Brown University map gives a very complete picture of what used to exist here.

High Place of Sacrifice

A popular early-morning hike is up to the High Place of Sacrifice (take the steps to the left just near the amphitheater and go to the right at the top of the stairs), which takes about 90 minutes each way. The site is at the top of the ridge, where you can see how

Great Temple

The Nabataean Capital

Petra is believed to be the capital city of the Arab tribe of the Nabataeans, who made their first appearance around the 6th century BC, just east of Jordan in the desert. Originating from the southeast of the Arabian Peninsula, they gradually expanded their territory and by the 2nd century BC had established a more organized society.

Highly independent and adept at dodging military conquest, the Nabataeans were influenced by Hellenistic culture, as can be seen in the remnants of their art and architecture. The Greek historian Herodotus refers to the Nabataeans and their capital city of Petra in 312 BC.

Petra has a long history of conquest. It was sacked in 312 BC by the army of King Antigonus. On its retreat, though, the army perished in the desert, hauling a massive load of treasure from the city. Around 63 BC, King Aretas III somehow managed to prevent a Roman military conquest of Petra. After Julius Caesar's assassination in 44 BC and the ensuing chaos, Petra had to begin paying tribute to Rome. Failure to pay resulted in two invasions, one by Herod the Great, who gained control of part of the Nabataean's territory and lucrative trade routes.

After the death of the final Nabataean ruler, Rabbel II, Rome annexed Petra and redesigned parts of it in the Roman style. It's believed that during Roman rule Petra's population grew to about 25,000. But over time and with shifts in trade routes, the Nabataeans profited less and less from trade and eventually abandoned Petra around the 4th century AD. Not much is known about the exact reasons Petra was abandoned, but very few possessions were left behind, suggesting a well-organized, planned departure.

animals were sacrificed in two large depressions with drains for their blood. An altar, obelisks, and the ruins of a building that was probably used by priests are just before where the path leads down to a stone fountain. If you continue walking, you'll see a few more complexes and the ruins of tombs, halls, and an ancient garbage dump.

★ Al-Deir Monastery

This final location requires a bit of a hike to reach, but the Al-Deir Monastery (up a flight of 800 rock-cut steps above the amphitheater) is worth every step. It takes about 90 minutes one way. The path is relatively easy to follow despite its many steps. You'll know you're on the right track when you see a sign to the Lion Tomb.

The monastery stands 164 feet (50 meters) wide and 147 feet (45 meters) tall, and the inner walls are marked with the symbols of crosses.

The highlight of Al-Deir is the crowning urn, which you can walk around the top of by going up some steps. The view of the surrounding landscape from the rim of the urn is fantastic.

Petra Nabataean Museum

tel. 03/215-6060; nabataea.net/museum.html; 9am-4pm daily; free with Petra entrance

Opened in 1994, the Petra Nabataean Museum houses over 600 artifacts that have been discovered in Petra over the years. The three main exhibition halls include a depiction of Nabataean history, specific exhibitions in the area, and a collection of Neolithic artifacts, Nabataean pottery, bronze statues, jewelry, coins, and ornaments.

Petra Archaeological Museum

tel. 03/215-6060; 9am-4pm daily; free with Petra entrance

The older and smaller of two museums in Petra is the Petra Archaeological Museum in an ancient Nabataean cave on the slope of Al-Habis. Opened in 1963, it has a main hall and two side rooms with finds from regional excavations that date to the Edomite, Nabataean, Roman, and Byzantine periods.

Three Cups of Coffee: The Bedouin Coffee Ceremony

If you get a chance to take part in a traditional Bedouin coffee ceremony while you're in Jordan, keep in mind that there will be three cups of (very strong) coffee. The Bedouin consider coffee to be a sacred beverage that is a symbol of wealth and hospitality.

The coffee ceremony is called a jaha, and can be extremely lengthy. Traditionally, it starts at dawn in a Bedouin tent, where water is boiled over coals, and the crushed arabica beans and cardamom are added to the water and left to steep.

When you finally get down to drinking the coffee, there will be three cups. The first cup of coffee is for the soul, the second cup of coffee is for the sword, and the third cup of coffee is in honor of your status as a guest. Another interpretation is that the three cups symbolize hospitality, welcome, and cheer. Asking for a fourth cup of coffee could be considered greedy (and bad for your blood pressure).

preparing Bedouin coffee

During the coffee ceremony, there is usually singing and the rattling of cups and thumping of a long wooden post. The singing was part of the Bedouin tradition in the past during long desert crossings.

Entertainment and Events

Throughout the year, Petra has some unusual entertainment offerings tailored around its sights. Neighboring modern-day Wadi Musa is a small Arab village that offers very little in the way of entertainment, other than eating out.

PETRA BY NIGHT SHOW

8:30pm Mon., Wed.-Thurs.; JD23, under 15 free

Petra shuts down early, but you can experience it by candlelight several nights a week during the Petra by Night Show. During the two-hour show, you can see the *siq* and the Treasury lit up with flickering light and listen to the ancient sounds of a Bedouin shepherd's flute for a soundtrack while local guides tell stories. On full moons, you can also get a guided night tour, but you must check with the Visitors Center and reserve in advance.

ANNUAL PERSEIDS METEOR SHOWER

The annual Perseids meteor shower (Aug., peak nights are Aug. 12-13) is an incredible natural phenomenon that is best seen from Wadi Rum because of the total lack of city lights and noise. At its peak, there are about 50-80 meteors per hour. Many tour companies have outings that you can join to see the showers.

Nabataean Pottery

Another enduring Nabataean treasure is their distinctive red clay pottery, which can be divided into two groups: coarser common wares and the more famous eggshell-thin wares embellished with black designs that range from very small saucers to trays about three feet across. Their pottery-making skills are believed to have been handed down to them from the Edomites.

The production source of Nabataean pottery was near Petra, and included oil lamps (thousands have been found throughout Petra), incense and perfume bottles (found throughout the former empire), and beautiful, thin serving dishes and platters.

Pottery kilns were discovered in the Ash-Sharah Mountains northeast of Petra in 1979, and at least a dozen kilns and portions of numerous on-site workshops have been found since then. At least one kiln was discovered in Wadi Musa as well.

Excellent examples of fine Nabataean pottery can be seen in the museum at Masada and at museums in Petra and throughout Jordan. The kilns can be seen in the Petra Archaeological Museum.

Shopping

Entering Petra is extremely cheap for Jordanians, which is part of the reason that you will see a huge number of locals, including young kids, selling all kinds of things from cheap necklaces to postcards.

GIFTS AND SOUVENIRS

There is no shortage of places to buy cheap, low-end gifts and souvenirs in Petra and the surrounding area. There are many shops just before the entrance to the site that sell all kinds of items and even more vendors inside Petra with makeshift stands selling everything from books about Petra to bottles of artistically arranged sand.

Feel free to bargain with vendors as they will start with a high price, but don't try to go lower than a third of the original price.

SAND CASTLE BAZAAR

tel. 776/389-398; http://petrasandcastle.com; 6:30am-5pm Sat.-Thurs.

Near the entrance to Petra is the well-known and family-owned Sand Castle Bazaar, which sells antiques, stone mosaic art panels, oil lamps, carpets, jewelry, silver, ceramics, and sand bottles. The bazaar has a second location near the Silk Road Hotel in Wadi Musa that ships items worldwide.

WADI MOUSA SILVER JEWELRY PROJECT

road just outside of Wadi Musa; 9am-6pm Mon.-Sat.

A silver workshop and large souvenir store with a small coffee stand can be found at popular pit stop the Wadi Mousa Silver Jewelry Project. The store has a silver craft workshop with the option to have a necklace custom-made (which you need to wait a few days for).

WADI MUSA

The modern village adjacent to Petra has basic amenities, as well as several shops selling souvenirs. Another specialty of shops in Wadi Musa is heavy silver antique necklaces.

LOCAL CRAFTS

Just next to the Visitors Center at the entrance to Petra are two crafts shops that sell many locally handmade products that support local women's organizations. One shop is run for the benefit of the **Rural Women of Jordan** and the other is for the **Ladies' Working Circle of Wadi Musa.** Beyond the more common embroidered items, both shops also sell jewelry boxes with inlaid mother-of-pearl, sand bottles, pottery, metalwork, and woven pillows.

Sports and Recreation

Petra's options for recreation are mostly related to outdoor sports, primarily well-established hikes. If you want to opt for something more luxurious, take in a spa or Turkish bath.

Horses, camels, and donkeys are all available for rent at the entrance of Petra and elsewhere throughout the site. However, many of them are not well cared for and have injuries acquired from being made to work in the tourism trade. This includes the horse-drawn carriages and donkey-drawn carts designed to take people in and out of the first main canyon, which in any case can be a bumpy and unpleasant ride. It's strongly recommended to walk on your own. If mobility is an issue, consider researching the use of animals at Petra online before you arrive, and if you decide using one is necessary, closely check the care and condition of any animal you hire.

HIKING

There are several good hikes in Petra that range from 30 minutes to 90-plus minutes. One of the best trails is at the entrance to Petra, just **above the Treasury.** There are several stops along the trail, which is about 90 minutes one way if you walk to the end.

You can also set out on the trail that starts near the amphitheater, just to the left, and leads to the Lion Tomb, the sacrificial altars, and Al-Deir Monastery.

If you are not an experienced hiker, a guide hired in advance to lead you through this part of Petra could be worth the extra cost. Inquire at the front desks of more than one hotel to get different recommendations and options for guides. Whether or not you go with a guide, try to set out early in the morning, by no later than 8am.

A couple of good choices are **Petra Moon Tours** (based in Wadi Musa, tel. 079/617-0666, www.petramoon.com) and **Bedouin Lifestyle** (Wadi Rum, tel. 077/913-1803, www.bedouinlifestyle.com).

hiking above the Treasury

TURKISH BATHS

SALOME TURKISH BATH

Wadi Musa; tel. 03/215-7342

For some relaxation, the family-owned and run Salome Turkish Bath offers a steam room, exfoliation, and massage. A treatment can be followed with herbal tea. Ask for transportation to and from your hotel when calling to make a reservation, as it is included with their services.

Food

If you eliminate the dozens of area hotels from the equation, Wadi Musa still has a nice range of at least 30 restaurants and eateries to choose from. Most of them are in the village center, and many are within easy walking distance of Petra.

ARABIC AND TRADITIONAL BEDOUIN

RED CAVE

near Petra Main Gate; tel. 03/215-7799 or 077/771-5223; 9am-11pm daily; JD10

A popular spot for a quick bite to eat, the Red Cave is a slightly more expensive option among a field of tourist-centric choices. But they serve generous portions of Bedouin-style dishes, including the rice-based dish with regional vegetables, spices, and meat called *gallayah*. It is very easy to spot with its red sign that hangs over the sidewalk and is one of the many stops to eat near Petra's main gate. They also have a wide selection of vegetarian dishes, including soups and stews.

★ SILK ROAD RESTAURANT

Silk Road Hotel; tel. 03/215-7222; www.petrasilkroad.com; 8am-9pm daily; JD10 for buffet

The Silk Road Restaurant has a tasty buffet in a large dining room, with a wide variety of salads and traditional, typical Arabic and Bedouin dishes. The hotel also has a traditional indoor-outdoor Bedouin-style café that is very small but beautifully decorated with tapestries. It makes a perfect spot for a quiet coffee or tea and a light snack.

AL ARABI

Shaheed roundabout; tel. 03/215-7661; yhamadeen@ link.net.jo; 6am-midnight daily; JD5

The Al Arabi restaurant has some seriously delicious dishes and is very centrally located, which makes it an easy choice for a place to try. For JD2 you can get a milk-and-fruit smoothie to go with the spicy Arabic food they serve.

BUFFET

PETRA ZAMAN

Main St.; tel. 079/553-6391; http://petrazaman restaurant.weebly.com; 9am-11pm daily; JD3

One of the best buffets in town with a nicely done strong Turkish coffee to finish, Petra Zaman serves a variety of salads and vegetarian dishes in their homey, central restaurant. They specialize in the regional favorite chicken-and-rice dish *maglubeh*, which comes in a pot and is flipped onto your plate upside-down when served.

BASIN RESTAURANT

Petra, near the monastery; tel. 03/215-6266; 11:30am-3pm daily; JD17 for lunch buffet

The Basin Restaurant is about 1 mile (1.6 km) past the Treasury in Petra and run by the Crowne Plaza Hotel group. It is the most up-scale option inside of the antiquities sites of Petra; you will see several other snack shops along the way. The restaurant serves a fairly large buffet, which includes several dessert options, and the typical offerings of hummus, salads, and some meat dishes. The patio seating is shaded and the restaurant has a great view of Petra, but they cater to groups and the prices are on the high end.

Bedouin Cuisine

fatteh

Traditionally cooked on an open fire, Bedouin food has a unique style worth sampling while you're in Petra. There are plenty of opportunities to try different Bedouin food, which is typically eaten with the hands, including dipping rolled-up rice balls into sauce.

- There are a few styles of bread that come with Bedouin meals: the more standard pita; the thin, crepe-like *shraak* cooked on a domed pan over a fire; and *taboon,* usually thicker and made from darker flour.

- *Mansaf* is a favorite dish usually reserved for special occasions or for special guests made of stewed lamb meat over rice with yogurt and pine nuts.

- *Maglubeh,* which translates to "upside-down," is a mixture of chicken, potatoes, peppers, vegetables, and rice stacked and layered in one pot and then flipped upside-down onto a plate after it is cooked. It is usually eaten family-style. Several restaurants in Petra serve *maglubeh.*

- *Fatteh,* easy to find and simple, is a delicious dish made from bread and yogurt, which some-times includes hummus, and is served with chopped raw onions and olive oil.

INTERNATIONAL FUSION
★ AL-WADI

Shaheed roundabout; tel. 077/633-1431 or 079/530-0135; mashalehl@yahoo.com; 7am-10:30pm daily; JD4

Serving everything from pizza and pasta to hearty omelets and Bedouin food, Al-Wadi is a popular choice for people who are not sure what they are in the mood to eat. The atmosphere is quaint, with an interior a bit on the dark and cool side, with Bedouin-style touches. Try the lamb casserole if you want some local home cooking.

Accommodations

As a tourist destination, Petra's adjacent village of Wadi Musa offers a variety of accommodations from lower-end to luxury, but the large majority of the approximately three dozen hotels in the area cost under US$100.

UNDER US$100
AMRA PALACE HOTEL
just up from the Shaheed roundabout next to Cleopatra Hotel; tel. 03/215-7070; US$87 d

Centrally and conveniently located, Amra Palace Hotel is also in walking distance to Petra and has a warm, modern exterior and interior with huge beds and a small sitting area in the rooms. The hotel's high points include an indoor pool, a spa, flat-screen satellite TVs, wake-up service, and a terrace for drinks that overlooks the garden. The restaurant offerings in the hotel differ a bit by the season, but in the summer they include an outdoor Bedouin restaurant serving traditional barbecued meat.

LA MAISON HOTEL
off Tourist St. behind Moevenpick Hotel; tel. 03/215-6401; www.lamaisonhotel.com.jo; US$50 d

The smaller 76-room La Maison Hotel has renovated rooms with mountain views, free wireless Internet, satellite TV, and minibars. The furnishings are spare and include only the basics with white tile flooring, giving the general environment a slightly sterile feeling. That said, everything that you do have in the rooms is top-notch and in good condition, including a minibar, air-conditioning, and safe deposit box. There is also a lobby lounge bar that serves food. It is just a five-minute walk to Petra.

AL RASHID HOTEL
Main St., at the Shaheed roundabout; tel. 03/215-6800; rashid@joinnet.com.jo; US$70 d

Known for its super-friendly staff, the Al Rashid Hotel is right near Wadi Musa's main offerings for shopping. The renovated rooms have free wireless Internet and are decorated very simply, but all include a private bathroom. The very small 28-room hotel serves lunch and dinner in its restaurant. It is about half a mile from Petra.

★ ROCKY MOUNTAIN HOTEL
Main St.; tel. 03/215-7393 or 03/215-5100; rockymountainhotel@yahoo.com; US$63 d

A 10-minute walk to Wadi Musa's center, the Rocky Mountain Hotel has some of the most fantastic views in town from its Bedouin-tapestry-decorated dining room and is one of the more attractive budget hotels in town.

The small hotel is popular for its rooftop terrace where you can dine on request, private bathrooms, free wireless Internet (as well as a lobby computer), and shuttle service to Petra. During the day, you can buy a lunch box or light snack and drink. The rooms are decorated with nice touches like fluffy, bright throw rugs and extra-thick blankets for the cold desert nights.

US$100-150
PETRA MOON HOTEL
Petra Visitors Center, Tourist St.; tel. 03/215-6220; www.petramoonhotel.com; US$145 d

Surprisingly upscale and modern for the price, the Petra Moon Hotel is a mere 100 yards (90 meters) from Petra. The rooms are spacious and have pretty, modern art deco touches, such as purple walls next to black-and-white furnishings, and private balconies. The rooms feature satellite TVs, DVD players, telephones, bathrobes, and bathtubs, as well as extra-long beds, minibars, and tea service. The five-story hotel also has a roof garden with an outdoor pool, buffet breakfast in the restaurant, and a small grocery store. You can set up excursions through the concierge desk.

MOEVENPICK RESORT PETRA

Tourism St., next to the Visitors Center; tel.
03/215-7111; www.moevenpick-hotels.com; US$145 d

The Moevenpick Resort Petra is a large five-star resort hotel, part of a regional luxury chain, with 183 rooms featuring a ton of outdoor access on the property. About as close as you can get to the entrance of Petra, the hotel features balconies for every room, a rooftop terrace, and two restaurants. The rooms themselves are pure luxury. Recently renovated, they all come with satellite TV, free wireless Internet, a desk, and every amenity you could need. The hotel also has a tearoom, a plush lobby bar, and a fitness center. The beautiful stone lobby has a massive arched colonnaded courtyard for sitting and relaxing with a tea or coffee.

US$150-200

MARRIOTT PETRA

Taybeh Rd., outside of Wadi Musa; tel. 03/215-6407;
www.marriott.com; $US 160 d

The Marriott Petra is one of the few high-end luxury accommodations in the area and just a 10-minute drive from Wadi Musa. Most of the hotel's rooms have views of Petra or Petra Valley. When you're not hiking, you can stay in the hotel and luxuriate in the outdoor pool, sauna, or Turkish bath, or eat in the hotel restaurant. There's no need to hire a taxi to drive you to Petra: The hotel has free shuttles to take you. The rooms are nice and spacious; they include huge windows for the panoramic views and comfortable touches like couches.

Information and Services

ONLINE RESOURCES AND TOURISM BOARDS

There are several very useful websites if you plan on doing any research about Petra and the surrounding area prior to or during your trip.

For local information, try the **Petra Development and Tourism Regional Authority** website (28 Wadi Musa, tel. 03/215-7093, www.visitpetra.jo), which has good general information about a wide range of things from currency rates to background information.

The website for the village of **Wadi Rum** (www.wadirum.jo) is also a good source for information about locals in the area and has a listing of tourism-related services.

For national information, the **Jordan Ministry of Tourism and Antiquities** (tel. 06/460-3360, www.tourism.jo) has tourism videos and statistics.

The official site of the **Jordan Tourism Board** (tel. 06/567-8294, www.visitjordan.com) is robust and has great photos and essential information.

Finally, the **Royal Society for the**
Conservation of Nature (www.rscn.org.jo) provides information about nature conservation and research, ecotourism, community projects, and handicrafts throughout Jordan.

For general background, **Nabataea.net** (nabataea.net) has quite a few external links and more information about the Nabataeans than you will need.

PRIVATE TOUR COMPANIES

There are quite a few tour companies that operate in Petra. If you are coming from Israel and pay a company there for services, don't be surprised if you are passed off to a gauntlet of different companies and guides before you actually reach your destination.

To make arrangements directly with a company that works in Jordan, there are several good options.

PETRA MOON TOURS

based in Wadi Musa; tel. 03/215-6665 or
079/617-0666; www.petramoon.com

One of the most popular and experienced at working with English speakers is Petra Moon

Tours. They offer a very wide variety of tours, including archaeological, experiential, participatory, and alternative. They also host an annual two-week writing workshop in Petra in June.

BEDOUIN LIFESTYLE

main tourist area at in Wadi Rum; tel. 077/913-1803; www.bedouinlifestyle.com

Run by two Bedouin guides who are lifelong residents of Wadi Rum, Bedouin Lifestyle specializes in tours that expose visitors to Bedouin customs and traditions, including hiking, camel rides, camping under the stars, and jeep rides through the desert.

JORDAN TRAVEL

locations in Petra and Annan; tel. 03/215-4666; www.jordantours-travel.com

Run by a Jordanian family and in operation since 1994, Jordan Travel provides customized, private tours of sites all throughout Jordan.

INSIDER'S PETRA

toll-free U.S. tel. 855/928-2538; www.insiderspetra.com

The U.S.-based Insider's Petra is an alternative for making tour arrangements in advance without the guesswork of dealing with someone in another country. The company can arrange individual and group travel experiences, and the founder and president is an American based in the United States.

VISITORS CENTER

PETRA VISITORS CENTER

outside of Petra Main Gate; tel. 03/215-6029; 6:30am-5pm Sat.-Thurs.

The Petra Visitors Center provides a variety of information about the site. Through the Visitors Center, you can also arrange to hire a **Bedouin guide** (about JD55) for the entire day or for a half day. A **Jordanian guide** (JD12-60) can also be arranged.

Transportation

Getting to Petra is relatively simple, though there are several steps for entry and re-entry when traveling from and to Israel. No vehicles are allowed inside the archaeological site at Petra. The simplest approach is to travel by car or bus from the border and then get around Petra by foot and taxi. Though the village of Wadi Musa is a bit isolated, it has plenty of options for hotels, restaurants, and many amenities. You can also fly from Tel Aviv to Jordan.

ENTERING AND EXITING JORDAN

Transportation options to and from Wadi Musa are limited, as many people arrive and leave with large tour buses. The unofficial public transportation stop is the Shaheed roundabout; just ask anybody and they will be able to point you in the right direction.

Air

Jordan has more than one airport, but the most common entry point is the Amman Airport, about 2.5 hours by car from Petra. Officially known as the **Queen Alia International Airport** (airport-authority.com/AMM), it offers flights between Amman and Tel Aviv on a regular basis.

Car

Aqaba is about a 10-minute drive from the Eilat border crossing and Wadi Musa is about two hours from Aqaba. If you are driving from Amman, it is about 3.5 hours to Wadi Musa.

After you cross into Aqaba, if you are driving yourself to Petra, you can visit one of the two **Hertz** locations (Alnahda St. and Aqaba Airport, tel. 03/201-6206, www.hertz.com, 8am-1pm and 4pm-9pm daily, Aqaba airport closes at 7pm, US$88 d).

Bus

If you are interested in getting to Amman, you can take the **JETT** bus (www.jett.com.jo), which is a big white vehicle that looks just like a tourist bus (rather than a public bus). The bus leaves from Wadi Musa once a day at 5pm and costs JD15. There are several stops in Aqaba where buses depart about half a dozen times a day (8am-6:30pm).

Border Control

Don't be surprised by the incredibly complex, circuitous route that you will need to take through border control when you are coming from Eilat and crossing into Aqaba. You will have your passport checked and stamped several times. Just follow the general flow of traffic or ask any one of the guards standing about if you are unsure about which window to stop at next.

The border opens at 8am, and it is best to be there before it opens to bypass the lines as much as possible.

GETTING AROUND

Once you are in Wadi Musa, it is easy and relatively cheap to take a **taxi** anywhere you need to go. If you do have a car, you won't be at much risk of getting lost. It is a fairly desolate area, and Petra and Wadi Musa are the only attractions for miles around.

Background

The Landscape

You will often hear Israelis say that theirs is a small country, and it's true. The total area of the State of Israel is 8,630 square miles (22,000 square kilometers), about the size of New Jersey in the United States, comprised mostly of landmass. At its widest it is 85 miles (135 km) across, and from the northernmost point to the southernmost point it is 290 miles (465 km).

GEOGRAPHY

Israel's western coast runs along the Mediterranean Sea, and elsewhere Israel is bordered by several other countries, not all of which can be characterized as friendly. In the north, its neighbors are Lebanon and Syria; on the east is the Hashemite Kingdom of Jordan; and Egypt is to the south. The majority (over 60 percent) of the country's 8.46 million people live in either the metropolitan Tel Aviv area or Jerusalem.

The West Bank, a landmass of about 2,270 square miles (3,650 square km), sits between Israel and Jordan; some refer to it as Judea and Samaria and others as the Palestinian Territories. To characterize the West Bank as part of Israel is a grave misnomer. The West Bank's three distinct divisions fall under the categories of A, B, and C: Palestinian Authority-controlled, joint Palestinian Authority and Israeli-controlled, and Israeli-controlled, respectively. About 60 percent of the West Bank is Area B or C, and there are 400,000 Israelis living there, including those who are residents of East Jerusalem.

The number of Arab residents of the West Bank is a matter of huge debate, but is usually cited as somewhere between 2.6 million and 2.7 million. Part of the dispute over accurate census numbers is due to inclusion of populations from East Jerusalem and Gaza.

As for the West Bank's landscape, a major feature in the summer and autumn months is the silvery-green olive trees. The terraced hillsides and fertile valleys have been farmed for generations. The gorgeous landscape of the West Bank is filled with rocky, rolling hills.

Distances in Israel are strikingly small, but the changes in weather and landscape can be drastic. In one hour, you can go from the cool, breezy mountains of Jerusalem to the flat, humid seaside town of Tel Aviv. The coastal plain of the north and its bordering rich farmland, with chalk and sandstone cliffs, is home to deepwater ports.

A number of mountain ranges run from north to south through the landscape. In the perpetually green north, the volcanic-eruption-created basalt Golan Heights tower over the Hula Valley. In the Galilee, where some elevations go as high as 4,000 feet (1,220 meters) above sea level, the hills are mostly dolomite and soft limestone.

Between Israel and the West Bank in the north is the Jezreel Valley, another fertile valley that is heavily cultivated.

Along the eastern side of Israel, part of the Syrian-African Rift that split the crust of the Earth millions of years ago, are the Jordan Valley and the Arava. The land ranges from semiarid in the south to fertile in the north.

The south of Israel is home to the Negev Desert, and although it accounts for about half of the country's landmass, it is the least inhabited. The extremely arid south is made up of low sandstone hills and plains with a huge number of canyons amid the sandstone landscape that are prone to flash flooding in the winter. Campaigns to make the desert green with tree plantings have gained in popularity and practice, but the region is still largely desert.

A bit farther south, the Negev is characterized by barren stone peaks and plateaus littered with rocks. Here you will find three erosive craters that are so huge that they are tourist attractions. The largest, Ramon Crater, is about 5 miles (8 km) across at its widest, about 24 miles (39 km) long, and about 1,600 (500 km) feet deep.

At the very south of Israel is Eilat and the Red Sea, where gray and red granite and sandstone form the base of the landscape.

SEAS AND RIVERS

One of the most significant bodies of water in the region is the Sea of Galilee. At 695 feet (212 meters) below sea level and between the hills of the Galilee and the Golan Heights, it is the most important source of water in Israel and home to several significant historic and religious sites.

The Sea of Galilee feeds the Jordan River and has a circumference of only about 30 miles (48 km). On the southern shore in the town of Tiberias, an electronic meter displays the sea's water level, a number of national interest. In early 2013, following weeks of heavy rain, the sea level was higher than it had been in several years and ended a seven-year drought. In 2016, however, the sea suffered one of its worst years on record, prompting the announcement of another drought.

Coming from the southern mouth of the Sea of Galilee, the Jordan River runs for about 186 miles (300 km), descending 2,300 feet (700 meters) from north to south through the Syrian-African Rift that split the crust of the Earth millions of years ago. The river is fed by tributaries from Mount Hermon and empties into the Dead Sea, the lowest point on Earth. The Jordan Valley ranges from fertile in the north to semiarid in the south.

The Dead Sea sits at 1,300 feet (395 meters) below sea level on the southern end of the Jordan Valley. Its waters have the highest level of salinity and density of any body of water in the world, and are famed for their rich mineral deposits (and mud), which include table and industrial salt, bromine, magnesium, and potash.

Since 1960, the water level of the Dead Sea has dropped by more than 35 feet (10 meters), partially caused by massive water diversion projects conducted by Israel and Jordan. The water diversion projects have reduced the amount of incoming water to the Dead Sea by 75 percent. In 2015, so many sinkholes had appeared in the land and sea from the lack of water that some public beaches and at least one hotel were closed for safety. Sinkholes continue to be a danger in the area.

South of the Dead Sea, which has separated into an upper section and a lower section over time, is the Arava, also part of the Syrian-African Rift and Israel's savanna region. The Arava continues to Israel's Red Sea outlet: the Gulf of Eilat, a subtropical region and home to some of the most remarkable coral reefs and unusual marine life in the world.

CLIMATE

The climate in Israel and the West Bank varies widely from temperate to tropical to alpine. There are two distinct seasons, though two additional very brief transitions are often evident between them.

November to May is the rainy season, or winter. Though it does not rain constantly, rainfall and lower temperatures (about 31°F, just under 0°C, at the lowest in some areas) predominate.

From June through October, there is little to no rainfall, and the temperature rises steadily to a daily low of 66°F (19°C) in some areas before starting its decline in late September. The average high throughout the country during the dry season ranges 84-104°F (29-40°C). The months of July and August are the most brutally punishing in terms of heat.

The variance in climate is marked by mild coastal winters, cooler summers in elevated regions (such as Jerusalem), and almost year-round semidesert conditions in the Negev.

ENVIRONMENTAL ISSUES

Drought and Flash Floods

One of the major environmental issues in the region is drought. The mean annual rainfall is a mere 8 inches (20 cm) in the south and about 28 inches (71 cm) in the north.

In the winter months, the rainfall that does come can sometimes cause flash floods, particularly in the south with its canyons of bone-dry rock. On occasion, a person or an animal will get swept away by one of these flash floods that seem to come out of nowhere, though that is rare.

Heat Waves

The punishing heat of the summer months (particularly during July and August) becomes more pronounced during a prolonged heat wave when the temperature can reach

95-105°F (35-40°C) and higher, even in typically temperate Jerusalem. The greatest risk during heat waves to humans is suffering from dehydration or heatstroke, of which some of the symptoms are dizziness, nausea, confusion, blurred vision, and vomiting. Left untreated, dehydration and heatstroke can lead to complications that can cause death. It is imperative to drink plenty of water while in the region and to protect yourself from the sun, even when there is no heat wave.

Sandstorms

On rare occasion the air in Tel Aviv and elsewhere will be filled with a very fine, yellow dust, typically at the end of a heat wave. It is not exactly a sandstorm, but it turns the air yellow and leaves a layer of dust on everything, including your skin. Sand in the air at the end of a heat wave typically indicates that the heat wave is about to break and is usually followed by a brief rainfall that turns things a bit muddy.

History

The histories of the regions of Israel, the West Bank, and Petra are long, winding, complex, and interconnected. In modern times, differing claims and versions of historical events are very much part of conversations, actions taken related to the land, and political stances on important issues. In other words, the history of this region is very much alive and plays an active role in dictating the future.

ANCIENT CIVILIZATION

Canaan is the area generally defined as Palestine in historical and biblical literature, and is known today as Israel and the West Bank (also called Judea and Samaria or Palestine). The names of Canaan and Canaanites for its inhabitants appear in Egyptian and Phoenician writings from approximately the 15th century BC and in the Old Testament of the Bible. The earliest human inhabitants of coastal Canaan go back to Paleolithic and Mesolithic times. Evidence of human settlements has been found in Jericho dating back to 8000 BC.

Israelites conquered Palestine around the late 2nd century BC or earlier, but there were others before and after them. The Egyptians, the Hyksos, and the Hurrians also invaded. During the Late Bronze Age, about 1550-1200 BC, the Egyptians were the main dominating power in the region, despite challenges from

the Hittites and the Habiru, who some believe were the original Hebrews.

Most archaeological excavations of the area have been conducted after the beginning of the 20th century, and the most significant literary texts on regional history are the Old Testament, the Ras Shamra texts, and the Amarna Letters, dispatches from the 14th century BC from Palestinian and Syrian governors to their Egyptian rulers.

The history and culture of the region has been influenced by a number of cultures, including Egyptian, Mycenaean, Cretan, Hurrian, Byzantine, Mesopotamian, Greek, Roman, and British. It is believed that the Canaanites were the first people to have used an alphabet, based on an archaeological discovery of a language that is widely recognized as a parent language to the Greek and Latin alphabets.

Around the time of the Early Iron Age, approximately 1250 BC, the Israelites came into Canaan after their exodus from Egypt and 40 years of wandering in the desert. In the next century, the Philistines invaded and established a strong hold over the region through a series of city-states, but it was broken under King David's leadership. King David also managed to capture Jerusalem from the Canaanites. The 10th century marked the beginning of the land being known as Israel.

Around the time of King David (about 1000-960 BC), the various tribes of Israel were consolidated into a united kingdom. King David made the Canaanite city of Jerusalem his capital, and according to tradition, moved the Ark of the Covenant, which was believed to contain the living presence of God, to the city. Around 960-920 BC, David's son, Solomon, carried out the wish of his deceased father to build a great temple to house the ark. The period of Solomon's rule is associated with the peak of Israelite grandeur; King Solomon oversaw the building of the First Temple, which was later destroyed. He also managed to forge treaties with neighboring kingdoms, including Egypt and Sheba, and create other important building projects in addition to the Temple.

The Kingdom of Israel was guided by strong, spiritual, monotheistic beliefs in one all-powerful God (Yahweh), the Lord Creator of the Universe. That belief was often used by rulers to help unify the kingdom and its people.

Around 920 BC, Solomon died, and the kingdom splintered into northern and southern halves. Israel was in the north with its capital Samaria, and the Kingdom of Judah was in the south with its capital Jerusalem. A period of frequent instability and lack of unity followed, and by 721 BC, the Neo-Assyrian Empire became the new ruling force, expelling people to make room for its own settlements. In 587 BC, Jerusalem was sacked by the Babylonian king Nebuchadnezzar II. The Temple was destroyed, and the ruling class and skilled craftsmen were deported to Babylon.

The deportation by the Neo-Assyrians and Babylonians of the people of the Kingdom of Israel was the end of the existence of the nation of Israel until the modern state's creation in 1948. It also marked the beginning of the Jewish diaspora and the start of the development of a religious framework in Judaism outside of the land of Israel. Connections between the ancient state and the modern state, including the name, remain an oft-debated and emotionally charged issue.

EARLY HISTORY

After the destruction of the First Temple, between 538-142 BC, there were several waves of tens of thousands of Jews who were allowed to return to Israel. They had varying degrees of self-rule over a period of about four centuries under Persian and Hellenistic authority.

Construction of a Second Temple on the site of the first one began in 521 BC and was finished in 516, during a period when Jerusalem's city walls were refortified.

Around 37 BC, Herod the Great was appointed king of Judea by the Romans and he launched a massive construction campaign, the evidence of which can be seen today in Caesarea, Masada, Jerusalem, and Herodium. Herod remodeled and renewed the Temple to a state of grandeur, but his efforts to appease the subjects to his rule failed to win their loyalty.

After a relatively brief period of rule by the Hasmonean dynasty of Seleucids, the Romans came into power around 40 BC, and Israel became a Roman province. It was not long after that Jesus appeared in Jerusalem and other areas in what is now Israel and the West Bank. By AD 66, ongoing violence and anger against Roman rule and oppression had erupted into full-scale revolt. By AD 70, Jerusalem, including the Second Temple, had been razed to the ground by the Romans.

Several hundred years later, after generations of Roman rule and the declaration of Christianity as the official religion of the Roman kingdom around AD 325, Helena, mother of Constantine the Great, came to the Holy Land to begin construction of some of the world's first churches. Helena supervised construction of several important churches in Jerusalem, and another structure near Hebron.

During the 7th century, Jerusalem was the object of military conquest multiple times. It was sacked and claimed first by the Persians, then taken back by the Byzantines, and finally claimed by the Islamic Empire. Around 690, under the rule of the Islamic Empire, the Dome of the Rock was built on the Temple Mount at the site of the First and Second Temples. According to Islamic tradition, the site is where Prophet Muhammad ascended to heaven. The region would remain under Islamic rule until about 1099.

Between the 8th and 9th centuries, the seventh of a series of historically massive and powerful earthquakes struck the region, destroying Tiberias, Beit She'an, Hippos, and Pella.

Between 1099 and 1291, the Crusaders and their multiple campaigns to reclaim the Holy Land dominated the region until the ancient city of Akko fell to the Egyptians and the Crusader kingdom of Jerusalem was ended. The land was under Mamluk rule until 1516 when the Ottomans took over and ruled until 1917.

MODERN HISTORY

Near the end of the 400 years of Ottoman rule, in 1860 the first neighborhood was built outside the Old City walls of Jerusalem, and the First Aliya, a large-scale immigration of Jews, came to Israel. The Second Aliya came between 1904 and 1914. Both groups were mainly from Russia and Poland. By 1909, the first modern all-Jewish city of Tel Aviv had been founded, and by 1917, British conquest had seized power from the Ottomans with the promise of a "Jewish national home in Palestine" by Foreign Minister Arthur Balfour.

The years between 1918 and 1948 were marked by British rule, and more groups of aliya from Europe. In 1922, the British granted the Mandate for Palestine, with 75 percent of the area going to Transjordan (modern-day Jordan) and 25 percent designated for Jews. In this period, major universities were established in Haifa (Technion) and Jerusalem (Hebrew University).

During the British Mandate prior to World War II, there were several instances of significant violence and fighting between Arabs, who had been living in the region for centuries, and Jews. By 1947, the United Nations proposed the establishment of both Arab and Jewish states in the land of Israel.

MODERN WARS

Achieving the seemingly elusive peace between Arabs and Jews in the region has been an incredibly long and drawn-out process that started before Israel was ever officially a state. In May 1948, the British Mandate ended and the State of Israel was established.

The day after the state was formally declared, five Arab countries invaded Israel, marking the beginning of the War of Independence, which lasted until 1949, when armistice agreements were signed with Egypt, Jordan, Syria, and Lebanon. Jerusalem was divided into east and west with East Jerusalem under Jordanian rule and West Jerusalem under Israeli rule. In 1948-1952, there were massive waves of immigration from European and Arab countries.

In 1967, the Six-Day War joined Jerusalem's east and west sides under Israeli control, though the east side is now either technically part of the West Bank or part of Israel, depending on who you ask. The Six-Day War was followed by the Egyptian War of Attrition (1968-1970) and the Yom Kippur War (1973). Following the Camp David Accords, the Israel-Egypt Peace Treaty was signed, normalizing relations between the two countries.

After peace with Egypt and Jordan, internal domestic violence erupted in 1987 in Israel-administered areas with the First Intifada, followed by another international conflict in the region with the start of the Gulf War (1991). On the verge of a domestic peace agreement in 1995, then-Prime Minister Yitzhak Rabin was assassinated in Tel Aviv. By 2000, the Second Intifada erupted, followed by years of violent regional instability.

In 2005, the highly controversial Gaza Disengagement Plan was carried out under the leadership of Prime Minister Ariel Sharon (who had a stroke and went into a coma almost immediately afterward), whereby Israel unilaterally withdrew all Jewish settlements in Gaza. Subsequently falling under the rule of the terrorist organization Hamas, Gaza has become a hotbed of violence and the center of destruction when fighting breaks out between Hamas and Israel.

Government and Economy

GOVERNMENT

There are two governments in the region, one for Israel and one for the West Bank: the government of the State of Israel and the Palestinian Authority. If and when there is an agreement made about a two-state solution for the region, it will be made between these two bodies. However, the major power in the region, politically, economically, legally, and militarily, is Israel.

Symbolism

The design of the flag of the State of Israel is based on the Jewish prayer shawl with the blue star of David in the center. Israel's official emblem is a menorah flanked by olive branches that represent Israel's desire for peace. The national anthem, *Hatikvah,* was penned by Jewish poet Naphtali Herz Imber in 1878, and the words express the hope of the Jewish people to live as a free and sovereign people in the land of Israel.

The flag used to represent the State of Palestine is a tricolor flag with three equal horizontal stripes of black, white, and green, with a sideways triangle of red on the left. It is based on a variety of different flags, including the one used during the 1916 Arab revolt.

Israeli Government Organization

The Israeli government is a parliamentary democracy, with free elections, a prime minister, and a president. The system is based on the concept of a division of powers between the legislative, executive, and judicial branches.

POLITICAL PARTIES AND ELECTIONS

Israel's unicameral parliament is called the Knesset, and functions in plenary sessions through 15 standing committees and 120 members. The Knesset generally runs for terms of four years, and its makeup is determined after general elections. Both Hebrew and Arabic are officially recognized languages of the Knesset, though debates on issues are conducted in Hebrew with simultaneous translation if a member wishes to speak Arabic.

The party with the most power in the Knesset following the 2015 elections is Likud, the party of Prime Minister Benjamin "Bibi" Netanyahu.

Israeli citizens are eligible to vote from age 18, and they vote for a political party to represent them in the Knesset, not for individuals. There are a wide range of political parties that run for seats in the Knesset representing a broad range of beliefs and positions on the issues.

Election Day in Israel is a national holiday, and if a voter is outside of their polling district, free transportation is provided to them. Polling stations are provided for military personnel, prisoners, hospital patients, merchant sailors, and Israelis on official work abroad.

ALLIANCES AND ENEMIES

Israel's political situation is characterized largely by a range of staunch advocates and lukewarm alliances. Immediately in Israel's neighborhood, Egypt and Jordan are border countries that have generally good relations with Israel. Relations with Turkey blow hot and cold, and Israel is not on good terms with Syria, Lebanon, or Iran.

The positions of western countries vary, but the United States is Israel's single greatest ally in the world. Other countries like Australia and Canada are basically supportive, but there is a great deal of political activism over the plight of Palestinians that originates in the west. The United Kingdom is on good terms with Israel, but its public discourse regularly challenges Israel's settlement policies in the West Bank and its human rights record vis-à-vis Arab residents of the West Bank and Israel.

JUDICIAL AND PENAL SYSTEMS

Israel's judiciary system is independent. Judges are appointed by the president after being recommended by a committee of Supreme Court judges, public figures, and members of the bar. Judicial appointments are permanent until mandatory retirement at age 70.

There are several types of courts, including special courts (such as traffic, labor, juvenile), religious courts, magistrates' court, district court, and the Supreme Court.

ISRAELI MILITARY

The Israeli Defense Force (IDF) has engaged in battle through several generations since the establishment of the State of Israel in 1948, and has fought in six major wars and numerous smaller ones. The highest-level public officials and politicians were often individuals who distinguished themselves during military service and in war.

Service in the IDF is compulsory for all eligible men and women at the age of 18. The male term of service is three years, while women serve for two years, and deferments can be made for students or new immigrants. Reserve duty obligations continue for men until age 51, and every soldier serves in a reserve unit that they are called to work for at least once a year. Ultraorthodox members of society are exempt from military service.

Palestinian Authority Government Organization

The Palestinian National Authority, also called the Palestinian Authority (PA), was established as an interim self-governing authority following the Oslo accords in 2003. The PA governs parts of the West Bank. It used to also govern Gaza, which is now under the control of Hamas.

The PA embodies many of the characteristics of a state, including a legislative and executive body, and a semi-independent judiciary.

Leadership includes a president, cabinet, and a prime minister.

PALESTINIAN AUTHORITY MILITARY

The Palestinian Authority military patrols certain areas of the West Bank, including some parts of Bethlehem, Hebron, Ramallah, and some checkpoints. They are largely a peacekeeping force.

ECONOMY

The Israeli economy was started virtually from scratch almost 70 years ago (officially) and has weathered crises and deprivation of various kinds. The modern free-market economy is bolstered by R&D, high-tech industries, nanotechnology, solar energy, irrigation innovation, agriculture, and a thriving start-up scene admired internationally.

Exports and Imports

In the past 30 years, significant free trade agreements have been made with the United States, the European Union, and a number of countries in Latin America. Israel's export of goods and services is about $80 billion annually.

Israel has struggled to balance its hefty trade deficit, which has been the price for its rapid economic growth. The somewhat limited domestic market and small economy mean that Israel must rely on expansion of exports, particularly industrial exports.

Most imports, about 85 percent, are production inputs and fuel, largely from Europe, followed by the Americas, then Asia and other countries. Most exports of goods go to the United States, Europe, and Asia. Excluding the export of diamonds, Israel's exports to the United States exceed its imports, but its overall imports exceed its exports.

Almost two-thirds of Israel's annual trade deficits have been covered through unilateral transfers, including foreign pensions, money brought in by immigrants, and hefty donations from overseas Jewish fundraising organizations that have gone straight into the coffers of health, education, and social service organizations and institutions. Grants from generous foreign governments, particularly the United States, have also bolstered the economy.

Agriculture

Scarce natural resources, particularly water and arable land, define Israel's production system in its agricultural sector. Aggressive innovation and ongoing cooperation between researchers, farmers, and agricultural industries drive the growth in agricultural production. The development and application of new methods across the board have fostered a sophisticated modern agricultural industry in a country where more than half of the land is desert.

The dogged innovation of the Israeli agricultural industry and its close cooperation with the R&D world have fostered a marketable international agribusiness export sector with agro-technology solutions. Particularly valuable to the outside and developing world have been innovations related to water.

The wide variety of creative solutions developed in response to extremely limited water resources include desalinization plants and drip agriculture.

Most of the country's food and flowers are produced domestically and supplemented by imports that mainly include grain, oilseeds, meat, coffee, cocoa, and sugar. Israel exports heavily to Europe during the winter, sending fruits, vegetables, and flowers.

Industry

Israel has overcome the small size of its country and its lack of raw materials and natural resources by focusing on its highly qualified workforce, R&D centers, and scientific institutes. The country's modern industry is centered around the manufacturing of products with added value. Today, over a quarter of the industrial workforce is employed in high-tech manufacturing.

Much of Israel's modern manufacturing base was developed straight out of 19th-century workshops that produced farming implements and processed agricultural products. When entrepreneurs and engineers with

years of experience immigrated to Israel in the 1930s, they were followed by an increased demand for industrial products during World War II.

Most of the industrial output from Israel centered around traditional products like food processing, furniture, chemicals, plastics, and other items, until the 1970s. This output was followed by a period marked by arms embargoes, which forced industrialization to focus on developing and manufacturing arms for self-defense. Massive investment in the arms industry and aviation gave life to new technologies that would later be the foundation of Israel's high-tech industries. These include medical devices, telecommunications, computer software and hardware, and more.

Two waves of human resources in the 1980s and 1990s bolstered the fledgling high-tech industries: first, the return of Israelis who had been working in Silicon Valley to open development centers for multinationals including Intel, Microsoft, and IBM; second, the huge wave of technicians, scientists, medical workers, and engineers who fled the former Soviet Union in the 1990s after its fall.

Another ace in the hole in Israel's industrial sector is the diamond industry. The country's reputation as a high-quality source for diamond manufacturing and trading has made it a leader in the industry. Tel Aviv's famed diamond district is just one of the ways that the country showcases its cutting-edge technologies, competitive prices, and high yield of polished diamonds from the rough. The Israel Diamond Exchange is the largest diamond trading floor in the world, and diamond exports are in the neighborhood of about $10 billion a year. Most diamond exports are sent to the United States, Hong Kong, Belgium, and Switzerland.

Entrepreneurship and Invention

Israel has earned a reputation for being a hotbed of entrepreneurship, innovation, and invention, bolstered in part by the publication of a book called *Start-up Nation: The Story of*

Israel's Economic Miracle, by Dan Senor and Saul Singer, which details the numerous ways in which the country has repeatedly innovated and invented its way into the 21st century.

The book is based on the remarkable fact that despite being a young country surrounded by enemies and with a population of just over 8.4 million, Israel is home to more start-up companies than Japan, China, India, Korea, Canada and the United Kingdom combined.

Distribution of Wealth

In 2011, massive, long-term public protests over Israel's distribution of wealth broke out throughout the country, centered mostly in Tel Aviv. The protests evolved into weeks-long encampments, mostly of young people, who demanded a more equitable distribution of economic wealth and a more equitable distribution of economic burden in their society.

Between 2005 and 2007, Israel had a millionaire boom, producing more millionaires per capita than any country in the world. The current estimated net worth of Israel's 500 richest people is in the neighborhood of US$140 billion (the country's GDP is about US$306 billion).

One of the most serious issues in the debate about the distribution of wealth stems from the perceived affordability of housing among the middle and lower class. The purchase of second homes in Tel Aviv and Jerusalem by wealthy foreigners is seen as having a major impact on housing prices. Over a span of eight years from 2011-2019, housing prices in some neighborhoods in Israel have risen by 25 percent. Settlements and apartment prices in the West Bank, on the other hand, remain extremely affordable.

Tourism

Israel's most frequently visited cities, Jerusalem and Tel Aviv, continue to work hard to become international tourist destinations. With the gradual stabilizing of internal security in Israel has come a stabilized tourism base. Since 2010, the average number of visitors to the country has been about three million people per year. Most visitors come from Europe, and about a quarter are from the United States. Since 2015, the numbers of tourists to some cities has dropped by as much as 40 percent, in large part due to spates of violence and conflict.

An average of about 30 percent of people visit Israel on a pilgrimage, while others come for leisure, to visit family, or on business. The vast majority of all tourists (about 80 percent), no matter what their reasons are for visiting the country, include Jerusalem as a destination. About 65 percent include Tel Aviv as a destination, about 45 percent go to the Dead Sea, and about 20 percent go to Tiberias and the Sea of Galilee.

People and Culture

DEMOGRAPHY

When the State of Israel was established, the country's population was about 806,000. Today it is more than 8.4 million. About 75 percent of residents are Jewish, over 20 percent are Arab, and all other groups make up just over 4 percent of the population. Over 70 percent of the total Jewish population was born in Israel; a native-born Jewish Israeli is known as a *sabra.*

Israel has 14 cities with over 100,000 residents; the six cities of Jerusalem, Tel Aviv-Yafo, Haifa, Rishon LeTsiyon, Petah Tikva, and Ashdod all have over 200,000 residents.

Israel has had periods of massive, concentrated immigration tied to world events. In 1990 alone, after the fall of the Soviet Union, more than 199,000 immigrants came to Israel, and another 176,000 in 1991. In the past few years, however, there has been an average of 16,500 immigrants to the country per year.

Israel suffers severely on the international stage from problems related to religious and ethnic tensions between the Jewish majority and Arab minority, which impacts its ability to attract a larger number of tourists and immigrants. Though daily life in major cities such as Tel Aviv, Jerusalem, and elsewhere is largely harmonious and various ethnicities and religions peacefully coexist, violence does erupt on a fairly regular basis. With the rule of neighboring Gaza in the hands of Hamas, the greatest domestic threat comes from attacks that originate in Gaza, such as rocket attacks. In recent years, isolated acts of violence carried out by individuals have also been on the rise, particularly beginning in 2015.

The West Bank, with its complex and multilayered governance and distribution of security between the Palestinian Authority and Israel, is also sometimes the source of religious and ethnic tension, protests, and violence.

Jews
As an ethnic group, Jews constitute about 75 percent of the population of Israel. Of those, about 72 percent are Israel-born and about 19 percent are European- or American-born. About 9 percent were born in Africa and Asia.

Arabs
The Arab population of Israel stands at about 23 percent and includes those who are Muslim, Christian, and Jewish. Bedouin and Druze peoples fall under the category of the Arab population.

RELIGION
Though Israel is officially a Jewish state, for all intents and purposes residents of Israel enjoy religious freedom to practice whatever faith they choose.

Those who are registered with the government as practicing Judaism comprise about 58 percent of the population, non-Arab Christians are about 2 percent, and those not

classified by religion are almost 5 percent. Of Israel's Arab population, 84 percent (about 20 percent of the population) are practicing Muslims, and almost 8 percent are Arab Christians. Another 9 percent are Druze.

Judaism
More than 58 percent of the people of Israel identify themselves as practicing the religion of Judaism, an ancient monotheistic faith with varying degrees of orthodoxy. The degree of orthodoxy of the Diaspora of people who practice Judaism around the world varies. The same is true in Israel, with pockets of people practicing orthodox, ultraorthodox, and reform Judaism, to name a few.

Particularly in Jerusalem but also throughout Israel and the West Bank, religious individuals can be somewhat identified by their dress. The men wear long, black coats and large black hats, and the women dress in long skirts and dresses with their arms and legs covered, and their heads covered with a hat, scarf, or wig.

On the day of worship on Friday, religious services are performed in synagogues. The more religious synagogues separate men and women into different worship areas. The holiest site in the holiest city to Jews is the Western Wall in Jerusalem (also known as the Kotel). It is the last remaining piece of the outer wall of the courtyard of the great temple that was twice built and destroyed on that spot in history.

Christianity
The Christian community in Israel, which is about 2 percent of the population, represents a wide variety of different sects from all over the world. There are Greek Orthodox, Russian Orthodox, Catholic, and others. Though they are only a small part of the population overall in the country, the Roman Catholic Church owns a large portion of land in Jerusalem.

Islam
About 20 percent of Israel's population practices the religion of Islam; they are known as

Muslims. The Islamic religion, in general, is fairly strict and generally forbids drinking alcohol. Friday is the day of prayer for Muslims, which makes it a difficult day to visit the larger mosques and the areas around them, such as Al Aqsa Mosque in Jerusalem's Old City, as they become very crowded.

Religious services are performed in mosques, which can often be distinguished by the nearby minaret (tower) from which the call to prayer is broadcast five times a day. In terms of dress, Muslim women (especially in more conservative areas like Nablus) dress in a very covered-up manner with headscarves, long sleeves, and covered legs. In some cases women's faces and hands are also covered.

LANGUAGE

Israel has two official languages: Hebrew and Arabic. But English is a compulsory second language taught throughout much of the secondary-level education system, so the majority of Hebrew speakers and many Arabic speakers also speak and understand English at least at a conversational level.

Almost all signs, menus, transportation tables, and tourist information are written in English.

THE ARTS

The arts in Israel are a well-developed and robust part of society. In addition to the many skills and traditions that generations of immigrants have brought with them from their original countries, the indigenous arts, crafts, and culture play a significant role.

Literature

Israel's literary culture is dominated by Hebrew-speaking authors, but in recent years the Arabic-speaking community has also made significant breakthroughs and contributions.

An ongoing issue in Israel's literary community is the slow death that independent booksellers are suffering due to the existence of a couple of major national chains. These chains are often accused of selling books at much less than their value, angering both authors and independent booksellers, who cannot compete with the prices. In recent years, many independent booksellers have been forced to close.

Despite the challenges to independent sellers, you can still find a variety of different types of bookstores in major cities that sell material in various languages including Hebrew, Arabic, French, and English. Major periodicals in English, Arabic, French, and sometimes Russian are also sold at national chain stores and smaller shops.

Jerusalem hosts a renowned international literature conference every year, but its reputation is sometimes overshadowed by authors who choose to publicly boycott the event because of their concerns over Israel's presence in the West Bank and its position on issues related to the Arab population. The largest Arab city of Ramallah also hosts an annual Literary Festival.

Visual Arts

The thriving visual arts scene in Israel is supported by the large number of museums, from the Israel Museum in Jerusalem to the Tel Aviv Museum of Art, to scores of venues of all sizes. Modern visual art in Israel shows international influences and the meeting of East and West, and reflects the influences of the land, traditions, and cultures.

Visual artists in Israel are engaged in a wide range of disciplines, including painting, photography, and sculpture. Part of what makes Israeli visual art unique is its emphasis and reflections on the local landscape, domestic social issues, and politics.

Music and Dance

The thriving dance scene in Israel has developed mainly in the Jewish folk dance genre and artistic dance centered around stage productions. The major influence of European dance began in the 1920s, and has developed to a highly professional level through a number of companies and ensembles. Dance in

Israel is influenced by the region's various social, cultural, and religious backgrounds.

There are currently over a dozen major professional dance companies in Israel, mostly in Tel Aviv, that perform domestically and internationally. There are also dance groups based in Ramallah.

The annual Israel Festival is the country's major multidisciplinary arts festival, held over a period of a few weeks in Jerusalem.

The music scene in Israel is just as vibrant as other places in the world, if not more. The country's offerings start with the world-class classical music of the Israeli Philharmonic Orchestra and the New Israeli Opera. The country's music scene has been enhanced by waves of European immigrants who brought along skills and influences from the best traditions in the world. The variations of music genres range from Arabic and Hebrew pop to Middle Eastern jazz, rock, and mainstream American music.

Essentials

Transportation

GETTING THERE

There are a variety of ways to get to Israel and the West Bank, though most visitors arrive by air through the international airport in Tel Aviv.

Air

Tel Aviv's **Ben Gurion International Airport** (tel. 03/975-2386, www.iaa.gov.il) is a massive, modern airport with flights to and from almost everywhere in the world. It is about a 15-minute drive from Tel Aviv and about one hour from Jerusalem. Once at the airport, you can

easily get to your destination by hotel shuttle, train, taxi, *sherut* (share taxi), or bus.

During the Jewish Sabbath—late Friday afternoon until Saturday night—things slow down considerably. The airport is still open, but certain airlines might not operate (such as Israel's El Al) and public transportation to and from the airport doesn't operate. Yom Kippur, when almost nobody drives and all public transportation shuts down, would present problems for travelers.

While you're on a flight to Tel Aviv, there are a few things to keep in mind that might be surprising. Airlines differ, but many flights into and out of Israel will serve customers eating kosher meals before other passengers. Some flights will also allow groups to pray during times designated by their religious beliefs at the back of the airplane. When you enter Israel, be prepared with the exact address of where you are going and a rough description of what you're doing in the country. Refrain from describing the details of your travel plans, as it's not necessary.

Jordan's international airport, **Queen Alia International Airport** (airport-authority. com/AMM), has flights between Amman and Tel Aviv on a regular basis. You can also fly into Amman and get to the West Bank by vehicle through one of the border crossings.

FROM NORTH AMERICA

Direct flights from North America to Tel Aviv come largely from East Coast hubs, including Toronto, all three New York City airports, and Miami. Flights with at least one stop also leave from airports in Los Angeles, San Francisco, Seattle, Dallas, and Chicago. The most typical flights from the East Coast are red-eye and take about 18-20 hours door-to-door. The flights from the Midwest or West Coast typically include at least one stop. For travel from the West Coast, expect about 20-24 hours door-to-door. If traveling with children, it can be worthwhile to spend the night in a hotel on

the East Coast before continuing on. The cost of flights vary from as low as $800 from the East Coast to $1,200 from the West Coast, and tend to go up several hundred dollars during summer and holiday seasons.

FROM EUROPE

Some of the most popular direct flights from Europe to Tel Aviv are out of Paris, London, Rome, Moscow, and Kiev. These flights can be done fairly easily in one day, and generally range from around $400-800 (€360-715) for a roundtrip flight out of these locations. The flights are about 4-8 hours, depending on the airline and number of stops. Since the flights are so short and the time difference with Europe is minor, red-eye flights are not relevant.

FROM AUSTRALIA AND NEW ZEALAND

From Australia, flights into Tel Aviv originate in Sydney, Melbourne, Perth, Brisbane, and Adelaide. The flights all have connections, and flight travel times are about 22 hours at a minimum. At least two days should be allowed for travel. In New Zealand, flights leave from Auckland. From Sydney the flights are $1,600-2,500. From Melbourne they are $1,400-2,400, and from Perth, Brisbane, and Adelaide tickets range from about $1,300-2,500.

FROM SOUTH AFRICA

From South Africa, flights into Tel Aviv with just one stop fly out of Johannesburg, Cape Town, Port Elizabeth, Durban, and Mbombela. Flight times from Johannesburg range about 8-10 hours and cost about $500-1200 (R7,190-17,250) roundtrip. Flights from Port Elizabeth and other cities in South Africa take about 14 hours.

Boat

Some people traveling by boat end up visiting Israel while on their way somewhere else, such as cruise ship passengers who stay for 1-2 days or longer, or ferry passengers who are traveling with cars. Both types of passengers go through the international **Port of Haifa** (www.haifaport.co.il). The port includes a large terminal with a wide variety of passenger facilities, including a waiting area, a duty-free shop, a souvenir shop, a cafeteria, a VAT (Value Added Tax) reimbursement counter and currency exchange, a Ministry of Interior services office, and other travel-related services.

Typical customs and immigrations procedures apply for passengers who want to exit the port and enter Israel. There is long- and short-term parking next to the passenger terminal. People on foot can walk about 10 minutes to the port's exit and take a taxicab to wherever they are going in Haifa.

Border Crossings

From **Jordan** (www.visitjordan.com) there are three land border crossings into Israel from the north, center, and south. The central and southern border crossings are the most convenient and frequently used, while the northernmost crossing is isolated from major cities and attractions.

A couple of hours from Petra, the **Wadi Araba Crossing/South Border** (6:30am-8pm Sun.-Thurs., 8am-8pm Fri.-Sat.) connects the resort towns of Eilat in Israel and Aqaba in Jordan. Visas are issued on the spot at the Eilat crossing, and you don't need to provide photographs.

The **Allenby/King Hussein Bridge** is in the southern Jordan Valley (8am-8pm for entering Jordan, 8am-2pm Sun.-Thurs., and 8am-1pm Fri.-Sat. for leaving Jordan). Private cars and tour buses are not allowed to cross, so you have to change vehicles when crossing the border. If coming from Israel and crossing at Allenby, pay for your visa in advance (about JD16) at the Jordanian embassy in Tel Aviv; you will need two photographs. You will receive a visa within 24 hours.

Americans and Canadians coming from Jordan into Israel do not need to apply for a visa in advance. They will be issued a visa at the crossing. There will usually be an exit fee of JD10 when coming from Jordan into Israel. Always travel with a passport that is valid for at least six months beyond your dates of travel.

GETTING AROUND

It is fairly easy to get around Israel because of the excellent bus systems that exist nationally and within the large cities. You can get almost anywhere you want to go by bus, including areas in the West Bank near Jewish settlements. The various train systems are less convenient because of their somewhat limited routes and slow pace, but they do offer a good option for transportation.

Train

The national train system, the **Israel Railways** (www.rail.co.il), is a fairly convenient way to get around many parts of Israel, particularly useful for north-to-south routes like Haifa to Tel Aviv. Just be aware that the railway system is also plagued by ongoing issues that include labor strikes and problems with keeping to the timetable. Daily and multi-journey tickets are available, and kids under the age of five travel for free; prices range from about NIS20-80 roundtrip.

If you go by train from the airport, you can be in Tel Aviv's city center in about 10 minutes and in Jerusalem, near City Center, in under 30 minutes, thanks to a high-speed rail line established in 2018. There are several train lines that leave every 20-30 minutes from the airport.

The two other station stops in Jerusalem are quite far off the beaten path, on the outskirts of town near the zoo and the Malha Mall. Just to get to and from the Jerusalem train station to the city center you will need to take a taxi, bus, or car. The station stops in Tel Aviv are numerous, convenient, and centrally located.

Train etiquette at crowded stops when passengers are boarding and disembarking is somewhat nonexistent. Basically, be prepared to shove your way on or off the train or risk getting stuck.

Light Rail (Jerusalem Only)

Though Haifa and Tel Aviv are in the process of establishing a light-rail train, currently the only city that has a functioning light rail is Jerusalem (tel. 073/210-0601 or *3686 from any local phone, www.citypass.co.il, 5:30am-midnight Sun.-Thurs., 5:30am-3pm Fri. and holiday eves, 7pm-midnight Sat., NIS5.9 for a single ride, discounted multi-ride on Rav Kav Card). Tourists get a discounted public transportation ticket, but there is not an extensive network of stops throughout the city. All tickets are valid for continued use for 90 minutes from the time they are purchased.

The route of Jerusalem's light rail is fairly limited, but there are plans to expand it. It runs roughly along the old border between East and West Jerusalem, and it is convenient if you want to get somewhere in East Jerusalem. It has stops next to the *shuk,* city center, Mount Herzl, and Yad Vashem.

Subway (Haifa Only)

The only subway in Israel is the six-station Haifa subway, the **Carmelit** (http://carmel-ithaifa.com, 6am-midnight Sun.-Thurs., 6am-3pm Fri., after sunset-midnight Sat., single ticket about NIS7). It is most useful for going between the lower city, Wadi Nisnas, and the top of the mountain until Hanassi Boulevard. You can buy a single, daily, or 10-ride ticket.

Bus

The main bus company that essentially comprises the national bus system of long-distance routes in Israel runs the green-and-white **Egged** (www.egged.co.il/Eng) buses. They can get you almost anywhere you want to go, including to some areas in the West Bank. Overall information about buses in Israel is online (http://bus.co.il).

You can pay cash for your bus ticket (about NIS7 within the city) while boarding the bus and do not need to wait at the ticket window if you are traveling from the central bus station. If you know you'll be making a return trip (say between Jerusalem and Tel Aviv),

buy your ticket on the bus and you will get a small discount. Central bus stations in major cities such as Tel Aviv, Jerusalem, and Be'er Sheva display route information in English and Hebrew on monitors in the station.

You can also buy a Rav Kav Card for 10 or 20 rides, also good for transfers, and each ride will be at a small discount.

Once you are on the bus, depending on where you are going, there are a few things to be aware of. First of all, the safety rules are fairly loose, and when seats are sold out on a long-distance bus, you can sit or stand in the aisle or the stairwell at the back of the bus. Eating and drinking are allowed, but if traveling with Jewish orthodox passengers (distinguishable by their black hats, black coats, beards, and white shirts), it is advisable to avoid sitting next to them.

The public transportation depot at the Tel Aviv airport is on the second floor near Gates 21 and 23. Buses go from there to the Egged station at nearby Airport City, and then you can transfer to regular Egged bus lines. The buses between Airport City and the airport are free. The Egged buses will get you to south Tel Aviv's central bus station.

You can also go between Jerusalem's central bus station and the airport by Egged bus. It takes about one hour in normal traffic. Try to avoid making the trip on a Friday afternoon, as traffic will typically be the worst at that time.

The Tel Aviv, Jerusalem, and Be'er Sheva central bus stations have tons of taxis available for hire, as do many of the smaller city bus stations.

In Tel Aviv, the city bus line, **Dan** (tel. 03/639-4444, www.dan.co.il/english), operates a series of very convenient lines throughout the city, and they have detailed information on their English-language website. The buses shut down on the weekend.

In Jerusalem, the bus system is extremely convenient, and the buses are frequent. There is a discounted public transportation ticket for tourists for public buses, operated by Egged. The one-stop shop for Jerusalem transportation information, including the buses, is **Jerusalem Transportation** (www. jet.gov.il).

Though there have been efforts in recent years to have some buses operate during the weekend in Tel Aviv, at the time of publication the only city in the entire country of Israel with buses that operate on the weekends (with partial service) is Haifa. The closest thing to public transportation that is available in other cities on the weekend is the *sherut* (share taxis), which are more expensive and less convenient.

Other bus operators work throughout the country. In the center of the country, bus operators include **Superbus** (www.superbus. co.il), as well as **Kavim** (www.kavim-t.co.il). Kavim also operates in the north. Other operators in the north include **Nazareth Buses** (www.ntt-buses.com) and **Golan Bus** (www. bus.co.il). In the south, the major bus operator is **Metropoline** (www.metropoline. com). Many of these bus operators do not have English websites available.

Taxi and Share Taxi

Throughout Israel, taxicabs are everywhere, but most cost 25 percent more on weekends and between 9pm-5am. One good option if you want to order a cab to come and pick you up (which will cost about NIS5 extra) is to ask any hotel front desk for the name of a taxi company. A company that operates nationally and is recommended by the Municipality of Jerusalem is **Rehavia Taxi** (Taxi Stand at 3 Agron St. in Jerusalem, tel. 02/625-4444 or 02/622-2444).

Sherut **(share taxis)** are an option in most parts of the country, and especially for travel between Tel Aviv and Jerusalem. On the weekend, they are your best (and almost only) option. A *sherut* from Jerusalem to Tel Aviv is about NIS35 or less, and leaves from the base of Tolerance Square seven days a week. The *sherut* from Tel Aviv leaves from the Central Bus Station (106 Levinski St.), just east of Neve Tzedek and Florentin. Keep in mind that a *sherut* will only depart when all of the

seats are full. Depending on how you time it, you might be waiting for 20-30 minutes for the taxi to fill up. While you're riding in the *sherut*, if you need to get out somewhere, it's perfectly acceptable to ask the driver to let you out as soon as possible; drivers stop upon request at the first chance they have to pull over.

Car

Foreigners traveling in Israel are allowed to drive with their foreign license for up to one year after arriving in the country, which is done on the right side of the road. There are quite a number of rental car companies that operate throughout Israel, the most prevalent of which are **Hertz** (19 King David St. in Jerusalem, tel. 02/623-1351, www.hertz.co.il) and **Budget** (23 King David St. in Jerusalem, tel. 03/935-0015), offering a wide variety of options; car rentals run about US$45/day after mandatory insurance is added. The largest domestic car rental company in Israel is **Eldan** (114 HaYarkon St. in Tel Aviv, tel. 03/527-1166, www.eldan.co.il); **Shlomo Sixt** (122 HaYarkon St. in Tel Aviv, tel. 03/524-4935, www.shlomo.co.il) is another good option. The central area for car rental offices in Jerusalem is on King David Street, just across from the King David Hotel, near Mamilla shopping center. In Tel Aviv, there is a stretch of car rental companies right on the promenade at the beach, around 114 HaYarkon Street.

The parking system throughout Israel is uniform and has strict rules, but there are many unspoken exceptions, especially during the weekend when parking rules are suspended. For instance, you might see cars parked on the sidewalk, or facing the wrong direction when parked along the street.

Red and white stripes mean no parking; blue and white stripes signify paid parking by a street meter (a machine that sometimes only takes cash); and gray means free. Other paid parking in certain neighborhoods or small lots will have a yellow-and-black sign with hours of paid parking where you must buy a ticket and leave it on your car dash with the date stamp showing. Paid parking costs approximately NIS10 for 90 minutes.

If you are going to be driving on a daily basis for an extended period of time, yellow gas stations sell an automatic pay-in-advance meter for parking, which you leave on the side of your vehicle. The meter costs NIS100 and you can pay for time on it as you go. If you have a smartphone, you may be able to install the Pango app, which you can use to pay for parking.

Driving yourself is fairly straightforward, as 99 percent of the road signs are posted in English, Hebrew, and Arabic. Don't panic if you think you're on the right road but don't see signs, or see signs for something with a different spelling. It is not uncommon to have no signage to a certain place until the last minute, or for signage names to change in their spelling of the place. The best thing to do is stop and ask for directions. But be prepared to stop more than once because when people give directions in Israel they typically tell you to go to a certain point and then ask someone else.

If you drive into Tel Aviv, take Highway 1 coming from the direction of Jerusalem, and Highway 2 when coming from the direction of Haifa. You will merge onto Highway 20, also known as the Ayalon Highway, which runs through the center of Tel Aviv; about half a dozen exits on the Ayalon get you into different parts of the city.

If you drive into Jerusalem, take Highway 1 and just follow the signs. There are several exits to Jerusalem, some of which will take you far into the outskirts and hills of town. Try to keep as close to the city center as possible, as that is where most hotels are, and where you will have the best luck getting your bearings. Driving within the city of Jerusalem can be extremely complicated and confusing, so take your time, and if you think you are lost, don't hesitate to stop.

TIPS FOR DRIVING

The key to driving while you're in the Middle East is to stay calm and focused, which will help you navigate the tricky road rules. The general guidelines are to keep moving, don't be afraid to improvise (especially in Jerusalem), and don't be afraid to honk your horn. Particularly for Americans, honking can be taken as rude, but it is an important mode of communication in the Middle East, where the roads are often older and narrower.

Some roads were built during times when they were used by donkey carts and horses, so they aren't quite wide enough for cars. Other roads were built up the side of mountains as cities grew over hundreds of years and are extremely steep. Take your time and have a GPS with you wherever you go.

There is no right turn on red, and you probably won't get a ticket if you park on the side of the street facing the wrong way.

CHECKPOINTS

There are checkpoints posted in various locations between Israel and the West Bank, inside the West Bank at the edge of Israel-controlled territory, at the Tel Aviv airport, and at Gaza. Sometimes officers at a checkpoint will ask you to open your trunk, so know where that release is located and be ready to open it. If you are stopped at the airport, you might be asked a series of questions. Don't panic if you are questioned. It is typically related to whatever the current security situation is and not you personally. There are also security checkpoints going into most major buildings where you will need to open your bag for inspection.

GAS CONVERSION

The price of 95 octane gas in the government-regulated system at gas stations throughout Israel fluctuates, but is about NIS6 per liter. At full-service gas stations, it costs 0.18 more per liter. The price of gas is updated by the government once a month and published in all daily newspapers.

Air

At Israel's domestic airport, **Dov Hoz** (www.iaa.gov.il), you can catch flights to the popular southern tourist city of Eilat and the **Eilat**

Domestic Airport (tel. 08/636-3800, www. iaa.gov.il), which takes flights from Arkia, El Al, Israir, and Sun Dor airlines. It is small and convenient, and a good option if you plan to also take in a trip to Petra, Jordan, while you're in the area. Most tour companies will pick you up directly from the airport.

Hitchhiking

Hitchhiking for a ride in Israel and the West Bank is fairly common, but carries the same risks as hitchhiking anywhere else. The regional signal for someone seeking a ride is to point their index finger at the ground in front of them. Especially on the weekend or on Friday afternoons, you will see more hitchhikers than usual.

If you are driving and see a soldier hitchhiking, understand that it is against military regulations for soldiers to hitchhike and they could face time in the brig if they are caught taking a ride.

Visas and Officialdom

Israeli bureaucracy is infamous, but getting into Israel from one of the many countries that they have a visa waiver program with is fairly easy.

VISAS AND PASSPORTS

If you have a passport that is valid for a minimum of six months after your date of exit from the country and you are coming from a visa waiver country, you do not have to arrange for a visa in advance to enter Israel. You will be automatically granted a three-month tourist visa upon entering Israel and there is no fee. The countries that have a visa waiver program with Israel include the United States, the United Kingdom, Australia, Canada, New Zealand, South Africa, and others.

The same six-month rule for passports applies to entering Jordan. If you plan to visit Arab countries (aside from Jordan) before your passport expires, ask for your visa stamp to Israel to be put on a separate piece of paper. It is not an uncommon request, as a passport with a stamp from Israel might make it very difficult or impossible to gain entry into many Arab countries.

Visas to Jordan are usually good for one month and can be obtained from the **Jordanian embassy in Tel Aviv** (14 Abba Hillel St., in the Tel Aviv suburb of Ramat Gan, tel. 03/751-7752), in your home country, or at the Wadi Araba Crossing/ South Border. Aqaba is a special economic zone and there should be no visa fee for Americans.

ISRAELI EMBASSIES AND CONSULATES ABROAD

Israel maintains embassies and consulates all over the world. In the United States, there are Consulate General offices of Israel in New York, Atlanta, Boston, Houston, Chicago, Miami, Philadelphia, San Francisco, and Los Angeles, as well as the Israeli Embassy in Washington, D.C.

FOREIGN EMBASSIES AND CONSULATES IN ISRAEL

Though Jerusalem is Israel's capital city and the seat of its federal government, countries with diplomatic relations with Israel maintain their embassies in Tel Aviv. The reason for this is related to Jerusalem's complicated international legal status. If a foreign government established its embassy in Jerusalem (instead of the consulates there now), it might be seen as an indication of the recognition of Jerusalem as the capital city of Israel. It would also seriously complicate matters in the event that an independent Palestinian state was established.

For that reason, embassies of foreign governments, except the United States, are located in Tel Aviv. Only some countries with an embassy in Tel Aviv also have a consulate in Jerusalem.

The **Embassy of the United States in Jerusalem** (main consulate at 18 Agron Rd., and consular services at 14 David Flusser St., Jerusalem, tel. 02/630-4000 or 02/622-7230 for emergencies and during nonbusiness hours, https://il.usembassy.gov/embassy; jerusalemvisa@state.gov for non-immigrant visa questions) essentially straddles the east-west "border" of the city. Appointments are mandatory for all visits to the consulate.

The **U.S. Embassy Branch in Tel Aviv** (71 HaYarkon St., Tel Aviv, tel. 03/519-7475 or 03/519-7575 for emergencies and during nonbusiness hours, http://il.usembassy.gov) has a useful email alert system that tells American citizens of serious security threats and advises areas not to travel in during times of violence and unrest in the region. Before traveling to Israel, you can register with the consulate or embassy for alerts.

The **U.K. Consulate General** (19 Nashashibi St. in Sheikh Jarrah, Jerusalam, tel. 02/541-4100, http://ukinjerusalem.fco.gov.uk, britain.jerusalem@fco.gov.uk) is in East Jerusalem.

The **Embassy of Canada** (3/5 Nirim St., Tel Aviv, tel. 03/636-3300, www.canadainternational.gc.ca/israel, taviv@international.gc.ca) is in Tel Aviv. Canada does not maintain a consulate in Jerusalem.

The **Embassy of Australia** (Discount Bank Tower, Level 28, 23 Yehuda Halevi St., Tel Aviv, tel. 03/693-5000, www.israel.embassy.gov.au) is in Tel Aviv. Australia does not maintain a consulate in Jerusalem.

The **Embassy of South Africa** (12 Abba Hillel St., Ramat Gan, Tel Aviv, tel. 03/526-2566, www.safis.co.il/sites) is also in Tel Aviv.

The **Embassy of the United Kingdom** (192 Hayarkon St., Tel Aviv, tel. 03/725-1222, www.gov.uk) has its offices in Tel Aviv.

TAXES

The Israeli taxing system uses what they call a Value Added Tax (VAT) of more than 16 percent for the purchase of goods and services. VAT is included in the price of many items (such as food at restaurants). However, if you purchase a more expensive item as a gift or souvenir while in the country (minimum NIS400), ask for tax refund forms. You will be eligible to get the VAT back when going through customs. Note that non-Israeli citizens or people who are not residents of Israel are not required to pay VAT for items like hotels and car rentals.

CUSTOMS

The standard fare of items are prohibited for import by Israeli customs, including weapons and drugs. They also restrict the import of games of chance, pornographic material, plants and soil, and pets. You can bring up to US$200 worth of tax-free gifts into Israel, 250 grams of cigarettes, and one bottle of liquor. You can convert up to US$3,000 in cash at the airport when you leave.

Be particularly careful about buying any kind of antiquities or archaeological artifacts and then transporting them out of the country; you must have a certificate that identifies the object in question. If you buy from a licensed antiquities dealer, they will provide you with such a certificate.

MEDICAL REQUIREMENTS

Inoculations and vaccinations are not required for entry to Israel and Jordan.

POLITICAL AFFILIATIONS AND AGENDAS

If you enter Israel with a specific intention or action that relates to a political agenda (particularly one that would be seen as against the state), you might be prevented from entering the country. This usually applies to large groups with a high profile, but you might be questioned by customs about the purpose of your trip to Israel.

POLICE

In some areas of Israel, there are **Tourist Police** (tel. 03/516-5382) who specifically work to serve tourists with any criminal matter (such as theft) or an emergency. There are tourist police offices in Tel Aviv near the beach, on the corner of Herbert Samuel and Geula Streets. You can also call the tourist police if you have an emergency. Areas without tourist police still have regular law enforcement.

Recreation

Though it is a small country, the options for outdoor recreation in Israel are staggering. In addition to a wide variety of archaeological sites that have national parks around them and serve as both hiking spots and sightseeing locations, there are nature reserves for hiking, biking, diving, camping, swimming, and many other sports.

The recreation opportunities in the West Bank are much less developed, but if you're an experienced hiker, you can find your way to some really nice spots and walk among groves of olive and lemon trees. Many groups organize hikes through social media, which is a great way to participate in a guided hike for a reasonable price with a group.

Petra and Jordan in general are home to vast expanses of desert that offer unique experiences, and they have a fairly well-developed tourism industry.

NATIONAL PARKS AND NATURE RESERVES

The **Israel Nature and Parks Authority** (3 Am Ve'Olamo St., Jerusalem, tel. 02/500-5444 or dial *3639 in-country, www.parks.org.il, moked@npa.org.il for information and tour reservations) maintains parks and nature reserves all over the country that vary widely in price. Many of these include archaeological sites. The least expensive are about NIS5 and the most expensive are about NIS50.

Jordan also has a nice national parks system, though it is recommended that you travel with a tour guide or go on a guided outing. The most highly recommended of Jordan's national park experiences is **Wadi Rum** (Rte. 15 between Aqaba and Petra, www.wadirum.jo), which is on the way to Petra from the border crossing at Eilat-Aqaba.

HIKING

Hiking in Israel, the West Bank, and Jordan is a very popular pastime and favorite family outing, particularly in the warmer dry season. Depending on the area you go hiking in, there are a few things to be aware of. Always bring water, sunscreen, and a hat, even if you are accustomed to being in a warm climate. If you get dehydrated or get sunstroke, the symptoms might not appear until you are in a dangerous condition. Experienced hikers will tell you that if you are drinking enough water, you should be looking for a restroom about every 90 minutes or so.

Along many hiking routes, there are places to swim that include streams, waterfalls, springs, and ancient cisterns (artificially constructed cave-like structures that were once used to gather water from the rainfall). It is culturally acceptable to swim in these areas, though you will always want to have some kind of swimwear or clothes you don't mind getting wet.

If you go for a hike in an area where you think there might be swimming, take some kind of shoes that you can wear while in the water, as the bottoms of water springs are often very rocky.

The biggest and most well-marked hike is the **Israel National Trail** (www.israelnationaltrail.net), a 620-mile (1,000-km) route that stretches from the Red Sea to Israel's border with Lebanon. The National Trail passes through many cities, including Tel Aviv, Haifa, and Netanya. It is possible to follow the trail for any portion you want.

BICYCLING

One of the best and least-advertised features of the boutique hotel industry is that they often offer **free bicycle rentals** to guests. The phrase bicycle rental is a misnomer that you might see on hotel websites; there is typically no fee involved. You can just borrow a bike for free for the day. This custom is particularly common among the boutique hotels in Israel's north coast, in the south, and in Eilat. Ask your hotel when booking if they let guests borrow bikes for free.

In Tel Aviv, the green bicycles of the **Tel-O-Fun** (www.tel-o-fun.co.il/en, NIS20 for a couple of hours) bike rental system can be found throughout the city, and you can pick up and drop off a bike at any Tel-O-Fun location. The first half hour of usage is free, and there is no law in Tel Aviv that requires bicyclists to wear a helmet.

SWIMMING

There are scores of places throughout Israel to swim that include the Mediterranean Sea, public pools, hotel pools (some of which you can use for a fee, even if you aren't a guest), springs and related streams, cisterns, the Sea of Galilee, the Dead Sea, and the Red Sea. In the hot summer month of August in Jerusalem, you might even see fully clothed ultraorthodox families swimming in the public fountains in the parks.

There are sometimes restrictions on swimming, with separated male and female times and areas when the pools are visited by orthodox Jews. If a pool has designated hours for male and female swimming, it will be listed on the schedule, but it is always best to ask. Some beaches, particularly along the Mediterranean, have designated male and female hours, or designated male and female beaches.

DIVING

The hottest diving spots in the region are in the **Red Sea,** with its world-renowned coral reef, year-round warm temperatures, and well-developed tourism industry that is able to cater to the needs of visitors.

COOKING OUT

In general, as with many other things in this region, the rules about cooking out are fairly loose. Basically, you can cook out almost anywhere you want to (within reason).

If you happen to be in Israel during the **Yom Ha'atzmaut** holiday (National Independence Day, around May 14, corresponding to the Jewish calendar), you will see cooking out like you have probably never witnessed. Most businesses shut down and people go out in droves to find any piece of ground they can to cook out on. Even the pristine grass on the grounds of the national rose garden next to the Israeli Knesset is fair game for setting up a small grill and starting a fire. If you pass by one of the large (or small) parks in any city, you will see a cloud of smoke hovering above it from the cookout frenzy.

If you want to take part, it is easy to buy a small grill (NIS20) prior to the holiday at most grocery stores and small convenience stores.

Festivals and Events

Spring

WHITE NIGHT FESTIVAL

Tel Aviv comes alive with festivals and events in the spring. The new Tel Aviv-Yafo White Night Festival (www.tel-aviv.gov.il, June, NIS40-120) features major international and Israeli acts covering a range of musical genres including jazz, funk, rock and roll, and ethnic world music.

TASTE OF TEL AVIV FOOD FESTIVAL

The Taste of Tel Aviv Food Festival (HaYarkon Park; tel. 03/642-2828; www.park.co.il; 8pm-midnight for three days in May; free entry) is the largest food festival in the country.

FELICJA BLUMENTHAL INTERNATIONAL MUSIC FESTIVAL

Also in May is the Felicja Blumental International Music Festival (Tel Aviv Museum of Art, https://en.fbmc.co.il, March, NIS100 per show), a weeklong classical array including chamber music, orchestras, solo ensembles, and folk music. Running since 1999, it's known for staging the debut of many Israeli artists who have gone on to become famous.

CULTURE OF PEACE FESTIVAL

Tel Aviv hosts the only festival of its kind in the Middle East, the annual Culture of Peace Festival (Tzavta Theater, 30 Ibn Gabirol St., tel. 03/695-0156, www.havatzelet.org.il under projects, three days in May, prices vary) includes Jewish, Muslim, and Christian traditional music.

JERUSALEM INTERNATIONAL WRITER'S FESTIVAL

The annual International Writer's Festival (Mishkenot Sha'ananim, Jerusalem, writers-festival.co.il, late spring, NIS140-300) is known for its breadth and length. The multiday festival is held in late spring at Mishkenot Sha'ananim in Jerusalem and features talks with a slew of well-known international authors, film screenings, and an extensive collection of books. Many of the events are in English.

PALFEST

The Palestine Festival of Literature, known as PalFest (various locations in the West Bank and Israel, usually Apr., http://palfest. org, free) was founded in 2008 and showcases the Middle Eastern love for the written word with domestic and international writers, poets, and songwriters through workshops and musical performances. Some events are in English, and the festival is held in various locations throughout the West Bank and East Jerusalem.

ZORBA THE BUDDHA FESTIVAL

In the spring, the big show in the south is the Zorba the Buddha Festival (Negev desert, tel. 08/632-6508, www.zorba.co.il, late Mar.-Apr., NIS450), which runs for four or five days and has a strong spiritual, Buddhist slant in the heart of Israel's southern desert.

Summer

OPERA IN THE PARK

The months of June through August are action-packed in Tel Aviv. The popular Opera in the Park (HaYarkon Park, Tel Aviv, tel. 03/692-7782, www.israel-opera.co.il, from 9pm in July, free) showcases performances by the renowned Israeli Opera. Typical crowds to the opera performances are about 80,000 or more from all across Israel, so go early and take a taxi or bus.

HAIFA INTERNATIONAL FILM FESTIVAL

Held in late September or early October annually, the Haifa International Film Festival (multiple venues, Haifa, tel. 04/801-3471, www.haifaff.co.il/eng, NIS46 and discounted bundles starting at NIS400) has been operating for more than 30 years. It includes events, lectures, and awards.

FESTIVAL OF FESTIVALS

This popular December event is a multicultural food and folklore festival that bills itself as the only one of its kind in the Middle East. Also known as the Holiday of Holidays, the Festival of Festivals (various venues, Haifa, tel. 04/853-5606, www.visit-haifa.org, 9am-8pm Thurs.-Sat. in Dec., free) spans several weekends throughout December, making use of the numerous religious holidays that occur among different faiths and cultures in the region in that month. The festival is held in the Wadi Nisnas neighborhood of Haifa, between the neighborhoods of Hadar and the downtown area around the German Colony. The main staging areas are on Khoury Street, Hatzionut Street, Shabbtai Levi Street, and HaWadi Street.

JERUSALEM INTERNATIONAL FILM FESTIVAL

The Jerusalem International Film Festival (Jerusalem Cinematheque, www.jff.org.il, mid-summer, NIS65-120) has been running for over 30 years and thus is a bit more traditional. The festival's flavor is primarily Israeli film, with a European flair.

JERUSALEM BEER FESTIVAL

Now a highly anticipated annual event, the Jerusalem Beer Festival (Independence Park, Jerusalem, tel. 050/594-8844, www.jerusalembeer.com/en, two days in late summer, NIS85) has been running for over 15 years. Centrally staged near Jerusalem's First Station, the festival features over 120 different beers, both international and local. The festival lasts two days and includes live music.

JERUSALEM WINE FESTIVAL

A bit more refined crowd can be found at the Jerusalem Wine Festival (Billy Rose Garden of the Israel Museum, Jerusalem, tel. 02/625-9703, 8:30pm-11pm, July, NIS80/evening pp, includes a wineglass, unlimited tasting, and admission to the museum's galleries until 9pm on Tues) takes place over three days at the end of July. The festival brings together some of the best wines from Israel's varied collection of local wineries.

END OF SUMMER FESTIVAL

The End of Summer Festival (20 David Marcus, tel. 02/560-5755, www.jerusalem-theatre.co.il, Aug., NIS40-110) is three days at the end of August and features Israeli and foreign artists and performers. The festival consists of some of the latest work in performance art and film. It's hugely popular amongst locals.

HAIFA BEER CITY FESTIVAL

During the last week of August thousands of people gather in Haifa for the annual Beer City Festival (Student's Beach, Haifa, www.visit-haifa.org, last week of August, free) that includes beers from all over Israel and the world and live music.

HAIFA FIRST FRUITS WINE AND CHEESE TASTING FESTIVAL

Held annually around May or June, the First Fruits Wine and Cheese Tasting Festival (Haifa Auditorium Park near the Haifa Cinematheque in the Hacarmel neighborhood, Haifa, tel. 04/853-5606, www.visit-haifa.org, May or June, 6pm-11pm daily) showcases regional wineries, wines, and foodstuffs with an emphasis on Haifa and the north. In addition to wines from vineyards of all sizes, there are booths of boutique cheese makers, chocolatiers, olive oil, and wine accessories; workshops and lectures are also given.

HAIFA PUPPET FESTIVAL

The end of August brings the completely free Puppet Festival (Haifa Auditorium in Central Carmel, Haifa, tel. 052/389-7487, yaeln@012.net.il, Aug, free), which includes children's performances, puppet shows, outdoor events, and an exhibition of masterpiece artistic puppets.

Fall

JERUSALEM INTERNATIONAL CHAMBER MUSIC FESTIVAL

The Jerusalem International Chamber Music Festival (YMCA Mary Nathaniel Hall, Jerusalem, tel. 02/625-0444, www.jcmf.org.il, Sept., NIS80-150) is a several-days-long concert series that highlights a different area of classical music every year.

PRESIDENT'S OPEN HOUSE

For an interesting peek at Israeli culture, head to the President's Open House (Presidential residence, Hanasi St. in Talbiyeh, Sukkot week, free) for photo taking, food, and live music. You can peek into the president's formal sitting room and wander a couple of tightly controlled hallways and rooms. The main events take place in the backyard of the house, just past the lavish Sukkah decorated for the Jewish holiday of Sukkot.

ABU GHOSH VOCAL MUSIC FESTIVAL

The Abu Ghosh Vocal Music Festival (Abu Ghosh, www.agfestival.co.il/en, spring, free) takes place every year in the Arab village of Abu Ghosh just outside of Jerusalem. Concerts are performed in the 12th-century Crusader-Benedictine Kiryat Ye'arim Church in the heart of the village.

Winter

JERUSALEM INTERNATIONAL BOOK FAIR

Now going for more than three decades, The Jerusalem International Book Fair (central locations throughout Jerusalem, www.jbookfair.com, spring, free) brings together agents, authors, and exhibitors of all kinds for a multiday event. The festival's Jerusalem Prize is awarded to a writer who exhibits the principles of individual freedom in society.

SHE'AN NIGHTS FESTIVAL

The annual She'an Nights Festival (Beit She'an National Park, Israel National Parks Service, Oct., free) is not to be confused with the She'an Nights multimedia show that runs in the evenings on a regular basis in Beit She'an National Park. The festival is held annually, usually around the time of Sukkot (Oct.) and includes food, wine, street performers, and music.

JACOB'S LADDER FESTIVAL

There is not a lot to speak of when it comes to entertainment and events in and around Tiberias. It is a fairly low-key area, but one exception is the annual Jacob's Ladder Festival (Ginosar, www.jlfestival.com, May and Dec., NIS170-540), a three-day festival twice yearly of food, wine, and live music in Ginosar, just a 15-minute drive up the Galilee shore from Tiberias.

TAYBEH BREWERY OKTOBERFEST

Yes, there is a beer festival in the West Bank even though it only has one brewery. The annual Oktoberfest (Taybeh, just outside of Ramallah; www.visitpalestine.ps; first Sat.-Sun. in Oct., free) features an interesting mix of local folk musicians, hip-hop, and brass bands as well as local dishes for the food portion of the two-day event.

PALESTINE INTERNATIONAL FESTIVAL

Founded in 1993 to host and showcase international arts in the West Bank, the Palestine International Festival (various locations, www.popularartcentre.org, spring, NIS25) includes a wide array of music, poetry, and performance events in surrounding Arab villages and refugee camps.

TAMAR FESTIVAL

Every year the Tamar Festival (multiple venues, southern Israel, www.tamarfestival.com, Oct., NIS180-250) lasts for several days in October during the Sukkot holiday and features performances by local and international artists. Events during the day include hikes, tours, and children's activities. The festival is known for its choice lineup of activities and music featured in various venues in the south of Israel, including the Botanical Garden at Ein Gedi, the Kikar Sdom villages, and Masada. If you plan ahead and pay a bit extra, you can camp in the midst of the event.

IN-D-NEGEV

For fans of indie rock music and camping in the desert, In-D-Negev (Mitzpe Gvulot, Rte. 234 to Ze'elim Junction, http://indnegev.co.il, Oct., NIS90-220) is three days of music, camping, and celebrating with a general spirit of togetherness and inclusion. The festival organizers even make allowances for kids, with activities and a play area. There is usually a crowd of about 4,000 people.

Food

The food in Israel and Jordan is basically a combination of a Mediterranean and Middle Eastern diet that emphasizes fruits, vegetables, whole grains, and non-processed foods, with a few common threads that can be found almost everywhere you go.

HUMMUS AND FALAFEL

Two of the most famous and favorite food dishes are hummus and falafel. Hummus is a sort of paste that is generally made from chickpeas, olive oil, and tahini. Hummus can be used as a dip on pita or on the side of your plate with main dishes, or as a sort of dressing on top of dishes like salad. It is also commonly used in shawarma sandwiches.

Falafel are deep-fried balls of mashed chickpeas that have been blended with onions and herbs. They can be bought from street vendors, in the *shuk,* and from small shops that specialize in falafel. Falafel is commonly served stuffed inside of a pita sandwich with lettuce, tomatoes, pickles, and tahini (a commonly served paste of sesame seeds and olive oil). It makes a filling and sometimes very cheap meal if you are not buying it in a tourist area.

SHAWARMA

The many shops that sell shawarma are distinguishable by the large chunk of lamb meat cooking on a spit in a prominent location. The meat is cut directly off the spit and typically served in a pita sandwich. You can usually tell if a shawarma shop is good by how juicy the meat is. If customers are not coming to eat frequently, the meat might look a bit dried out.

KNAFE

One of the region's most famed sweets is *knafe,* a traditional Arab sweet cheese treat that comes in various forms.

BEDOUIN

Bedouin food, which can be found throughout the region but particularly in the south of Israel and in Jordan, is traditionally cooked on an open fire and eaten with the hands. Common Bedouin meals include the more standard pita; the thin, crepe-like *shraak* pita that is cooked on a domed pan over a fire; and *taboon,* which is usually thicker and made from darker flour. Other typical Bedouin ingredients and dishes focus on lamb meat, rice, and yogurt.

DRUZE

Arab people of Syrian descent, the Druze are known for their delicious dishes that include many typical facets of Middle Eastern food, such as pita, hummus, vegetables, and lamb and chicken dishes. Druze stew, a delicious combination of meat, potatoes, and vegetables, is worth trying when you're in the region.

KOSHER AND NONKOSHER

Some areas of Israel have a multilayered system for following the religious dietary laws of being kosher. The level to which the restaurant follows kosher regulations determines the type of certificate it will display. Kosher certifications are always posted in public view and are often advertised on websites.

Particularly in Jerusalem, most restaurants are kosher, so they will either serve milk or meat, but not both. At a kosher restaurant that serves meat, for example, you will not be able to get a latte or ice cream for dessert. They might serve milk-substitute dishes, though, so it is always worth asking.

The production of kosher food is overseen by a rabbi who certifies the food as being kosher according to Jewish law. The level of supervision and adherence to religious dietary law determines the differing types of kosher certification. The three levels from least restricted to most restricted are kosher, glatt kosher, and *mehadrin* kosher.

Some hotels cater to religious Jewish customers and adhere to kosher religious laws. These establishments will basically not serve a hot meal on Friday night (unless it was cooked hours earlier and kept warm somehow) or on Saturday until nighttime. Restaurants that keep kosher close on Friday in the late afternoon (depending on the time of the year, around 3 or 4pm). Some will not open again until Sunday morning, but many open later in the evening on Saturday after the Sabbath has ended, generally around 9pm, and then stay open later than usual.

Accommodations

There are several different types of accommodation options when traveling throughout Israel, the West Bank, and Jordan. Options range from five-star resorts to extremely casual accommodations, such as renting a room in someone's home.

GUESTHOUSES (ZIMMERS)

The fairly ubiquitous and lovely option of a *zimmer* (also spelled *tsimmer*) is one of the best ways to experience regional hospitality, food, and culture. A *zimmer* is typically family-owned and operated, and set up as a series of private cabins or bungalows spread across the *zimmer* grounds and centered around a main building where meals and sometimes recreation can be found.

There are two main categories of *zimmers*: luxury and luxury-rustic. The luxury-level *zimmers* include amenities such as a large flat-screen TV and a whirlpool hot tub. The rustic *zimmers* usually won't include any kind of TV and will emphasize a more natural, country experience. *Zimmer* cabins often have private porches, but ask in advance about bathing accommodations, because the bathtub (and sometimes the toilet) are often placed in a prominent spot in your room and not inside a closed-off bathroom.

While the north, in the Galilee and Golan Heights, is full of *zimmers*, they can be found throughout Israel. The website for **Rural Tourism in Israel** (www.zimmeril.com) is an invaluable resource, as many *zimmers* don't maintain their own website, social media pages, or even an email address and can only be reached by telephone.

Some *zimmers* are located in *moshavs*, which are basically cooperative neighborhoods that are sometimes a bit off the beaten path.

GUEST ROOMS

Arranging for a guest room is a tricky matter, and you probably need to be in the country already or have a trusted go-between like a tour guide to make arrangements for one.

Particularly in the West Bank, you can inquire at the shops that cater to tourists (especially in Bethlehem) if they know of any houses in town that rent rooms out.

BUDGET, MIDRANGE, BOUTIQUE, AND HIGH-END HOTELS

The range of hotels in Israel, the West Bank, and Jordan is just as broad as any other region that caters to tourists, but the main thing to be aware of is that the size of rooms, even in higher-end hotels, are often on the smaller side, more in accordance with European standards. Budget hotels and midrange hotels will often be a bit sparse on furnishings and will have tile floors (not carpeting), but they usually have free wireless Internet. High-end and luxury hotels, in turn, will usually charge for Internet access, but have every amenity you can imagine, down to the smallest detail.

There are a couple of common features for the majority of hotels in the region. One is that breakfast is included with the rate of your room. In some cases, you can upgrade your room rate to have all meals included. Once in a blue moon, the standard breakfast-included practice is not kept at a hotel, so it is always best to ask in advance.

The included breakfast is typically served around 7am-9am, but always ask in advance. It includes hot and cold drinks, salads, eggs, toast, and more. If you try to take food out of the breakfast area, hotel staff will charge you extra.

The general practice for room service in midrange hotels and up is that you can often get at least hot and cold drinks delivered to your room.

HOSTELS

The hostel system in Israel is surprisingly well-developed and the best of the hostels book extremely far in advance, sometimes as far as six months. Hostel options in Jerusalem include places to stay in the Old City as well as near the city center. The Israel Youth Hostel Association (IYHA) (tel. 059/951-0511, www.

iyha.org.il/eng) has English-speaking hotline representatives and a very easy-to-use booking website for hostels throughout the region. Though the hostel listing is not comprehensive, it includes hostels that are sanctioned members of the IYHA.

FIELD SCHOOLS

The Society for Protection of Nature in Israel (tel. 03/638-8653, www.natureisrael.org) is more than just a resource for nature activities in Israel. They also maintain a group of affordable, hostel-like accommodations throughout Israel that are called field schools. Many field schools are located near major tourist destinations and offer an excellent alternative to a more expensive hotel. The organization's emphasis on nature preservation also means that field school staff are knowledgeable about outdoor activities in the region where they are located.

KIBBUTZIM

There are a number of Israeli communal kibbutzim (members of collectives who live in communities throughout the country) that generate part of their income from operating luxury resort-like hotels or more midrange accommodations. When you stay at one of these kibbutz hotels (Ramat Rachel on the outskirts of Jerusalem is a good example), you will typically have access to certain kibbutz amenities, including a swimming pool, playgrounds, and the like.

CAMPING

You will be hard-pressed to find a clearinghouse of published information in English about camping in Israel, the West Bank, and Jordan. Though there are many, many excellent camping sites throughout the area, and particularly in Israel, information about campsites, costs, and regulations is generally only published in Hebrew.

The two best resources to check for camping information are the Israel National Parks (tel. 02/500-5444 or dial *3639 in-country, www.parks.org.il) and the Society for **Protection of Nature in Israel** (tel. 03/638-8688, www.natureisrael.org).

ARAB AND BEDOUIN GUEST ENCAMPMENTS

Throughout the south of Israel, the Negev, in the Golan Heights, and in Petra, you can experience Arab and Bedouin culture by visiting a **Bedouin tent.** The easiest areas to find these are in the Negev at Sefinat Hamidbar, Khan Hashayarot, and Khan Beerotayim, as well as at the Mashabei Sadeh junction, near the ancient city of Avdat and the village of Ezuz. Petra and the surrounding area are also excellent places to find Bedouin tent encampments, in which you can stay overnight.

Conduct and Customs

The general rule with conduct and customs in Israel, the West Bank, and Jordan balances on two ends of the spectrum: live and let live or extremely strict. In general, the more religious the area you are in (Jewish, Muslim, or Christian), the more strictly the conservative conduct and religious customs are adhered to. This includes everything from clothing to food, and it particularly applies to women.

ETIQUETTE

There are a few things to keep in mind when navigating the general regional etiquette of the Middle East. One is that you will likely encounter at least one person who is unwilling to shake your hand for religious reasons, again, particularly if you are a woman.

Also in a general sense, people are more direct, less prone to affected pleasantries, and often more willing to get involved in other people's personal affairs (including giving unsolicited advice or directions). This directness and familiar approach to communicating takes some getting used to.

CONVERSATION

When talking with people, it is advisable to speak up and be as direct and decisive as possible. If you know what you want or what you are after in a conversation or interaction, you're likely to get better results than if you hesitate or are timid about what you're saying. Don't be alarmed or intimidated if someone speaks to you in a loud voice that sounds like yelling. It is just conversation.

In Israel, the common greeting is "shalom," which means *peace*. In Arabic, it is "as-salaam alaikum," which means *peace be upon you*. If you say nothing else in the native languages, try these two phrases out.

CLOTHING

Before you travel to any area, check in advance what the customs regarding clothing are. In some towns in the West Bank, women don't show their bare arms and legs and a man in shorts would stick out. In the ultraorthodox areas of certain towns in Israel, people also dress extremely conservatively. It's not advisable to walk through these areas in shorts and a tank top on a hot summer day. In Jerusalem, there have been cases of women being accosted and even physically attacked for dressing in a manner that is considered immodest by the religious.

Jerusalem is more conservative, while Tel Aviv is a bit wild.

RELIGIOUS SITES

Most religious sites have signage to explain the site's expectations. Depending on the site, this can include covering your head, taking off your hat, covering your shoulders, having covered legs, keeping your cell phone off, refraining from flash photography, refraining from photography completely, keeping your speaking voice low, no public displays of affection, and on and on.

Mosques

Visitors to mosques in this region need to be aware of several things. Shoes are not worn inside, legs and arms should be covered, women and men worship separately, women cover their heads, and non-Muslims in general should not enter areas of prayer without an official guide or escort. If men are praying in protest on the streets, as happens in Jerusalem from time to time, don't stand in front of them for too long.

Temples

Visitors to temples can expect, depending on the sect of Judaism, to wear modest clothing and be designated to areas of prayer for men and women. Men typically wear a skullcap and women sometimes cover their head in the more religious temples.

Churches

Conduct in churches in this region varies depending on the sect of Christianity. Modest clothing is generally expected, but in general most churches maintain a relaxed and welcoming atmosphere to visitors from around the world.

DINING

When you go out to eat, you can stay as long as you want. It is the rare waiter who will approach you in any eating establishment to ask if you want the check, unless the restaurant is extremely busy. The custom is to let customers sit as long as they want until they are ready to leave. The waiter might continue to come back and ask if you want more of something, but they will not prompt you to leave.

The one exception to this is the preemptive measure some places will take during Shabbat (particularly in Jerusalem) if you come in without a reservation. The customary approach is to explain that you don't have a reservation, to which the host or hostess might say they have a table for you but it is reserved for a group that is arriving in a certain amount of time. That is your cue to understand that you can sit and eat, but you must leave within the allotted time.

SHABBAT (SABBATH)

The Jewish Shabbat (or Sabbath) starts on Friday at sundown and ends on Saturday night after three stars are out in the sky (when it is fully dark). Depending on how religious someone is, Shabbat can involve restrictions on using motorized transport, electricity, working, and handling money. Taxicabs still operate, but their fees are higher than normal. The one exception to public transportation shutdowns is in Haifa, where some public buses run on a limited schedule throughout Shabbat.

In Israel, Shabbat is the weekend for everyone except Muslims and most Arabs, whether they are religious or not. All government offices and services stop, including public transportation. One exception to a major shutdown is East Jerusalem, which is predominately Arab, and where everything continues to hum along as normal. Arab areas shut down on Friday afternoon, which is their major prayer time during the week. Also, any restaurant that is kosher is closed. In Jerusalem, that means that all but about 15 restaurants shut down for more than 24 hours.

RAMADAN

The holy month of Ramadan is generally from early July to early August; the exact dates vary slightly every year. Ramadan involves fasting from morning until evening, when a large meal is eaten. It is the one time of the year during which it would be quite inconvenient to visit a predominantly Arab area, as many things close or operate on a special schedule.

Health and Safety

MEDICAL CARE IN ISRAEL

Israel's health care facilities are modern, world-class operations, and if you need medical service, you can go to one of its many hospitals. Dial 101 from any phone at any time if you have an emergency (most people speak English). Some cities also have pharmacies and drugstores that operate 24 hours a day.

VACCINATIONS

You do not need vaccinations to enter Israel or Jordan, but it is best to travel with valid health insurance. You can get travel insurance for your trip, which will protect you in the case of any major mishaps.

You will see signs posted from the Israeli Ministry of Health reminding people to carry water with them and drink it regularly (even if they're not thirsty) to avoid dehydration and heatstroke. Tap water is perfectly safe to drink in all parts of Israel.

BOMB SHELTERS AND ALARMS

Many houses, buildings, and hotels have bomb shelters. If you don't know where a bomb shelter is, the next safest place is in a stairwell as far from windows as possible.

The sound of a wailing bomb alarm is unmistakable and could go off at any time of day or night. From the time you hear the sound of the alarm, you have about two minutes to get to a bomb shelter or safety before impact.

Israel's highly sophisticated Iron Dome system (partly funded by the U.S. government) has been tested plenty in recent years, and it is very effective at intercepting and detonating incoming rockets while they are still in the air. Most of them never hit the ground.

CONTACT LENSES AND GLASSES

If you wear contacts lenses or glasses, note your prescription level in advance, as you will be able to easily buy contacts or glasses in any drugstore, optometrist shop, or glasses store once you are in the country. There is no doctor's prescription required.

STRAY CATS

You might notice a large number of stray cats wandering around different cities, particularly in areas where there are more people. Most of these cats are not only strays, they were born on the streets and might carry disease. Don't pet stray cats or try to feed them.

Practical Details

WHEN TO GO

You will generally want to avoid traveling to Israel, Jordan, and the West Bank during major religious holidays. Jewish, Muslim, and Christian calendars are available online, but the biggest holidays are Passover and Easter, Hanukkah, Sukkot, Ramadan, and Christmas. Hotel rates will be higher during these times, and many venues will be closed in certain areas.

The month of August is not an advisable time to visit Jerusalem. It is a time of year when many children are not in camp, day care, or school, and it is also a major holiday for the ultraorthodox community. Jerusalem becomes extraordinarily crowded (including the museums, roads, and restaurants) during this time.

WHAT TO PACK

There are a few items that are must-haves, and most are easily replaceable if something gets lost. Take at least one cotton scarf, shoes that can handle uneven, slippery surfaces, a serious hat, and a trusted indigestion medication.

Bringing the right clothing is incredibly important, particularly **comfortable shoes,** as there is a lot of rough terrain and bumpy cobblestones at various tourist sites, parks, and some cities. In some places you will need to **dress conservatively,** particularly if you're a woman. A few long-sleeve shirts, pants, and long skirts should suffice. At least one cotton scarf to guard against dusty winds, chills, and sweat is a must for men and women. A scarf can be easily purchased once there, too.

Stick to skirts that are either below the knee or more fitted, and lower-heeled or flat shoes, preferably with more support so you won't twist your ankle while walking on the uneven stones.

No matter when you go, take some kind of **light jacket** (heavier in the winter months), as it can get cool in many areas during the evening. You will also need a **hat, sunglasses, sunscreen,** and a **good water canister** if you have one. Beyond that, you will just need a sense of adventure and a **good guidebook.**

MONEY

At the time of writing, exchange rates for the New Israeli Shekel (NIS) were approximately:

- 4 NIS = 1 U.S. dollar, 1 Euro
- 5 NIS = 1 pound sterling
- 1 NIS = 4 South African Rand
- 10 NIS = 4 Australian dollars
- 10 NIS = 4 New Zealand dollars

Israel

The Israeli currency is the New Israeli Shekel (NIS or shekel), and it is divided into 100 Agorot. The most current exchange rates are available from the **Bank of Israel** (tel.

02/655-2211, www.boi.org.il/en). The U.S. dollar generally hovers around an exchange rate of US$1 to NIS4. Major tourist areas have currency exchange services.

Israeli banks are open Sunday-Thursday about 9am-noon, then close for a few hours, and open again about 2pm-5pm. Cash can be withdrawn from ATMs 24 hours a day.

Non-Israeli citizens can get a VAT (Value Added Tax) refund if they don't have an Israeli passport and are visiting Israel as a tourist. The goods should have been bought in a store included in the VAT refund program and the purchase amount in one tax invoice including VAT must exceed NIS400.

The West Bank

You can pay for goods and services in the West Bank using U.S. dollars or Israeli shekels, though it is best to use shekels.

Jordan

The official currency of Jordan is the Jordanian dinar (JD), and it is divided into 10 dirham, 100 qirsh (or piasters), or 1,000 fils. Half-dinar and one-dinar coins are most common, and bills come in 1 dinar, 5 dinars, 10 dinars, 20 dinars, and 50 dinars denominations. JD1 is typically worth about US$1.40 or NIS5.20.

If you are coming from Israel, change your shekels to Jordanian dinars before crossing the border, or at one of the money-changing desks that are along the way as you pass through the many stops that you need to make it through the border (Eilat-Aqaba border crossing). If you are trying to pay in shekels after entering Jordan, it will really put a damper on your trip, as most people will have no idea what to charge you.

ATMs and Credit Cards

It's possible to pay for goods and services with major credit cards and even some debit cards throughout the region. The farther off the beaten path or into the West Bank you travel, the more vital it will be to have cash on hand.

BUDGETING

There are a few workarounds to save money when traveling in the region, particularly when traveling in more expensive places like cities and tourist-centric areas. Look for hotels that include breakfast in the room rate; they are largely the norm in the region. Many higher-end restaurants, including those in hotels, offer business lunch specials. Bus tickets include transfers if used within 90 minutes of change. Happy hour is not very common, but some hotels do offer it. If you're in an indoor-outdoor market (*shuk*) near closing time, many vendors will sell at reduced prices. Below is a list of average prices (NIS) to expect for common purchases throughout the region:

- cup of coffee NIS 8-14
- hotel room NIS350-1,000
- falafel NIS8-12
- breakfast NIS 15-25
- lunch NIS12-20
- dinner NIS 40-60
- pint of beer/glass of wine NIS12-20
- public transport ticket NIS5-10
- museum entrance fees NIS10-20

SHOPPING AND BARGAINING

There are a few unique aspects to shopping in the region. One is that if you are in Tel Aviv or Jerusalem, there are numerous Israeli designers who design and make wonderful clothes, shoes, bags, and other accessories. These are unique, domestically produced items that are largely sold only in Israel. They are typically extremely well made, durable, and attractive. Made-in-Israel products are sold everywhere from large shopping malls to small boutique stores on the street.

One of the worst places to shop is in tourist areas. The prices, quality, and selection are often worse than elsewhere, and vendors will often try to convince you that something is antique or much more valuable than what they are selling it for. The upside, however, is that if you have the stamina, you can drive a pretty hard bargain with shopkeepers, particularly in Jerusalem's Old City shops. Shop owners might chase you after you start walking away in refusal of a price they offered, shouting out an even lower price. The general rule of thumb is not to expect to negotiate the price down by more than a third.

When buying antiquities of any kind, always get the certificate of authenticity from the seller, as grave robbers and antiquities thieves are a major regional problem. If an antique item you bought is discovered by customs, you will not be able to leave the country without a certificate from the seller.

If someone buys you a present while you are in the country, don't leave it wrapped; be prepared to have it scanned for bombing materials by the Israeli security personnel at the airport if you mention you are carrying a gift someone gave you.

TIPPING

It is customary to tip about 15 percent to service personnel, including waiters and bellhops, but it is not customary to tip taxi drivers. In restaurants, you will often see a note on your receipt that says *Service is Not Included*, which means that they want your money.

OPENING HOURS

Attractions and businesses are open during typical business hours of 9am-5pm; It's 10am-10pm for most restaurants. Most museums keep 10am-5pm hours, but are often closed on Mondays. Restaurants that keep kosher close early-to-mid-afternoon on Fridays, depending on the time of year. Generally, closing time is several hours before sunset, which varies based on the time of year. Establishments like this reopen when it's fully dark and a few stars are showing in the sky. During the month of Ramadan, Muslim restaurants do not serve food and many businesses are closed during the day but open at night.

Public Holidays

Dates and times of major public holidays vary slightly based on the calendar year. Following is a list that gives a general sense of when the holiday occurs.

- Purim – March
- Passover – March
- Easter – April
- Shavuot – May
- Ramadan – July
- Rosh Hashanah – September
- Yom Kippur – September
- Sukkot – September/October
- Hanukkah – December
- Christmas – December

COMMUNICATIONS
Phones and Cell Phones

Phone numbers in the region are typically 10 digits, often starting with the number 05 for cell phones and 02 for landlines. When you are in the country you need to dial the 0 if calling from a cell phone, but not if you're calling from overseas. The country code is 972. There are differences in cell phone networks in Israel and the West Bank. Cell phone service in general is much better in and near larger cities like Jerusalem and Tel Aviv, and the deeper in the West Bank you travel, the worse the cell reception and wireless network service. Some fairly large cities have extremely limited cell service. Essentially, don't rely on your cell as your only source of information for maps and travel.

Pre-paid cell phones can be purchased at the airport for about NIS300-500, depending on the pre-paid minutes, and most electronics stores also sell them.

Internet Access

One of the best features of Israel is the fact that you get free wireless Internet almost everywhere you go. Most restaurants, cafés, and coffee shops have free wireless Internet, so as long as you have a computer you can get Internet access. Internet cafés are much less common, but most large luxury hotels with business centers will agree to let you use their business center computers for a small fee.

Shipping and Postal Services

Postal services in Israel are fairly reliable and easy to find, though it may take several weeks for anything you mail to reach its destination. It's not recommended to mail packages, especially if the contents include any type of antique, which requires a customs stamp at the airport. A postcard stamp costs about NIS8 to an international address.

Printed and Online News

There are several major newspapers in English, Arabic, Hebrew, and Russian that are distributed throughout Israel and the West Bank. Those published in English and Hebrew include the *Jerusalem Post, Ha'aretz,* and *Yedioth Ahronoth* (known online as Ynet), among others. The *International New York Times* is published only in English, and *The Jerusalem Report* is an English-only magazine sold in bookstores and on newsstands.

Arabic publications include *al-Sennara* and *al-Ittihad,* among others.

MAPS AND TOURIST INFORMATION
Maps

Israel's **Ministry of Tourism** (https://info.goisrael.com) has online maps of major cities and pilgrimage sites as PDF files that can be easily printed. **Eye on Israel** (www.eyeonisrael.com) has interactive maps of Israel and major cities, including tourist sites, hotels, geographical information, and a historical atlas. Hard copy maps, including city maps, road maps, touring maps, and hiking maps are available for online purchase on the Ministry of Housing and Construction's website (www.gov.il).

Tourism Offices

There are tourist offices located throughout Israel in major cities, including in **Tel**

Aviv (Ben-Gurion International Airport, tel. 03/975-4260, doritk@tourism.gov.il, open 24 hours a day), **Jerusalem** (Jaffa Gate, tel. 02/628-0403, orenm@tourism.gov.il, 8:30am-5pm Sat.-Thurs., 8:30am-1pm Fri.), **Nazareth** (58 Casanova St., tel. 04/675-0555, ronnye@tourism.gov.il, 8:30am-5pm Mon.-Fri., 9am-1pm Sat.), **Eilat** (8 Beit Hagesher St., tel. 08/630-9111, eilatinfo@tourism.gov.il, 8:30am-5pm Sun.-Thurs., 8am-1pm Sat.), and **Haifa** (48 Ben-Gurion St., www.tour-haifa.co.il/eng, 9am-5pm Sun.-Thurs., 9am-1pm Fri., 10am-3pm Sat.).

WEIGHTS AND MEASURES

The Israeli system of weights and measures is based on the metric system. The most common conversions include 1 kilogram (2.2 pounds), 1 meter (1.1 yards), 1 liter (1 quart), 1 dunam (0.22 acres), and 1 kilometer (about 0.6 miles).

ELECTRICITY

Similar to most European systems, Asia, and the Middle East in general, Israel uses a 220V system (220V-240V) at 50 Hz. European visitors shouldn't have any trouble, except for a possible converter for the unique Israeli outlet system of a type H plug that has two flat prongs that form a V and one vertical grounding prong on the bottom. You can buy a converter for an American plug at any electronics store for about NIS4.

Visitors from the United States will need to make a few adjustments because they use 110V appliances, and need to be aware that Israel's 50 Hz system might cause some problems with certain items (such as analog clocks), even with a transformer. Don't plug your 110V directly into an Israeli outlet, and be careful bringing a hair dryer from the United States.

TIME ZONES

Israel, the West Bank, and Jordan all operate three hours ahead of Greenwich Mean Time (GMT+3), but only Israel and the West Bank also operate on daylight saving time. They switch to daylight saving time on the last Friday before April 2 and switch back on the last Sunday before Yom Kippur (about late Sept.-Oct.) every year.

Traveler Advice

OPPORTUNITIES FOR STUDY AND EMPLOYMENT

There are many work and study opportunities in Israel, but unless you plan on staying long-term, most of the work opportunities are voluntary and unpaid. There are several types of programs such as international volunteer advocacy programs, religious study programs with cooperation between universities, and others that allow visitors to participate in the local culture. Experiences can include internships and fellowships in Tel Aviv, touring and experiential activities, volunteering programs, Hebrew language programs, Arabic language programs, academic programs, Jewish studies programs, and activist-based travel (similar to volunteer experiences).

ACCESS FOR TRAVELERS WITH DISABILITIES

Israel is pretty well-equipped for travelers with disabilities, but the older sections of cities and archaeological sites, such as Jerusalem's Old City, are less so.

The West Bank and Jordan are not really set up to serve travelers with disabilities, though some of the nicer hotels do make certain accommodations.

TRAVELING WITH CHILDREN

Though it might seem like a tricky area to travel with children, nothing could be further from the truth. As long as adequate preparations are made for sun protection and hydration, it is very easy to travel in the region with a child. The general culture in this part of the world is centered on family life (including extended families), and people are accustomed to families that have at least 3-7 children.

For this reason, it is easy to be accommodated with children in hotels, restaurants, and tourist destinations. One caveat to this is that the public safety standards are not as strict as North Americans are accustomed to, so it's best to be a bit more alert about what's going on around you. Most hotels will have very nice cribs (some, but not all, charge a bit extra) that you can use in your hotel room. Ask for the crib in advance and it will be set up in your room on arrival.

The general regional atmosphere in regard to children is accepting also in restaurants, where something like a crying baby likely won't cause any of the customers to even bat an eye. The typical sounds and actions of babies and children are so familiar in the culture that you can usually expect a very understanding and helpful reaction when traveling with children.

WOMEN TRAVELING ALONE

It can be a bit tricky for a woman to travel solo in certain parts of Israel, and in the West Bank and Jordan. The best way to keep a low profile is to dress conservatively. There aren't any real dangers for a woman traveling alone in this region, but it is also not that common, and it is a male-dominated society with widely varying expectations about the role women play.

SENIOR TRAVELERS

The most important thing for senior travelers to keep in mind while traveling in the region is to be cautious about the potential dangers of the Middle East sun. In the hottest summer months, it's advisable to conduct outdoor activities before 10:30am and after 3pm. When it's hottest, always drink plenty of water and wear a hat and sunscreen.

LGBT TRAVELERS

The main place in the region where LGBTQ people are openly accepted is Tel Aviv and its immediate suburbs. The city caters to gay and lesbian travelers so openly that its municipal website has a special section for gay and lesbian travel.

In much more conservative Jerusalem, there are some gay bars and clubs, but in day-to-day life, gays and lesbians are very much under the radar. Jerusalem is a city where you will seldom see anybody, gay or straight, making public displays of affection.

TRAVELERS OF COLOR

The complex and ever-evolving socio-political situation in this region means that travelers of color may encounter some profiling and harassment. The most common scenarios involve moving between points of transit, border crossings, and entering and exiting the airport. Keeping your answers simple and resisting the urge to argue is usually the best course of action if any issues arise. Also, it's culturally acceptable, or at least typical, for strangers to ask about ethnic, religious, and political affiliations.

Resources

Hebrew Phrasebook

PRONUNCIATION

Hebrew is, for the most part, a straightforward language that is logical and doesn't have very many exceptions.

Consonants

Aleph	Ah-lehf
Bet	BEHT
Gimel	GEE-mel
Dalet	DAH-let
Hey	Hay
Vav	Vahv
Zayin	ZAIN
Khet	het
Tet	TEHT
Yud	YOOD
Kaf	KAHF
Lamed	LAH-med
Mem	Mehm
Nun	NOON
Samech	Sah-Mekh
Ayin	Ah-yeen
Pe	PEH
Tsadi	SAH-di
Quf	KOOF
Resh	Rehsh
Shin	SHEEN
Tav	TAHV

Accent

Through the ages, as the Jewish population spread throughout the world, different accents developed. Most people who speak Hebrew today speak what is known as modern Hebrew, which is the Hebrew that is used in Israel. The variance in pronunciations is seen primarily during religious ceremonies, especially when reading from the Torah.

COMMON PHRASES

Hello, good-bye, or peace Shalom
Good morning Boker tov
Good evening Erev tov
See you soon L'hitra'ot
What's up? Ma nishma?
Yes Ken
No Lo
Thank you Toda
Excuse me/I'm sorry Slicha
Please/You're welcome Bevakasha
What is your name? (male/female) Eich korim lecha/lach?
My name is... Shmi...
How are you? (male/female) Ma shlomcha/shlomech?
Fine, OK B'seder
Not good Lo tov
Excellent Metzuyan
I'm tired (male/female) Ani ayef/ayefa

BASIC, COURTEOUS, AND RELIGIOUS EXPRESSIONS

Please excuse me Slicha bevakasha
Just a minute Shneeyah
Just hold on a minute Shneeyah rega
No thank you Lo toda
Thanks to God Toda le-El
Happy holiday Hag sahmeah

EATING AND SHOPPING

Do you have...? (male/female) Yesh
lecha/lach...?
How much? Kama zeh oleh?
I want... (male/female) Ani rotzeh/rotzah...
I don't want... (male/female) Ani lo
rotzeh/rotzah...
Money Kesef
Change (literally, "leftovers") Odef
Waiter/waitress Meltzar/meltzarit (though
you will always just say Slicha)
Water Mayim
Coffee Kafeh
Latte Kafeh Afuh
Tea Tay

GETTING AROUND

I'm going to...(male/female) Ani nose'a
l'.../Ani nosa'at l'...
There is... Yesh...
There is no... Ain...
**Do you know where...is? (male/
female)** Aht yoda'at eifoh nimtza...?/Ata
yodea eifoh nimtza...?
Wait/Just a moment Rega
Restaurant Mis'adah
Bathroom (services) Sherutim
Post office (mail) Do'ar
Street Rechov
Boulevard Sderot
Market Shuk
Museum Muzion
Synagogue Beit knesset
Church Knaissia
Central bus station Tachana merkazit
Taxi (regular) Monit
Shared taxi Sherut
Automobile Mechonit
Train Rakevet
Bus Otoboos
Hotel Malon
Hostel Akhsaniya
Room Cheder
Beach Chof
Grocery store Makolet
**What is this?/What is the reason for
this?** Mah zeh?
Food Okhel

Right Yemina
Left Smola
Straight Yashar

AT THE BORDER AND AT CHECKPOINTS

Passport Darkon
Open (your trunk) Leef to ach
Are you American? Ahtah Amerikai?

EMERGENCIES

**Do you speak English? (male/
female)** Ata medaber Anglit?/Aaht
medaberet Anglit?
**I don't speak Hebrew (male/
female)** Ani lo medaber Ivrit/Ani lo
medaberet Ivrit
Police Mishtara
Doctor Rofe
Hospital Beit cholim
Passport Darkon

USEFUL QUESTIONS

Who Mi
What Mah
When Matai
Where Fh-fo
Why Lama
What is this? Mah zeh?
How Eich
How much does it cost? Kamah zeh oleh?
Where are the restrooms? Eifo
hasherutim?
What time is it? Mah hasha'ah?
What happened? Mah karah?

NUMBERS

One Achat
Two Shtayim
Three Shalosh
Four Arba
Five Chamesh
Six Shesh
Seven Sheva
Eight Shmone
Nine Tesha
Ten Eser
Eleven Achat esrey

Twelve Shtem esrey
Thirteen Shlosh esrey
Fourteen Arba esrey
Fifteen Chamesh esrey
Sixteen Shesh esrey
Seventeen Shva esrey
Eighteen Shmoneh esrey
Nineteen Tsha esrey
Twenty Esrim
Thirty Shloshim
Forty Arbaim
Fifty Chamishim
Sixty Shishim
Seventy Shivim
Eighty Shmonim
Ninety Tishim
One hundred Mea
Two hundred Mataim
Three hundred Shlosh meot
Four hundred Arba meot
Five hundred Chamesh meot
Six hundred Shesh meot
Seven hundred Shva meot
Eight hundred Shmone meot
Nine hundred Tsha meot
One thousand Elef
Two thousand Alpayeem
Three thousand Shloshet alafim

DAYS OF THE WEEK

Sunday Yom rishon
Monday Yom shenee
Tuesday Yom shlishi
Wednesday Yom revi'i
Thursday Yom chamishi
Friday Yom shishi
Saturday (Sabbath) Shabbat

TIMES

Hour, time Sha'a
Day Yom
Week Shavua
Month Chodesh
Year Shana
Today Ha'yom
Yesterday Etmol
Tomorrow Machar

GLOSSARY

Hello, good-bye, or peace Shalom
Saturday (Sabbath) Shabbat
Shared taxi Sherut
Market Shuk
Boulevard Sderot
Guesthouse Zimmer

Arabic Phrasebook

PRONUNCIATION

The Arabic alphabet is written from right to left in a cursive style and has 28 letters. Each symbol can be written in several different ways according to its position in a word.

Consonants

a/ā/l	alif
b	bā'
t	tā'
ṯ	thā'
j	jīm
ḥ	ḥā'
kh	khā'
d	dāl
ḏ	dhāl
r	rā'
z	zayn/zāy
s	sīn
š	shīn
ṣ	ṣād
ḍ	ḍād
ṭ	ṭā'
ẓ	ẓā'
c	'ayn
gh	ghayn
f	fā'
q	qāf
k	kāf
l	lām

m	mīm
n	nūn
h	hā'
w/ō/ū	wāw
y/ē/ī	yā'

Other Symbols

ā	alif maddah
n/a	tā' marbūṭah
ā/ỳ	alif maqṣūrah

Accent

As the population of the world grew and spread throughout eons of human civilization, the Arabic language grew with it. Today, it is spoken by over 300 million people in 22 countries in North Africa and the Middle East. As such, accents and dialectical variations are vast. In Israel and the West Bank, the accent is considered to be Palestinian.

BASIC PHRASES

Hello, nice to meet you Marhaba ana saeed b-mareftak
Do you speak English? Hal tatakallam al ingliyziyya?

Do you understand English? Hal tafham al ingliyziyya?
Yes Na-am
No Laa
I understand Fahamt
I do not understand Laa afham
Please repeat Aiyd law samaht
Good morning Sabaah il-khair
Good evening Masa il-khair
Good night Tisibh ala khair
Hello Marhaba
Hello (response) Ahlan
Goodbye Ma-a is-salaama
How are you? (male/female) Kayf haalak/haalik?
Fine Bikhair

ASKING FOR HELP

I don't speak Arabic Ana laa atahadith al-arabiya
Please speak more slowly Laww samaht tahadith ala mahil
Where is the bathroom? Ayn il-hammaam?
I'm sorry Ana aasiff

Suggested Reading

MODERN HISTORY AND CURRENT AFFAIRS

There are numerous books about the current affairs and modern history of Israel and the region, but a few stand out. Also, once you are in Israel, look for the fairly robust selections in the English sections of bookstores that have titles by regional authors.

Carter, Jimmy. *Palestine: Peace Not Apartheid.* Simon and Schuster, 2006. A controversial look by former president Carter on how to bring peace to Israel and justice to Palestine.

Cohen, Rich. *Israel Is Real: An Obsessive Quest to Understand the Jewish Nation and Its History.* Picador, 2009. An entertaining yet scholarly look at the history of the Jewish people from the time of the destruction of the Second Temple through the modern era.

Oz, Amos. *How to Cure a Fanatic.* Princeton University Press, 2010. Amos Oz is a beloved Israeli author and also internationally acclaimed. This pair of essays is about how to settle the question of real estate to bring peace to the Israeli-Palestinian relationship.

Senor, Dan, and Saul Singer. *Start-up Nation: The Story of Israel's Economic Miracle.* Twelve, 2009. A comprehensive and illuminating look at how Israel, a country of just over seven million people and limited resources, manages to produce more start-ups than more stable and well-developed countries like Japan, Canada, and the United Kingdom.

Zertal, Idith, and Akiva Eldar. *Lords of the Land: The War for Israel's Settlements in the Occupied Territories, 1967-2007*. Nation Books, 2009. The tragic yet gripping story of Jewish settlement in the West Bank and Gaza Strip and how it has impacted every facet of modern Israeli life, as told by a professor (Zertal) and a leading journalist (Eldar).

HISTORICAL CHRONICLES

Among the mountains of historical chronicles that have been published, there are several that are must-reads.

Collins, Larry, and Dominique LaPierre. *O Jerusalem!* Simon and Schuster, 1972. This extremely thick book is an account of the bitter 1948 dispute between the Arabs and Jews over Jerusalem and emphasizes prominent individuals and the British in the process.

Flavius, Josephus, and William Whiston (translation). *The Wars of the Jews*. Digireads.com, 2010. One of the most frequently referenced historians of his time, Flavius Josephus was a Jewish historian and Roman citizen who wrote detailed (and some say questionable) accounts of the events of his time in AD 75.

Oren, Michael. *Six Days of War: June 1967 and the Making of the Modern Middle East*. Presidio Press/Random House, 2002. This international best seller by the U.S. ambassador to Israel details six days of the definitive Arab-Israeli battle in June 1967 and its lingering impact on the peace process and the world.

Suha, Sabbagh. *Palestinian Women of Gaza and the West Bank*. Indiana University Press, 1998. A collection of insider-perspective essays on the roles of women in Gaza and the West Bank and their approach to dealing with issues of gender, feminism, and politics.

LITERATURE

The literary scene in Israel and the West Bank is robust, but there are a few voices who dominate the industry.

Grossman, David. *Someone to Run With*. Farrar, Straus and Giroux, 2000. The fictional story of life and love on the streets of Jerusalem, told from the perspective of a 16-year-old boy.

Oz, Amos. *Scenes from Village Life*. Houghton Mifflin Harcourt, 2011. A collection of essays set in a bygone era in a fictitious pioneer village.

FOOD

A great selection of books on food in the region can be found at local bookstores.

El-Haddad, Laila, and Maggie Schmitt. *The Gaza Kitchen: A Palestinian Culinary Journey*. Just World Books, 2013. Full of rich illustrations, this book explores the culinary heritage of people living in Gaza and the West Bank using recipes from their kitchens.

Ottolenghi, Yotam, and Sami Tamimi. *Jerusalem: A Cookbook*. Ten Speed Press, 2012. Jerusalem locals Ottolenghi and Tamimi explore the cuisine of their home city with its varied cultural and religious influences.

TRAVEL AND EXPLORATION

Insider guides to the region are largely published in Hebrew, and there are a few specialized guides to specific regional travel experiences.

Saar, Jacob. *Israel National Trail and the Jerusalem Trail (Hike the Land of Israel)*. Gefen, 2011. A full guide to the Israel National Trail and the Jerusalem Trail and the hiking experiences they present, including maps and tips for the trail.

Szepsi, Stefan. *Walking Palestine: 25 Journeys into the West Bank*. Interlink Books, 2012. An alternative look at how to skip the politics of the West Bank and just experience its natural beauty through beginner walks and more advanced hikes, including information for local guides, restaurants, and accommodations.

POLITICAL

The plethora of political books related to Israel and the West Bank is astounding, but you can start with some classics, old and new.

Said, Edward. *Orientalism*. Vintage Books, 1979. From one of the region's most noted critics and authors comes an examination of how the West observes Arabs.

Shehadeh, Raja, and Penny Johnson. *Shifting Sands: The Unraveling of the Old Order in* the Middle East. Profile, 2015. A collection of essays edited by Shehadeh and Johnson about the shifting power paradigm in the Middle East.

Yousef, Mosab Hassan, and Ron Brackin. *Son of Hamas: A Gripping Account of Terror, Betrayal, Political Intrigue, and Unthinkable Choices*. Tyndale, 2010. A controversial, real-life account from the eldest son of a founding member of Hamas.

THE HOLOCAUST

The number of books written on the Holocaust is almost countless, and titles continue to be published every year.

Range, Peter Ross. *1924: The Year That Made Hitler*. Hachette Book Group, 2016. The dark story of Hitler's life in the year 1924 and how it shaped the monster that he would become.

Safdie, Moshe. *Yad Vashem: Moshe Safdie—The Architecture of Memory*. Lars Mueller Publishers, 2006. Israel's most famous and prolific architect examines his painstakingly designed project: the Yad Vashem Holocaust memorial in Jerusalem.

Suggested Viewing

MODERN CULTURE AND CURRENT AFFAIRS

The Israeli movie industry is very active and films often become nominees for Academy Awards. Following are a few selections.

Binisty, Thierry. *A Bottle in the Gaza Sea*. 100 minutes, 2011, Hebrew and Arabic subtitled in English. Two teenagers, a Jewish girl in Israel and an Arab boy in Gaza, change the course of their lives after becoming pen pals.

Burshtein, Rama. *Fill the Void*. 90 minutes, 2012, Hebrew and French subtitled in English. A young orthodox woman is pressured into marriage with a widower.

Yedaya, Keren. *Jaffa*. 106 minutes, 2009, Hebrew and Arabic subtitled in English. A look at the intersecting lives of Jews and Arabs in Tel Aviv's Jaffa.

Internet Resources and Apps

There are a good number of websites with useful information about Israel, the West Bank, and Jordan in English. Some websites are slow to update or are missing information, so it's always a good idea to cross-reference information. The following is a selection of the best, most relevant, and most useful.

JERUSALEM

www.gojerusalem.com

A private venture dubbed simply GoJerusalem. com contains helpful, descriptive, and fairly up-to-date listings on hotels, tours, and sightseeing, though much of the information has been republished on iTravelJerusalem.

www.itraveljerusalem.com

The official tourism website of the city of Jerusalem was launched in 2012 and has current information on food, accommodations, sightseeing, and events.

www.jerusalem.muni.il

The Municipality of the City of Jerusalem website has basic information about the city and some resources for visitors.

Jerusalem Audio Walking Tours App

The Jerusalem Development Authority has created a free app that guides visitors on routes through the Old City.

Waze Driving App

Born and raised in Israel before it went international, never be without the Waze app if you drive anywhere in Israel and the West Bank.

GOVERNMENT

www.gov.il

The Israeli government portal is a good jumping-off point for any branch of the Israeli government online.

www.mfa.gov.il

The official site for the Israeli Ministry of Foreign Affairs has domestic facts, issues, statistics, and foreign-government-relations information.

TOURISM AND CITIES

www.tour-haifa.co.il/eng

The City of Haifa's official tourism website is a good resource for navigating the city.

www.tel-aviv.gov.il

The City of Tel Aviv's official website also has useful information, maps, and tips.

www.eyeonisrael.com

The private enterprise Eye on Israel offers interactive maps of Israel and its major cities, including tourist sites, hotels, geographical information, and a historical atlas.

https://info.goisrael.com

The official Israeli Ministry of Tourism website has online maps of major cities and pilgrimage sites as PDF files that can be easily printed.

www.visit-tel-aviv.com

The Tel Aviv Tourism Board's official website has every kind of information you could possibly need to enjoy the city by day or night.

PARKS AND RECREATION

www.parks.org.il

The official website of the Israel Nature and Parks Authority contains a comprehensive listing of the names, locations, admission fees, descriptions, and contact information for national parks and nature reserves throughout Israel (if you can get the spelling of the park's name right).

www.israelnationaltrail.com
A useful guide to the Israel National Trail, with maps, information, and guidelines to taking the hike.

ACCOMMODATIONS

www.iyha.org.il
The official website of the Israel Youth Hostel Association (IYHA) is easy to use and allows you to check the availability of youth hostels in Israel by region.

www.zimmeril.com
Though not an official site for *zimmers,* this site has a fairly comprehensive listing of *zimmers* (guesthouses) throughout the country, including their contact information, which can be very hard to find otherwise.

TRANSPORTATION

www.dan.co.il
The official website of the Tel Aviv city bus line Dan has route and ticketing information.

www.egged.co.il/Eng
The official website of Israel's national bus company Egged, which also operates throughout Jerusalem, has route and ticket information, but you need to dig a bit to get the right bus number.

www.rail.co.il/en
The official website of Israel's national train system has convenient and easy-to-use listings of times and prices for rail tickets.

www.citypass.co.il
Jerusalem's official light rail website has schedules, ticketing, a route map, and news updates for passengers.

www.tel-o-fun.co.il/en
Tel Aviv's citywide bicycle rental website for the green Tel-O-Fun Bikes has detailed instructions and payment and usage information for bike rentals.

WEST BANK

www.thisweekinpalestine.com
The website of the weekly publication *This Week in Palestine* is a useful guide for events and things happening in the West Bank.

http://travelpalestine.ps
The official tourism website for the West Bank is not as robust or user-friendly as it could be, but it is one of the few online resources of its kind available in English.

www.visitpalestine.ps/en
A tourism website that's a level above anything else available, Visit Palestine is detailed and comprehensive and very easy to use.

JORDAN

www.tourism.jo
The official website of the Jordan Ministry of Tourism and Antiquities is particularly useful for background and historical information.

www.visitjordan.com
The official tourism website of Jordan has the basic information you might need before visiting.

www.visitpetra.jo
The official website of the Petra Development and Tourism Regional Authority has good general information about a wide range of things from currency rates to background information.

http://international.visitjordan.com
Petra's neighboring village Wadi Rum has a website that is a good resource for local information on restaurants, hotels, and resources.

Index

UV

W

List of Maps

Photo Credits

All photos © Genevieve Belmaker except: title page photo © Mirovic | Dreamstime.com; page 2 © Natalia Volkova | Dreamstime.com; page 3 © Alexirina27000 | Dreamstime.com; page 6 © (top left) Khmarskyi Maksym | Dreamstime.com; (top right) Viculia | Dreamstime.com; (bottom) Dorinmarius | Dreamstime.com; page 7 © (top) Amit Erez | Dreamstime.com; (bottom left) Inge Hogenbijl | Dreamstime.com; (bottom right) Serhii Liakhevych | Dreamstime.com; page 8 © (top) Rafael Ben Ari | Dreamstime.com; page 9 © (top) Xantana | Dreamstime.com; (bottom left) Kushnirov Avraham | Dreamstime.com; (bottom right) Krystsina Ivanch | Dreamstime.com; page 10 © Masar1920 | Dreamstime.com; page 12 © (top) Rndmst | Dreamstime.com; (bottom) Alefbet26 | Dreamstime.com; page 13 © Antonella865 | Dreamstime.com; page 14 © Klaus Hoffmann | Dreamstime.com; page 15 © (top) Aleksandar Todorovic | Dreamstime.com; (middle) Linda Johnsonbaugh | Dreamstime.com; (bottom) Rita Phessas | Dreamstime.com; page 16 © (top) Evgeniy Fesenko | Dreamstime.com; (bottom) Hitmans | Dreamstime.com; page 17 © Mindauga Dulinska | Dreamstime.com; page 18 © (top) Kobby Dagan | Dreamstime.com; (middle) Lev Tsimbler | Dreamstime.com; (bottom) Daniel Weishut | Dreamstime.com; page 19 © (top) Lukas Bischoff | Dreamstime.com; (bottom) Buurserstraat386 | Dreamstime.com; page 20 © (bottom) Rafael Ben Ari | Dreamstime.com; page 22 © (bottom) Rndmst | Dreamstime.com; page 24 © (bottom) Rudi1976 | Dreamstime.com; page 25 © Rostislav Glinsky | Dreamstime.com; Sean Pavone | Dreamstime.com; page 26 © (bottom) Steven Cukrov | Dreamstime.com; page 27 © (top) Richie Chan | Dreamstime.com; page 29 © Kushnirov Avraham | Dreamstime.com; Vladimir Blinov | Dreamstime.com; page 30 © (top) Moreno Soppelsa | Dreamstime.com; page 32 © (bottom) Rafael Ben Ari | Dreamstime.com; page 33 © (top) Rafal Kubiak | Dreamstime.com; page 34 © (top) Evan Spiler | Dreamstime.com; page 36 © (top) Inna Felker | Dreamstime.com; page 38 © (bottom) Wilting | Dreamstime.com; page 40 © (top) Jnkoste | Dreamstime.com; page 41 © Rafael Ben-Ari/123rf.com; page 42 © (top left) VanderWolfImages | Dreamstime.com; (top right) rndms/123rf.com; page 57 © (top left) Leonid Andronov | Dreamstime.com; (top right) Engin Korkmaz | Dreamstime.com; (bottom left) Ryszard Parys | Dreamstime.com; page 60 © (top) Dmitrii Melnikov | Dreamstime.com; (left middle) Gorshkov13 | Dreamstime.com; (right middle) Serge Novitsky | Dreamstime.com; (bottom) Wing Travelling | Dreamstime.com; page 65 © (top) Vladimir Blinov | Dreamstime.com; (bottom) Bargotiphotography | Dreamstime.com; page 69 © (top left) Lev Tsimbler | Dreamstime.com; (top right) Philippians44 | Dreamstime.com; (bottom) Lev Tsimbler | Dreamstime.com; page 73 © Nancy Anderson | Dreamstime.com; page 83 © (top) Alefbet26 | Dreamstime.com; (bottom) Serhii Akhtemiichuk | Dreamstime.com; page 91 © (top) Fotokon | Dreamstime.com; (left middle) Rotgerbesch | Dreamstime.com; (right middle) Nikoletta Muhari | Dreamstime.com; (bottom) Rafael Ben Ari | Dreamstime.com; page 106 © Alexandr Makarenko | Dreamstime.com; page 109 © Bogdan Lazar | Dreamstime.com; page 110 © (top left) TEL AVIV, ISRAEL - May 6 2016: Lake, bench, girls with dog, and relax in Yarkon Park; (top right) Vadim Lerner | Dreamstime.com; page 113 © Evgeniy Fesenko | Dreamstime.com; page 115 © Jasmina | Dreamstime.com; page 124 © (top) Engin Korkmaz | Dreamstime.com; (left middle) Irina Opachevsky | Dreamstime.com; (right middle) Shai Radoshitzky | Dreamstime.com; (bottom) Stanislav Samoylik | Dreamstime.com; page 128 © (top) Richie Chan | Dreamstime.com; (bottom) Engin Korkmaz | Dreamstime.com; page 133 © (top left) Lev Tsimbler | Dreamstime.com; (top right) Dnaveh | Dreamstime.com; (bottom) Inge Hogenbijl | Dreamstime.com; page 138 © Vitaly Sosnovskiy | Dreamstime.com; page 145 © Evgeniy Fesenko | Dreamstime.com; page 158 © liorpt/123rf.com; page 159 © (top left) Vienybe | Dreamstime.com; (top right) Maurizio Giovanni Bersanelli/123rf.com; page 162 © Leonid Andronov | Dreamstime.com; page 169 © (top) Gelia | Dreamstime.com; (left middle) Lev Tsimbler | Dreamstime.com; (right middle) Benary Image | Dreamstime.com; (bottom) Engin Korkmaz | Dreamstime.com; page 173 © (top left) Rndmst | Dreamstime.com; (top right) Rndmst | Dreamstime.com; (bottom) Rndmst | Dreamstime.com; page 179 © Evgeniy Fesenko | Dreamstime.com; page 185 © (top) Ilia Torlin | Dreamstime.com; (left middle) Ilia Torlin | Dreamstime.com; (right middle) Rafael Ben Ari | Dreamstime.com; (bottom) Rafael Ben Ari | Dreamstime.com; page 189 © Viculia | Dreamstime.com; page 194 © (top) Beatrice Preve | Dreamstime.com; (bottom) Rndmst | Dreamstime.com; page 200 © Tsafreer Bernstein | Dreamstime.com; page 201 © (top left) K45025 | Dreamstime.com; (top right) Rndmst | Dreamstime.com; page 204 © Leonid Pilnik/123rf.com; page 207 © Tsafreer Bernstein | Dreamstime.com; page 210 © (top) Aliaksandr Mazurkevich | Dreamstime.com; (left middle) Rontav123 | Dreamstime.com; (right middle) Lev Tsimbler | Dreamstime.com; (bottom)

MOON

AMALFI COAST
With Capri, Naples & Pompeii
LAURA THAYER

ARUBA

BAHAMAS

Beachy
Getaways

MOON.COM
@MOONGUIDES

BAJA

BELIZE

COASTAL
CALIFORNIA

COSTA RICA

DOMINICAN
REPUBLIC

FIJI

FLORIDA

HAWAII

JAMAICA

MAUI

TULUM

YUCATÁN
PENINSULA

GO BIG AND GO BEYOND!

These savvy city guides include strategies to help you see the top sights and find adventure beyond the tourist crowds.

OR TAKE THINGS ONE STEP AT A TIME

Packed with colorful photos, helpful lists of top experiences, and strategic tips for visiting America's National Parks, this top-selling travel guide is a practical keepsake.

Moon USA National Parks includes a pull-out souvenir map and a designated section to collect each park's stamp.

5 ³⁄₈" x 8 ³⁄₈" • 700pp • $24.99 US | $32.49 CAN

MOON
TRIP OF A LIFETIME
ANGKOR WAT

MOON
TRIP OF A LIFETIME
GALÁPAGOS
ISLANDS

MOON
JAPAN
JONATHAN DEHART

MOON
TRIP OF A LIFETIME
MACHU
PICCHU

MOON
MOROCCO

MOON
NEW
ZEALAND
JAMIE CHRISTIAN DESPLACES

MOON
NORWAY

MOON
TRIP OF A LIFETIME
PATAGONIA
Including the Falkland Islands
WAYNE BERNHARDSON

MOON
VIETNAM
DANA FILEK-GIBSON

MOON
YELLOWSTONE
& GRAND TETON
Including Jackson Hole
BECKY LOMAX

MOON
ZION &
BRYCE
Including Arches, Canyonlands, Capitol Reef, Grand Staircase-Escalante & More
W. C. McRAE & JUDY JEWELL

MOON
Drive & Hike
APPALACHIAN
TRAIL

THE BEST TRAIL TOWNS, DAY HIKES,
AND ROAD TRIPS IN BETWEEN
TIMOTHY MALCOLM

MOON
ROUTE 66
Road Trip

JESSICA DUNHAM

MOON
YELLOWSTONE TO
GLACIER NATIONAL
PARK
Road Trip

JACKSON HOLE, CODY, THE GRAND TETONS
& THE ROCKY MOUNTAIN FRONT
CARTER G. WALKER

MAP SYMBOLS

≡	Expressway	○	City/Town	✈	Airport	⚲	Golf Course
≡	Primary Road	◉	State Capital	✈	Airfield	🅿	Parking Area
≡	Secondary Road	◉	National Capital	▲	Mountain	⬟	Archaeological Site
⋯	Unpaved Road	★	Point of Interest	✦	Unique Natural Feature	⯅	Church
—	Feature Trail	•	Accommodation			🛢	Gas Station
----	Other Trail	▾	Restaurant/Bar	🝊	Waterfall	⬭	Glacier
⋯⋯	Ferry	▪	Other Location	⯅	Park	▨	Mangrove
≡	Pedestrian Walkway	Λ	Campground	❶	Trailhead	◱	Reef
▥	Stairs			⛷	Skiing Area	▱	Swamp

CONVERSION TABLES

°C = (°F – 32) / 1.8
°F = (°C x 1.8) + 32
1 inch = 2.54 centimeters (cm)
1 foot = 0.304 meters (m)
1 yard = 0.914 meters
1 mile = 1.6093 kilometers (km)
1 km = 0.6214 miles
1 fathom = 1.8288 m
1 chain = 20.1168 m
1 furlong = 201.168 m
1 acre = 0.4047 hectares
1 sq km = 100 hectares
1 sq mile = 2.59 square km
1 ounce = 28.35 grams
1 pound = 0.4536 kilograms
1 short ton = 0.90718 metric ton
1 short ton = 2,000 pounds
1 long ton = 1.016 metric tons
1 long ton = 2,240 pounds
1 metric ton = 1,000 kilograms
1 quart = 0.94635 liters
1 US gallon = 3.7854 liters
1 Imperial gallon = 4.5459 liters
1 nautical mile = 1.852 km

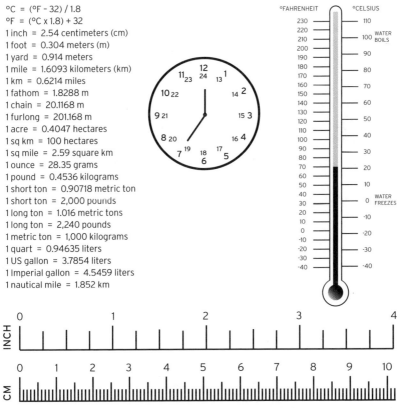

MOON ISRAEL & THE WEST BANK
Avalon Travel
Hachette Book Group
1700 Fourth Street
Berkeley, CA 94710, USA
www.moon.com

Editor: Megan Anderluh
Copy Editor: Julie Meade
Graphics Coordinator: Rue Flaherty
Production Coordinators: Rue Flaherty
  and Kit Anderson
Cover Design: Faceout Studios, Charles Brock
Interior Design: Domini Dragoone
Moon Logo: Tim McGrath
Map Editor: Albert Angulo
Cartographer: John Culp
Proofreader: Lina Carmona
Indexer: François Trahan

ISBN-13: 978-1-64049-097-0

Printing History
1st Edition — 2016
2nd Edition — November 2019
5 4 3 2 1

Text © 2019 by Genevieve Belmaker.
Maps © 2019 by Avalon Travel.
Some photos and illustrations are used by
permission and are the property of the original
copyright owners.

Front cover photo: Dome of the Rock, Jerusalem ©
  Photography by Daniel Frauchiger, Switzerland
  / Getty Images

Back cover photo: Petra, Jordan © Sviatlana
  Barchan | Dreamstime.com

Printed in China by RR Donnelley